The INDUSTRIAL RAILWAYS of BOLTON, BURY and the MANCHESTER COALFIELD

Part 2

The Manchester Coalfield

by

C.H.A. Townley

C.A. Appleton

F.D. Smith

J.A. Peden

Townley etc
The Industrial Railways of Bolton, Bury
and the Manchester Coalfield
Pt. 2 The Manchester Coalfield
1.
I. Title

ISBN 1–870754–32–8

Typeset and printed by
Stroud Printing Services Ltd.

Runpast Publishing
10 Kingscote Grove
Cheltenham
GL51 6JX

CONTENTS

Howe Bridge Colliery in November 1956, looking north. The Bolton and Leigh line of British Railways is on the left and the pit headgear and screens are on the right, in the middle distance. The well tank locomotive, built by Hawthorns and Company of Leith in 1861, is shunting in the NCB sidings.

Bernard Roberts

CHAPTER 7

CLIFTON, PENDLEBURY AND AGECROFT

In the first chapter of Part 2, we return to Clifton. Here, and in the adjacent township of Pendlebury, Andrew Knowles opened out several coal mines early in the nineteenth century. His Pendlebury Colliery, latterly known as Wheatsheaf, survived to be taken over by the National Coal Board in 1947 and did not close until 1961.

From Pendlebury we turn to the area around Clifton Junction, where several industrial concerns, not directly associated with the coal industry, were located. Two, the Chloride battery works and Magnesium Elektron Ltd, survive to the present day, but no longer make use of rail transport.

We then move south to Agecroft, where pits were sunk by Andrew Knowles in the 1820s. Although Knowles' Agecroft Colliery ceased production in 1932, it was reopened by the National Coal Board. When it finally closed in July 1990 it was the last mine to be worked in the Manchester Coalfield.

We conclude the chapter with the three electricity works which were established to the east of the Manchester and Bolton railway. The first was constructed by Salford Corporation in the 1920s. After the second world war, two further power stations were built on an adjacent site and have only recently closed.

KNOWLES' CLIFTON AND PENDLEBURY COLLIERIES

Clifton Moss Colliery

Andrew Knowles, who was already well established as a colliery proprietor in the neighbourhood of Bolton, turned his attention to the Clifton area shortly after 1810. There are records of mining leases taken up by him in Clifton in May 1814 [1] and in Pendlebury in 1825 [2], but details are insufficiently precise to be able to say where the individual pits were situated.

In the late 1830s Andrew Knowles took his sons Robert, Thomas, John and James into partnership and set up the firm of Andrew Knowles and Sons. Control passed to the four sons after Andrew's death in 1847. John died in July 1852, leaving Robert, Thomas and James to carry on the firm. As mentioned in an earlier chapter, there was a family dispute about the inheritance in 1872 and this resulted in the assets being transferred to members of the third generation - Andrew and Kay Knowles, sons of Robert; Andrew and Robert Millington Knowles, sons of James; and John Knowles, son of Thomas [3 to 8]. Andrew Knowles and Sons Ltd was formed in September 1873 [9].

The Clifton Moss pits were possibly sunk to work the coal which was leased in 1814 [1]. They were sufficiently important to attract the attention of the early railway promoters. The Manchester and Preston Railway proposals of 1830 included a branch from Clifton to Little

Hulton which passed nearby [10]. Although the Manchester and Preston scheme failed to gain Parliamentary approval, a line to Clifton Moss Colliery was authorised by the Manchester, Bolton and Bury Act of 1831 [11]. This was intended to leave the Farnworth Branch near the top of the Unity Brook incline and cut across country past Fletcher's Doe and Buss Pits, but was never built.

As it turned out, road transport proved sufficient to distribute the whole of the coal production, most of which was probably sold locally. There were no further schemes by the main line companies to provide rail access nor does there seem to have been any proposal by Andrew Knowles and Sons to build a private line.

Clifton Moss Colliery, which in its heyday had employed between 200 and 300 men, closed at the end of 1891 [12]. Some twenty years later, the Earl of Ellesmere's mining engineers carried out some exploratory work with a view to reopening it. The Mines Lists record that this took place over the over the period from 1910 to 1921, but was abandoned in 1922.

Clifton Hall and Wheatsheaf Collieries - 1820 to 1892

Clifton Hall Colliery, in the Irwell valley below Pendlebury, dates from the 1820s, if not earlier. It was linked to the Manchester, Bolton and Bury Canal by a short horse worked tramroad. The colliery was certainly in existence in 1830, as it is shown, together with the tramroad, on the Deposited Plans of that date for the railway from Manchester to Preston [10]. According to a historical article on Knowles' collieries which appeared in the Eccles and Patricroft Journal [13] two shafts were sunk at Clifton Hall in 1838, which suggests that some modernisation was carried out at that time. There were 30 oblong coke ovens using crushed small coal. The Clifton Branch of the London and North Western Railway, which was opened in February 1850 [14], ran past the colliery and we assume that a siding was provided. Clifton Hall Colliery later gained notoriety as being the scene of one of the worst mining accidents in Lancashire. An explosion took place in the Trencherbone seam in 1885, causing the deaths of 186 men and boys.

The original colliery at Pendlebury was situated south of the Manchester to Bolton Turnpike, alongside Bury Lane, later to become Swinton Hall Road. There are records of a lease here in 1825 [2], but the pits may have been sunk earlier. The Manchester and Preston Railway proposals of 1830, which we have mentioned earlier and which were not pursued, included a short branch to the colliery from the Clifton to Little Hulton line. However, by the mid 1840s, when the surveys were made for the first edition of the 6" map, Andrew Knowles' first Pendlebury colliery had closed and the map shows "old pits" on the site.

A new Pendlebury Colliery was sunk on the north side of the main road and came into production in 1846 [13,15]. It became better known as Wheatsheaf Colliery, taking its name from the adjacent public house. Originally all the coal was sold at the pit yard and it was only later that arrangements were made to send any away by rail.

A new screening plant and washery were built on the west side of the LNWR line at Clifton Hall, probably in 1873, as the sidings which served them were laid in under an agreement dated 15th April of that year [16]. The original sidings appear to have been on the opposite side of the main line, adjacent to Clifton Hall Colliery, and were removed as part of the alterations.

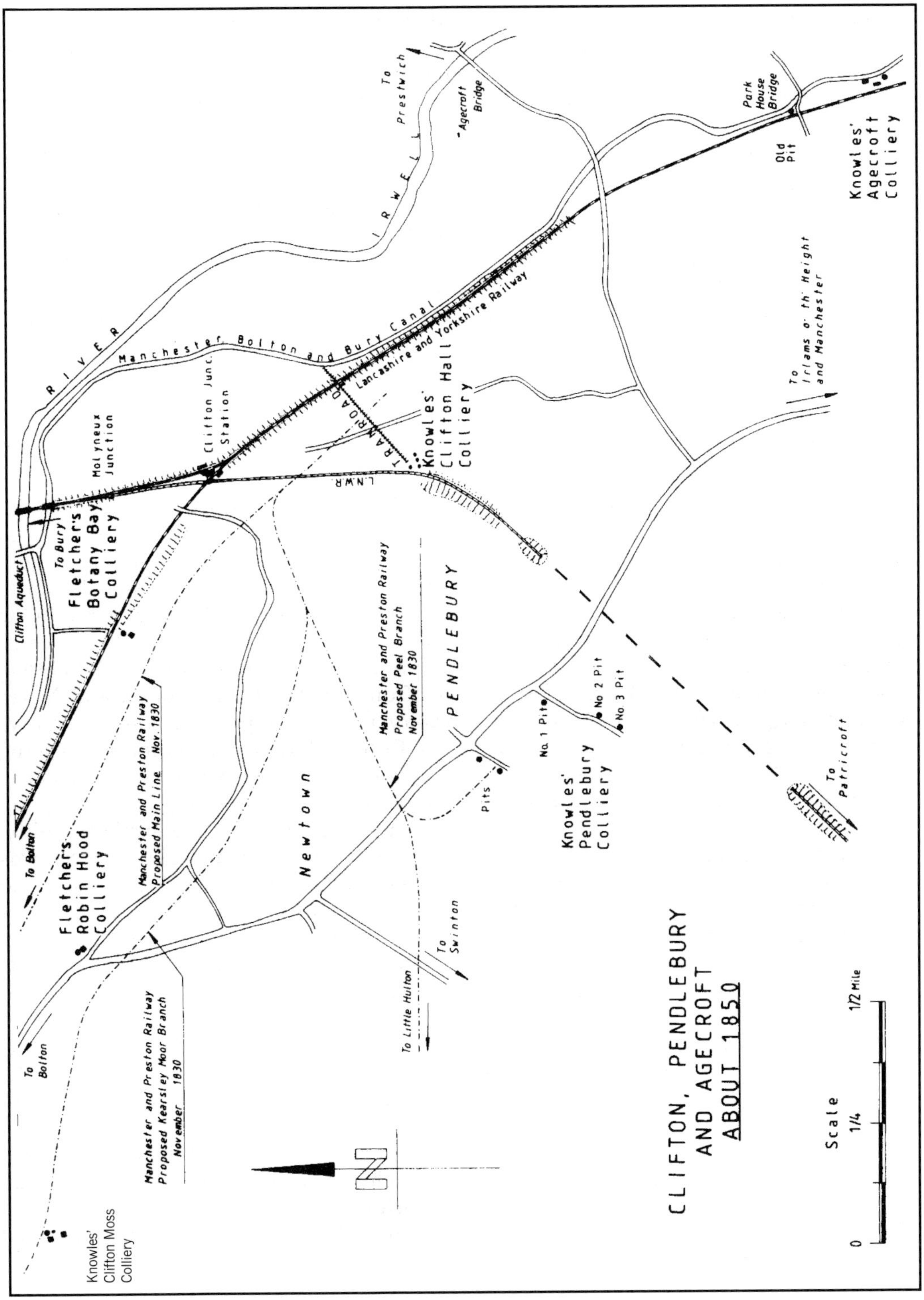
CLIFTON, PENDLEBURY
AND AGECROFT
ABOUT 1850
Scale
0
1/4
1/2 Mile
N
Knowles' Clifton Moss Colliery
To Bolton
Manchester and Preston Railway Proposed Kearsley Moor Branch November 1830
Fletcher's Robin Hood Colliery
Manchester and Preston Railway Proposed Main Line Nov. 1830
Newtown
To Little Hulton
To Swinton
Pits
Knowles' Pendlebury Colliery
No. 1 Pit
No 2 Pit
No 3 Pit
PENDLEBURY
Manchester and Preston Railway Proposed Peel Branch November 1830
To Patricroft
Clifton Aqueduct
To Bury
Fletcher's Botany Bay Colliery
Molyneux Junction
Clifton Junc. Station
L.N.W.R.
TRAM ROAD
Knowles' Clifton Hall Colliery
RIVER IRWELL
Manchester, Bolton and Bury Canal
Lancashire and Yorkshire Railway
To Irlams o' th' Height and Manchester
To Prestwich
Agecroft Bridge
Park House Bridge
Old Pit
Knowles' Agecroft Colliery

A tubway was installed to bring coal from Wheatsheaf Colliery to the new coal preparation plant. The first edition of the 25" map, surveyed 1889 to 1891, shows a single track from the pit yard, passing through a tunnel as it approached the washery.

An article describing the colliery states that a vertical table engine was provided for haulage purposes [13]. Presumably the loaded tubs ran down by gravity, taking the rope from the engine with them, so that the empties could be drawn back to the top of the incline.

Under the new arrangements, coal from the Clifton Hall pits was conveyed in tubs to the preparation plant across a bridge over the main line. The horse worked tramroad from Clifton Hall to the canal was also replaced by a tubway, presumably at the same time.

Although it seems likely that a locomotive would have been needed after the Clifton Hall sidings at were extended in 1873, we have been unable trace any before 1890. In that a year a six coupled saddle tank, named CLIFTON HALL, was delivered by Peckett and Sons of Bristol.

This photograph was taken from above the northern portal of Pendlebury Tunnel in 1957. Clifton Hall Sidings Signal Box on the former LNWR branch from Patricroft to Molyneux Junction can be seen in the centre. The NCB line to Wheatsheaf screens curves away on the left. The waste tips in the middle distance are on the site of Clifton Hall Colliery. The associated screens and washery were on the left of the main line, hidden beyond the hill. Harry Townley

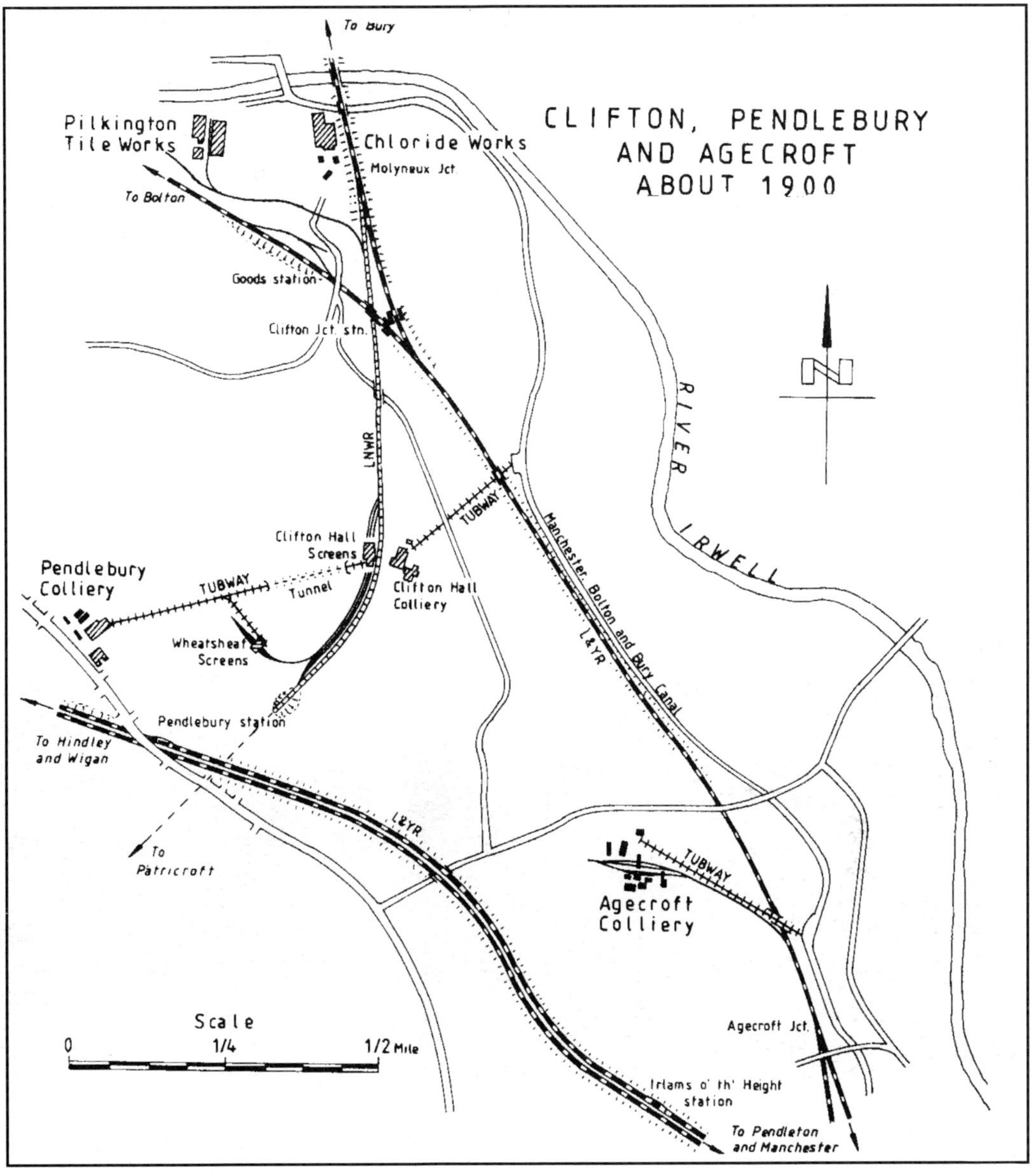

Clifton Hall and Wheatsheaf Collieries - 1892 to 1929

Wheatsheaf Colliery was redeveloped towards the end of the century [15], leading to a significant rise in output. Much of the coal continued to be screened at the pit head and sold for local consumption from the landsale yard at the colliery [17] but an increasing amount was sent out by rail, including some which went for shipment at Weaste Wharf.

As the existing facilities at Clifton Hall were no longer adequate to cater for the increased railway traffic, an additional screening plant was erected, exclusively for coal from Wheatsheaf Colliery. The siding layout at Clifton Hall was extended to link up with the new Wheatsheaf screens and the connections with the London and North Western Railway were altered under an agreement dated 31st December 1892 [16,18,19].

The earlier tubway was retained, so that Wheatsheaf coal could still be dealt with at Clifton Hall washery, and a branch was constructed, from a point above the tunnel entrance, leading to the new screens. The second edition of the 25" map, revised in 1907, shows that the tubways to both the old and the new screens were still single track.

A second engine shed was built near the Wheatsheaf screens, to supplement the original shed at the north end of the Clifton Hall sidings [16], but it is not clear whether two locomotives were regularly in use.

Following the closure of Knowles' Radcliffe collieries in the mid 1890s, RADCLIFFE, the six coupled Manning Wardle, and the unnamed Peckett four wheeler were transferred to the Wheatsheaf - Clifton Hall site. Thereafter it seems to have been the practice to keep the firm's spare locomotives here and it is likely that one or other of them would have been sent to the Agecroft and Pendleton Collieries from time to time on a temporary basis when the regular engines were under repair.

Coal being loaded into a sailing vessel on the Manchester Ship Canal by Knowles' crane at Weaste. A turn of the century photograph which shows the steam crane which hoisted the wagons into position over the hold so that the coal could be discharged through the end doors. The tipping operation was controlled by the workman in the centre of the picture, using a rope attached to one of the buffers. Note the early Manchester Ship Canal locomotive on the left, which was being used to shunt the wagons on and off the turntable leading to the crane. Alex Appleton collection

The Peckett engine from Radcliffe features in a letter of 18th February 1918 from Andrew Knowles and Sons to the makers about spare parts [20]. The engine was stated to have been out of use for some time, but it was now to be fitted up for government use. It was presumably this engine which an old employee remembered as having been sent from Wheatsheaf to Middlesbrough during the first world war.

RADCLIFFE remained at the Wheatsheaf-Clifton Hall complex and was regularly employed there, along with CLIFTON HALL, up to March 1929, when the firm of Andrew Knowles and Sons Ltd was merged into Manchester Collieries Ltd.

Clifton Hall and Wheatsheaf Collieries - 1929 to 1961

Clifton Hall Colliery was closed soon after the amalgamation. The Mines Lists show that coal production was discontinued on 9th November 1929, one of the pits being retained as a ventilating shaft for Wheatsheaf Colliery. Wheatsheaf Colliery itself was reconstructed in the 1930s [21]. The washery at Clifton Hall was taken out of use and an increasing amount of small coal was sent by rail to Outwood for processing.

The tubway system had already been modernised by Andrew Knowles and Sons. The 1926 revision of the 25" map shows that the tunnel had been opened out and that there was now a double line from the colliery to Clifton Hall washery with a double track branch to the Wheatsheaf screens. There were also alterations to the standard gauge sidings, covered by agreements with the LNWR dated 1st July 1914 and 4th April 1917 [18,19].

In parallel with the 1930s modernisation of the colliery, the Wheatsheaf screening plant was enlarged. The 1935-6 revision of the 25" map shows that the engine shed here had to be removed to make way for the extensions. It was replaced by a new one a short distance away, where the working locomotive was kept.

The engine shed at Clifton Hall was demolished and the wagon repair shop, now no longer needed for its original purpose, was then used to house the spare locomotive.

CLIFTON HALL was fitted with a new boiler, supplied by Peckett and Sons of Bristol, in 1930 [22] and was subsequently transferred to Agecroft Colliery, to be described later in the chapter. AGECROFT, another six coupled saddle tank, built by Manning Wardle and Company in 1889, came to Wheatsheaf in exchange, perhaps after its overhaul at Walkden Yard at the end of 1933 and the beginning of 1934 [22] or perhaps a few years earlier, as has been suggested to us by a former employee.

LMS railway company records which were inspected by the authors some years ago show that CLIFTON HALL was returned to Wheatsheaf Screens in December 1937, after a short spell of duty at Bradford Colliery. AGECROFT was then taken out of service and was scrapped in 1938. According to an old employee, it was broken up by George Cohen, Sons and Co Ltd in July and August.

RADCLIFFE and CLIFTON HALL, which had lost its name by 1937, were the regular engines throughout the war years and were at Wheatsheaf Screens when the coal industry was nationalised on 1st December 1947.

The colliery itself subsequently underwent considerable development and, in 1957, the underground workings were linked with those of Newtown Colliery. Coal from both collieries was then wound at Wheatsheaf, much of it still being sold in the landsale yard. Such coal as was sent away by rail went down the tubway to the Wheatsheaf screens and thence to Outwood washery. The tubway to the old Clifton Hall Colliery was retained to convey waste to a disposal site on the east of the railway.

The six coupled Peckett locomotive, formerly CLIFTON HALL, working from Wheatsheaf shed, photographed at the north end of the sidings in October 1948. Alex Appleton

FAILSWORTH photographed at Clifton Hall Sidings in March 1951, shortly after its transfer from Moston Colliery. Alex Appleton

Following its spell of work at Wheatsheaf Screens WESTWOOD went to Walkden Yard for overhaul. This photograph was taken shortly after it had left the workshops.
Industrial Railway Society Ken Cooper collection

RADCLIFFE was sent to Walkden Yard on 10th May 1948, returning to Wheatsheaf after repairs were completed towards the end of the year. By early 1952 it was laid aside and was scrapped by Thomas W Ward Ltd at Clifton Hall in September of that year.

CLIFTON HALL left Wheatsheaf for Walkden Yard on 4th January 1950. After repairs, when the new name PECKETT was painted on the saddle tanks, it was sent to Outwood Washery. It returned to Wheatsheaf under its own steam on 8th December 1955 after a further overhaul at Walkden Yard. It was at Wheatsheaf until the end of 1956 or early in 1957, when it once more was sent to Walkden Yard. It remained there, out of use, until it was finally cut up in January 1962 by the Central Wagon Co Ltd, which had purchased it for scrap.

FAILSWORTH arrived on 1st February 1951 from Moston Colliery, as a welcome replacement for RADCLIFFE, which was in poor condition. FAILSWORTH had been built by Hawthorn, Leslie and Company of Newcastle in 1907 and had been taken over by the National Coal Board from Platt Brothers (Holdings) Ltd. It remained at Wheatsheaf for the rest of its life, apart from two spells at Walkden Yard for repairs, from 3rd to 12th August 1953 and from 12th January to 23rd June 1955. It was condemned in December 1957 and was broken up at Wheatsheaf in September 1958.

A succession of other locomotives were drafted in when the regular engines were out of service. ROBIN HOOD, the four coupled saddle tank taken over by Manchester Collieries Ltd from Outwood Collieries Ltd, was here towards the end 1949, from May to August 1950 and in April and May 1952.

OUTWOOD, the Peckett saddle tank, also taken over by Manchester Collieries Ltd from Outwood Collieries Ltd, was at Wheatsheaf from March to June 1954.

COLONEL, a six coupled Hunslet saddle tank originally owned by Fletcher, Burrows and Co Ltd, was at Wheatsheaf temporarily between January and September 1955. It returned on a more permanent basis towards the end of 1957, along with WESTWOOD, to replace PECKETT and FAILSWORTH. Apart from a short visit to Walkden Yard in 1959, COLONEL remained at Wheatsheaf until the colliery closed.

WESTWOOD was a four coupled saddle tank, built by Hudswell Clarke and Company in 1913, and, like FAILSWORTH, had originally been the property of Platt Brothers (Holdings) Ltd. Since nationalisation it had spent most of its time on the Bridgewater Collieries railway system. It was at Wheatsheaf for a short period early in 1952 and from mid 1957 until 3rd September 1959, when it left for Walkden Yard under its own steam.

KEARSLEY, the Kerr Stuart locomotive bought by Bridgewater Collieries Ltd for use at Robin Hood Screens, came early in 1959, after repairs at Walkden Yard, as a replacement for WESTWOOD. It had previously spent a short period at Ashton Moss Colliery, while the regular engine there was under repair.

Wheatsheaf Colliery closed in June 1961 and was demolished. The site was later occupied by a car sale room. The Wheatsheaf Screening Plant and the remaining buildings at Clifton Hall Colliery were cleared away and the area landscaped. The waste dumps lower down the valley, which had also served Agecroft Colliery, were removed and the area is now used as a refuse tip by the City of Salford.

COLONEL left under its own steam for Walkden Yard on 5th July 1961. It was later transferred to Bedford Colliery and was scrapped there in August 1966. KEARSLEY was also sent to Walkden Yard, where it stood out of use until it was broken up in February 1967.

AROUND CLIFTON JUNCTION

Chloride Industrial Batteries Ltd

A factory alongside the Manchester, Bolton and Bury Canal previously occupied by the Truby Chemical Co, but sometimes ascribed to the Manchester Aniline Company, was acquired in 1892 for the manufacture of electric storage batteries. The Chloride Electrical Storage Syndicate Ltd had been registered on 12th December 1891 and was originally a subsidiary of Mather and Platt Ltd. Production commenced in 1893 and in 1903 the firm was reorganised as the Chloride Electrical Storage Co Ltd.

Until the second world war all manufacture was concentrated on the west side of the East Lancashire line, with the exception of a blast furnace for lead recovery, erected in the early 1930s. After the war the east side of the site was developed and in 1972 part of the old East Lancashire Railway embankment was demolished to give better access.

On 1st January 1950 Chloride Electrical Storage Ltd became a holding company and the Clifton works then traded as Chloride Batteries Ltd. In 1965 there was a merger with Electric Power Storage Ltd and from 1971 the works came under the control of a subsidiary, Chloride Industrial Batteries Ltd.

The works never had its own private sidings, but at one time made considerable use of the the adjacent Clifton Junction Goods Yard for incoming and outgoing traffic. There was also a wharf on the Manchester, Bolton and Bury Canal, where, in the early days, pig lead brought by barge from Manchester Docks was unloaded. From the mid 1930s much of the output was despatched by road, although the some still went by rail. Submarine batteries, for example, were sent away in complete train loads. Incoming traffic consisted latterly of raw materials and included tank wagons conveying sulphuric acid.

Within the works a narrow gauge railway system, on which small bogies were propelled manually, had been used for a time to convey materials from one shop to another. This had ceased to operate by 1930.

In 1961 a 2'6" gauge line about 600 yards long was constructed to take scrap lead to a reverbertory furnace for remelting. A Greenwood and Batley battery electric locomotive and 152 old mining wagons, previously used at Mosley Common Colliery, were purchased from the National Coal Board. Before entering service the locomotive, which was named SATURN at Clifton, was renovated by the makers. The system was discontinued at the end 1969 or early 1970 and the locomotive and wagons disposed of.

Previous to this, in June 1950, two other battery electric locomotives had been briefly at the Clifton works, when a temporary display was put on for a visit by the Institution of Mining Engineers. One, on the 2ft gauge, had been built in 1950 by the Logan Mining Machinery Co Ltd of Dundee and was subsequently employed by the contractors working on the Manchester Corporation's Haweswater Aqueduct. The other, on the 3'6" gauge had been built by Greenwood and Batley Ltd, of Leeds, in 1949. Each was run up and down about 75ft of track to demonstrate the use of battery powered locomotives in mines.

The works is still in production, although manufacture of motive power batteries was transferred to a new works at Over Hulton in 1980. The Clifton works was sold in 1991 to Hawker Siddeley Ltd, a firm which was taken over by the BTR Group almost immediately afterwards.

Use of the railway for outgoing goods and incoming raw materials ceased when Clifton Junction Goods Yard closed in August 1965 [23]. The site of the yard was cleared to make way for a warehouse for Rowntree Mackintosh Ltd where products coming from this firm's factories were transhipped from rail to road for local distribution. The depot was opened in 1965 and vacated by Rowntree Mackintosh in 1975, following a move to a new site at Warrington. The building, no longer served by a siding, has subsequently been occupied by various firms.

Lancashire and Yorkshire Railway Power Station, Clifton Junction

In December 1913 [24] the Lancashire and Yorkshire Railway Board authorised the conversion of the Manchester and Bury line to electric traction. A site at Clifton Junction was chosen for the central power station, supplying current to two sub stations at Radcliffe and Manchester Victoria. Construction contracts were let on 21st May 1914 for completion within eleven months. The plant comprised three Babcock and Wilcox boilers and two Dick Kerr 5,000 KW turbo-generators; cooling water was taken from the nearby canal [25,26].

Sidings were laid in from the adjacent Manchester and Bolton line and a fleet of hopper wagons was built to bring in the coal. For the first few years, shunting in the sidings was carried out using five electric capstans. These were replaced in July 1917 when a battery electric locomotive was delivered. Numbered 2 in the L&Y stock, it had been built by the railway company at its Horwich works and had been designed specially for use at the power station.

The power station became the property of the London, Midland and Scottish Railway in 1923. It was closed in 1931, when arrangements were made to take electrical supplies from the grid. The locomotive was transferred to Greenhill Sleeper Depot, near Falkirk, in Scotland and by May 1946 it had been sent to Derby Works. It was still there in November 1947 prior to being broken up.

A works photograph of the battery locomotive built by the Lancashire and Yorkshire Railway at Horwich for use at Clifton Power Station. Industrial Railway SocietyBrian Webb collection

Magnesium Elektron Ltd

Magnesium Elektron Ltd was formed in 1934 by a Mr F A Hughes to acquire the patents of the German I G Farbenindustrie for the production of magnesium. A plant was constructed at Clifton Junction with the help of some German personnel and in part utilising the former L&YR Power station buildings. The first metal was produced in 1936.

The sidings which had originally served the L&Y power station were taken over under an agreement with the LMS Railway dated 11th November 1937 [27]. Shunting was performed by a four coupled diesel electric locomotive which had been built by Armstrong, Whitworth and Company of Newcastle on Tyne in 1933. Before the second world war there was a certain amount of inwards traffic in Continental wagons which came from Germany via the train ferries.

To cater for the increased war time demand for magnesium, additional production facilities were provided in the early 1940s. The new factory, on the low lying ground to the north of the original premises, was provided with its own internal railway system. Extra siding accommodation was laid in alongside the former East Lancashire line, linked to the firm's existing sidings and connecting with the new factory down a steep gradient. Additional main line connections were provided adjacent to the up Bury line platform at Clifton Junction Station, under an agreement with the LMSR dated 18th September 1942 [27].

To supplement the diesel locomotive and to cater for the additional traffic, a four coupled saddle tank was purchased from Andrew Barclay Sons and Company of Kilmarnock in 1942. Lettered MEL No 2, this was the sister engine of MEL No 1, delivered at about the same time to the shadow factory at Hapton, East Lancashire, operated by Magnesium Elektron for the Ministry of Aircraft Production.

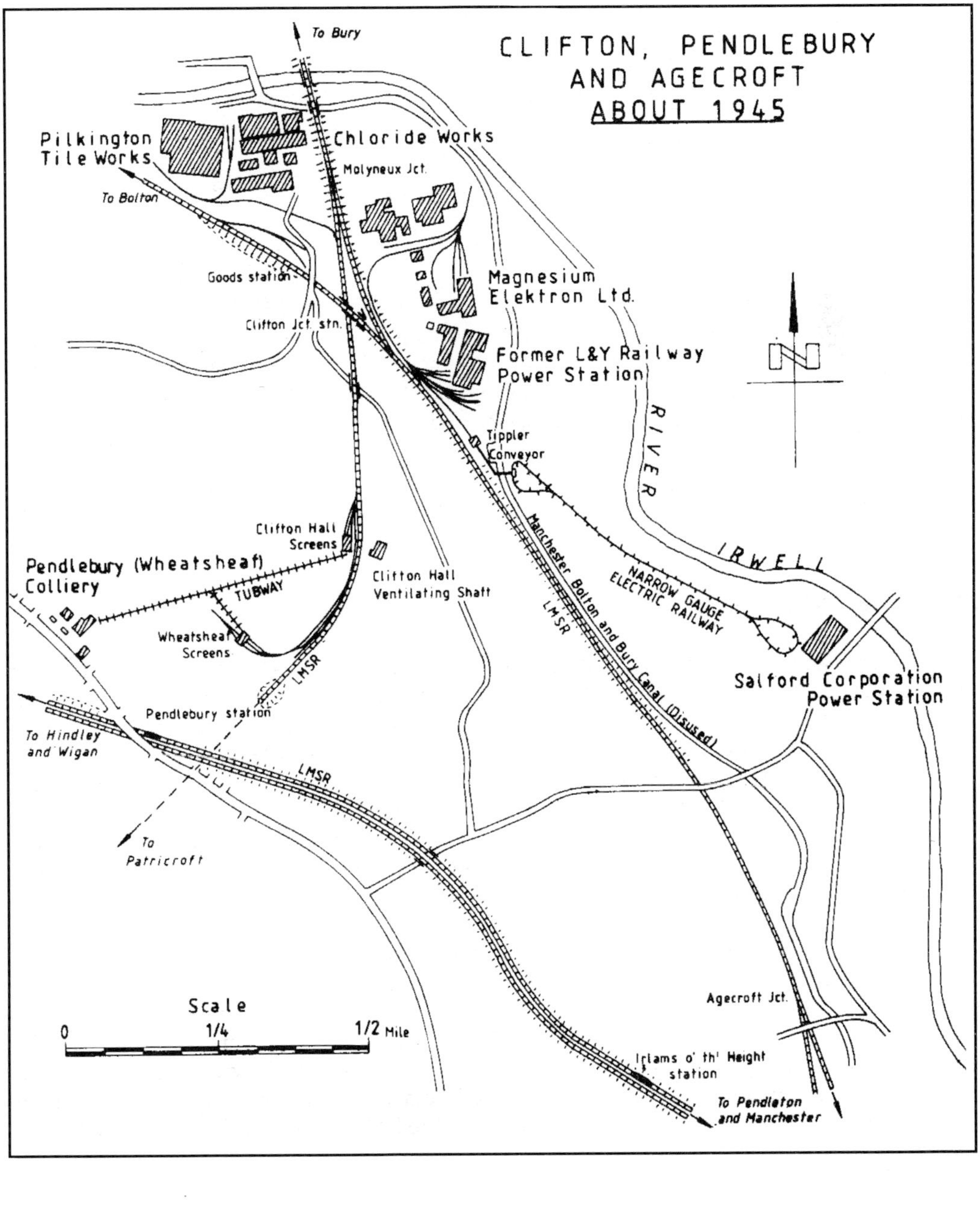

The opening of the new factory at Clifton Junction led to the closure, for the duration of the war, of a portion of the LMSR Patricroft and Clifton line south of Clifton Hall Siding. One of the raw materials used in large quantities in the magnesium production process was chlorine, which was delivered in liquid form in rail tankers. To minimise the risk of widespread loss of life and disruption which would have occurred if loaded tank wagons had been damaged in an air raid, they were stabled until required in Pendlebury Tunnel.

The Armstrong Whitworth diesel locomotive and MEL No 2 continued in use at Clifton Junction until 1961 or 1962, although other locomotives were hired from time to time. A four coupled saddle tank, British Railways No 51230, built by the Lancashire and Yorkshire Railway at Horwich in 1906, was observed at work here in March 1957.

In July 1961, a four coupled diesel mechanical locomotive, built by John Fowler and Company of Leeds in 1939, was acquired from the Newport works of the British Aluminium Company. This replaced the two earlier locomotives, which were subsequently broken up.

Rail traffic ceased a few years later, the agreements in respect of the main line connections being terminated on 25th June 1966 [27]. The Fowler diesel locomotive was sold and, by mid 1967, had become the property of H P Bulmer and Co Ltd of Hereford.

The factory is still in production at the time of writing, the firm latterly being a subsidiary of Distillers Company Ltd and British Aluminium Co Ltd [28].

AGECROFT

Agecroft Colliery up to 1937

Andrew Knowles obtained a lease of coal under the Agecroft Hall Estate in August 1823 [29]. His Agecroft Colliery is shown on two Deposited Plans of 1830 [10,30] on a site alongside the Manchester, Bolton and Bury Canal, near the boundary of Pendleton township. There may also have been earlier workings a little further to the north, near Park House Bridge, where an old pit is marked on the first edition of the 6" map.

A new Agecroft Colliery was developed by the firm of Andrew Knowles and Sons, on the opposite side of the railway, in the Park Meadows. Hayes [15], possibly quoting from a historical article which appeared in the Eccles and Patricroft Journal in 1892 [13] states that work started in 1844 to sink new shafts. However, the 6" map, surveyed in 1845, shows Agecroft Colliery on the same site as the 1830 Deposited Plans and there is no evidence of any new pit at Park Meadows.

It is not clear how quickly development took place here. A new winding engine was erected in 1855 [15], but the first edition of the 25" map, surveyed in 1888 and 1889, suggests that the colliery site was not then in production. The map shows a single standard gauge connection with the Manchester and Bolton line. It also shows the formation for a tubway, with no track laid, leading from the pit yard to the canal and crossing the Lancashire and Yorkshire Railway on an overbridge.

We can only assume that the first colliery at Park Meadows had a restricted output and that what the map records is the major reconstruction which took place around 1890, when the surface plant was modernised, new screens were erected and the railway sidings extended [15]. This preceded the sinking of two new shafts, on which work started in 1896 [31], and the purchase of a large mineral estate at Pendleton in 1897 [32].

We have been unable to trace any locomotives associated with the colliery before 1889, which tends to confirm our view that such railway sidings as existed previously were on a modest scale. In that year a six coupled saddle tank, carrying the name AGECROFT, was delivered by Manning, Wardle and Company of Leeds.

We have no record of other locomotives employed by Andrew Knowles and Sons Ltd at the colliery. Presumably during those periods that AGECROFT was out of service, an engine would have been temporarily transferred from one of the firm's other pits.

Agecroft Colliery became the property of Manchester Collieries Ltd in 1929, but production ceased soon afterwards. The Mines Lists show that Nos 1 & 2 Pits were closed in 1930, followed by Nos 3 and 4 Pits on 29th July 1932. The tubway to the canal seems to have continued in use until a late date, perhaps until the closure of the colliery. In the years immediately before the war the remains of the bridge over the Manchester and Bolton line were still in evidence and there were several derelict barges in the basin.

Nos 3 and 4 pits were retained for pumping purposes, to provide drainage for other collieries in the area. The surface plant was not demolished until the late 1930s.

AGECROFT seems to have been the regular engine at the time of the merger. It was overhauled at Walkden Yard between September 1933 and February 1934 [22] and was then sent to work at Wheatsheaf Screens.

There is photographic evidence that KNOWLES, another Manning Wardle six coupled saddle tank, was at Agecroft for a time. It appears to have been transferred from the nearby Pendleton Colliery in the late 1920s or early 1930s. KNOWLES was later sent to Walkden Yard, where it was broken up in 1936.

The Manning Wardle KNOWLES at Agecroft Colliery, probably taken around 1930.
Alex Appleton collection

There is also a suggestion, which we have been unable to confirm, that THE SIRDAR, a Vulcan Foundry four coupled saddle tank, taken over by Manchester Collieries Ltd from John Speakman's Bedford Colliery, was here for a short time in the early 1930s, before going to Robin Hood Sidings.

CLIFTON HALL, a third of Andrew Knowles and Sons' six coupled Manning Wardle saddle tanks, was transferred from Wheatsheaf to Agecroft in the early 1930s. It was observed here, out of use, as late as April 1937. Shortly afterwards it seems to have gone to Bradford Colliery for a short period, as LMSR records show that it was subsequently sent from Bradford to Clifton Hall sidings on 7th December 1937.

Agecroft Colliery 1953 to 1990

In the early 1950s, a decision was taken by the National Coal Board to reopen Agecroft Colliery to tap seams on the north side of the Irwell as well as the south. The original No 3 and 4 pits were reconstructed and a new No 5 shaft was sunk. Work started in July 1953 and was substantially complete by December 1960 [21] although some development was still taking place in 1961 [33].

New sidings were laid in alongside the British Railways' Manchester and Bolton line. Coal was brought by conveyor from the pit head to a bunker for loading into railway wagons, while a second conveyor led directly to the coal handling plant in the sidings serving the adjacent power station. A connecting line was laid in between the colliery and the power station sidings, which could be used to transfer coal when the conveyor was not available.

There was also an extensive 2'6" gauge system on the surface, which appears to have been used to assist with the construction work. It later served to transport materials from the stock yards to the pit head.

The standard gauge sidings were worked by two six coupled diesel electric locomotives, both built by the Yorkshire Engine Company of Sheffield. The first to arrive came new in 1960, carrying works number 2745. The second, carrying works number 2660, was built in 1957 and had been used on the Bridgewater Collieries railway system before coming to Agecroft around 1962. Two four wheeled diesel mechanical locomotives, built by Ruston and Hornsby of Lincoln in 1955 and 1956, were used on the narrow gauge lines.

Despatch of coal by rail ceased in the early 1980s and the sidings were being dismantled in April 1983. No 2745 was acquired by the Chatterley Whitfield Mining Museum, in Staffordshire, while No 2660 was noted out of use at Agecroft as late as 1987.

The colliery continued in production until July 1990, with most of the output going to direct to the power station by conveyor belt. The German built winding towers were demolished in January 1992 [34] and the site has now been cleared. The part adjacent to Agecroft Road is being developed as a business park - Agecroft Enterprise Park - by British Coal Enterprises Ltd.

Agecroft Power Stations

The first power station in Salford was opened under the auspices of the Corporation Gas Committee at Wallness Road in August 1895. It was taken over by the newly formed Electricity Committee in May 1897 and was replaced by a station at Frederick Road, which began supplying electricity in 1901 [35]. We think it likely coal supplies were brought in by the Manchester, Bolton and Bury canal, which ran near to both of the works.

In January 1921 preliminary work started on a new site at Agecroft, to the east of the Manchester and Bolton railway and the canal. The first plant was commissioned in December 1924, with the official opening on 23rd September 1925 [35]. The Frederick Road works, where the original buildings still survive, was then converted to a sub-station.

New sidings were provided for the Salford Corporation at Clifton Junction, adjacent to those serving the former Lancashire and Yorkshire Railway power station, under an agreement with the London, Midland and Scottish Railway dated 29th August 1926 [36].

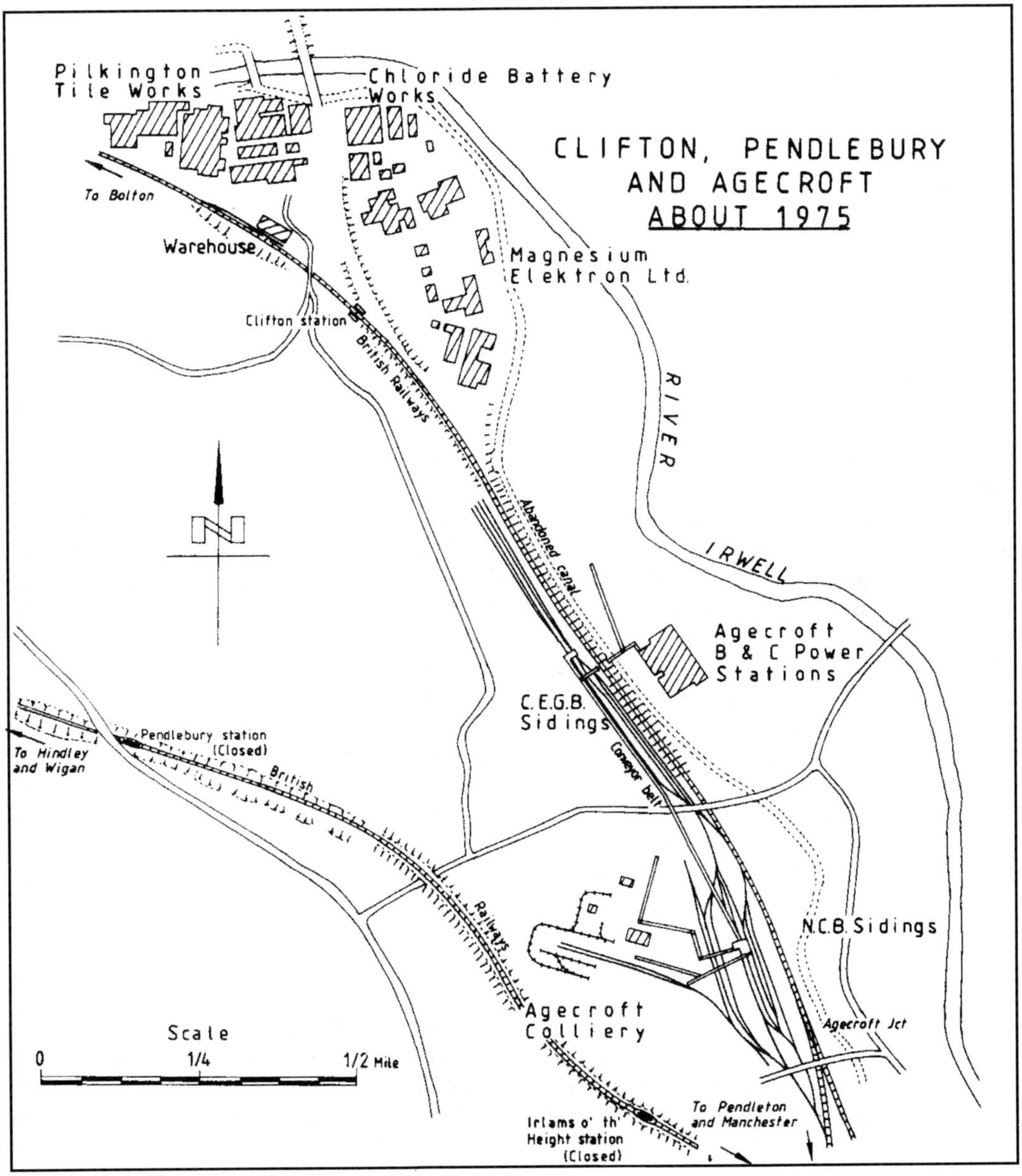

Coal was discharged from incoming railway wagons at tipplers and then taken by conveyor belt to a hopper on the opposite bank of the canal. From here a 2′6" gauge railway ran to the boiler house. The line was operated by electric traction, using overhead wire current collection, and was worked by two locomotives built by the English Electric Company in 1925.

After the second world war, Salford Corporation drew up plans for a new power station on an adjacent site. Sidings were built on the west side of the Manchester to Bolton railway and a conveyor was provided to take coal to both the old and new power stations. The conveyor passed over the main line and was covered by an agreement with the London, Midland and Scottish Railway dated1st January 1947 [27]. As a result of these developments, the narrow gauge railway and the associated sidings at Clifton Junction were closed early in 1947. Until the sidings serving the new "B" station had been completed, coal was brought in by road as a temporary measure.

With the nationalisation of the industry, the project was taken over by the British Electricity Authority as from 1st January 1948 and Agecroft "B" power station came into operation in December 1950.

To work the new sidings, two four coupled saddle tanks were obtained from Robert Stephenson and Hawthorns Ltd. Built in 1948, they carried nameplates with the inscriptions AGECROFT No 1 and AGECROFT No 2. They were delivered before the sidings had been completed and were stored for several months in the old L&Y power station buildings at Clifton Junction, by this time the property of Magnesium Elektron Ltd. When new, they were in a green livery, with black, yellow and red lining. Latterly, No 1 was painted unlined red and No 2 unlined blue.

A third identical engine came in 1954. It had been built by Stephenson and Hawthorns in 1951 for Back o' th' Bank Power Station at Bolton, but had seen little use there. It carried the name BOLTON No 1, but later became AGECROFT No 3. It was still in its original pale blue livery when it arrived, but was later painted unlined green.

With the reorganisation of the electricity industry, the Agecroft installations passed to the Central Electricity Authority on 1st May 1955 and to the Central Electricity Generating Board on 1st January 1958. Meanwhile, construction of a third power station, the "C" station, had commenced. It was officially opened on 24th May 1962.

Even after coal started to be delivered by conveyor belt direct from Agecroft Colliery, a considerable amount still came in by rail, mainly from Bickershaw and collieries in Yorkshire. Towards the end of 1961 a six coupled diesel mechanical locomotive was transferred from Bromborough Power Station on the Wirral to supplement the steam engines. It had been built by Robert Stephenson and Hawthorns Ltd and still carried the name BROMBOROUGH No 2 when it worked at Agecroft. It did not prove satisfactory and was sent to Whitebirk Power Station at Blackburn in July 1963.

When the conveyor from Agecroft Colliery was out of action, coal was transferred in internal user wagons over the connection with the colliery sidings. Initially the power station engines were used, but latterly the the work was performed by one of the NCB diesel locomotives [35].

The "A" station of the 1920s closed in March 1970, but with the "B" and "C" stations in operation, one locomotive was fully employed seven days a week in winter and two or three days a week in summer [35].

The "B" station ceased generating in 1980. Rail traffic finished in 1981 or 1982 and the sidings were removed. Thereafter, coal came in by road transport, although some continued to be supplied from Agecroft Colliery until production finished there in 1990.

No 3 shunting wagons under the tippler at Agecroft Power Station in May 1976 Adrian Booth

The modern locomotive shed at Agecroft Power Station showing the Stephenson and Hawthorns engines, taken in April 1979. Nos 1 and 3 stand outside, while No 2 is inside. The conveyor belt from Agecroft Colliery runs over the concrete viaduct in the background. Jim Peden

The "C"station closed in 1993 [37], having been taken over by National Power plc when the industry was privatised. The cooling towers and chimneys were demolished on 8th May 1994 [38]. The site is due to be cleared by May 1995.

Latterly the Central Electricity Generating Board had organised open days, when the locomotives had been on view to the public. The last was held on 12th and 13th September 1981, when Nos 2 and 3 were in steam, with No 1 on display [39].

Following the closure of the railway system, all three locomotives were sold for preservation. No 1 went to Mr P Clark, of Fulstow, near Grimsby, No 2 to Steamport Southport and No 3 to the Greater Manchester Museum of Science and Industry.

LOCOMOTIVE SUMMARY

Clifton Hall and Wheatsheaf Collieries

Various Knowles family partnerships until 1873
Andrew Knowles and Sons Ltd 1873 to 1929
Manchester Collieries Ltd 1929 to 1947
National Coal Board 1947 to 1961

Locomotives originally kept at Clifton Hall and at Wheatsheaf Screens from about 1892
Shed at Clifton Hall later closed, but spare engine kept in former wagon shop

Andrew Knowles and Sons Ltd and Manchester Collieries Ltd

CLIFTON HALL 0-6-0STIC P 518 1890 13"x18"
New to Andrew Knowles and Sons Ltd,Clifton Hall. xL class. Ex works 29-12-1890
Transferred to Agecroft Colliery, probably about 1933, but possibly before 1929
Name removed by 4-1937
Temporarily transferred to from Agecroft Colliery to Bradford Colliery mid /late 1937
Transferred from Bradford Colliery to Wheatsheaf Screens 7-12-1937
To N C B at Wheatsheaf Screens

0-4-0STOC P 502 1890 10"x14" 2'6"
Transferred from Knowles' Radcliffe collieries about 1895
Probably sold to Government Factory in 1918, see text

RADCLIFFE 0-6-0STIC MW 1192 1890 12"x17" 3'0"
Transferred from Knowles' Radcliffe collieries about 1895
To NCB at Wheatsheaf Screens

AGECROFT 0-6-0STIC MW 1120 1889 12"x17" 3'0"
Transferred from Agecroft Colliery probably about 1930, but possibly in 1928
Scrapped at Clifton Hall by George Cohen Sons and Co Ltd 7 and 8 -1938

National Coal Board

PECKETT 0-6-0STIC P 518 1890 13"x18"
First carried name in 1950s Originally named CLIFTON HALL
Ex Manchester Collieries Ltd at Wheatsheaf Screens
To Walkden Yard for repairs 24-11-1948, returned to Wheatsheaf 4-1-1950
To Walkden Yard for repairs 4-1-1950 and later at Outwood Washery
Returned to Wheatsheaf Screens 8-12-1955 after repairs at Walkden Yard
To Walkden Yard 3-1957 and scrapped there 1-1962

RADCLIFFE 0-6-0STIC MW 1192 1890 12"x17" 3'0"
Ex Manchester Collieries Ltd at Wheatsheaf Screens
To Walkden Yard for repairs 10-5-1948 and returned to Wheatsheaf Screens late 1948
Scrapped at Clifton Hall by T W Ward Ltd 9-1952

FAILSWORTH 0-6-0STOC HL 2727 1907 15"x22" 2'9"
Transferred from Moston Colliery 1-2-1951
To Walkden Yard for repairs 3-8-1953 and returned to Wheatsheaf Screens 12-8-1953
To Walkden Yard for repairs 12-1-1955 and returned to Wheatsheaf Screens 23-6-1955
Condemned 12-1957 and scrapped at Wheatsheaf 9-1958

ROBIN HOOD 0-4-0STOC CF 1200 1901 14"x19" 3'2"
Temporarily at Wheatsheaf Screens late 1949, May to August 1950 and April and May 1952

OUTWOOD 0-6-0STOC P 923 1901 14"x20" 3'7"
Temporarily at Wheatsheaf Screens March to June 1954

COLONEL 0-6-0STIC HE 1459 1927 15"x20" 3'7"
Temporarily at Wheatsheaf Screens January to September 1955, after repairs at Walkden Yard in 1954
Transferred to Wheatsheaf Screens late 1957, after repairs at Walkden Yard
To Walkden Yard for repairs 2-1959 and returned to Wheatsheaf 6-1959
To Walkden Yard 5-7-1961

WESTWOOD 0-4-0STOC HC 1036 1913 16"x24" 3'8"
Here temporarily early 1952
Transferred from Central Railways system mid 1957, after repairs at Walkden Yard late 1956 and early 1957
To Walkden Yard 3-9-1959

KEARSLEY 0-4-0STOC KS 3123 1918 15"x20" 3'2"
Transferred to Wheatsheaf after repairs at Walkden Yard, early 1959. Previously at Ashton Moss Colliery
To Walkden Yard 9-1961 and laid aside. Sold to Maudland Metals Ltd for scrap 2-1967

Chloride Batteries Ltd

Demonstration of battery powered mines locomotives June 1950

2'0" gauge

4w BE LMM 1056 1950
Later Edmund Nuttall Sons and Co (London) Ltd and used on contract for construction Haweswater Aqueduct

3'6" gauge

4w BEF GB 2221 1949
Ex Greenwood and Batley Ltd and returned to the firm
In 1-1951 to NCB Cowdenbeath Central Stores

2'6" gauge system to convey scrap lead to reverbatory furnace (in use 1961 to late 1969, early 1970)

SATURN 4w BE GB 2514 1954
Ex NCB 1961, formerly used at Mosley Common Colliery
Scrapped or sold about 1970

Lancashire and Yorkshire Railway Power Station

Transferred to London Midland and Scottish Railway in 1923
Closed 1931 and premises taken over by Magnesium Elektron Ltd

2 4wBE Hor 1917
New
Transferred to Greenhill Sleeper Depot, near Falkirk after closure
Broken up at Derby Works about 1947

Magnesium Elektron Ltd

0-4-0DE AW D26 1933
New (?)
Scrapped about 1962

MEL No 2 0-4-0STOC AB 2150 1942 14"x22" 3'5"
New
Scrapped about 1962

51230 0-4-0STOC Hor 923 1906 13"x18" 3'0 3/8"
On loan early 1957

0-4-0DM JF 22871 1939 60/66 HP
Ex British Aluminium Co Ltd, Newport, Mon 7-1961
Later at H P Bulmer and Co Ltd, Hereford.

Rail traffic ceased about 1965

Agecroft Colliery

Various Knowles family partnerships until 1873
Andrew Knowles and Sons Ltd 1873 to 1929
Manchester Collieries Ltd from 1929
Colliery closed July 1932, but loco kept on site until mid/late 1937
Reopened by National Coal Board - work started July 1953
Rail traffic ceased early 1980s
Colliery closed July 1990

Andrew Knowles and Sons Ltd and Manchester Collieries Ltd

AGECROFT 0-6-0STIC MW 1120 1889 12"x17" 3'0"
New to Andrew Knowles and Sons Ltd. Class K. Delivered to Agecroft Colly. Ex works 9-7-1889
Transferred to Wheatsheaf Screens possibly about 1928 or possibly about 1930

KNOWLES 0-6-0STIC MW 1520 1901 12"x17" 3'0"
Transferred from Pendleton Colliery probably about 1928
To Walkden Yard about 1930 and stored out of use
Sold to Harry Stephenson and Sons Ltd on 8-5-1936 and scrapped by them at Walkden Yard

CLIFTON HALL	0-6-0STIC	P	518	1890	13"x18"	

Name removed by 4-1937
Transferred from Wheatsheaf Screens probably about 1933, but possibly before 1929
Transferred from Agecroft to Bradford Colliery mid /late 1937
Transferred from Bradford Colliery to Wheatsheaf Screens 7-12-1937

THE SIRDAR	0-4-0STOC	VF	1541	1897	15"x20"	3'7"

The ILS lists show this locomotive as transferred from Bedford Colliery to Agecroft before going on to Robin Hood Screens. This had not been confirmed.

National Coal Board

LO 52	0-6-0DE	YE	2745	1960	280HP

63.000.401
New to Agecroft
To Chatterley Whitfield Mining Museum

LO 61	0-6-0DE	YE	2660	1957	280HP

63.000.402
Transferred from Central Railways system, Walkden, about 1962

2'6" gauge

No 1	4wDM	RH	387816	1955

New to Agecroft
Scrapped or sold about 1971

No 2	4wDM	RH	393331	1956

New to Agecroft
Scrapped or sold about 1971

Agecroft Power Stations

"A" Station
Salford Corporation 1921 to 1948
British Electricity Authority 1948 to 1955
Central Electricity Authority 1955 to 1958
Central Electricity Generating Board from 1958

"B" Station
British Electricity Authority until 1955
Central Electricity Authority 1955 to 1958
Central Electricity Generating Board from 1958

"C" Station
Central Electricity Authority 1955 to 1958
Central Electricity Generating Board from 1958

2'0" gauge line built for Salford Corporation's "A" Station

No 1	4wOHWE	EE	693	1925

New
Scrapped 10-1946

No 2	4wOHWE	EE	694	1925

New
Scrapped 10-1946
Track lifted 1947

Standard gauge system installed for "B" and "C" Stations

AGECROFT No 1	0-4-0STOC	RSH	7416	1948	14"x22"
New					
To P Clark, Fulstow, Nr Grimsby for preservation 12-1982					
AGECROFT No 2	0-4-0STOC	RSH	7485	1948	14"x22"
New					
To Steamport Southport 14-12-1982					
AGECROFT No 3	0-4-0STOC	RSH	7681	1951	14"x22"
Formerly BOLTON No 1, ex Back o' th' Bank Power Station, 9-1954					
To Greater Manchester Museum of Science and Industry, 11-5-1982					
BROMBOROUGH No 2	0-6-0DM	RSH	7746	1954	
Ex Bromborough Power Station about 11-1961					
To Whitebirk Power Station, Blackburn 7-1963					

Rail Traffic ceased 1981 or 1982

REFERENCES TO CHAPTER 7

1 LRO DDX/29/4
2 LRO DDX/29/50
3 LRO DDX/29/64
4 LRO DDX/29/65
5 LRO DDX/29/66
6 LRO DDX/29/67
7 LRO DDX/29/68
8 LRO DDX/29/69
9 MJ 20-9-1873
10 LRO PDR 195
11 1&2 Wm 4 cap lx; 23rd August 1831
12 EPJ 20-11-1891
13 EPJ 23-9-1892
14 *"Chronology of the Railways of Lancashire and Cheshire"* - M D Greville - Railway and Canal Historical Society, 1981
15 *"Collieries in the Manchester Coalfields"* G Hayes - De Archaeologische Pers, Eindhoven, nd
16 LNWR Sdgs Diag at GMRO A19/4/61
17 EPJ 30-4-1894
18 LNWR Sdgs Diag 248 dated 12.1916
19 LNWR Sdgs Diag 248 dated 7.1918
20 Letter Andrew Knowles and Sons Ltd to Peckett and Sons Ltd, 18th February 1918, copy supplied by Mr Ken Plant
21 *"Coalmining in Salford"* - G Preece - City of Salford Cultural Services, 1985
22 *"From Walkden Yard Records - Part Two"* - C A Appleton - *"Industrial Locomotive"* Vol 6, No 63, 1991
23 *"Register of Closed Passenger Stations and Goods Depots, 1830-1970"* - C R Clinker and J M Firth - publ by the authors, 1971
24 *"The Lancashire and Yorkshire Railway, Vol 2"* - John Marshall - David and Charles, Newton Abbot, 1970
25 *"Clifton Junction Power Station"* - D Chaplin - Platform 29, Spring 1989
26 *"Electric Locomotive No 2"* - B C Lane - *"Platform 29 "*, Spring 1989
27 Line Plan of Bolton to Manchester Line and Kearsley Branch - BR, LMR, Euston, 2 chains to 1 inch - at BRPB Manchester Office
28 *"Swinton and Pendlebury Journal"* 4-6-1975
29 LRO DDX/29/49
30 LROPDR 208
31 FJ 22-2-1896
32 FJ 11-12-1897
33 *"Guide to the Coalfields"* - Colliery Guardian, London, 1961
34 *"The Advertiser"* 9-1-1992
35 *"Agecroft Power Station"* - P Teather - Industrial Railway Society Journal, Vol 7 No 75, February 1978
36 LMSR Sdgs Diag 4421, 7-1928
37 *"Agecroft Power Stations 1924 to 1993"* - Peter Hooton - National Power plc, 1993
38 *"The Advertiser"* 12-5-1994
39 BLN 424

CHAPTER 8

PENDLETON, SALFORD AND ECCLES

We continue along the former Lancashire and Yorkshire Railway to Pendleton and Salford. Here, where the principal industries were textiles and engineering, the majority of the works had no rail connection. We shall be directing our attention to the few that did.

We start at the northern end of the old Pendleton Township, where a paper mill and an iron works were erected in the 1870s and where the firm of Andrew Knowles and Sons and its predecessor had been working a colliery since the 1830s. The sites here, still rail served, were redeveloped several times from the 1930s onwards for other industrial uses.

Nearer to the centre of Pendleton, William Barningham set up a works to manufacture wrought iron in the 1850s and went on to establish an engineering works to supply equipment for his later developments at Darlington. Three or four locomotives were built here in the 1860s. The works continued until about 1930, albeit under new management. The site was then taken over for use as scrap yard, which is still in existence.

We move next to the three Gas Works established by Salford Corporation, the first two of which, dating from the 1860s and the 1870s, were on sites alongside the former London and North Western Railway line near Ordsall Lane. Latterly operated by the North Western Gas Board, rail traffic did not cease until the early 1980s. We then follow the LNWR line to Weaste, where J E C Lord set up a tar distillation works in the 1890s. We conclude the chapter at Patricroft. James Nasmyth, later to become famous for the development of the steam hammer and the steam pile driver, established the Bridgewater Foundry at Patricroft in the 1830s. Locomotive construction started at an early date and, under the auspices of Nasmyth, Wilson and Company, who took over in 1867, it became the main line of business at the works. The firm ceased trading in 1939 and the works was later taken over by the Government for use as an ordnance factory.

Our final section deals with Patricroft and Monton Collieries, worked by the Lancaster family in the 1830s and 1840s. A later unsuccessful venture at Patricroft is noteworthy as being the only example of iron ore mining in South Lancashire.

PENDLETON

Agecroft Hall Paper Mill

The first edition of the 25" map, surveyed in 1888 to 1889, marks a paper mill on the east side of the Manchester and Bolton railway, immediately to the south of the boundary between the former townships of Agecroft and Pendleton. The map shows that there were a number of sidings serving the the various parts of the factory and connecting with the main line near Brindle Heath Siding Signal Cabin.

The works was probably established in the mid 1870s by William Chadwick and Sons, who are shown here in directories from 1879 [1] to 1893 [2]. It passed into the hands of the Sun Paper Mill Co Ltd in the mid 1890s, a new agreement in respect of the siding connection with the L&YR being signed by that firm on 24th December 1896 [3].

Towards the end of the first world war, the factory was taken over by Smith, Stone and Knight (Manchester) Ltd who entered into a new sidings agreement on 10th May 1918 [4]. The mill seems to have closed around 1925. It still appears in a directory of that year [5] but is not shown in one of 1926 [6]. Subsequent development of the site is dealt with later in the chapter. We have found no record of any locomotive associated with any of the owners of the factory, although the internal sidings were sufficiently large to have justified the use of one.

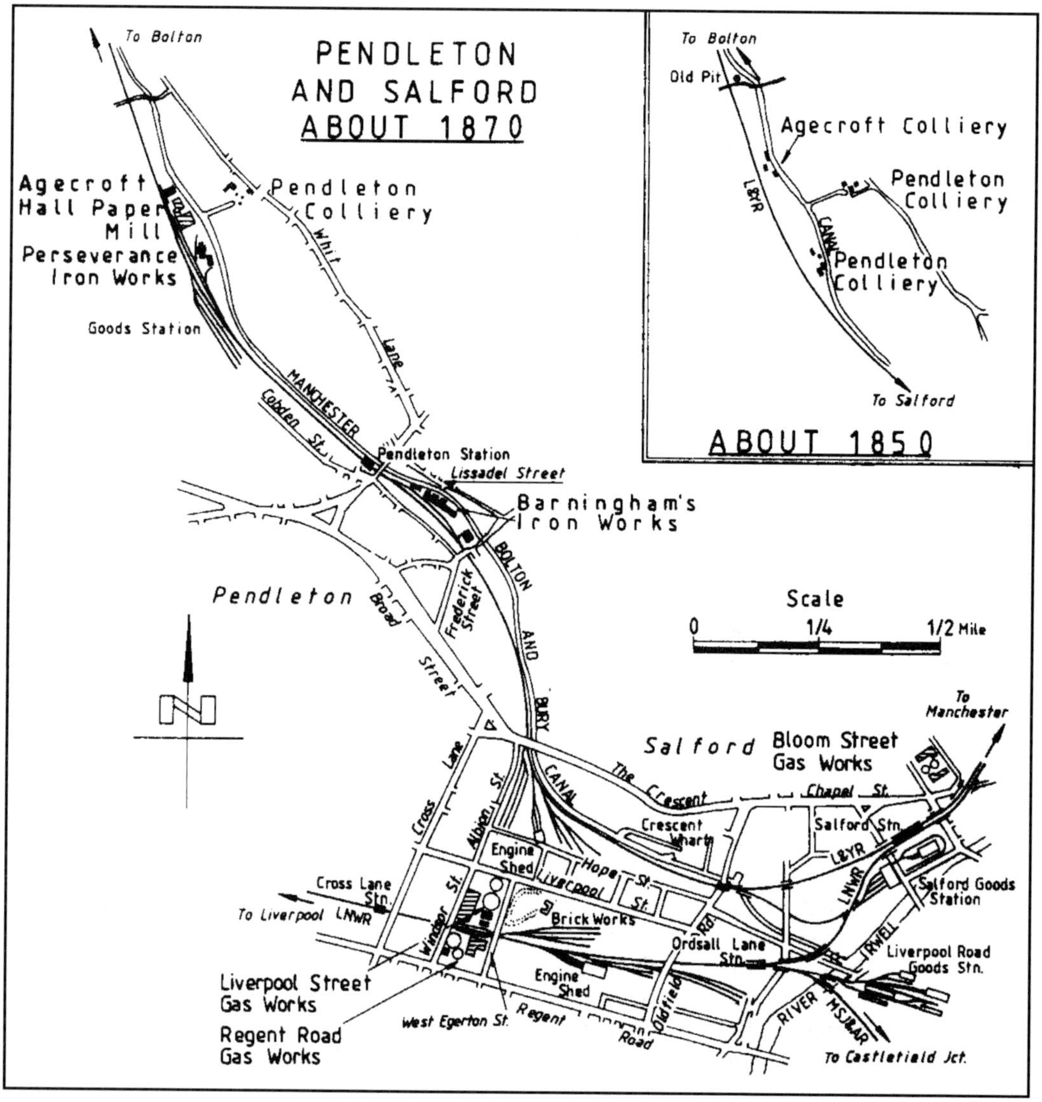

Perseverance Iron Works

The Perseverance Iron Works was located immediately to the south of Agecroft Hall Paper Mill, on a site between the Lancashire and Yorkshire Railway and the Manchester, Bolton and Bury Canal. It seems to have been established in the early 1870s by Maybury, Matthews and Company for the manufacture of wrought iron. The works is listed in a directory of 1871-2 [7] and first appears in the Mineral Statistics for 1873, when eight puddling furnaces are recorded on the site. From 1875 the owners are shown as Maybury, Matthews and Sharpe and, when the Statistics ceased to be published in 1881, the works had expanded to include 18 puddling furnaces and 2 rolling mills.

The firm opened up another factory at Huyton Quarry, near Liverpool, around 1879 [8] and in 1887 it was reported to be putting down additional sheet rolling mills at both works [9]. Between 1887 and 1889 contemporary directories [10,11] record a change in the name of the owners to Maybury and Marston, who are described as steel and iron hoop manufacturers and ironmasters.

The first edition of the 25" map, surveyed in 1888 to 1889, shows a small internal railway system, connecting with the Lancashire and Yorkshire Railway near Brindle Heath Siding Signal Cabin. We have been unable to discover if the firm possessed a locomotive.

The works appears to have closed around 1890 and is not shown in directories after 1891 [2,12]. The buildings were demolished and the site redeveloped to provide a screening plant serving Pendleton Colliery.

Pendleton Colliery

In the late 1820s [13], at about the same time that Andrew Knowles was starting his operations at Agecroft, John Purcell Fitzgerald sank two pits on a site a little further south. The Deposited Plans, prepared in 1830, for the proposed railway from Manchester to Preston, show that these were on the west bank of the Manchester, Bolton and Bury Canal, at the south end of the property later occupied by Maybury, Matthews and Company [14]. It is of interest to note that, until his death in February 1837, Robert Stephenson, younger brother of George Stephenson, was engineer and manager for Fitzgerald.

In July 1837, Fitzgerald started to sink a third pit on the east side of the canal and reached coal in 1840 at what was for the time an almost record depth of 464 yards [15,16]. The first edition of the 6" map, surveyed in 1845, shows that the new sinking was served by a short branch canal which terminated in a loading basin in the pit yard.

On 1st August 1843, there was serious flooding and it was at first thought that the colliery was totally destroyed [17]. Inspection showed that the damage was not as serious as first feared [18] and by December of that year a beam engine with a 75½" cylinder had been installed in an attempt to clear the water [19]. Production restarted in 1846, but ceased again in 1848 [13,20].

In 1852 the property was purchased by the firm of Andrew Knowles and Sons [20,21]. New shafts were sunk in 1857 [21] on the site to the east of the canal, where coal was reached at 3600 feet [13]. The earlier workings, west of the canal, were abandoned.

Until the mid 1890s, much of the coal was distributed by road transport for local domestic and industrial use and the remainder was despatched by canal. A newspaper article of 1892 [22] stated that there were three screens at the pit bank for loading coal into boats or carts and that there was no railway connection.

At this time modernisation was in hand. In 1891 two new shafts had been commenced but were abandoned before completion due to surface flooding and subsidence [13]. A little later a screening plant and loading facilities for railway wagons were built on the opposite side of the canal, adjacent to the Manchester and Bolton railway line, on the Perseverance Iron Works site. An overhead tubway was constructed to link the colliery to the new plant, the bridge over the canal being built in 1894 [23].

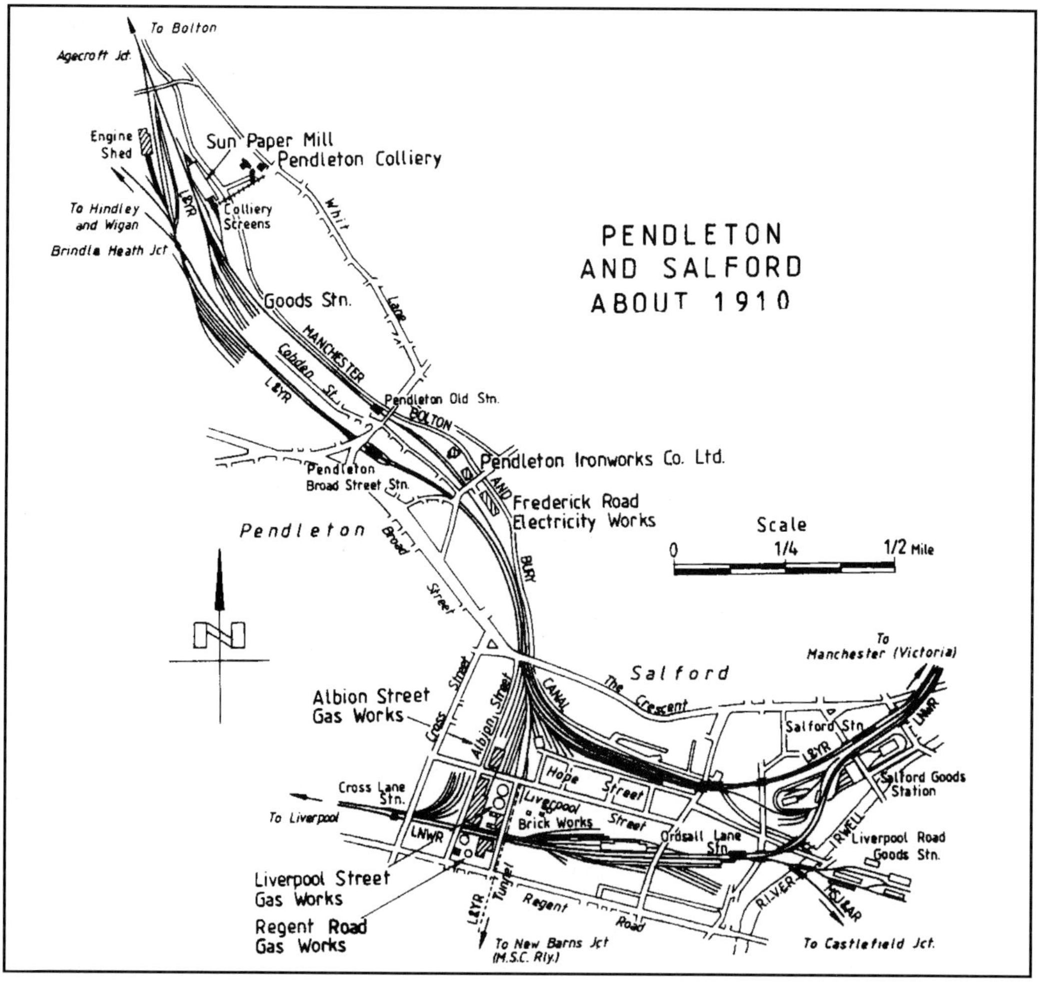

The connection between the sidings serving the screens and the Lancashire and Yorkshire Railway was provided under an agreement dated 23rd January 1895. A contemporary sidings diagram marks a small locomotive shed on the colliery company's property [24], but we have been unable to discover anything about the engines used at that time.

The manufacturer's records show that a six coupled saddle tank was purchased from Manning Wardle and Company of Leeds in 1901. Named KNOWLES, it appears to have been delivered to Pendleton Colliery. Before that it seems likely that shunting was performed by one of the engines made redundant by the closure of Andrew Knowles and Sons' Radcliffe Collieries.

Pendleton Colliery was taken over by Manchester Collieries Ltd in 1929. Workings in the Albert and Crombrouke seams had been abandoned in 1915 [13] and, although coal production was declining, new steel headgear was fitted to No 1 Pit in 1931 [25]. The colliery eventually closed in April 1939, with the exhaustion of the Rams seam [13].

We do not know if the rail connected screening plant remained in use until the end. The bridge carrying the tubway over the canal was rebuilt in 1927 [23], but we think the screens may have been taken out of use shortly after the amalgamation.

There is photographic evidence that KNOWLES was at Agecroft Colliery, probably in the late 1920s. According to old employees, KNOWLES arrived at Walkden Yard about 1930 and stood out of use for several years. Walkden Yard records [26] show that it was purchased by Harry Stephenson and Sons Ltd, of Hindley, on 8th May 1936 and was subsequently broken up.

Manchester Oxide Co Ltd

The derelict land formerly occupied by the Pendleton Colliery screens was taken over during the second world war by the Manchester Oxide Co Ltd. The firm, which had a factory for the manufacture of prussian blue at Miles Platting [27], set up a plant to process spent iron oxide which arrived by rail from gas works in South Lancashire and elsewhere. New sidings were laid in under an agreement with the London, Midland and Scottish Railway, dated 15th May 1942 [28,29].

Soon after taking over the site, the Manchester Oxide Company obtained a small four coupled locomotive for shunting its very limited internal railway system. Named MARCIA, it was purchased second hand from the West of Scotland Shipbreaking Co, of Troon in Ayrshire. It had been built by Peckett and Sons of Bristol in 1923 and had previously been used at the Mauchline quarries of Marcus Bain Ltd. It was first observed at Pendleton on 7th November 1943.

When MARCIA was undergoing repair, it was necessary to find a replacement. According to the Industrial Railway Society lists MONARCH, a four coupled saddle tank built by Peckett and Sons, was hired in 1945 from Cudworth and Johnson Ltd, the Wrexham machinery merchants. The lists also show that another four coupled saddle tank, also of Peckett's make, came from Murgatroyds Salt Co of Middlewich at an unspecified date.

By 1948 the Manchester Oxide Co Ltd had been taken over by Hardman and Holden Ltd, an old established Manchester chemical firm [30]. The Pendleton plant continued to operate under the new owners until the early 1960s. Rail traffic is believed to have ceased late in 1962 or early in 1963, although the sidings agreement was not formally terminated until 31st December 1968 [29].

MARCIA was sold to the Kent and East Sussex Railway Preservation Society at Tenterden and had left Pendleton by July 1963.

Later developments

The 1/2500 Ordnance Survey map published in 1952 shows that some of the buildings of the former Agecroft Hall Paper Mill had been taken over for what is described as an Asphalt Works. The two long sidings running northwards from Brindle Heath Siding Signal Cabin, which had previously served the paper mill, were still in situ as were several of the shorter lines within the mill area itself.

We think that the works was operated by Asphaltic Roadways Ltd and Highways Construction Ltd. Both firms are shown in a directory of November 1957 [31] with an address at the Agecroft Commercial Estate, which we presume was a new name for the paper mill premises, now let out to light industry. We have no record of a locomotive belonging to either of these firms and, if the sidings were still in use, we think it likely that the shunting was performed by the engine belonging to the Manchester Oxide Company.

By 1961 [32] the Amalgamated Asphalte Co Ltd had taken over the land vacated by Hardman and Holden. Stone and possibly other raw materials were brought in by rail. There was a new agreement with British Railways dated 24th September 1964 and a revised Siding Diagram was issued in November 1964 [33]. The business still continues under the ownership of the Permanite Asphalt Company, but there has been no rail traffic for some years.

Between 1970 [34] and 1972 [35] operations on the site of the now demolished Agecroft Hall Paper Mill were taken over by Tarmac Roadstone Holdings Ltd. In 1977, this firm applied for a grant under the 1974 Railways Act [36] to extend its railway facilities [37]. The two long sidings near the main line were brought back into use and new equipment for unloading stone from railway wagons was erected.

The diminutive eight inch Peckett locomotive MARCIA at Hardman and Holden's Manchester Oxide works at Brindle Heath in June 1959.
Jim Peden

A four wheeled diesel electric locomotive was purchased from W Bush and Co Ltd of Alfreton. It arrived at Pendleton in December 1978 and was used to shunt at the stone terminal. It also shunted at the neighbouring scrap yard of Arnott Young and Co Ltd, which had been moved here from Trafford Park between 1976 [38] and 1978 [39]

Rail traffic ceased towards the end of 1981, although the sidings and the wagon discharging equipment are still in situ at the time of writing. By December 1981 the diesel locomotive was stored off the track. It was noted to be still here on 24th May 1982, but had gone by 26th August, following its purchase for preservation.

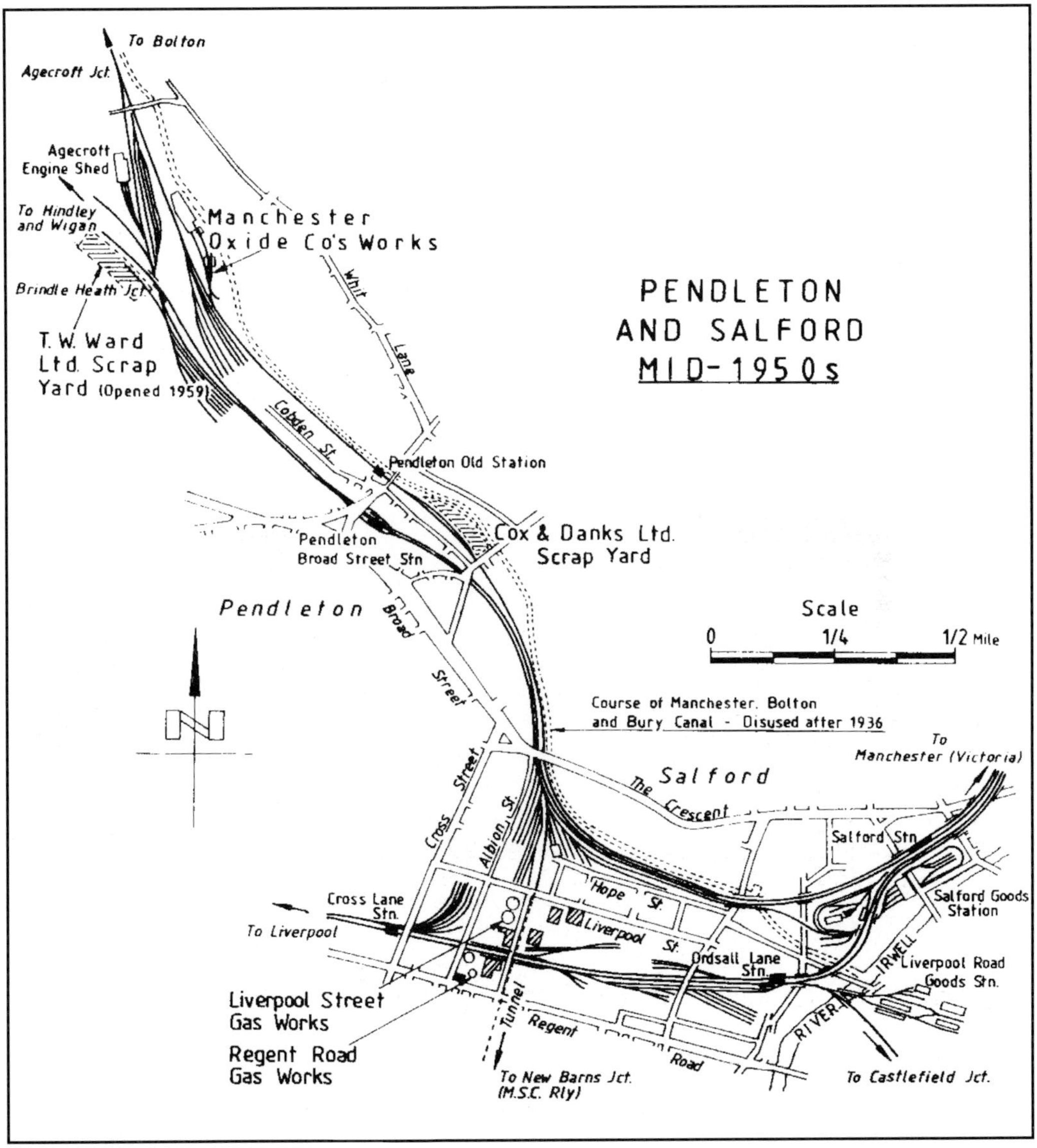

T W Ward Ltd's Scrap Yard at Brindle Heath

A scrap yard was established by Thomas W Ward Ltd, the Sheffield based machinery and scrap merchants, on vacant land on the south side of the Pendleton to Hindley line. Sidings were provided which connected with the main line near to Brindle Heath Junction. The yard was noted to be under development in April 1959, with a new looking steam crane at work. It was still active in June 1982, but by August 1983 the site had been cleared.

Machinery was mainly brought in by road, but both main line and industrial locomotives were also broken up from time to time. A list of those observed by the authors is given in the Locomotive Summary at the end of the chapter.

Diesel locomotives were used for shunting wagons within yard. The first to arrive, in March 1959, had been built by John Fowler and Company of Leeds in 1957 and came from the firm's Templeborough Works at Sheffield. After that a succession of other diesel locomotives were employed, some of which had been purchased for scrap and some of which came from other of Ward's sites.

Awaiting the scrap man's torch at T W Ward's yard at Brindle Heath in 1960. Left to right - SIR ANDREW NOBLE, SIR WILLIAM KAY and RICHARD BURTLES. Harry Townley

Greater Manchester Refuse Disposal Authority's Siding

The most recent development in the Pendleton area has been the Refuse Transfer Station, constructed on the site of a former railway goods yard. Originally built for the Greater Manchester County Council it later passed into the ownership of the Greater Manchester Waste Disposal Authority. Here, rubbish brought by road is pulverised and loaded into containers.

The containers, which are which mounted on flat wagons, are taken by rail to various landfill sites. The small amount of shunting which is required is performed by the British Rail engines which work the trains.

The connection with the Manchester and Bolton line was placed on to TOPS (British Rail's computerised data bank of sidings) on 6th October 1985 [40]. The transfer station was noted to be complete by 12th December 1985, when wagons and containers were present in the sidings.

The Transfer Station closed temporarily in the summer of 1993 when the quarries at Appley Bridge had been filled up. It was expected to reopen during 1995, following negotiations to use old ironstone workings near Scunthorpe for landfill.

William Barningham's Pendleton Ironworks

We now move further south and to an earlier period in time, to William Barningham's Pendleton Ironworks. This was established in the early 1850s on a site north of Frederick Road, between the Lancashire and Yorkshire Railway and the canal.

William Barningham had come to Manchester in the early 1840s, after working on the Paris and Rouen Railway, and had established a brass and iron foundry at Collyhurst with his brothers James and Christopher. The business does not seem to have been a success and the partnership was dissolved on 4th August 1845 [41]. William Barningham is next heard of in Middlesbrough, where he had set up a works for the manufacture of railway switches and crossings.

In 1851 he entered into another partnership with his brother James with the object of returning to Manchester. The Pendleton Iron Works was erected in 1852 as the result of a large contract from the Lancashire and Yorkshire Railway to supply 4000 tons of rails and 2000 tons of chairs, reworking old material supplied by the railway company [42]. The partnership was dissolved 27th April 1853, when James withdrew, leaving William in sole control [43].

In May 1858, William Barningham started construction of a new iron works at Albert Hill, Darlington, for which he had purchased a large building originally used to house the Exhibition of Art Treasures of the United Kingdom which had been held in Manchester the previous year. A few years later there were further developments at Darlington, when the Springfield Works was established nearby. In 1872, the Darlington establishment was described as the largest works in the country manufacturing wrought iron, with a total of 192 puddling furnaces and associated rolling mills [44]. The works was stated to have six miles of railway tracks and four locomotives were employed there.

The Pendleton Iron Works, where Barningham had his headquarters, was a much smaller affair, with around 20 puddling furnaces. It specialised in the manufacture of railway equipment, whereas the Darlington works made a very wide range of plates, bars and similar products. Most of the equipment needed by the firm was made in-house in an engineering shop which had been set up adjacent to the Pendleton works. In January 1867 [45] it was reported that work was in progress on several new rolling mills for the Darlington works, a beam blowing engine with a 46" steam cylinder and a number of steam hammers. There is also a tantalising statement that "amongst other articles now in progress are three small locomotives for use at the Darlington establishment". No other information seems to have survived, in Lancashire or at Darlington, about these engines. It has been suggested [46] that at least two other locomotives built by the firm were employed at Darlington, but we have been unable to confirm this.

William Barningham seems to have retired from active participation in the business in the early 1870s. He sold the Darlington works in 1872 or 1873 [43,47] although he appears to have retained some financial interest in the successor company, the Darlington Iron Co Ltd, a firm which went bankrupt early in 1881 [47].

Isaac Bowes, who had joined the firm in 1851 and had later risen to the position of manager, formed the firm of William Barningham and Co Ltd to purchase the Pendleton works. The new owners took possession of the premises on 1st November 1872, when the plant included 20 puddling furnaces and four forges. In 1874 a public company was created with the same title [48].

By late 1880s the company was in financial difficulty and the works was advertised for sale by auction on 21st to 23rd September 1886 [49]. There was no acceptable bid and subsequent attempts to sell by private treaty were equally unsuccessful. In 1888 the firm gave up the part of the works devoted to wrought iron manufacture, but retained the offices and the engineering shops.

The ironworks reverted to the William Barningham's executors, the ground landlords. It does not seem to have reopened and remained derelict until 1892, when it was reported that the works was being dismantled to make way for a new factory for a firm making steel axleboxes [50]. The Steel Railway Journal Box Co Ltd is listed here in directories between 1894 [51] and 1925 [5].

Isaac Bowes continued to run the engineering works until March 1893. The liquidation of William Barningham & Co Ltd was complete by November 1893 and the building and site reverted to Barningham's trustees. Isaac's son Alfred and a Mr Kay formed the Pendleton Iron Works Co Ltd to carry on the business of switch and crossing makers and iron and steel merchants in premises leased from the Trustees. The works was extended in 1900, when a large constructional shop was added for the manufacture of roofs, bridges and similar steel structures.

The constructional works seems to have closed around 1926, the last year that it appears in the Trade Directories [52,53]. The single siding parallel to the main line, which had presumably been laid in for William Barningham's iron works, was retained by the various successor companies. There is no evidence that a locomotive in use at the works at any time and, indeed, the siding was too restricted in size to warrant such a provision.

One locomotive did, however, pass through the books of Isaac Bowes' firm. William Barningham and Co Ltd were awarded the contract to construct and equip the 2'6" gauge railway system which the Manchester Corporation Cleansing Department established on Carrington Moss in the 1880s. A four coupled saddle tank, named WINDSOR and later HUGO SHAW, was ordered by Barninghams from Black Hawthorn and Co Ltd of Gateshead on behalf of the Corporation. It was used by Barningham on the construction of the railway system at Carrington before being handed over to the Corporation.

Cox and Danks Ltd's Scrap Yard at Pendleton

The Barningham site was taken over by Cox and Danks Ltd as a scrap yard around 1935 [54,55]. Much of the machinery bought for dismantling came by road but the siding was retained to despatch scrap metal. Following a merger around 1979 [39,56], the yard became the property of the Cox and Danks Division of George Cohen, Sons and Co Ltd. The scrap yard still remains in use at the time of writing. Since 1989 or 1990, following a take-over by the Sheppard Group, it has been operated under the name of George Cohen Ltd.

After the second world war a number of industrial locomotives came here to be broken up. The first two arrived by rail in October 1955, from Imperial Chemical Industries Ltd, which was then replacing steam locomotives by diesels at its Mid Cheshire works. Named KELVIN and FARADAY, they were both four coupled well tanks, built by Borrows of St Helens. They were followed by four more engines of the same type, but of a later series, built by Kerr, Stuart and Company of Stoke in Trent. They arrived, again by rail, in October 1956 and all had had their nameplates removed. Three were identified as ROSCOE, BOYLE and JOHN BRUNNER. The fourth was probably LUDWIG MOND.

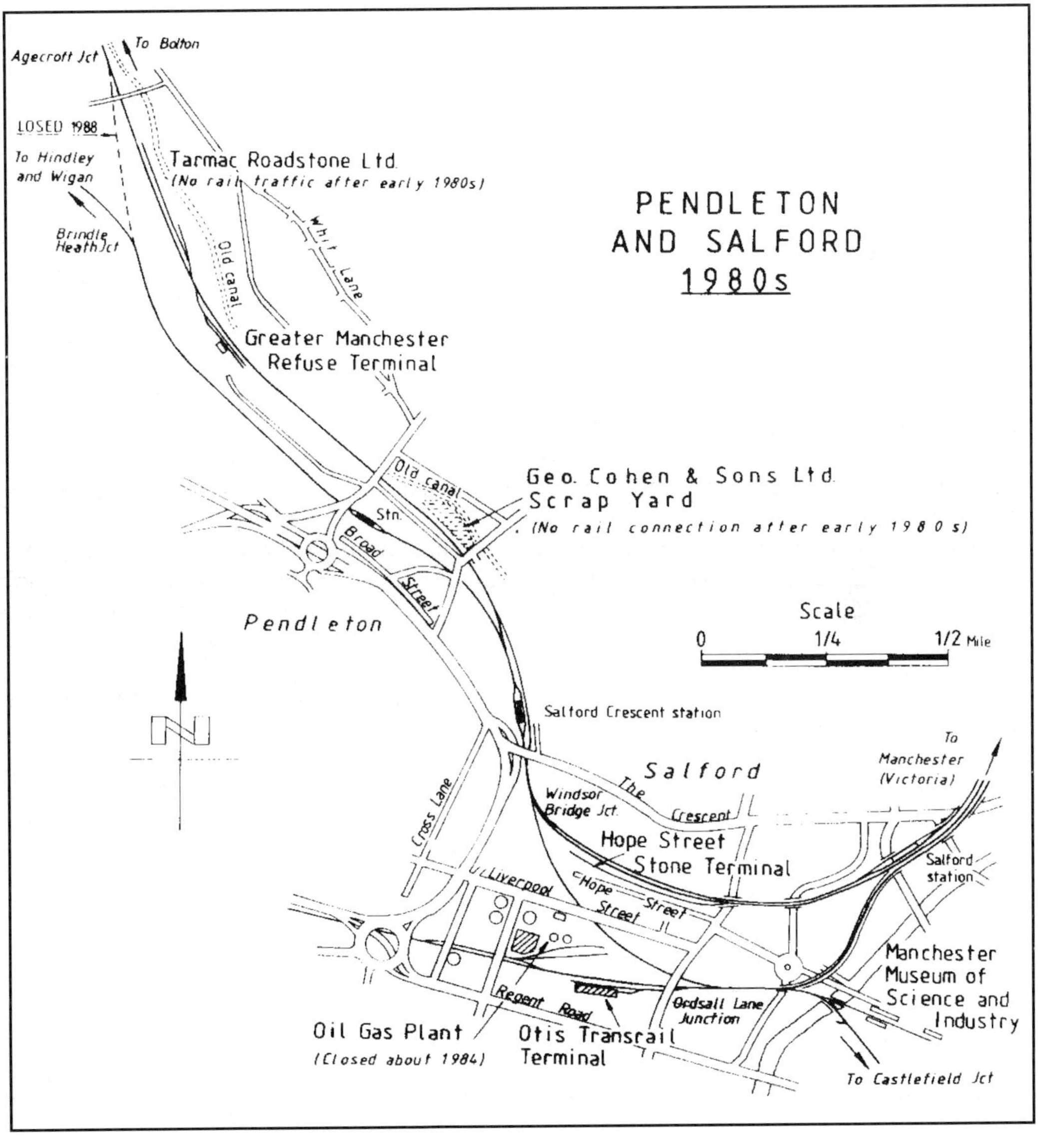

Until the late 1970s, the yard relied on rail mounted cranes for shunting purposes. By June 1976 a Fowler diesel locomotive, originally built in 1945 for the Air Ministry, had been acquired from the Cransley depot of George Cohen and Sons Ltd. By March 1980 it was out of use, standing under Frederick Road Bridge. Its place as working locomotive had been taken by another Fowler, which had come from the London Brick Company's Calvert works.

Rail traffic ceased during 1981, the siding being noted out of use in December of that year. The main line connections had been taken out by September 1983. By January 1984 the ex Air Ministry engine was the only locomotive at the site and had been moved into the works yard to be broken up.

An October 1956 view of Cox and Danks' yard at Pendleton, on the site of Barningham's iron works. Three well tanks, DYAR, JOHN BRUNNER and probably LUDWIG MOND, have recently arrived for scrap from ICI's Winnington Works. They were built by Kerr, Stuart and Co of Stoke to a design which originated with Edward Borrows of St Helens. Frank Smith

SALFORD

Hope Street Stone Terminal

One of the more recent developments has been the construction of a terminal for off-loading stone brought in by rail on the south side of the former Lancashire and Yorkshire line at Hope Street. This appears to have opened shortly after 1970, the first year that the owners, Kingston Minerals Ltd, are shown in the directories [57,58].

The development of the site can be traced on contemporary versions of the 1/1250 map. That issued in 1970 shows that the tracks leading to the former Hope Street goods yard had mostly been cleared away. The southernmost pair of main line tracks, the former goods lines, were then taken out of use and, as can be seen from the 1982 map, converted into sidings serving the terminal. Wagon discharging equipment was built on what had been the up goods line, and from here stone was taken by a conveyor belt to the storage area.

By 1985 [59,60], the site had been taken over by the A.R.C. Group and is now operated by R.M.C. (North West) Ltd. Although there was some reduction in traffic in 1990 [61], the terminal is still served by trains conveying stone from the Peak District. Wagons are placed in position by British Rail locomotives and no private shunting engine is employed.

Duncan Transrail Terminal

Another recent development has been the rail served warehouse established by Duncan Transrail Ltd in 1983 on the south side of the former LNWR Manchester to Liverpool line, west of Oldfield Road bridge. The firm obtained a grant in 1982, under Section 8 of Railways Act 1974 [36], to provide terminal facilities where goods could be transhipped from rail to road for local delivery. A second grant was obtained in 1986 to extend the facilities.

Duncan Transrail Ltd was acquired by the Faber Prest Group in 1988 and since February 1989 the terminal has been operated by Otis Euro Transrail Ltd. In 1990, it was serviced by a daily trip working from Arpley Yard, Warrington. Traffic included barrelled beer from London and paper imported from Austria in VTG wagons [62].

A four coupled diesel mechanical locomotive was purchased in 1983 from the Purfleet Deep Wharf and Storage Co Ltd, at Erith in Kent. Named TAURUS and carrying the number 2, it had been built by the Vulcan Foundry of Newton le Willows in 1951.

A second locomotive was obtained second hand from British Railways in May 1989. This was a six coupled diesel machine, with mechanical drive, built at Swindon in 1960 and numbered 03170 in BR stock.

At the time of writing the terminal still in use and and at least one of the locomotives remains in service.

Salford Gas Works

A public supply of gas was inaugurated in 1819 from a works in Clowes Street. A second works was brought into production a few years later on land between Green Bank and Back Hampson Street.

In 1830, the Salford Improvement Commissioners were established by Act of Parliament [63]. They were empowered to manufacture and supply gas and a new works was built at Bloom Street, which commenced operation in 1835. The two original works were closed in the course of the next few years [64], and the Bloom Street Works became the property of Salford Corporation when the Borough was incorporated on 16th April 1844.

Coal for the Bloom Street Works was delivered by horse and cart, presumably from the nearby canal wharves. With an increasing demand for gas and with an enlarged area of supply, which by the 1850s included Pendleton, Broughton, Eccles, Patricroft, Swinton and Pendlebury, the decision was taken by the Corporation to build a new works with rail access.

Land was purchased on the south side of the LNWR Liverpool and Manchester line, between Windsor Street and West Egerton Street, in 1858 and the Regent Road Works came into operation a year or so later. Two short sidings were built adjacent to the main line, from which turntables gave access to the retort houses. The connection with the LNWR, to the east of Egerton Street bridge, was provided under an agreement dated 28th March 1860 [65].

Construction of the Liverpool Street Works, on the opposite side of the London and North Western Railway, was authorised by Parliament in 1867 [66]. Work started in 1868 and was completed in 1869. As at Regent Road, two short sidings were provided running parallel to the main line, with turntables to serve the retort houses. Connections with the LNWR were laid in at each end of the works under an agreement dated 21st September 1870 [65].

In 1891 land north of Liverpool Street was purchased from the Lancashire and Yorkshire Railway and in 1893 construction of the Albion Street Works was started [64]. Coal came in by rail over a siding which connected with the adjacent Lancashire and Yorkshire sidings.

To enable the Liverpool Street works to be supplied by the L&YR as well as by the LNWR, the siding serving the Albion Street works was extended southwards, crossing Liverpool Street on the level. This was apparently done during the early years of the present century. The level crossing over Liverpool Street is not shown on the second edition of the 25" map, revised in 1894 but appears on the 25" map revised in 1916 and published in 1922.

There were extensions at Liverpool Street 1900 and 1901, followed by modernisation of the earlier plant in 1905 and 1906, which included the provision of new stoking machinery and new coke handling equipment [67]. By 1920 two 20 ton hydraulic hoists had been installed which lifted wagons from the sidings to an elevated railway over the coal stores [64].

There were extensions at Albion Street in 1902, 1903 and 1909. At Regent Road, the construction of new retorts, started in 1914, was not completed until 1920. Meanwhile, plant was installed by the Ministry of Munitions in March 1916, to extract toluene and benzine for the manufacture of explosives [64].

Plans had been drawn up for a new works on the north side of the London and North Western line, east of West Egerton Street, before the first world war. Land near Wilma Terrace and Barlow's Road had been purchased from the Earl of Ellesmere in 1912 and 1913, but building work did not start until the early 1920s. The railway sidings and the weighbridge house were reported to be complete by the end of 1925 [67]. At the Regent Road Works, there were extensions and reconstruction of the older plant in 1935 and 1936 [67].

There was further development at the Liverpool Street works, on the site east of West Egerton Street, during the second world war. The plant erected in the 1920s was demolished to make way for a new works, with up to date coal handling plant and a revised siding layout. The Corporation's first locomotive was delivered in 1943 for use here. Built by Ruston and Hornsby of Lincoln, it was one of that firm's standard 48 HP four wheeled diesel engines. Prior to this shunting operations at the various works had been performed by means of capstans and ropes.

The industry was nationalised on 1st May 1949 and the Salford undertaking was absorbed into the North Western Gas Board. At Regent Road a new plant had been been erected in the period immediately after the second world war. By June 1953, when the survey was made for a revision of the 1/1250 map, the Albion Street works had been closed and the plant at the original Liverpool Street works site, west of West Egerton Street, had been demolished, leaving only the gas holders.

As far as railway operations were concerned, shunting at the Regent Road works was still carried out using capstans. On the north side of the main line, a second and more powerful Ruston and Hornsby locomotive was put into service in 1950 to supplement the one delivered in 1943.

With a run down in gas production and with increasing amounts of coal coming in by road, the locomotives became redundant in the early 1960s and were transferred to other North Western Gas Board establishments. The wartime plant east of West Egerton was demolished in the late 1960s and the site had been cleared by the time a revision of the 1/10,000 map was published in 1972. The carbonisation plant at Regent Road seems to have remained in operation, closing on 25th March 1973 [68].

A new works to manufacture gas from oil was erected on the site north of the main line, east of West Egerton Street. By August 1978, this was being served by two trains of tank wagons each week, which ran from Washwood Heath, Birmingham [69]. However, the new plant did not have its own locomotives, the wagons being placed at the unloading point by the incoming British Railways trains.

Natural gas had already started to be supplied in Salford in 1975, making the new works largely redundant. It continued in operation until about 1984 [70], when the plant was mothballed. The siding connection with the main line was was retained for a few years and was taken off TOPS on 3rd June 1988 [71]. The private sidings agreement was determined on 9th March 1989 [70].

Two gas holders on the original Liverpool Street site and a Gas Board stores east of West Egerton Street are all that now remains. The Regent Road site has been redeveloped as offices.

ECCLES AND PATRICROFT

Mode Wheel Sewage Works and Weaste Tar Works

In 1876, Salford Corporation took a decision to provide a plant for the treatment of sewage, which had previously been discharged direct into the River Irwell. A site adjacent to the river, at Mode Wheel, was selected and the construction contract was let to S W Pilling of Manchester a few years later. A pair of compound vertical pumping engines was supplied by James Watt and Company of Birmingham. The works was complete by January 1883 [72] and were formally opened, with much ceremony, on 6th July of the same year by the Mayor of Borough, Alderman R Husband [73].

Following the completion in 1895 of the London and North Western Railway's branch from Eccles to join the Manchester Ship Canal Company's system at Weaste Junction, a connection was provided to serve the sewage works. The date when this was opened has not been recorded, although it may have been earlier than the formal agreement between Salford Corporation and the LNWR, dated 2nd November 1900 [74].

The private siding left the LNWR near the bridge under Eccles New Road and ran past the precipitation tanks to the east end of the works, where there were spurs to the pump house and other plant. Beyond here it extended into the John Edward Calvert Lord's Ship Canal Tar Works.

Lord's firm had been founded in 1896 [75] and the works, at the corner of Clowes Street and Borough Road, was in operation by 1899 [76]. Crude liquor, brought in by rail tanker from various gas works, was processed to recover a variety of chemical products.

We have been unable to discover what motive power was used in the earliest days and how the two operators shared the working of the siding. The first locomotive which we have on record was a small M5 class four coupled saddle tank obtained by J E C Lord in 1906 from Peckett and Sons of Bristol, named LORD WEASTE. Lords then took over responsibility for working the Corporation traffic to and from the LNWR exchange point as well as their own.

There were extensions to the sewage works in 1909 and a major reconstruction after the first world war. Work started in July 1920 and there was a formal opening ceremony by Alderman Littler, Chairman of Irwell Conservancy Commission, on 22nd October 1925 [77].

LORD WEASTE which came from Peckett and Sons in 1906. The name was a play on words. Mr J E C Lord was never elevated to the peerage ! Alex Appleton collection

A narrow gauge railway system had been installed at the sewage works around the turn of the century and is shown in some detail on the second edition of the 25" map, revised 1905. We presume that the wagons were originally propelled manually or were hauled by horses, but during the reconstruction of 1920 to 1925, the contractors, Wellerman Bros Ltd, of Sheffield, are said to have made use of a steam locomotive which worked over temporary tracks which gave access to the construction site.

From information which we obtained during a discussion with the tar works locomotive driver in 1947, this appears to have been one of the 4-6-0 tank locomotives, nearly 500 of which were supplied by the Baldwin Locomotive Works at Philadelphia for service with the British Army during the first world war. A number were returned to this country after hostilities ceased and were resold for industrial use.

The steam locomotive, which was never the property of Salford Corporation, left Weaste when the contract was completed. We were told, however, that the Corporation then purchased a petrol locomotive for its own use, although we have been unable to confirm this. The narrow gauge system was taken out in the late 1930s or early 1940s.

Returning now to developments at Lords, a Creosote Works was built at the west end of the sewage works site, probably towards the end of the war. Two sidings were laid in to connect with the Corporation's line and are shown on the relevant LNWR Siding Diagram dated 1919 [78]. In the early 1920s the firm was turned into a limited liability company with the title of J E C Lord (Manchester) Ltd. This in turn became part of Lancashire Tar Distillers Ltd, which was formed in 1929 through the amalgamation of the leading north west firms engaged in this line of business [75].

The Peckett locomotive of 1906 was replaced in 1924 by a larger R2 class four coupled saddle tank from the same makers. Unlike its predecessor, it was not named. The new engine continued in service until 1959, when it, in turn, was replaced by a "Planet" diesel locomotive supplied by F C Hibberd and Co Ltd, of Park Royal, London.

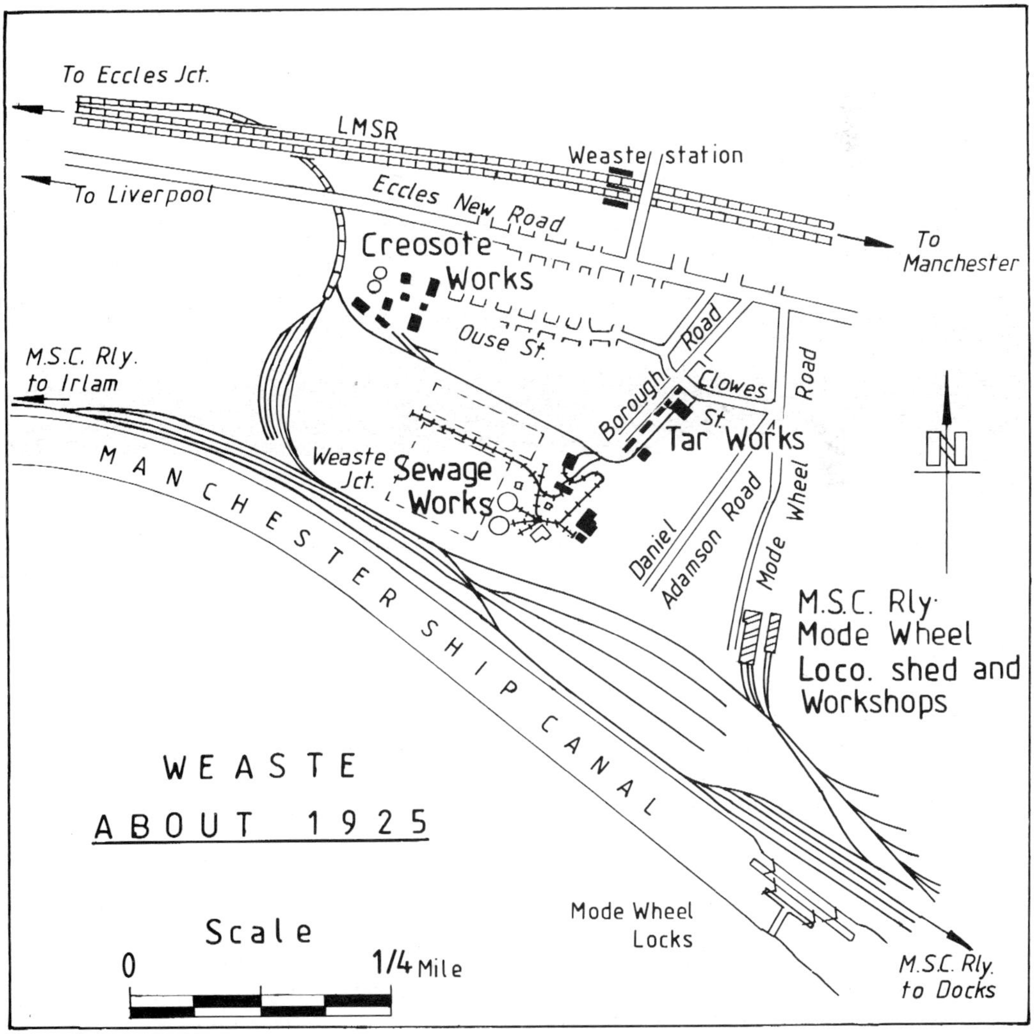

Rail traffic is said to have ceased in 1974 when the "Planet" locomotive was transferred to the firm's Cadishead Works. The tar works and the creosote works at Weaste seem to have ceased production at about the same date, although the Borough Road address appears in the Yellow Pages until 1981.

The Sewage Works, now owned by North West Water plc, is still in operation at the time of writing. The Creosote Works has been demolished, while the site of the Tar Works at Borough Road has been taken over by British Fuels Ltd. Along with a small tank farm nearby, which had previously been used for storing edible oils, it now forms this firm's Weaste terminal.

Fuel oil was delivered to the terminal by rail but the sidings serving the tar works and the sewage works were not brought back into use. Instead, two, and later three, sidings were provided on the south of the Manchester Ship Canal lines leading across Daniel Adamson Road to the Mode Wheel locomotive depot and workshops.

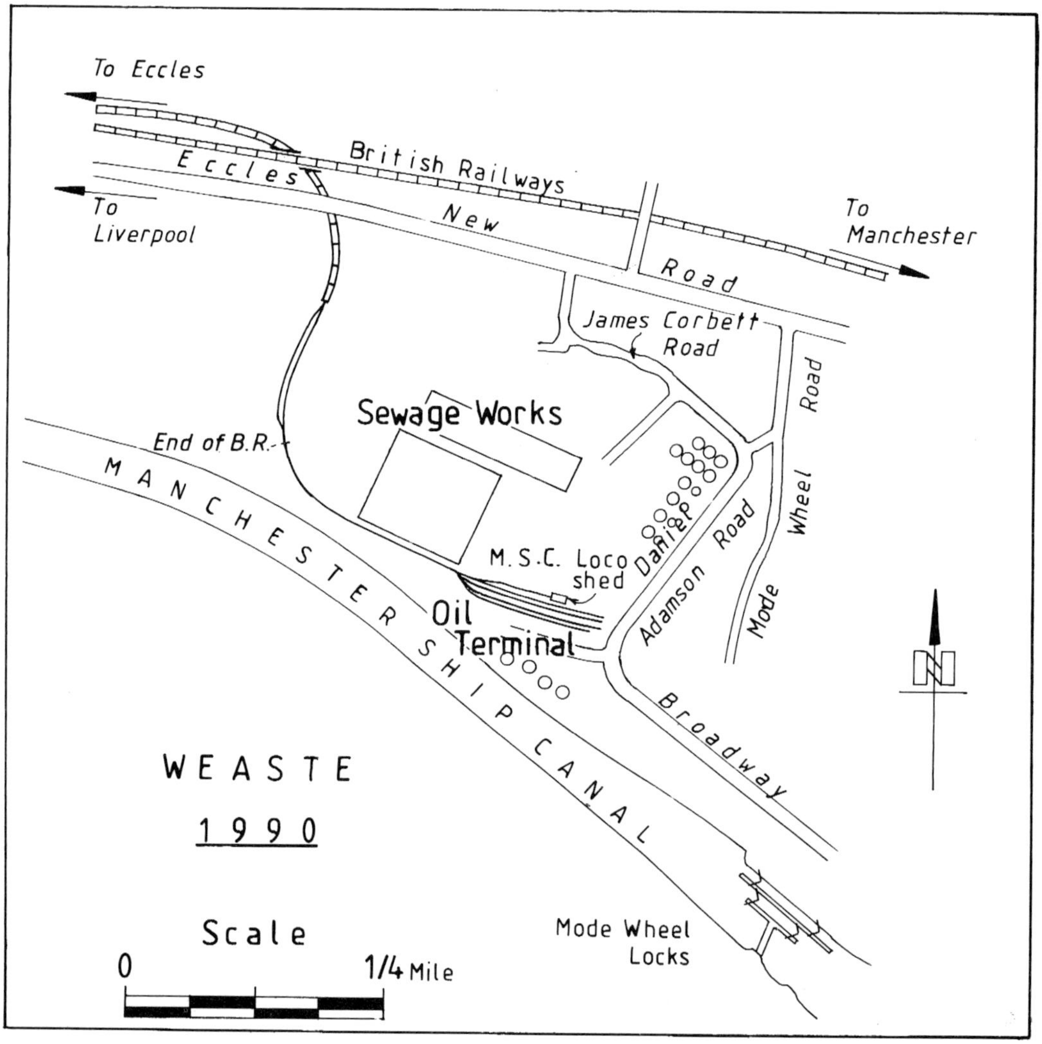

Tank trains were handed over by British Railways at Weaste Junction from where they were hauled the short distance to the terminal by Ship Canal Company's engines. This practice continued after all other rail traffic at Manchester Docks had ceased and, following the closure of the Mode Wheel depot, a small shed was built adjacent to the oil terminal sidings to house the Ship Canal Company's diesel engines used on the tank trains.

Oil deliveries by rail ceased in March 1994 [79], leading to the demise of the last Ship Canal railway operations in Manchester and the closure of the British Railway's line from Eccles to Weaste Junction.

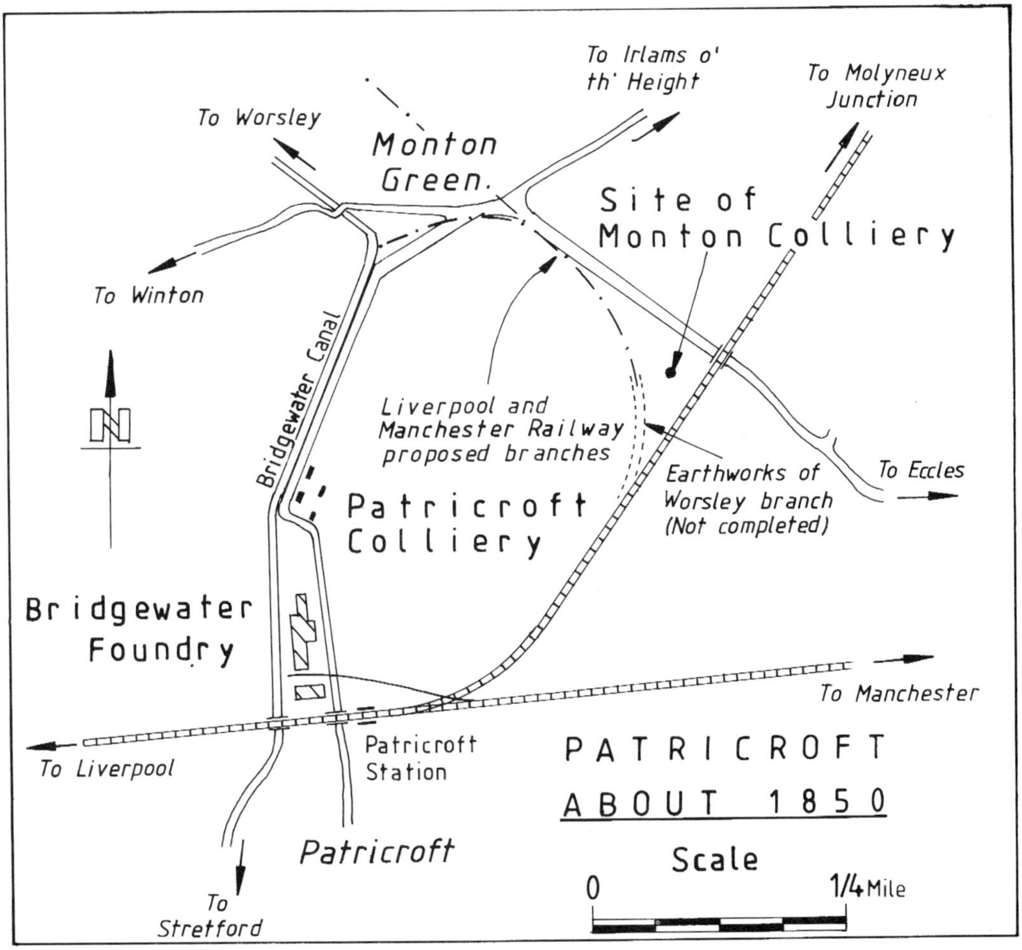

The Bridgewater Foundry

The Bridgewater Foundry was established by James Nasmyth and his brother George on a plot of land on the north side of the Liverpool and Manchester Railway at Patricroft, adjacent to the canal. It has been the subject of a recent publication by J A Cantrell [80]. This deals with the period up to the 1850s and provides a comprehensive study of all aspects of the enterprise. We have used it as the main source of information about the early history of the works in the account which follows.

Land on the west side of Green Lane was leased on 31st December 1835 from Thomas Joseph Trafford and there was second lease of an adjoining plot from George Cornwall Legh on 30th May 1836. The main part of the works was built between the beginning of 1836 and the middle of 1838. In 1839 a siding was constructed which crossed Green Lane on the level and joined the Liverpool and Manchester Railway to the east of Patricroft Station.

Holbrook Gaskell, later to become a well known figure in the chemical industry, joined the partnership in October 1836, the firm thereafter trading as Nasmyth, Gaskell and Company. Finance was initially provided by H H Birley, an important cotton manufacturer, and by members of his family. The Birleys withdrew in June 1838 and their places as sleeping partners were taken by George Humphrys and Henry Garnett.

The firm's products included machine tools, stationary steam engines and a wide range of equipment for use in textile mills, in coal mines and in other branches of industry. Construction of locomotives started in 1838 and was almost entirely confined to orders from the main line railway companies.

The steam hammer, which brought world wide recognition to James Nasmyth, was invented at the end of 1839 and was subsequently developed into a practical working tool with the assistance of Robert Wilson, the works manager. The first commercial machine was set to work in October 1843 and, by 1856, over 500 had been sold. Steam pile drivers, operating on a similar principle, were also manufactured in large quantities.

In February 1843, George Nasmyth left to set up in business as a consulting engineer and agent. George Humphrys retired from the partnership in June 1848 and Holbrook Gaskell in June 1850. On 1st January 1851 [81], the firm, in which James Nasmyth and Henry Garnett were now the sole partners, changed its name to James Nasmyth and Company.

James Nasmyth sold his share in the business and retired from the firm on 31st December 1856. Henry Garnett and his sons, Charles and Robert, together with Robert Wilson, continued to run the Bridgewater Foundry, trading under the name of the Patricroft Iron Works. By now the works seems to have been fully committed to the manufacture of steam hammers and pile drivers. Locomotive production came to an end in 1853, except for three small industrial engines for the Kirkless Hall Coal and Iron Company, turned out in 1862 and 1863.

On 30th October 1867, Nasmyth, Wilson and Company was formed to take over the business, with Robert Wilson and members of the Garnett family among the partners. The new firm revived the locomotive building side of the business, which steadily expanded. By the time that Nasmyth, Wilson and Co Ltd was registered as a private company on 25th April 1882 [82], the works must have been given over almost entirely to locomotive construction.

There were major extensions in the years immediately before the first world war when the site to the east of Green Lane was developed. Land here had been leased by James Nasmyth and Holbrook Gaskell in June 1841 from Thomas Joseph Trafford and had been used to build dwelling houses for workmen employed at the Bridgewater Foundry. Many of these were now demolished to make way for a new erecting shop, boiler shop and paint shop. The original buildings, to the west of Green Lane, were given over entirely to casting, forging and machining of smaller components. A multi-gauge track was laid out in the yard of the new works to test completed engines and an extra level crossing was laid in across Green Lane [81].

When Nasmyth, Wilson and Co Ltd was reformed as a public company in 1919, the firm could be counted as one of the leading locomotive manufacturers in the country. However, the works was unable to survive the depressed state of the market for railway equipment in the years preceding the second world war. The last locomotive was completed in 1938 and the company was wound up in 1939 [83].

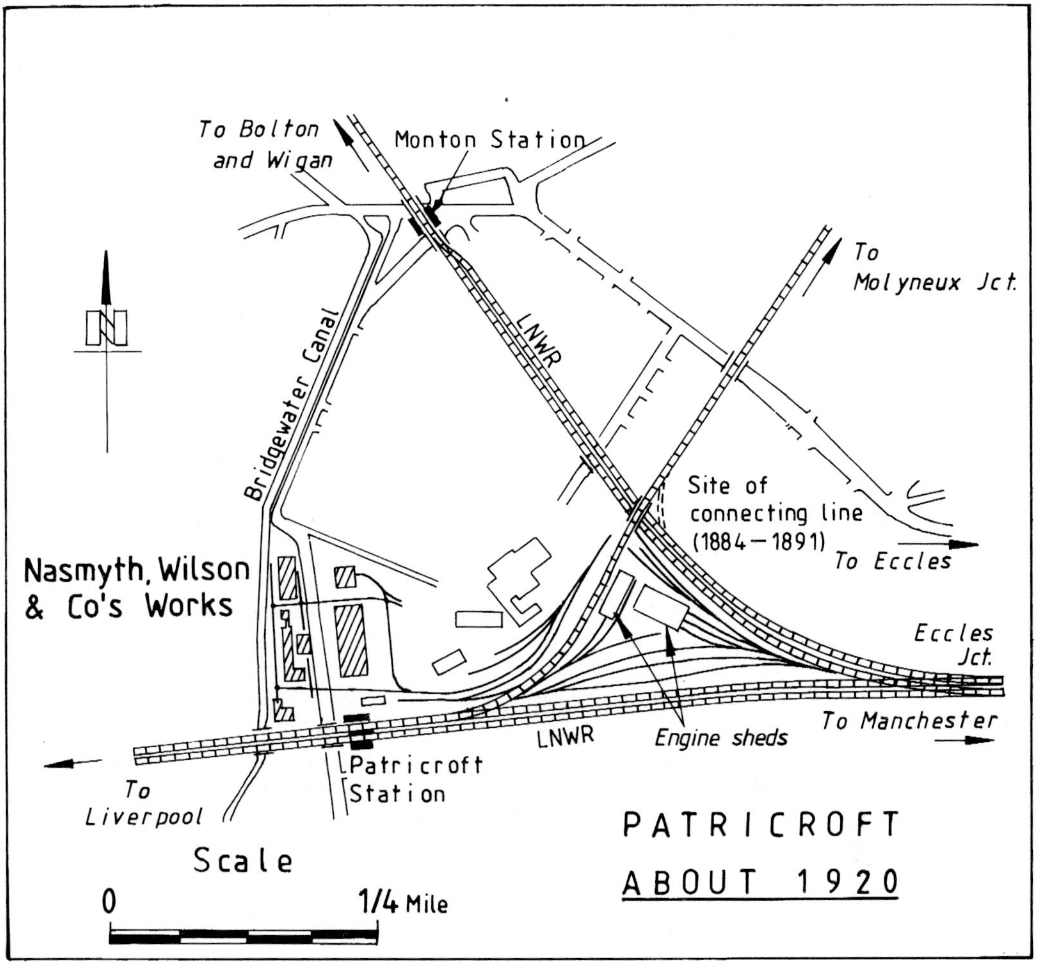

A considerable amount of material relating to the early years of the Bridgewater Foundry, including order books and sales books, has survived and is now deposited at the Salford Local History Library. Information about the locomotives constructed in the period up to 1853 is contained in Cantrell's work referred to earlier. Those built after that date, as well as earlier, are listed in *"Nasmyth, Wilson & Co Ltd"* by G S Moore [84].

In all 1632 engines were built, 338 for Great Britain (including 132 for the Ministry of Munitions and the War Department), 34 for Ireland, 113 for Continental Europe, 837 for Asia (including India), 141 for Africa, 102 for Central and South America and 77 for Australia and New Zealand.

For internal shunting and for working to and from the main line sidings, the firm designed and built a special locomotive, JAMES NASMYTH, which was completed in 1921. This was a six coupled side tank with a steam operated crane mounted above the boiler which enabled heavy loads to be moved around the the works yard. Following the closure of the works, it was sold to the Cowpen Coal Co Ltd in Northumberland, where the crane was removed.

We have no record of what motive power was used within the works before 1921. Perhaps before the extensions on the east side of Green Lane had been completed, it was not necessary to employ a locomotive.

An official photograph of JAMES NASMYTH, the six coupled crane tank built by Nasmyth, Wilson and Co for their own use.
Jim Peden collection

Patricroft Royal Ordnance Factory

The former Nasmyth, Wilson works was taken over by the Ministry of Supply for conversion to a Medium Machine Shop. The contract was placed with G Gerrard and Sons. Work started in June 1940 and was completed early in 1941 [85].

After the end of the second world war the works was retained by the Ministry of Supply, and later by the Ministry of Defence, as a Royal Ordnance Factory, although there was some diversification. For example, in June 1947, it was reported to be making parts for 16 ton steel wagons for British Railways.

Very little has survived about the locomotives which were used at the Ordnance Factory.

A four coupled diesel locomotive with an MAN engine was reported to have been in use in June 1947. There is some circumstantial evidence to associate this with a locomotive built by John Fowler of Leeds in 1933. After being used for demonstration purposes for a few months it had been purchased by the Great Western Railway and put into Departmental Stock as No 1. It was sold by the GWR in March 1940 to George Cohen, Sons and Co Ltd of Stanningley, and was resold to the Ministry of Supply on 12th October 1940 [86]. However, we been unable to confirm that it was this engine which was employed at Patricroft.

A four coupled saddle tank, built by W G Bagnall of Stafford, was observed here in 1948, carrying a plate which read ROF 5 No 1. By August 1952 this had been changed to ROF 16 No 1.

The engine had been delivered in 1941 to the Royal Ordnance Factory at Bescot and is believed to have arrived at Patricroft about 1946 either from Bescot or the ordnance factory at Swynnerton [87]. It was transferred from Patricroft to the ordnance factory at Rotherwas, near Hereford in 1955 [87] and was later sold to Fred Watkins (Boilers) Ltd, machinery merchants of Coleford in the Forest of Dean.

This locomotive was replaced at Patricroft by LAUREL, built by Hawthorn, Leslie and Company, which came from the Royal Arsenal at Woolwich in October 1954. The Industrial Locomotive Society's lists state that it was returned to Woolwich in May 1956, but according to an official at the works it was sold by auction.

We have been unable to discover if there was a locomotive at Patricroft after this. Perhaps none was needed, as already in August 1952 it was noted that the main line connections to Patricroft Goods Yard were still in place, although the sidings between the works and the Clifton branch were seldom used. Such shunting as was performed was mainly confined to the eastern part of the works but the locomotive worked across the street at irregular intervals, about once a week, to deliver fuel to the part of the works alongside the Bridgewater Canal.

The date when rail traffic ceased has not been recorded. In June 1987 the track within in the factory was still in place, as was the connection with the main line, but the rail system was completely disused. By this date operation of the works was in the hands of Royal Ordnance Ammunition Ltd, a subsidiary of Royal Ordnance PLC, which in turn was a member of the Rolls Royce Group and later British Aerospace PLC. In October 1988 [88] it was announced that the works was to be closed. Today the premises are occupied by a number of light industrial firms.

Monton Green and Patricroft Collieries

In *"The Industrial Railways of the Wigan Coalfield"* [89] we have described how John Lancaster played a leading role in setting up the Kirkless Hall Coal and Iron Company and its successor, the Wigan Coal and Iron Company Ltd and how, after leaving Wigan, he became one of the foremost colliery proprietors of the Victorian era. Before starting out on his own career, he had been involved with his father, John Lancaster Senior, and his brothers, William and Robert, in mining ventures at Monton and Patricroft.

Monton Green Colliery was on land owned by John Willis and was located to the south of Slack Lane (the present Monton Road) in the neighbourhood of the later Belmont Street. Sinking appears to have begun in the mid 1830s and a high pressure steam engine was supplied by James and George Nasmyth in September 1837.

A second colliery was sunk at Patricroft, not far from the Bridgewater Canal, under a lease granted on 16th February 1838 to John Lancaster Senior by J T Trafford [90]. Sinking began on 2nd March of the same year, coal was proved, at 420 yards, on 5th February 1841 and production started on 5th August 1841 [90]. The workings were later extended under land owned by the Trustees of the Duke of Bridgewater, under a lease dated 20th May 1845 [91].

Meanwhile, in 1839, James King, who also features prominently in later developments at Wigan, had joined the firm of John Lancaster and Company. John Lancaster Senior died on 15th March 1845 [92] and the partnership was formally dissolved on 17th March, leaving James King in sole control [93]. Monton Green Colliery had already been closed, probably in 1842 and is not shown on the 1st edition of the 6" map, surveyed in 1845.

Patricroft Colliery was put up for auction as going concern on 3rd August 1845 [94] but the sale must have fallen through. Shortly afterwards James Hodgkinson was taken into the partnership, the firm subsequently trading as James King and Company, although the it also seems to have been known as King and Hodgkinson.

In July 1847 James King retired from the business and it was decided to close the colliery. Preparations were made towards the end of the year to sell the winding engine and other items of equipment [90]. The remaining plant was auctioned on 19th January 1848 [95] and included 15 narrow boats carrying 22 to 25 tons and several broad barges carrying 40 tons. It appears that the canal craft and some of the machinery was taken over by the Bridgewater Trustees in lieu of outstanding royalties and in payments to break their lease. The final rent to J T Trafford was paid in September 1847 [90] and the Bridgewater Trustees lease was surrendered on 20th March 1848 [91].

Patricroft Colliery despatched much of its coal by the Bridgewater Canal as is evidenced by the canal boats offered for sale in January 1848 and the "roomy basin" mentioned in the advertisement of the previous August. There had also been several attempts to provide rail access. In December 1843 [90] plans by John Lancaster and Company to construct a line to join the Liverpool and Manchester Railway were held up because of a dispute with the the landowners.

In 1844 the Liverpool and Manchester proposed a connection of its own to Patricroft Colliery, as is shown on the Deposited Plans for its Clifton Branch [96], but this was never built. Subsequently, King and Hodgkinson must have started to build their own line to join the Clifton Branch, then under construction. The sales notice of August 1848 refers to a "short branch railroad, partly made"

Monton Green Colliery was too small to justify a tramroad to the Bridgewater Canal and all its output seems to have been sent away by horse and cart.

Ironstone had been discovered in 1846, when Patricroft Colliery was being sunk [97] and, in 1857 or 1858, Samuel Lancaster, a younger brother of John Junior, and Thomas Marsland set up the Patricroft Ironstone Company to reopen the shaft and work the ore. Thomas Marsland retired on 14th November 1858 [98], leaving Samuel Lancaster as the sole proprietor. An agreement dated 27th April 1859 with Sir Humphrey de Trafford permitted Samuel Lancaster to work the mine for one year on a trial basis, with the option to take out a 21 year lease. Work began on 12th May 1859 and the iron ore which was produced seems mainly to have been sent by canal to John Lancaster's Kirkless works at Wigan [99].

On the expiry of the agreement, de Trafford refused to grant the lease to Samuel Lancaster. It appears that he was looking for better terms elsewhere as a 60 acre plot of ironstone and coal at Patricroft was advertised to be let or sold in August 1861 [100]. Lancaster took de Trafford to court in attempt to enforce the agreement, but lost [101]. He was forced to vacate the property and was declared bankrupt on 24th September 1862 [102, 103]. The pit never reopened.

LOCOMOTIVE SUMMARY

Pendleton Colliery

Various Knowles family partnerships to 1873
Andrew Knowles and Sons Ltd 1873 to 1929
Manchester Collieries Ltd from 1929

KNOWLES 0-6-0ST IC MW 1520 1901 12"x17" 3'0"
New to Andrew Knowles and Sons Ltd, Pendleton Colliery Class K. Ex works 12-6-1901
Transferred to Agecroft Colliery probably about 1928
Sent to Walkden yard about 1930 and scrapped there 1938

Manchester Oxide Ltd, Brindle Heath, later Hardman and Holden Ltd

MARCIA 0-4-0T OC P 1631 1923 8"x12" 2'3"
Ex Marcus Bain Ltd, Mauchline, 1943, via West of Scotland Shipbreaking Co, Troon
To Kent and East Sussex Railway 18-7-1963

The Industrial Railway Society also lists the following :

0-4-0ST OC P 905 1901 12"x18" 3'0"
Ex Murgatroyds Salt Co, Middlewich loan and return

MONARCH 0-4-0ST OC P 503 1892 10"x14" 2'6"
Hired from Cudworth and Johnson, Wrexham, 1945

Tarmac Roadstone Ltd

D3 0-4-0DE RH 398119 1957 200DE Class
Ex W Bush etc, Alfreton 12-1978
To Staffordshire Public Works Ltd for preservation by late 1982, early 1983

T W Ward Ltd, Brindle Heath Scrap Yard

Working locomotives

0-4-0D JF 21942 1957 80HP
Ex T W Ward Ltd, Templeborough Works, Sheffield, 3-1959, previously Shell, Stanlow No 11
Scrapped about 4-1979

MERSEY 0-4-0D JF 21909 1938 60HP
Ex N Greening (Warrington) Ltd in 1966
Scrapped or sold about 1967

47068 0-4-0D HC D622 1942
Ex T W Ward Ltd, Templeborough Works, Sheffield, 1967
Scrapped 9-1978

4wD RH 299098 1950 88DS Class
Ex T W Ward Ltd, Tinsley Works, Sheffield about 8-1973
Returned to Tinsley Works 1974

ARMY 113 4wDM RH 201980 1940 80/88HP
Ex Royal Ordnance Factory, Radway Green, 1975
Scrapped about 10-1981

0-4-0DE RH 381752 1955 165DE Class
Ex T W Ward Ltd, Templeborough Works, Sheffield 8-1978, previously Port of Tyne Authority
Scrapped 10-1981

0-4-0DM HC D1009 1956
Ex Cadbury Schweppes Ltd, Somerdale, 5-1979
To T W Ward Ltd, Silvertown, 20-8-1980

BELFAST 0-4-0DM JF 4210109 1956 150HP
Ex T W Ward Ltd, Preston, about 8-1980
Scrapped or sold in 1982

F.W.W. 4wDM MR 9930 1966
Ex T W Ward Ltd, Barrow, about 8-1980
Scrapped 10-1981

DH3 0-4-0DH YE 2838 1961 170HP
Ex Lowton Metals Ltd, Haydock about 6-1981
Scrapped or sold in 1982

Locomotives brought in for scrap

52360 0-6-0 Hor 523 1897 18"x26" 5'1"
Ex British Railways by 4-5-1959

52120 0-6-0 Hor 78 1891 18"x26" 5'1"
Ex British Railways by 7-5-1959

SIR ANDREW NOBLE 0-4-0STOC HL 2914 1912 14"x22" 3'6"
Ex English Steel Corpn Ltd, Openshaw by 2-1960

0-4-0STOC AB 1375 1914 12"x20" 3'2"
Ex North Western Gas Board, Bradford Road Works, Manchester, by 3-1960
Named SIR WILLIAM KAY

0-4-0STOC AB 1646 1919 10"x18" 3'0"
Ex North Western Gas Board, Bradford Road Works, Manchester, by 3-1960
Named RICHARD BURTLES

0-4-0STOC P 1770 1929 12"x18" 3'0"
Ex North Western Gas Board, Partington Works, by 5-1960
Named SIR WILLIAM KAY

G T 3 4-6-0 EEV 1959
Experimental 2750 HP Gas Turbine locomotive
Ex English Electric, Vulcan Works, 2-1966, in partly dismantled state

4wDM RH 262997 1949
Ex CEGB, Walsall Power Station, about 7-1982

Cox and Danks Ltd, Pendleton Scrap Yard

Cox and Danks Ltd until about 1979
George Cohen, Sons and Co Ltd until about 1989
Sheppard Group from about 1989

Working locomotives

	0-4-0DM	JF	23009	1945	150HP

Ex Cohen's Cransley Depot, Northants, about 9-1974, formerly MOD Air Force Dept, Hartlebury, Worcs.
Scrapped 3-1985

	0-4-0DM	JF	22895	1940	80HP

Ex London Brick Co Ltd, Calvert Brickworks, 4-1980
Scrapped 3-1985

Rail traffic ceased 12-1981. BR siding closed 24-12-1981

Locomotives brought in for scrap

Two 0-4-0WTs arrived on 29th October 1955 from ICI Ltd, Winnington Works. These can be identified as FARADAY (Borrows 31 of 1891) and KELVIN (Borrows 51 of 1908).
Four similar engines from ICI Ltd arrived in October 1956, two on 17th, one on 19th and one on 20th. Three have been identified as BOYLE (KS 3049 of 1917), JOHN BRUNNER (KS 4198 of 1920) and ROSCOE (KS 2485 of 1917). The fourth was probably LUDWIG MOND (KS 1271 of 1912).

Duncan Transrail Ltd, Oldfield Road Terminal

Duncan Transrail Ltd to 1988
Otis Euro Transrail Ltd from 1988

2 TAURUS	0-4-0DM	VF	D139	1951	
		DC	2273	1951	

Ex Purfleet Deep Wharf and Storage Co Ltd, Erith, about 6-1983

03170	0-6-0DM	Swindon		1960	204HP

Ex British Railways, Chester, 9-5-1989

Salford Gas Works

Salford Corporation to 30-4-1949
North Western Gas Board from 1-5-1949

Locomotives used at Liverpool Street Works

	4wDM	RH	218050	1943	Class 48DS

New
To White Lund Gas Works, Lancaster, 1962

	4wDM	RH	284838	1950	Class 88DS

New
To Wigan Gas Works, 1964

J E C Lord's Weaste Tar Works

J E C Lord until early 1920s
J E C Lord (Manchester) Ltd from early 1920s until 1929
Lancashire Tar Distillers Ltd from 1929

LORD WEASTE	0-4-0STOC	P	1079	1906	10"x15"	2'9"

M5 Class, new
To Vernon and Sons, Birkenhead, 1924 via Cudworth and Johnson, Wrexham

	0-4-0STOC	P	1665	1924	12"x18"	

R2 Class, new
Believed scrapped about 1959

	4wDM	FH	3906	1959		

New
To Lancashire Tar Distillers Ltd, Cadishead Works, 1974

Rail traffic believed to have ceased in 1974

Nasmyth Wilson and Co Ltd. Patricroft

JAMES NASMYTH	0-6-0CT	NW	1268	1921	13"x22"	3'0"

New for use as works shunter
To Cowpen Coal Co, Northumberland

Royal Ordnance Factory, Patricroft

	0-4-0DM					

Some evidence to suggest that this may have been JF 19451 of 1933, sold by Great Western Railway to Ministry of Supply in 1940 (see text)
Left Patricroft about 1947

ROF 5 No 1	0-4-0STOC	WB	2653	1941	14½"x22"	3'6½"

Ex Royal Ordnance Factory, Bescot, or Royal Ordnance Factory, Swynnerton, about 1946
Plates changed to read ROF 16 No 1 by 8-1952
To Fred Watkins (Boilers) Ltd, Coleford, Gloucestershire, by 11-1955

LAUREL	0-4-0STOC	HL	3091	1914	14"x22"	3'6"

Ex Royal Arsenal, Woolwich, 10-1954
Possibly sold, or alternatively returned to Woolwich Arsenal, 5-1956

References to Chapter 8

1 *"Royal National Commercial Directory of Manchester and Salford"* - Isaac Slater, Manchester, 1879
2 *"Manchester, Salford and Suburban Directory"* - Slater & Kelly and Co Ltd, Manchester, 1893
3 L&YR Sdgs Diag 128, 31st March 1897
4 L&YR Sdgs Diag 128A, 31st December 1921
5 *"Slater's Directory of Manchester, Salford and Suburbs"* - Kelly's Directories Ltd, 1925
6 *"Slaters's Directory of Manchester, Salford and Suburbs"* - Kelly's Directories Ltd, 1926
7 *"General and Classified Directory of Manchester and Salford"* - Isaac Slater, Manchester, 1871-2
8 *"Directory of Liverpool and its Environs"* - J Mawdesley and Sons, Liverpool, 1879
9 BC 31-12-1887
10 *"Manchester, Salford and Suburban Directory"* - Isaac Slater, Manchester, 1887
11 *"Manchester, Salford and Suburban Directory"* - Isaac Slater, Manchester, 1889
12 *"Manchester, Salford and Suburban Directory"* - Isaac Slater, Manchester, 1893
13 *"Coalmining in Salford"* - G Preece - Salford City Cultural Services, 1985
14 LRO PDR 195
15 MJ20-6-1840
16 Procedings of Lit and Phil Soc, 1854
17 MJ5-8-1843
18 MJ 12-8-1843
19 MJ 30-12-1843
20 *"Collieries in the Manchester Coalfields"* Geoff Hayes - De Archaeologische Pers, Eindhoven, nd
21 *"Carbon"* April 1933
22 EPJ 23-9-1892
23 *"Towpath Guide to the Manchester, Bolton and Bury Canal"* - Steven Parker and Richard Chester-Browne - Manchester, Bolton and Bury Canal Society, 1989
24 L&YR Sdgs Diag 58, 22nd Feb 1896
25 *"Carbon"* Jan 1932
26 Copy inauthors' possession
27 *"Slater's Directory of Manchester, Salford and Stretford and Suburbs"* - Kelly's Directories Ltd, 1945
28 LMS Sdgs Diag No 4450, nd
29 BR Sdgs Diag No 4450, 5-1950
30 *"Slater's Directory of Manchester, Salford and Stretford and Suburbs"* - Kelly's Directories Ltd, 1948
31 Classified Telephone Directory, November 1957
32 Classified Telephone Directory, 1961
33 BR Sdgs Diag 4463, 11-1964
34 Yellow Pages, 1970
35 Yellow Pages, 1972
36 1974 Chap 48
37 BLN 333
38 Yellow Pages, 1976
39 Yellow Pages, 1978
40 BLN 537
41 LG 15-8-1845
42 *"The Pendleton Iron Works of William Barningham"* - P Bowes, 1979 - Manuscript at Salford Local History Library
43 LG 3-5-1853
44 CG 1-11-1872
45 *"Engineering"* 4-1-1867
46 *"Industrial Locomotives of Durham - Pocket Book L"* - Industrial Railway Society, Market Harborough, 1977
47 Mancr Courier 5-3-1881
48 Iron 14-11-1874
49 Iron 3-9-1886
50 Iron 7-12-1892
51 *"Manchester, Salford and Suburban Directory"* - Slater & Kelly and Co Ltd, Manchester, 1894
52 *"Slater's Directory of Manchester, Salford and Suburbs"* - Kelly's Directories Ltd, 1926
53 *"Slater's Directory of Manchester, Salford and Suburbs"* - Kelly's Directories Ltd, 1927
54 *"Slater's Directory of Manchester, Salford and Suburbs"* - Kelly's Directories Ltd, 1934
55 *"Slater's Directory of Manchester, Salford and Suburbs"* - Kelly's Directories Ltd, 1935
56 Yellow Pages 1980
57 *"Directory of Manchester, Salford and Suburbs"* - Kelly's Directories Ltd, 1969
58 *"Directory of Manchester, Salford and Suburbs"* - Kelly's Directories Ltd, 1970
59 Yellow Pages, 1983
60 Yellow Pages, 1985
61 BLN 630
62 *"Modern Railways"* Oct 1990,p 543.
63 11 Geo IV cap viii; 19th March 1830
64 *"Report on the Gas Undertaking"* - Salford Corporation,1920 - at Salford Local History Library
65 LNWR Sdgs Diag No 253, 12-1916
66 30 Vic cap lviii; 31st May 1869
67 Annual reports of Salford Corporation Gas Department - at Salford Local History Library

68 Information supplied by North West Gas Historical Society

69 BLN 352 23rd Aug 1978

70 Information suppled by Mr Richard Maund

71 BLN 589

72 Salford Weekly News 27-1-1883

73 Pendleton Times and Reporter 14-7-1883

74 LNWR Sdgs Diag No 252, 12-1916

75 *"A History of the Modern British Chemical Industry"* - D W F Hardie and J D Pratt - Pergamon, 1966

76 *"Manchester, Salford and Suburban Directory"* - Slater and Kelly's Directories Ltd, Manchester, 1899

77 Salford Reporter 24-10-1925

78 LNWR Sdgs Diag No 252, 3-1919

79 Industrial Railway Society Bulletin No 577, July 1994

80 *"James Nasmyth and the Bridgewater Foundry"* - J A Cantrell - The Chetham Society - Manchester - 1984

81 *"The New Extensions of the Bridgwater Foundry - Nasmyth Wilson and Co Ltd"* in Railway Gazette Vol XVIII No 26, 27th July 1913, pp 779-790

82 CG 19-5-1882

83 *"British Steam Locomotive Builders"* - Lowe - Goose and Sons, Folkestone, 1975

84 *"Nasmyth, Wilson & Co Ltd"* - G S Moore -nd

85 Schedule of Ordnance Factory Construction - copy in authors' possession

86 *"Locomotives of Great Western Railway - Part Eleven"* - Railway Correspondence and Travel Society, 1952

87 *"The R O F Bagnalls"* - Allan C Baker - *in "Industrial Locomotive"*, No 52,Winter 1989

88 MG 7-10-1988

89 *"The Industrial Railways of the Wigan Coalfield - Part Two"* - Townley, Smith and Peden - Runpast Publishing, Cheltenham, 1992

90 LRO DDX/Tr - Diary of Thomas Ayre, Traffords' agent

91 Bridgewater Estates archives

92 MG 19-3-1845

93 Manc Courier 22-3-1845

94 *"Mining Journal and Railway and Commercial Gazette"* 24-7-1847

95 MG 12-1-1848

96 LRO PDR 390

97 *"Mining Journal and Railway and Commercial Gazette"* 7-3-1846

98 LG18-12-1858

99 *"The Lancashire and Cheshire Coal-Fields"* - Edward Hull - in CG 8-2-1862

100 WO 30-8-1861

101 Law Journal Reports Court of Chancery 1862, Vol 31, pp 554 to 557 - Lancaster v De Trafford

102 LG 26-9-1862

103 MG 29-9-1862

CHAPTER 9

ATHERTON, LEIGH AND TYLDESLEY

We start our explorations at Atherton, where there are records of coal mining in the first decades of the eighteenth century. The Bolton and Leigh Railway, opened in 1830, and the Kenyon and Leigh Junction Railway, opened in 1831 and connecting with the Liverpool and Manchester Railway, provided access to more distant markets. First under the control of John Fletcher and then under the firm of Fletcher, Burrows and Company, the industry here showed continuous growth until the 1920s and did not come to an end until 1966. The early history of the collieries is outside the scope of the present work. Those who wish to explore the subject will find further information in *"The Coal Pits of Chowbent"* [1]. There is also much interesting material in *"Carbon"*, the house journal of Fletcher, Burrows and Co Ltd, particularly the issue for February 1923.

From Atherton we move on to Bedford Colliery, to the east of Leigh, sunk by the Speakman family in the 1870s. As at Atherton, coal production continued until recent times and the colliery did not close until November 1967.

To the south of Speakman's pits there had been an earlier Bedford Colliery, which dated back to the 1830s. There were also the mines which John Darlington opened up in the 1840s to the north of Astley village. For many years output was restricted by the lack of a proper rail outlet, with all coal not sold locally being conveyed by tramroad to the Bridgewater Canal.

The opening of the LNWR's Eccles, Tyldesley and Wigan line in 1864 provided the incentive to expand. Under new ownership, the Astley pits were reconstructed and a new colliery was built at Tyldesley. Further expansion took place in the period up to the first world war and again production continued until the 1960s.

THE ATHERTON COLLIERIES

John Fletcher's Collieries

The Fletcher family's connections with Atherton go back to the latter half of the eighteenth century, when John Fletcher (1727-1806), who had colliery interests at Haulgh, near Bolton, opened up mines in the district. There are records of the partnership of Fletcher and Fildes working two pits here in 1769 and of a lease obtained in 1776 by John Fletcher and Thomas Guest [1]. Thomas Guest's interest in the firm passed to his son John, who retired from the partnership in 1803. He was replaced by Ralph Fletcher (1757-1832), son of John Fletcher [1,2].

When Colonel Ralph Fletcher died in 1832 the interest in his Bolton collieries passed to his son John (1807-1876), who also inherited three shares in the Atherton collieries. Shares in the Atherton collieries also went to the Colonel's younger sons, Ralph Fletcher, (1815-1886) and James Pearson Fletcher (1818-1872), and to his nephew, John Langhsaw [1]. The firm subsequently traded under the title John Fletcher and Others.

During the first quarter of the nineteenth century, the Fletchers were working some six or eight small pits. These mainly supplied local demand but in addition some coal seems to have been shipped by canal. It has been suggested [1] that a branch was laid from their Lover's Lane Pit to the Blackcroft Colliery tramroad for this purpose. The tramroad led from pits at Westleigh to a wharf on the Leeds and Liverpool Canal [3], but it seems unlikely that the Fletchers actually made use of it. It was not until 1857 that they ceased to employ road transport to take their coal to the canal.

Meanwhile, the opening of the Bolton and Leigh Railway in 1830 and its extension to Kenyon Junction a year later, led to an expansion of trade. A new colliery was sunk alongside the site of the new railway at Gibfield in 1829 [4]. The sidings which were put in to serve it were in use by 1831, as there is reference to an accident in July of that year. The locomotive LIVERPOOL, hauling a luggage train from Liverpool, was thrown off the rails at the turn-out near Bag Lane Station leading to the colliery [5].

To serve the town of Leigh a coal yard was established at Stock Platt Bridge and a private branch about half a mile in length was constructed to join the Bolton and Leigh Railway north of Kirkhall Lane. The Atherton Tithe Map of 1839 [7] shows that the line was standard gauge. We presume that the wagons from Gibfield were conveyed by Bolton and Leigh trains from to the junction and that from there they were hauled by horses.

By 1845 and 1846, when the surveys were made for the first edition of the 6" map, many of the earlier pits had been abandoned. Lovers Lane Colliery was still at work, although not at that time provided with a rail connection. There was also a group of pits between Gadbury Fold and the Leigh to Atherton road which were probably approaching closure. The Bolton and Leigh Railway had originally proposed a short branch to reach this area [6], but it was not built.

In 1845, work started on a new colliery at Howe Bridge [1] and eventually there were three shafts here, the Victoria, the Puffer and the Volunteer, as well as a drift, the Crombrouke Day Eye. The site was adjacent to the Bolton and Leigh line and seems to have been provided with standard gauge sidings from the beginning.

Howe Bridge was also the starting point of a narrow gauge tramroad which superseded the earlier branch to Stock Platt Bridge. A plan of the Bolton and St Helens Turnpike drawn up in 1856 by J Lomax, the Bolton land surveyor, [8] shows that for the first half mile the tramroad followed a course alongside the Bolton and Leigh railway. Beyond there it took the route of the original line to Stock Platt Bridge. The plan gives a gauge of 2'2", but it is apparent from the standard gauge lines which are shown elsewhere that Lomax took his measurements over the outside of the rails. This would suggest a gauge of 2 feet or a little under for Fletcher's tramroad, using the more conventional definition.

In 1857, work was put in hand to extend the line from Stock Platt Bridge to the Bridgewater Canal. On 7th February, the tender of Mr Saville of Chorley was accepted, which included excavation of a new basin at Bedford, 150ft long, 90ft wide and 6ft deep, and the construction of a tunnel, 880 ft long, under a built up area to the north of the basin [9]. We have been unable to locate the precise route between Stock Platt Bridge and the tunnel. It appears to have been a little to the north of the later Henrietta Street.

The first sod was cut on Monday 6th April 1857 on the site of the new basin [10]. The line was operational by the end of September of the same year, when it was reported that the coals arrived in much better condition than by the old method of carting them to the canal. It was stated that the railway avoided congestion on the roads, saved on horse labour and gave John Fletcher and Others a 6d per ton advantage over their competitors [11]. From the evidence in a court case [12], we learn that coal for shipment by canal, and presumably that going to the sale yards, was conveyed along the railway in the same tubs which had been used to raise it up the pit. The tubs were made up into short trains which were drawn by horses [13].

By the end of February 1858, 6ft, 7ft and Gibfield coal was advertised as being available at the wharf, which we assume to mean the landsale yard at Henry Street, adjoining the canal basin [14]. The Gibfield coal must have been transferred from standard gauge to narrow gauge wagons at Howe Bridge, as Deposited Plans dated November 1860 show the tramroad terminating here [15].

The tramroad crossed the Bolton and St Helens Turnpike north of Kirkhall Lane at an acute angle and this caused inconvenience to road users which the Turnpike Act of 1860 [16] sought to remedy . Sections XV and XVI made specific reference to the line, stating that it was of the narrow gauge, adapted to the passage of small wagons.

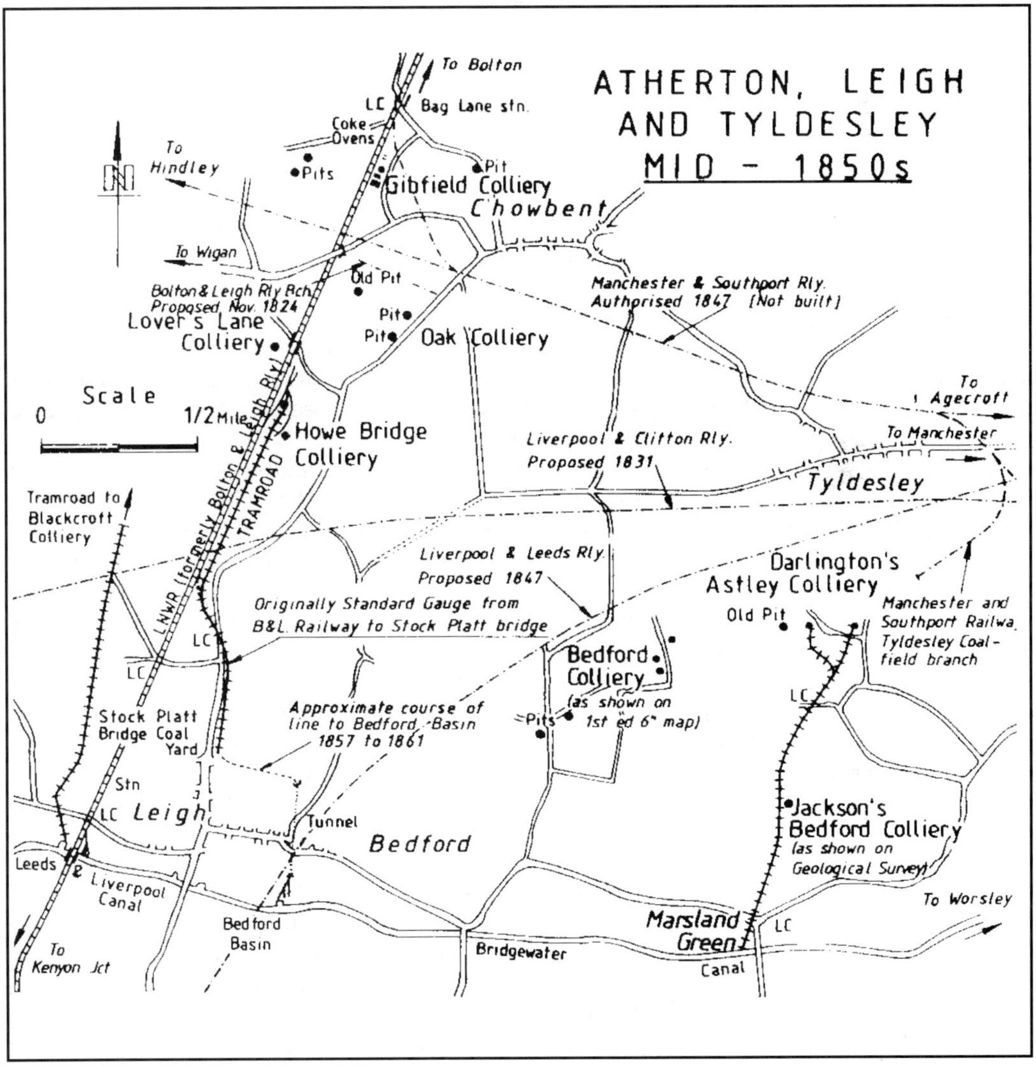

Powers were granted to John Fletcher and Others to alter their tramroad so that it crossed the road at angle of not less than 60 degrees, or to substitute an underbridge. They were given two years to do this and failure to comply meant that the Turnpike Trustees could remove the line.

Instead of carrying out the alterations, John Fletcher and Others opted to abandon the route through Stock Platt Bridge and to construct a direct line from Howe Bridge Colliery to the north end of the tunnel and thence to Bedford Basin. The new railway was to be standard gauge throughout and involved conversion of the narrow gauge track through the tunnel and at the basin. By September 1860, plans were well advanced and the firm was negotiating to cross two fields near the workhouse, leased by the Board of Guardians from Lord Lilford [17].

Bedford Basin, photographed from the towpath of the Bridgewater Canal in 1952, Coal shipments had finished before the war and rail traffic to the landsale yard a few months previously. The entrance to the tunnel can just be seen in the centre of the photograph, below the bridge carrying the ex-LNWR line

Harry Townley

Two locomotives, named LILFORD and ELLESMERE, were purchased from Hawthorns and Company of Leith, near Edinburgh, to work over the new line. Because of the restricted dimensions of the tunnel, the overall height of the engines was only some ten feet above rail level, considerably less than normal. It was not possible to provide full cabs and only weatherboards were fitted. Water was carried in tanks between the frames instead of in the more usual saddle tanks above the boiler.

There was a trial trip on 27th May 1861 and the formal opening of the line took place on the following day, accompanied by much ceremony. The first train, consisting of six open trucks fitted out with seats for members of the Fletcher family and their guests, accompanied by the band of the local volunteer force and hauled by LILFORD, arrived at the wharf at 4 pm. It was followed by ELLESMERE drawing four large wagons of coal [13,18].

Newspaper reports of the opening suggested that the locomotives would also be employed in conveying coal to Fletcher's coal yard in Bolton [13]. We have found no evidence that they actually did so. Later, they were permitted to run over the LNWR lines between Gibfield, Howe Bridge and Chanters Collieries and this practice continued until around 1960.

By this time, Lover's Lane Colliery, on the opposite side of the Bolton and Leigh Railway to Howe Bridge, had been provided with a railway connection. There was a fatal accident,in March 1862, to a man employed as horse driver on the line from Lovers Lane siding to the junction with the firm's locomotive railway [19].

This delightful view of No 3 ATHERTON, the well tank of 1867, is taken at Gibfield. It is one of a series of postcards of Fletcher, Burrows and Company's collieries. Jim Peden Collection

Concurrently with these developments, work was being undertaken at the new Chanters Colliery. Sinking of the two shafts here commenced around 1860 [1] and the colliery came into operation in 1864 or 1865. It was connected to the LNWR Eccles, Tyldesley and Wigan line by a private branch about three quarters of a mile long, built at the expense of the LNWR under the Railway Clauses Consolidation Act of 1845. Construction was undertaken by Mr Tredwell, who used the spoil on his contract for the Eccles, Tyldesley and Wigan line [20].

A third locomotive, named ATHERTON, came from Hawthorns and Company in 1867, identical to those delivered in 1861. We assume that this was intended for use at Chanters Colliery as we have no record of any other locomotive available to the firm at this time to work the branch to the main line sidings. A more conventional six coupled saddle tank, named COLLIER, was purchased from Manning, Wardle and Company of Leeds in 1878.

Fletcher, Burrows and Company

By 1870 the partners included James Pearson Fletcher, Ralph Fletcher Senior, Ralph Fletcher Junior, John Fletcher and John Langshaw. James Pearson Fletcher died on 2nd August 1872. Abraham Burrows joined the partnership on 31st December 1872, when John Fletcher retired. John Langshaw retired on 31st December 1874, when the firm changed its title to Fletcher, Burrows and Company [21]. Ralph Fletcher Senior died on 13th June 1886. Fletcher, Burrows and Co Ltd was registered on 14th April 1892 [22].

The collieries continued to expand during the latter part of the nineteenth century and into the twentieth. At Howe Bridge a new fan pit was opened in 1874 [1]. At Gibfield Colliery, the Arley Pit was sunk in 1872 and a third shaft in 1909 [4].

Lovers Lane Colliery, made redundant by these new developments, finally ceased production in 1898 [1], although one pit there had closed as early as 1862. Surplus plant including a 30 HP marine engine and an egg ended boiler was offered for sale in December of that year [23]. The Crombrouke Day Eye at Howe Bridge closed in 1907 [1].

Chanters Colliery was redeveloped towards the end of the century. A screening plant was erected in 1890, followed by others in 1896 [1] and 1904 [24], A washery was provided in 1901 [24]. No 1 Pit was modernised in the 1890s [4]; in 1904 the original wooden headgear was replaced in steel [24] and a new winding engine installed [1]. At No 2 Pit, a new winding engine had been provided in 1894 [24], at the time the shaft was being deepened [4].

It was at this period that a new railway was proposed which would have broken the monopoly held in the district by the LNWR and would have provided a direct link between the Atherton Collieries and the Manchester Ship Canal at Partington. The Bill for the Leigh and South Central Lancashire Railway, which was brought before Parliament in 1895, included a branch to connect with Fletcher, Burrows' line from Howe Bridge to Bedford Basin at a point north of the tunnel [25]. As described in Chapter 2, the scheme fell through.

The increased coal output resulting from the colliery developments towards the end of the century required additional locomotives. One, a four coupled saddle tank, was constructed in the firm's workshops at Gibfield.

There is some uncertainty about the date when it was built. The Industrial Railway Society lists give 1888, while another version is that it was completed during the miner's strike of 1893 [26]. It was named ELECTRIC and it has been suggested by old employees that this was to commemorate the opening of the power station at Howe Bridge. We were also told that it was low-built so that it could work through the tunnel to Bedford Basin and this seems to be confirmed by a photograph of the engine. Only a weatherboard was fitted, not a full cab, and the chimney was of reduced height.

In 1892 the Vulcan Foundry of Newton-le-Willows supplied a six coupled sadle tank which, appropriately enough, was named VULCAN.

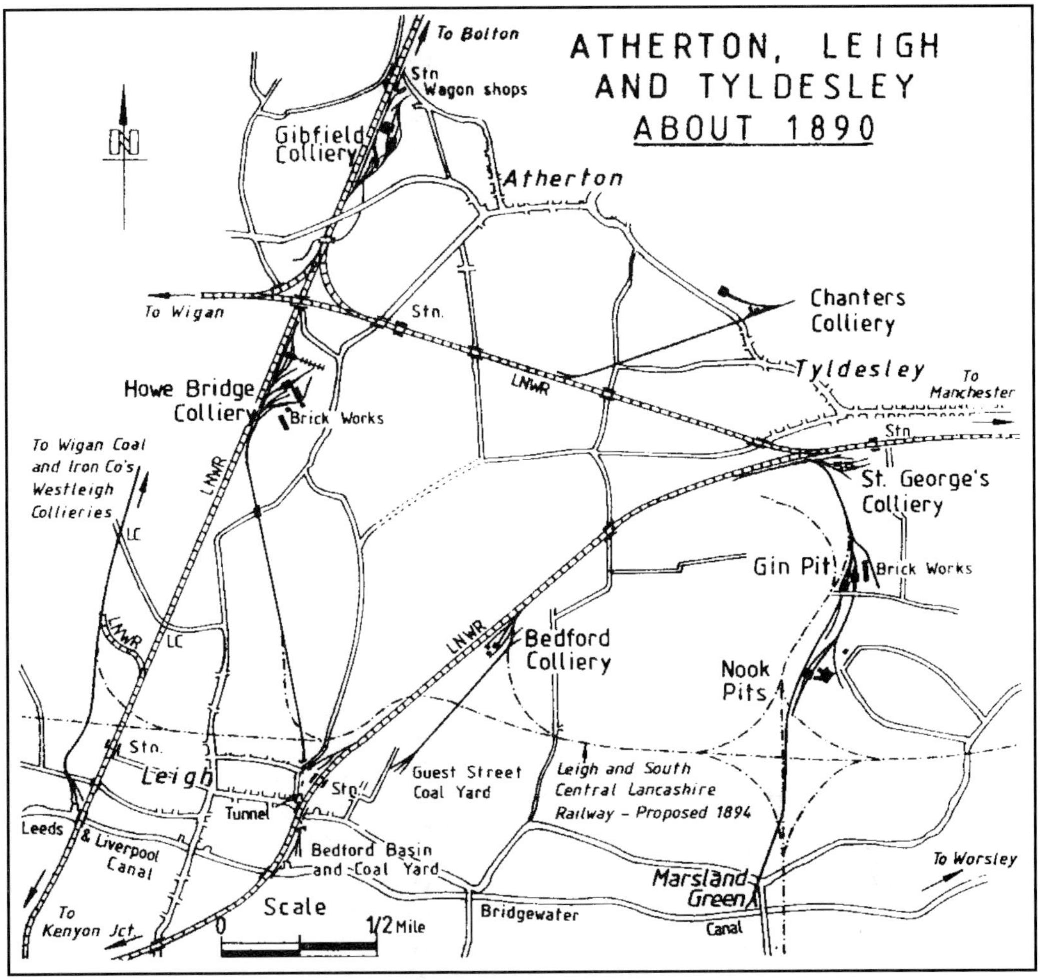

LILFORD, the well tank of 1861, was sold to Thomas Mitchell and Sons Ltd, the Bolton machinery dealers, late in 1898 or early in 1899. The name was transferred to a six coupled saddle tank which is said to have arrived in 1897 [27]. The new LILFORD was built by the Hunslet Engine Company of Leeds in 1892 and had been used at Hemsworth Colliery in South Yorkshire before coming to Atherton.

Finally, in 1909, a six coupled saddle tank, named ATLAS, was purchased from Peckett and Sons of Bristol. It was one of the largest of the Fletcher, Burrows' locomotives and was employed on working trains of slack coal from Gibfield and Howe Bridge over the LNWR lines to the washery at Chanters.

After the first world war there was further modernisation at the collieries. New headgear was installed at Chanters in 1926 [28] and a new washery was completed in 1928 [29]. A new brickworks, capable of producing 100,000 bricks per week, was built at Gadbury Fold, south of Gibfied, in 1925 and replaced an earlier works on the same site [30].

There was modernisation on the locomotive side as well. CARBON, a four coupled saddle tank, came from Andrew Barclay Sons and Company of Kilmarnock in 1920, followed by CHOWBENT, a six coupled saddle tank from the same makers in 1923. COLONEL, another six coupled saddle tank, was purchased from the Hunslet Engine Company in 1927.

At this period, or perhaps a little earlier, Fletcher, Burrows and Co Ltd adopted the practice of allocating numbers to their locomotives as well as names. Details are incomplete and such information as is available is given in the Locomotive Summary.

With the influx of new engines, ELECTRIC, VULCAN and COLLIER were taken out of service. ELECTRIC was sold, in 1926 or 1927, for use at Netherseal Colliery, near Burton on Trent. We think that the deal was negotiated by Mr F N Siddall who was a director of the Netherseal Colliery Co Ltd and also manager of the Gibfield Arley and Victoria Pits [31]. VULCAN seems to have broken up in the late 1920s. COLLIER may have survived until 1930.

According to old employees, the engines normally employed at Chanters Colliery at this time were CARBON, CHOWBENT and, before it was withdrawn, VULCAN. COLLIER was possibly here as well. LILFORD, ELECTRIC and ATLAS were stationed at Gibfield, while ELLESMERE and ATHERTON were normally to be found at Howe Bridge, as least one engine of this type was needed there for working through the tunnel to Bedford Basin and to the landsale yard at Henry Street. COLONEL was also here in 1928 [32].

The Atherton Collieries 1929 to 1946

In 1929, Fletcher, Burrows and Co Ltd amalgamated with neighbouring mining concerns to form Manchester Collieries Ltd. Robert Burrows, chairman of the firm, had been the prime mover behind the scheme. The proposal was first discussed at a meeting called by Robert Burrows in September 1927 [33] and by the end of the year the merger had been approved in principle. As a result, Manchester Collieries Ltd was registered on 4th March 1929.

Following the amalgamation a certain amount of rationalisation took place. The wagon shops at Gibfield were closed by the end of 1931 and all repairs were concentrated at Walkden Yard [34]. Major overhauls of locomotives at Gibfield also ceased at this time and were transferred to the central workshops at Gin Pit [34]. Light engines proceeding to and from Gin Pit were permitted to travel under their own steam between the Atherton Collieries and Jackson's Sidings, subject to a payment of £1 per annum, under an agreement of 14th December 1933 with the London Midland and Scottish Railway [35]. A pilot driver was provided by the railway company and paid for by the colliery company.

During the same period, Gibfield Colliery lost its permanent allocation of locomotives. The engine used to shunt the colliery yard was supplied from Howe Bridge Colliery. It remained at Gibfield during the week, returning to Howe Bridge at week-ends, running over the main line.

Several of the locomotives taken over from Fletcher, Burrows and Co Ltd were moved to other collieries belonging to the new concern.

LILFORD was sent to Gin Pit between April and June 1938, presumably for repair, but was broken up there in December of the same year [36].

CARBON went to Astley Green Colliery in the early part of 1938.

CHOWBENT, which was at Chanters Colliery in 1938 and 1939 [36], was sent to Gin Pit sometime during the first few years of the war and subsequently used on the Astley and Tyldesley collieries railway system.

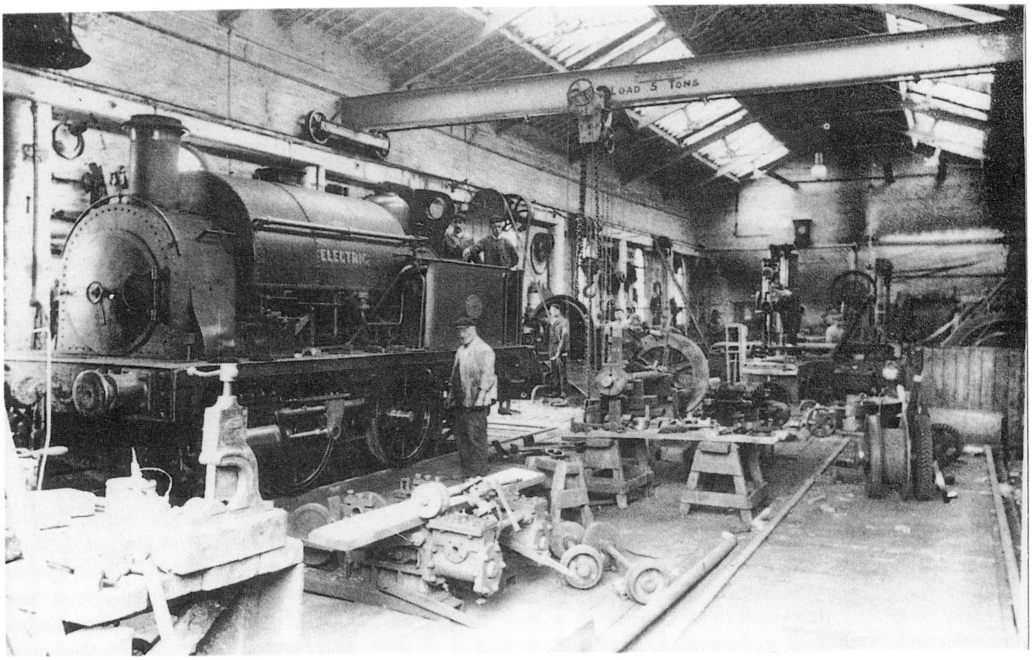

ELECTRIC, the locomotive built by Fletcher, Burrows and Co, taken in the repair shop at Gibfield.
Lancashire Mining Museum

COLONEL moved to Gin Pit in the mid 1940s. Prior to that it seems to have been mainly employed at Howe Bridge and Gibfield, apart from a period in 1938 when it was noted under repair at Gin Pit [36].

The remaining locomotives belonging to Fletcher Burrows and Co Ltd continued in service at the Atherton collieries throughout the Manchester Collieries era.

ELLESMERE and ATHERTON were kept at Howe Bridge for their special duties on the line to Bedford Basin. To avoid confusion with the former Bridgewater Collieries engine of the same name, ELLESMERE became "1861" in the official records after the amalgamation. ATHERTON also lost its name, but continued to be referred to as such in the records. It was noted at Gin Pit in March 1940, presumably for repairs.

ATLAS was noted at Howe Bridge in August 1938, but had moved to Chanters by March 1940. It was at Gin Pit in 1946, presumably for overhaul, and was back at Chanters by the end of the year.

Various locomotives were brought in by Manchester Collieries Ltd to replace the engines which had been transferred elsewhere. GOWER, a six coupled saddle tanks built by Sharp, Stewart and Company in 1882 for the Bridgewater Trustees, came from the Walkden railway system. It arrived at Chanters Colliery in July 1930 [37], possibly as a replacement for COLLIER, which seems to have been scrapped at about this time. GOWER moved on a few years later and in June 1938 it was noted at Bedford Colliery [36].

Another of the Bridgewater Collieries Sharp Stewart locomotives, CERBERUS, was also briefly at Chanters Colliery. It was despatched there from Walkden 10th March 1937 [37], but does not seem to have proved satisfactory. It had been sent to Gin Pit by January 1938 and worked on the Astley and Tyldesley collieries system until June of that year. By December 1938 it had been dismantled and was subsequenlty scrapped.

The Sharp, Stewart engines were followed by two six coupled saddle tanks built by Nasmyth, Wilson and Company for the Bridgewater Collieries. MADGE was despatched from Walkden Yard to work at Chanters Colliery in March 1938 [37]. Later the same year it was under repairs at Gin Pit [36] and T.B.WOOD was sent from Gin Pit to Chanters as a temporary replacement [36]. The sister engine, VIOLET, arrived at Chanters Colliery in 1943 or 1944. It had previously been working from the shed at Gin Pit, where it had been sent from Walkden Yard in June 1937 [37].

EDITH and SHAKERLEY, two six coupled saddle tanks built by the Hunslet Engine Company in 1887 and 1901 respectively, arrived at the Atherton collieries, the former during 1939 and the latter towards the end of 1938. They had previously been used at William Ramsden and Company's Shakerley Colliery at Tyldesley, taken over by Manchester Collieries Ltd in March 1935 and closed in October 1938. Both seem to have been employed mainly at Howe Bridge and Gibfield, although SHAKERLEY was sent to Chanters towards the end of 1946 [38].

In 1938 or 1939, coal shipments on the canal at Bedford Basin, which had been at a reduced level since the formation of Manchester Collieries Ltd, finally ceased [39]. The line from Howe Bridge through the tunnel, however, remained open to serve the landsale yard.

Early in 1943 changes were made to the method of disposing of dirt at Gibfield Colliery, which must have reduced the work performed by the locomotives. It was found to be more economical to take the material to the tip in motor lorries instead of railway wagons [39]. By September 1943, the new system had been introduced at Chanters Colliery as well [41].

ATLAS photographed at Howe Bridge Colliery in January 1939. This engine was used for many years on the trains which ran over the main line between Gibfield, and Chanters Collieries Bernard Roberts

The Hunslet locomotive COLONEL, photographed in August 1952 at Sandhole shed, after its transfer to the Bridgewater Collieries railway system. Alex Appleton

CARBON, by now carrying a "home made" chimney, photographed at Tyldesley in May 1955, when it was working at Cleworth Hall Colliery. David Chatfield

A view of Gibfield Colliery, looking north, showing LILFORD at work. Note the wagons in Manchester Collieries livery and the short train, with brake van in rear, which has been marshalled ready for a trip over the main line to Chanters. Lancashire Mining Museum

There was a certain amount of redevelopment at Gibfield in the war years. The Plodder Mine came into production on 17th July 1944, together with new surface plant which replaced the old screens and washery, erected in 1890. Dirt was conveyed in railway wagons over the LMSR Bolton and Leigh line to a bunker, from where it was taken by lorry to the tip [42].

In the immediate post war period there were several changes to the locomotive stock. MADGE was broken up at Gin Pit in 1946 and was used to provide spares for VIOLET, which continued in service at Chanters until 1962.

The replacement for MADGE was an austerity saddle tank, built by Robert Stephenson and Hawthorns in 1944 as War Department No 71479. Purchased by Manchester Collieries Ltd, it had arrived on 8th April 1946 at Walkden Yard, where the name GORDON had been painted on. It was despatched from Walkden to Chanters on 18th April [37].

The Atherton Collieries under the National Coal Board - 1947 to 1966

1947 to 1952 - No 1 (Manchester) Area

When the industry was nationalised on 1st January 1947, the mines belonging to Manchester Collieries Ltd, including those at Atherton, were absorbed into the No 1 (Manchester) Area of the National Coal Board's North Western Division. Also included in the No 1 Area were the Bickershaw Colliery Co Ltd's pits, the Parsonage Colliery of the Wigan Coal Corporation, and the Cleworth Hall Colliery of the Tyldesley Coal Co Ltd. We have already dealt with history of the railway systems at Bickershaw and Parsonage in the *"Industrial Railways of the Wigan Coalfield"* [3]. The Tyldesley Coal Company appears in Chapter 10.

The locomotives at the Atherton Collieries absorbed into the stock of No 1 (Manchester) Area can be identified from records formerly held at Walkden Yard [38]. 1861 and ATHERTON were then at Howe Bridge, with EDITH at Gibfield. Chanters had ATLAS, VIOLET, SHAKERLEY and GORDON.

A second austerity locomotive arrived at Chanters at the end of 1948. Built by Robert Stephenson and Hawthorn Ltd for the War Department as No 71484, it had been purchased by Manchester Collieries Ltd in March 1946 and given the name HUMPHREY. It had been used intially at Astley Green Colliery and on the Bridgewater railway system and was sent to Chanters on 31st December 1948 [37] before being transferred to Howe Bridge Colliery in 1949. There it was used on the slack coal trains which ran over the main line between Gibfield, Howe Bridge and Chanters.

COLONEL, which had been moved to Gin Pit during the war, returned to the Atherton collieries, probably in 1947. By November 1950, it had been transferred to Parsonage Colliery. It was sent from there to Gin Pit for repairs in the summer of 1951 and subsequently saw service on the Bridgewater railway system and at Wheatsheaf Screens before being sent to Bedford Colliery in January 1962. It was broken up there in August 1966, after being out of service for several years.

SHAKERLEY was transferred to Cleworth Hall Colliery around 1949. It never returned to Atherton and was broken up at Cleworth Hall in January 1962. Its sister engine, EDITH, was for most of the time allocated to Howe Bridge Colliery and was often employed on shunting duties at Gibfield.

ATHERTON was at Ashton Moss Colliery for a short time 1947, when the regular engine there was out of service. ATLAS went to Gin Pit in 1948 for repairs, followed by GORDON.

1952 to 1961 - No 2 (Wigan) Area

Subsequent history is complicated by a reorganisation of the area boundaries which took effect on 1st January 1952. Howe Bridge, Gibfield and Chanters Collieries, along with Bickershaw, Parsonage and Bedford, were transferred to the No 2 (Wigan) Area. The locomotives which were taken over from the Atherton Collieries comprised 1861, ATHERTON, ATLAS, VIOLET and the two Austerity tanks, GORDON and HUMPHREY.

Under the new arrangements, overhauls were now carried out at the Kirkless Works at Wigan or in the workshop at Parsonage Pit, instead of at Walkden Yard or Gin Pit. Several of the Atherton locomotives were repainted in the No 2 Area livery, with green saddle tanks and black cab, black bunker and black underframing. Previously they had been been either unlined black or black with red lining, this being the paint scheme adopted at Walkden Yard.

The two well tanks, dating from the 1860s, were no longer required for their special duties following the closure of the line from Howe Bridge through the Bedford Tunnel. Coal traffic to the landsale yard at Henry Street had ceased towards the end of 1951 and the railway track was lifted in January 1952 [39,43]. ATHERTON had already been transferred to Gibfield Colliery before May 1951. By April 1952 it was out of use and was eventually broken up later that year.

1861 remained at Howe Bridge as the yard shunter until the middle of 1957, apart from a visit to Gin Pit for overhaul in 1951. It was sold to a consortium of railway societies for £1 and was despatched on a well wagon on 18th September 1957 to Bruce, Peebles works at Leith under the care of the Edinburgh Society of Model Engineers. After being stored at various locations, it has recently has been taken over by the Royal Scottish Museum.

The two surviving well tanks at Howe Bridge Colliery. Note the detailed differences between the 1867 engine on the left and the 1861 engine on the right. Also note the old egg ended boiler in use as a water tank alongside the engine shed.
Neville Fields

HUMPHREY working a train of coal from Gibfield Colliery to Chanters Washery, passing through Howe Bridge Station on the former LNWR line in June 1951.
W S Garth

Of the other Atherton Collieries engines taken over by No 2 Area, EDITH worked variously at Gibfield and Howe Bridge until it was taken out of service at the latter colliery at the end of 1956. After standing derelict for several years, it was finally broken up there in May 1959 [44].

ATLAS seems to have been employed mainly at Chanters until it was sent to Bedford Colliery during 1953, when JAMES LORD was under repair. On its return from Bedford ATLAS spent most of its time at Howe Bridge and Gibfield. In 1956 it suffered a major boiler problem [44] and, following repairs, it was at Chanters Colliery for a period in 1958. It was then transferred on a more permanent basis to Bedford Colliery and its subsequent history appears later in the chapter.

HUMPHREY and VIOLET were employed regularly at Chanters. HUMPHREY was repaired at Parsonage workshops in the summer of 1954, when it was repainted in the Wigan Area livery. VIOLET also appears to have been overhauled, either at Kirkless or Parsonage, in the late 1950s, as it was observed repainted in the Wigan Area livery in August 1959.

GORDON remained at Chanters until 1954. It went to Parsonage workshop late in 1954, and was then sent on to Kirkless, where the repairs were completed in April 1955. It was used on the Standish railway system until further repairs were undertaken at Kirkless in 1958. It then had a spell at the Wigan Junction and Maypole Collieries, working from Low Hall shed, before being transferred back to Chanters Colliery in the summer of 1959. It was temporarily at Gibfield from September 1959 to January 1960 and in September 1960 went to Bickershaw Colliery [44].

During this period, several of the six coupled saddle tanks designed by the Wigan Coal and Iron Company were transferred to Atherton from other collieries in the No 2 Area.

LINDSAY, built by the Wigan Coal and Iron Company in 1887, was the first to arrive, early in 1957. It was sent to Howe Bridge after an overhaul at Kirkless Works, to take over from ATLAS [45]. It was used as the main line locomotive, working the slack coal trains between Gibfield, Howe Bridge and Chanters for a few months. It returned to the Standish railway system on 18th April. Its subsequent history has been recorded in *"Industrial Railways of the Wigan Coalfield"* [3] and in a series of recent articles in *"Industrial Railway Record"* [45,46,47]

LINDSAY was replaced by CRAWFORD, built by the Wigan Coal and Iron Company in 1883, which had also been overhauled at Kirkless before being sent to Howe Bridge in March 1957 [45]. Like LINDSAY, CRAWFORD was employed on the slack coal trains over the main line.

The smaller ACHILLES, built by Hudswell, Clarke and Rodgers in 1880 , came from John Pit, Standish, to Howe Bridge early in May 1957 [45]. It took over from 1861 as the pit shunter. Following the closure of Howe Bridge Colliery in September 1959 [4], it was sent to Chanters Colliery.

1961 to 1965 - East Lancashire Area

There were further changes to the National Coal Board's organisation on 1st January 1961, when the North Western Division was reformed into the West Lancashire Area, the East Lancashire Area and the North Wales Area.

The East Lancashire Area, as well as taking in Burnley and West Cumberland, included all the remaining collieries in the the No 1 (Manchester) Area and also Gibfield, Chanters and Bedford, which were transferred from the No 2 (Wigan) Area. The West Lancashire Area took over the No 3 (St Helens) Area and the majority of the collieries in No 2 (Wigan) Area, including Parsonage and Bickershaw.

As a result of these changes, the locomotives at the Atherton Collieries once again came under the jurisdiction of the railway headquarters at Walkden Yard. All major overhauls were subsequently carried out there, as the repair shops at Gin Pit had been closed in the late 1950s

By the time of the reorganisation, coal production was being run down. Howe Bridge Colliery had, as noted earlier, already closed in September 1959 [4]. By February 1963, demolition was well in hand [48] and the site was later landscaped. The last coal was wound at Gibfield 30th August 1963 [48]. No 1 Pit at Chanters, the last of the former Fletcher, Burrows' collieries, ceased work on 25th January 1964. Final closure came when No 2 Pit there was stopped on 24th June 1966.

Four locomotives at the Atherton Collieries were taken into the stock of the East Lancashire Area - VIOLET, HUMPHREY, ACHILLES and CRAWFORD. GORDON, which was at Bickershaw Colliery on 1st January 1961, remained with the West Lancashire Area until it was withdrawn from service in 1968.

ACHILLES which had been out of use for several years at Chanters Colliery was cut up in January 1962. CRAWFORD was at Gibfield Colliery up to the closure in August 1963. After being used for another month or so on salvage operations it was laid to one side [48]. It was still there in a derelict condition in January 1964 and was broken up a few months later.

VIOLET was sent to Walkden Yard in the summer of 1962, in a bad condition after 20 years of service at Chanters. After repairs had been started it was decided that it was not worthwhile to continue. It was left in a dismantled state alongside the running shed until the end of 1966, after which the remains were cut up.

The brake van, marked "Allowed to work Gibfield Howe Bridge and Chanters", owned by the National Coal Board and used on the trains which ran over the main line was sent to Walkden where it was seen in February 1964.

In the declining years of Chanters colliery, the traffic was worked by two austerity saddle tanks. HUMPHREY and WITCH. HUMPHREY had been here, as mentioned earlier, since 1948, while WITCH was transferred from the Bridgewater railway system in 1962 as a replacement for VIOLET.

HUMPHREY was at Walkden Yard for overhaul from November 1961 to May 1962 and again from May to November 1965. STANLEY was brought in on a temporary basis on the first occasion and RENOWN on the second.

WITCH left Chanters a year or so before the colliery closed, being transferred to the Bridgewater railway system towards the end of 1964 or early 1965. HUMPHREY left under its own steam for Gin Pit in July 1966.

JOHN SPEAKMAN'S BEDFORD COLLIERY

Bedford Colliery 1874 to 1929

John Speakman started sinking his Bedford Colliery in 1874 [34], on the south side of the London and North Western Railway near Wood End. His father, who died in March 1873, had been the proprietor of mines at Westleigh [3] and it seems that the younger John Speakman had been manager of the Bankfield Colliery there [34].

Production at Bedford, which commenced about 1876 [4], seems to have been at a relatively low level until the shafts were deepened between 1883 and 1886. It is likely that a siding was provided to connect with the adjacent main line when the pits were first opened.

However, the earliest agreement which we have been able to trace is dated 31st July 1882 [49], coinciding with the later developments.

John Speakman died on 3rd June 1893 and the property was inherited by his sons, Harry and Fred, [50], the firm then becoming John Speakman and Sons. A limited liability company of the same name was formed on 1st August 1914 [51].

The private line, some half a mile in length, which ran from the colliery to a landsale yard at the end of Guest Street in Leigh, was probably contemporary with the colliery expansion of the 1880s. It had certainly been completed when the second edition of 6" map was surveyed in 1888 to 1892. Later, the line also served a brickworks and a patent fuel works. The brickworks, located alongside the LNWR line but not connected to it, was erected around the turn of the century and did not close until during or immediately after the second world war. The patent fuel works dated from the first world war period and closed around 1930. The site was later occupied by a small housing estate.

Bedford Colliery was amongst those which would have had direct access to the Manchester Ship Canal, if the proposal for the Leigh and South Central Lancashire Railway scheme of 1895 had come about. The main line would have crossed Speakman's railway to Guest Street and there would have been a spur leading towards to the colliery [25].

The earliest locomotive which we have been able to trace at Bedford Colliery was a six coupled saddle tank. Apart from the fact that it was sold to Thomas Mitchell and Sons Ltd, of Bolton, around 1898, we have little further information. It was listed in Mitchells' catalogues from July 1899 to January 1905, but its subsequent disposal is not known. The catalogues show the builder as Barclay, indicating that it had been built at Kilmarnock, either by Andrew Barclay, Sons and Company or the rival firm of Barclays and Company.

BEDFORD built in 1865 by Manning, Wardle and Company for the Potteries, Shrewsbury and North Wales Railway and later the property of John Speakman and Sons Ltd. Photographed here in August 1948 at Walkden Yard after it had been withdrawn from service. Norman Allcock

As a replacement, a powerful four coupled side tank was obtained in 1897 from the Vulcan Foundry. Named THE SIRDAR, it had a long career with John Speakman and Sons Ltd and later with Manchester Collieries Ltd.

Finally, there was the locomotive BEDFORD. It was one of a batch of three six coupled side tanks built for the Potteries, Shrewsbury and North Wales Railway by Manning, Wardle and Company of Leeds in 1865. According to Walkden Yard records, inspected by the authors in the 1950s, it had been purchased in 1910. The engines were originally named POWIS, SIR WATKIN and VISCOUNT although there is some doubt about which engine was acquired by John Speakman and Sons.

BEDFORD has often been associated with SIR WATKIN, which was sold by the railway in the early 1870s to the Norton Cannock Colliery Company. Evidence to support this is that some of the working parts were stamped 167, the Manning, Wardle works number for SIR WATKIN. However this is not conclusive, as other parts were stamped 151, the works number for POWIS, which was auctioned, along with VISCOUNT, by the railway in 1888.

Bedford Colliery 1929 to 1947

John Speakman and Sons Ltd was one of the founder firms when Manchester Collieries Ltd was formed in March 1929. By the end of 1931, new screening plant had been erected and No 2 Pit equipped with new headgear [34]. A railway was built across country to link up with the former Astley and Tyldesley Collieries Company's system near Gin Pit, so that Bedford coal could be be sent to the Nook Pit washery and also to the Bridgewater Canal at Marsland Green. The line was completed in 1930 [52] or perhaps a year or two later.

THE SIRDAR left Bedford Colliery around 1930 and, as we have described in Chapter 6, spent much of the remainder of its life at Robin Hood Sidings, where it was broken up early in 1946. BEDFORD was sent to Astley Green Colliery around the same time. It worked there until it was withdrawn from service in 1947.

After the rail link had been completed to Gin Pit, it was still the practice to keep one locomotive at Bedford Colliery on a permanent basis. Throughout the 1930s and the early 1940s, the regular engine here was GOWER, which had to have its chimney shortened to fit the shed. It was one of the Sharp, Stewart six coupled saddle tanks delivered to the Bridgewater Trustees in 1882. It left Walkden Yard on 25th July 1930 and was briefly at Chanters Colliery before coming on to Bedford.

GOWER was withdrawn from service towards the end of the war and sent to Gin Pit, where it was broken up in April 1945. It was replaced at Bedford Colliery by JAMES LORD, a six coupled side tank. This engine had formerly belonged to Astley and Tyldesley Collieries Ltd and had been built by the Lowca Engineering Company of Whitehaven in 1903.

Bedford Colliery 1947 to 1967

Bedford Colliery passed to the National Coal Board on 1st January 1947 and became part of the No 1 (Manchester) Area of the North Western Division. In the rationalisation of arrangements for coal sales which followed, the Guest Street landsale yard at Leigh was closed. The railway to there from the colliery was taken out of use on 15th June 1949 [53]. Locomotive requirements were further reduced when the screening plant was shut down.

As with the Atherton Collieries, Bedford was transferred to the No 2 (Wigan) Area on 1st January 1952 and came under the control of the East Lancashire Area on 1st January 1961. With further reorganisations in the industry it was transferred to the North Western Area of the National Coal Board which was formed on 26th March 1967. The colliery closed in November of the same year [52] and the agreement in respect of the siding connection was terminated on 31st December 1967 [49].

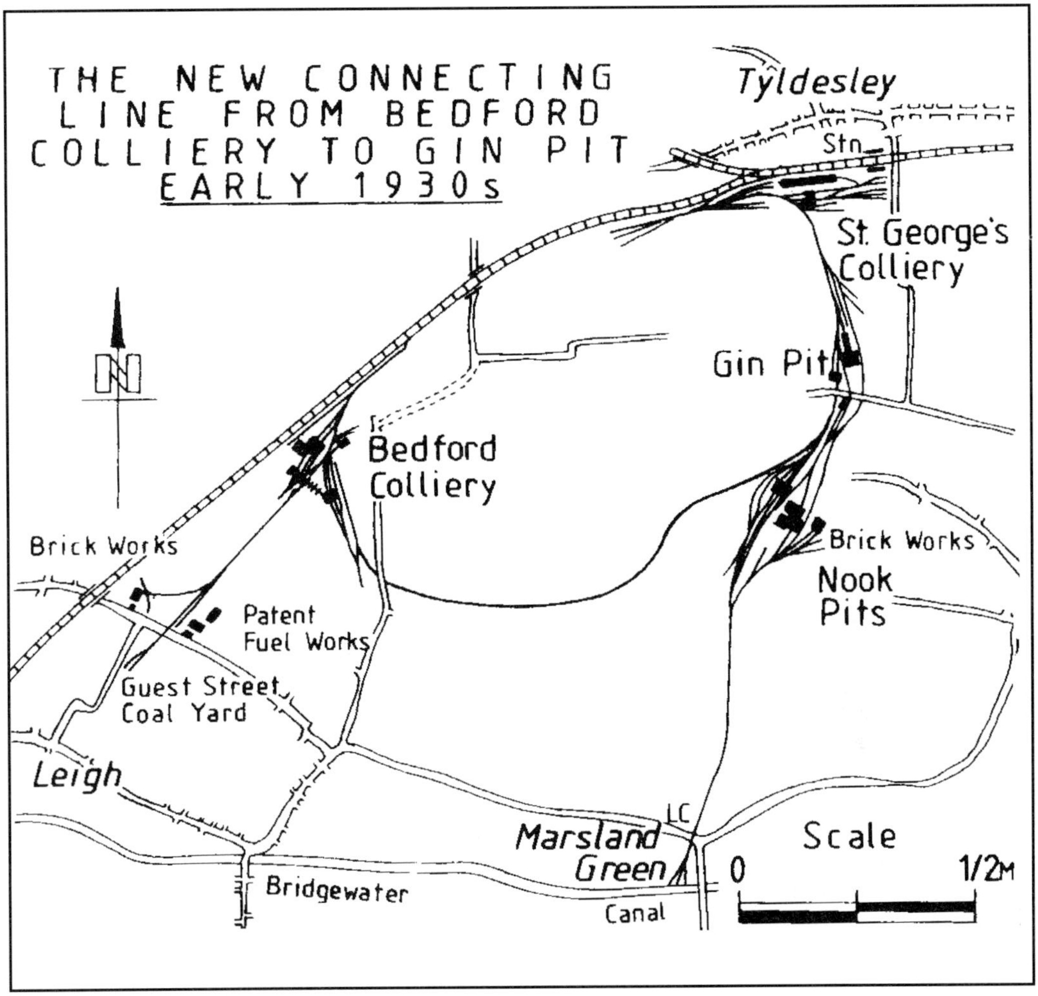

On vesting day, JAMES LORD was at Bedford Colliery and remained the regular engine here until it was broken up on site in December 1960. It was noted under repairs at Gin Pit in June 1947 and presumably one of the Gin Pit locomotives was sent temporarily to Bedford as a replacement.

From January 1952 onwards, during the period that Bedford Colliery was included in the Wigan area, replacements no longer came from Gin Pit, which remained in the No 1 (Manchester) Area. In the summer of 1953, when JAMES LORD was under repairs, ATLAS the ex Fletcher Burrows locomotive was sent from Chanters Colliery to take its place. ATLAS was back at Bedford again early in 1959, when JAMES LORD was again taken out service for overhaul.

It was eventually decided not to proceed with the repairs and JAMES LORD was broken up on site towards the end of the following year. ATLAS remained at Bedford and was there when the colliery was absorbed into the East Lancashire Area, with its locomotive headquarters at Walkden.

ATLAS continued as the regular engine at Bedford. It was sent to Walkden Yard for overhaul in April 1962. It returned in December 1962, repainted in the new maroon livery usually reserved for engines working on the Bridgewater system and at Astley Green. It was not put into traffic until February 1963 on account of the very cold weather.

COLONEL arrived at Bedford Colliery in January 1962 from Wheatsheaf Screens to take over while ATLAS was away at Walkden. It proved too small for the work and was laid aside. RENOWN, one of the austerity saddle tanks, was sent from Gin Pit in its place. COLONEL was eventually was scrapped at Bedford Colliery in August 1963, while RENOWN returned to Gin Pit as soon as ATLAS was put to work.

ATLAS remained at Bedford for another three and a half years, until it was sent to Walkden Yard in November 1966 for repairs to its boiler. These were not carried out and the engine lay out of use for several year outside the running shed at Walkden, being broken up towards the end of 1968.

ATLAS was replaced by RODNEY another austerity saddle tank, which had previously been used at Bickershaw Colliery, and which came to Bedford in the late summer or early autumn of 1966 after an overhaul at Walkden Yard. Soon after it arrived, RODNEY managed to demolish part of the engine shed and had to go to Gin Pit for attention. It stayed at Bedford until March 1967 when it was sent back to Walkden Yard.

RENOWN was back at Bedford in March 1967 and stayed here until the colliery closed. At the end of October 1967, it ran light engine to Gin Pit. In December it was coupled bunker to bunker to HUMPHREY, the last remaining locomotive at Gin Pit, and the two engines then made their way under their own steam over the British Railways line from Jackson's Sidings to Walkden.

THE ASTLEY AND TYLDESLEY COLLIERIES

Up to 1864 - Milner's Bedford Colliery and Darlington's Astley Colliery

There are several references to mining in the Bedford district of Leigh in the first half of the nineteenth century, but this seems to have been in an area to the south-east of Speakman's activities.

A Bedford Colliery, lately worked by Richard Pickering Higginson and leased from the devisees of the late J Bourne, was advertised for sale on 15th August 1839 [54]. There was a further sale on 22nd April 1841, when Bedford Colliery was still in the possession of Richard Pickering Higginson [55].

This was presumably the colliery marked on the on the 2" drawings and on the first edition of the 6" map near Lower Fold. The pits here also appear on the Bedford Tithe Map of 1847 [56], which attributes ownership of the land to Joseph Eckersley.

Following the sale of 1841, the colliery was acquired by William Edward Milner, in partnership with James Morris and Joseph Hill. William Milner became sole proprietor following a dissolution of the partnership on 8th October 1845 [57], and Bedford Colliery appears under his ownership in directories for 1848 [58] and 1851 [59]. It was being worked by Milner's executors in 1853 when it was advertised to be let [60].

John Darlington, who owned mines at Coppull and was a leading proprietor of the Ince Hall Coal and Cannel Company [3], also had interests in the area. During the 1840s he took out a lease at Astley, to the east of Milner's Bedford Colliery, from the Trustees of Colonel Malcolm Nugent [61] and sank what later became known as Gin Pit.

At this date there were no main line railways which served the district. Although there had been a number of proposals in the 1830s and 1840s these had all fallen through. A branch to serve the Tyldesley Coalfield [62] had been authorised by Parliament in 1847 as part of the Manchester and Southport Railway [63], but was never built.

To provide an outlet for his coals, John Darlington built a tramroad from Gin Pit to the Bridgewater Canal at Marsland Green, passing through land owned by Colonel Nugent's Trustees. We can date its construction fairly precisely. The line is not shown on the first edition of the 6" map, surveyed in 1845 and 1846, but appears on the Astley Tithe Map of 1847 [61]. It was presumably narrow gauge and, at this date, worked by horses.

The tithe map shows a short branch at the northern end of the line leading to pits near Meanleys Farm, on land owned by the Bridgewater Trustees. It was presumably this branch which was covered by an agreement with the Bridgewater Trustees dated 24th December 1847 [64].

It appears that William Milner may also have made use of Darlington's tramroad to reach the canal. Although we have found no map showing a line serving his Bedford Colliery, an advertisement of February 1853 relating to the lease of the colliery [61] says that "permission may be granted for conditional use of the railway."

In 1851, Darlington was trying to dispose of his interests at Astley. Towards the end of the year, he approached the Bridgewater Trustees with a view to a sale. The correspondence [65] makes specific reference to the tramroad and mentions 2 cranes for lifting out boats and 2 tipplars (sic) at the pier head.

Negotiations with the Bridgewater Trustees fell through. However, John Darlington eventually succeeded in disposing of his property to Samuel Jackson and Company, who had also acquired William Milner's Bedford Colliery from his executors in 1853.

1864 to 1900 - The Astley and Tyldesley Coal and Salt Co Ltd

The improved transport facilities, available after the London and North Western Railway's Eccles, Tyldesley and Wigan line opened in 1864, provided the impetus for an expansion of the collieries. Samuel Jackson formed the Astley and Tyldesley Coal and Salt Company in the early 1860s.

Work started about 1866 on the first two shafts at St George's Colliery, south of the new railway, near Tyldesley Station [4] . Nook No 1 Pit was sunk in 1866 [4], on a site to the south of the original Gin Pit. A new pit was was also sunk at Cross Hillock, near Astley Village a little later, but seems only to have been served by road transport.

With the new collieries coming into production, the older pits were abandoned. Bedford Colliery, taken over from William Milner, is last shown in the Mines Lists for 1864. Astley Colliery, which presumably comprised the pits formerly worked by John Darlington, is last shown in 1868, but was subsequently redeveloped. A new shaft at Gin Pit, the only one in use there in later years, was completed in 1872 [4]. A second shaft was sunk at the Nook Pits in 1873 [4].

The Astley and Tyldesley Coal and Salt Co Ltd was registered in the early 1870s to take over from the existing partnerhsip , the new title first appearing in the Mines Lists for 1874. A contemporary description of the firm's activities appears in the Mining Journal for 2nd

May 1874. Jackson's Pit and Bedford Pit had finished working some time previously. Gin Pit was standing because of water problems. Coal was being produced at at the old and new Nook Pits, at the two pits at Tyldesley and at Cross Hillock, which was also used for pumping. Two locomotives were employed, one on the standard gauge and the other on a gauge of about 2'0", conveying coal to the canal.

The standard gauge extended from Jackson's Sidings on the LNWR at Tyldesley as far the Gin and Nook Pits. The sidings serving St George's Colliery are shown on a Line Plan of 1868 [66] and we assume that the rest of the private line had been completed by that date. The narrow gauge tramroad, which ran from the Nook and Gin Pits to the canal at Marsland Green, had evidently been reconstructed for locomotive working. We have, however, been unable to find any confirmatory evidence that the gauge was as small as that quoted by the Mining Journal's correspondent. Nor have we been able to find out anything more about the locomotive which was used on it, except that, according to old employees, it may have been named GORDON.

The standard gauge engine was presumably TYLDESLEY, a six coupled K Class saddle tank, supplied by Manning Wardle and Company of Leeds in 1868. According to the manufacturer's records, the name was changed to JACKSON prior to May 1872. Certainly old employees whom we interviewed in the 1940s remembered an engine of this name which, according to them, was taken out of service in the 1890s.

They recalled another standard gauge locomotive named LADY CORNWALL, which they said was a 2-2-0 well tank, built by Bury, Curtis and Kennedy and also taken out of service in the 1890s. LADY CORNWALL appears to have been the engine sold by the Lancashire and Yorkshire Railway to George Peace, Managing Director of the Astley and Tyldesley company, in November 1874 for £150 [67]. It had been built as a 2-2-0 tender locomotive for the Preston and Wyre Railway by Bury, Curtis and Kennedy in 1846. It had been acquired by the Lancashire and Yorkshire Railway in 1849, when the Preston and Wyre was taken over jointly by the L&YR and the LNWR, and had later been rebuilt as a tank engine.

A further standard gauge engine, MADEN, was purchased in 1875 from Manning, Wardle and Company of Leeds. It was one of the firm's Class O six coupled saddle tanks. It had been built originally for Logan and Hemingway, the public works contractors, but the order had been cancelled. It must have arrived at Tyldesley towards the end of the year. The Bolton Chronicle [68], reporting on a dinner held at Queens Head Tyldesley on 22nd December, to celebrate the opening of the new Nook Pit and improvements to Cross Hillock Pit, mentions that MADEN had recently been delivered.

An estimate was prepared in March 1876 for the conversion to standard gauge of the narrow gauge line to the canal [69]. Several other estimates followed. The final one is dated 27th March 1884 [69] and we believe that the work was put in hand shortly afterwards. The conversion had certainly been completed when the survey was made for the first edition of the 25" map in 1892.

A new locomotive was acquired in 1886, possibly to coincide with the extension of the standard gauge system to the canal basin. Named ASTLEY, it was a six coupled side tank and came from Sharp Stewart and Company, of Manchester.

Another locomotive was added to the stock in 1894, when TYLDESLEY, a six coupled side tank, was purchased from Peckett and Sons of Bristol. JACKSON was taken in part exchange and was resold by Pecketts to the Sussex Portland Cement Co Ltd, Heighton, Sussex where, according to Manning, Wardle records, it was renamed EDITH.

The installations at Marsland Green photographed in March 1959. This was originally the terminus of the narrow gauge tramroad, later converted to standard gauge. Note the building in the foreground, where coal was tipped from railway wagons into barges, and the elevated line in the background, serving the landsale yard. Jim Peden collection

Peckett and Sons' official photograph of TYLDESLEY, the side tank supplied to the Astley and Tyldesley Coal and Salt Co Ltd in 1894. Frank Jones collection

There were further colliery developments towards the end of the century. No 3 Pit at St George's Colliery was sunk in 1883 and No 2 Pit there was enlarged about 1893 [4]. Nook No 3 Pit, where sinking started in 1895, was completed in 1899 [4]. Meanwhile coal production had ceased at Cross Hillock Colliery, which is last shown in the Mines Lists for 1887.

The Leigh and South Central Lancashire Railway proposals of 1895, which we have noted earlier, would have caused major changes to the Astley and Tyldesley company's system. The hub of the railway was to have been south of the Nook Pits, where the branches from Ince and Walkden converged into the main line leading south to the Cheshire Lines Railway at Glazebrook and to the Manchester Ship Canal at Partington [25]. Junctions were intended with the Astley and Tyldesley company's lines north of Gin Pit and near Marsland Green.

1900 to 1929 - The Astley and Tyldesley Collieries Co Ltd

In 1900 the property was transferred to a new company, the Astley and Tyldesley Collieries Co Ltd, which was registered on 4th December. T B Wood was the Chairman and G H Peace the Secretary [70]. Further developments at the Nook Pits followed, No 4 Pit there being sunk in 1914 [4].

The new company also set about improving the railway system and its locomotives. Extensions and alterations were made to Jackson's Sidings at Tyldesley, where traffic was exchanged with the LNWR. The revised arrangements were covered by agreements dated 7th November 1906 and 29th February 1912 [71].

Three new locomotives were purchased from the Lowca Engineering Company of Whitehaven, partly to replace the firm's earliest engines and partly to cater for the increased work load. They were all six coupled side tanks. The first, of the maker's class H design, was named T.B.WOOD. It carried the date 1899 on its works plate and had presumably been ordered by the old company. JAMES LORD, another Class H followed in 1903.

GEORGE PEACE, which was built in 1906, was of the manufacturer's Class D design. It soon gained a reputation for being a poor performer and it is clear that there were a number of design faults. One unusual feature was the Joy valve gear, driving piston valves above the cylinders. The two Class H locomotives, which were more satisfactory, had slide valves actuated by the conventional Stephenson gear. There seem to have been other differences in the blast pipe and smokebox arrangements which affected steaming.

The next two locomotives represented a departure from the usual practice on colliery railways, where only four coupled and six coupled designs were normally employed. Apart from another example at the Bridgewater Collieries, to be described in Chapter 11, they were unique in having eight coupled wheels and were specially designed by Nasmyth, Wilson and Company of Patricroft. MADEN was delivered in 1910, replacing the earlier engine of the same name. The second eight wheeler, EMANUEL CLEGG, came in 1924. ASTLEY of 1886 and TYLDESLEY of 1894 were withdrawn from service during the first world war or shortly afterwards.

Manchester Collieries Ltd 1929 to 1947

The Astley and Tyldesley Collieries Co Ltd merged with other neighbouring firms to form Manchester Collieries Ltd in March 1929. The firm's pits, together with the Atherton collieries of Fletcher, Burrows and Co Ltd and the Bedford Colliery of John Speakman and Sons Ltd, formed the Western District of the new organisation.

Coal was wound at St George's Colliery, at Nook Nos 1 and 4 Pits and at Gin Pit. There was a landsale yard at St George's, which was kept quite busy with deliveries to Tyldesley and district, together with smaller yards at the Nook Pits and Marsland Green. Coal not sold locally was sent away by rail through Jackson's Sidings or was loaded on to barges on the Bridgewater Canal at Marsland Green. The sawmills and pit-prop yard was located at Gin Pit and there was a brickworks at the Nook Pits.

The locomotive depot was at Gin Pit, where a three road building with a north light roof was provided. Two roads were used by the working engines, while the third housed the steam cranes which were used on such jobs as unloading timber and stores, emptying the slurry pits and maintenance of the railway tracks. There was a separate repair shop where, after the amalgamation, heavy overhauls on all the Western District locomotives were carried out.

The locomotive stock employed on the Astley and Tyldesley system changed little between 1929 and the second world war. The two eight coupled engines, MADEN and EMANUEL CLEGG, were used on the heaviest duties, including working over the new line to Bedford Colliery, which was steeply graded.

The three Lowca engines were used for the lighter work. T.B.WOOD was temporarily at Chanters Colliery at the end of 1938 and the beginning of 1939 as a replacement for MADGE, which was undergoing overhaul at Gin Pit workshops.

Towards the end of the war time period, JAMES LORD was transferred on a permanent basis to Bedford Colliery to replace GOWER, leaving T.B.WOOD and GEORGE PEACE on the Astley and Tyldesley system. GEORGE PEACE was something of a black sheep. Modifications were made about 1944 in an attempt to improve its performance. New cylinders and valves were fitted. The side tanks were shortened and an extra water tank was put under the bunker. The smokebox was lengthened, the blast pipe altered and the chimney was changed. All this had little effect and the engine was confined, as far as possible, to shunting duties in the pityard at St George's Colliery, where no lengthy runs were involved.

In June 1937 VIOLET, one of the six coupled saddle tanks built by Nasmyth, Wilson and Company for the Earl of Ellesmere arrived from the Bridgewater railway system [37]. It left Gin Pit for Chanters Colliery late in 1943 or early in 1944 after an overhaul. We have described its subsequent history earlier in the chapter.

Its place was taken by CHOWBENT, transferred from Chanters Colliery to Gin Pit in the early years of the war. As noted earlier, CHOWBENT was a six coupled saddle tank built by Andrew Barclay, Sons and Company in 1923 for Fletcher, Burrows and Company.

The closure of St George's Colliery in 1941 [4] must have led to some reduction in the shunting which was required, but, nevertheless, one further locomotive was transferred to the Astley and Tyldesley system. COLONEL came from one of the Atherton Collieries, probably Howe Bridge, at some date after March 1943.

The National Coal Board 1947 to 1967

The Nook and Gin Pits were taken over by the National Coal Board on 1st January 1947. They formed part of the No 1 (Manchester) Area of the Board's North Western Division, and unlike the Atherton and Bedford Collieries were not transferred to the Wigan Area on 1st January 1952. They became part of the East Lancashire Area on 1st January 1961.

Four of the former Astley and Tyldesley Collieries Company's locomotives were based at the Gin Pit shed on vesting day - T.B.WOOD, GEORGE PEACE, MADEN, and EMANUEL CLEGG.

The Lowca locomotive T.B.WOOD and its crew pause for the photographer in the landsale yard at St George's Colliery
Frank Jones

EMANUEL CLEGG, one of the two unusual eight coupled locomotives built by Nasmyth, Wilson and Co for the Astley and Tyldesley Collieries Co, photographed at Gin Pit in August 1965. The Nook Pit washery can be seen in the background.
Bernard Mettam

GEORGE PEACE photographed in August 1950. Note the extended smokebox and short chimney fitted towards the end of the war in an attempt to improve the steaming capability of the locomotive.
Frank Jones

Gin Pit locomotive shed in October 1967, taken soon after the closure of the railway system, when RENOWN and HUMPHREY were locked away inside. The original roof was one of the "northlight" pattern and was replaced following storm damage in May 1956.
Philip Hindley

A fifth of the Astley and Tyldesley engines, JAMES LORD, was at Bedford Colliery when it was taken over by the National Coal Board. Apart from an overhaul in the summer of 1947, it never returned to Gin Pit and passed into the stock of the Wigan Area in 1952. It was broken up at Bedford in 1960.

The Gin Pit allocation was completed by COLONEL and CHOWBENT, which had been transferred from the former Fletcher, Burrows and Company's Atherton Collieries a few years earlier.

COLONEL had left the Astley and Tyldesley railway system by July 1947. It was at Parsonage Colliery November 1950, but may have spent some time at one of the Atherton Collieries before that. It was back at Gin Pit for overhaul in the summer of 1951, but apparently did not see further service there, except perhaps on trial following completion of the repairs. As recounted previously, it was subsequently used on the Bridgewater railway system, at Wheatsheaf Screens and at Bedford Colliery.

CHOWBENT was transferred to Parsonage Colliery and was taken into the stock of No 2 (Wigan) Area on 1st January 1952. It never returned to Gin Pit, being broken up at Parsonage in 1958.

The two Lowca built locomotives T.B.WOOD and GEORGE PEACE and the two Nasmyth, Wilson eight coupled engines EMANUEL CLEGG and MADEN remained at Gin Pit, supplemented by austerity saddle tanks, which took over the heaviest work. The first of these to arrive was W.H.R., which had been purchased second hand from the War Department and was still in WD livery. It was delivered to Walkden on 18th June 1947 and was sent from there to Jackson's Sidings on 30th September 1947.

W.H.R. was followed by GORDON, which came to Gin Pit from Chanters Colliery in 1950. It did not stay long and was returned in 1951. By August 1951 it had been replaced by RENOWN, which was transferred from Parsonage Colliery.

The pattern of locomotive working at this time is described in article by Steven Oakden in the *"Industrial Railway Record"* for September 1988 [52]. Additional information is provided in the a follow up article in the same journal for March 1990 [72]. W.H.R. was normally employed working traffic between the Nook Washery and Jackson's Sidings. MADEN shunted at the washery while the other eight-wheeler, EMANUEL CLEGG performed general shunting duties and also worked twice a day to Marsland Green with coal for the landsale yard and for transhipment to the canal. One of the six coupled Lowca engines, usually T B WOOD, shunted at Jackson's Sidings.

Although dumpers were reported to have replaced rail transport for the disposal of waste [73] in 1945, there was still a certain amount being conveyed to the tips alongside the line to Bedford Colliery in special internal user wagons with sloping floors and side doors. Rakes of up to 33 wagons of dirt were propelled on to the tips in the morning and at lunch time by the engine which shunted at the Nook Pit washery.

In the 1950s locomotive repairs at the Gin Pit workshops were phased out. EMANUEL CLEGG was the last locomotive to have a heavy overhaul, in 1952. Light repairs continued to be undertaken for a few more years, for example to W.H.R. in the summer of 1953 and again in June 1955 and to RENOWN also in June 1955. The last overhaul for which we have records was to MADEN. The boiler was taken out at the end of 1958 or early in 1959, and sent to Hough and Sons Ltd, of Wigan, for repair. There was some damage, fortunately mainly superficial, to the working locomotives when the roof of the engine shed collapsed during a gale in May 1956.

The 1950s saw the withdrawal of the two Lowca engines. GEORGE PEACE, which had been temporarily at Astley Green Colliery in 1952, was taken out of service in the summer of 1955. It then stood out of use until it was scrapped in November or December 1957.

T. B. WOOD worked until 1957 when it broke a driving axle. It was sent to Walkden Yard, but was found not to be worth repairing and was scrapped there in June 1958.

At this period three locomotives seem to have been needed cover the work, W.H.R., RENOWN and one of the eight wheelers being normally in use. When RENOWN was under repair at Walkden Yard in 1956 and when W.H.R. was there in the following year, both the eight coupled engines were needed.

EMANUEL CLEGG and MADEN were both taken out of service in 1958, the former in the summer and the latter towards the end of the year. EMANUEL CLEGG stood out of use for several years and was broken up in June 1965. MADEN was eventually returned to traffic and lasted until 1962.

Further austerity saddle tanks were brought in. WEASEL arrived at Gin Pit in May 1958. It was relatively new engine, built by the Hunslet Engine Company to the War Department design. It had been delivered to Walkden Yard in March 1957 and had spent the intervening period on the Bridgewater railway system.

WASP, built by the Hunslet Engine Company in 1954, was also at Gin Pit for a short time. It was transferred temporarily from Bridgewater system from August 1959 to May 1960. RENOWN was sent to Walkden Yard for repair in December 1960 and returned in May 1961, WEASEL was there in the middle of 1961 and W.H.R. from December 1961 to March 1962.

Coal production had ceased at Gin Pit in 1958 and by 1962 was being run down at the Nook Pits. Out of the three locomotives still at the Gin Pit shed, two were in regular use from Mondays to Fridays, with one only on Saturdays. Their work had been reduced significantly now that all dirt was taken to the tips by road transport. The line to the canal at Marsland Green was still busy, with coal being despatched by barge to Westwood and Barton Power Stations.

RENOWN was sent to Bedford Colliery in the summer of 1962 to deputise for ATLAS, which was sent for overhaul at Walkden Yard. It returned to Gin Pit in February 1963, thus allowing WEASEL to go to Walkden for repairs the next month. On WEASEL's return towards the end of the year, RENOWN itself was sent to Walkden. It was noted there in the December, but was back at Gin Pit by January 1964. W.H.R. was at Walkden from January to May 1964 and returned briefly to Gin Pit. By the autumn of the same year it had been transferred to work at Astley Green Colliery and on what remained of the Bridgewater railway system.

Another austerity tank arrived in June 1964 under its own steam from Peel Hall Opencast Disposal Point, still carrying its WD number 71499. It had evidently been sent to Gin Pit for storage following closure of the disposal point and was not intended to be used.

However, the story goes that the fitters at Gin Pit removed a number of parts to keep RENOWN and WEASEL working. They were told to stop and the engine was a patched up and sent to Walkden Yard either late in 1964 or early in 1965. It was transferred from the National Coal Board's Opencast Executive to the East Lancashire Area, overhauled at Walkden, repainted in the Area's maroon livery and given the name HARRY.

The remaining Nook Pit ceased winding on 6th August 1965 [52]. RENOWN and WEASEL were kept busy for the next two months, clearing stock-piled coal and also dealing with coal brought in by road from Chanters Colliery. The preparation plant there had broken down and, with the imminent closure of the colliery, it was more economical to make use of the Nook Washery than to carry out repairs.

The two locomotives left Gin Pit for Walkden Yard towards the end of 1965 and were replaced by HARRY, the erstwhile Opencast engine, which was employed for a further two or three months. By March 1966, it had been returned to Walkden Yard for repairs following an accident.

The Gin Pit railway system then seems to have been in state of suspended animation until until a decision was taken to use the Nook Washery to process slack coal from Bedford Colliery, which had previously been sent to Sandhole [52]. The railway from Bedford Colliery to the Nook Washery had not been used for some time and work to refurbish it started at Easter 1966, using one of the Gin Pit steam cranes. The austerity saddle tank HUMPHREY was transferred from Chanters Colliery to Gin Pit under its own steam in July to work the re-opened line. According to Steven Oakden [52], the washed coal was taken to Marsland Green to be loaded on to barges. By this time the there had been subsidence at Jackson's Sidings which meant that they could not be used for traffic purposes.

WEASEL leaving the Nook Pits and climbing past Gin Pit village with the steam sanding gear in full operation
Jim Peden collection

Bedford Colliery closed just over a year later, in October 1967, and the railway system finally ceased operations. As recounted earlier HUMPHREY, and RENOWN from Bedford Colliery, left for Walkden Yard in December 1967, The agreement with British Railways in respect of the main line sidings was terminated on 14th November 1968 and the whole of the railway system was dismantled using road transport.

LOCOMOTIVE SUMMARY

Atherton Collieries

Various Fletcher family partnerships to about 1832
John Fletcher and Others from about 1832 to 31-12-1874
Fletcher, Burrows and Company 1-1-1875 to 13-4-1892
Fletcher, Burrows and Co Ltd 14-4-1892 to 3-3-1929
Manchester Collieries Ltd 4-3-1929 to 31-12-1946
National Coal Board 1-1-1947 to 1966
No 1 (Manchester) Area 1-1-1947 to 31-12-1951
No 2 (Wigan) Area 1-1-1952 to 31-12-1960
East Lancashire, Burnley and Cumberland Area after 1-1-1961

Howe Bridge Colliery closed September 1959
Gibfield Colliery closed October 1963
Chanters Colliery closed June 1966

Locomotives used at Howe Bridge, Gibfield and Chanters Collieries up to 1947

LILFORD 0-4-0WTOC H(L) 1861 12"x18"
New to John Fletcher and Others
Sold to Thomas Mitchell and Sons Ltd, dealers, Bolton about 1899

ELLESMERE 0-4-0WTOC H(L) 244 1861 12"x18" 3′6½"
New to John Fletcher and Others
No 2 in Fletcher, Burrows' stock
Name removed in 1929 or 1930 and afterwards known as 1861
To NCB at Howe Bridge 1-1-1947

ATHERTON 0-4-0WTOC H(L) 340 1867 12"x18" 3′6½"
New to John Fletcher and Others
No 3 in Fletcher, Burrows' stock
Name removed by 1938, probably earlier, but still known as ATHERTON afterwards
To NCB at Howe Bridge 1-1-1947

COLLIER 0-6-0STIC MW 698 1878 15"x22" 3′9"
New to Fletcher, Burrows and Co. Class O. Ex works 24-5-1878
New boiler and copper firebox ordered in 4-1905
Scrapped about 1929

ELECTRIC 0-4-0STOC Gibfield
Built in 1888 or 1893. See text
Sold to Netherseal Coliery Co Ltd about 1926 or 1927

VULCAN 0-6-0STIC VF 1350 1892 16"x22" 3′9"
New to Fletcher, Burrows and Co Ltd
Scrapped about 1929

LILFORD 0-6-0T IC HE 561 1892 15"x20" 3′4"
New to Hemsworth Colly Co Ltd "KINSLEY" 23-3-1892 and sold Fletcher, Burrows Ltd between 2-1900 and 1-1901
Sent to Gin Pit between April and June 1938. Dismantled by December 1938 and scrapped early in 1939.

ATLAS 0-6-0STIC P 1177 1909 16"x22" 3′10"
New to Fletcher, Burrows and Co Ltd
No 7 in Fletcher, Burrows' stock
To NCB at Chanters 1-1-1947

CARBON	0-4-0STOC	AB	1704	1920	14"x22"	3'5"

New to Fletcher, Burrows and Co Ltd
Maker's records show as No 8 when new, but later No 6 in Fletcher, Burrows' stock
Transferred to Astley Green Colliery between January and March 1938

CHOWBENT	0-6-0STOC	AB	1802	1923	16"x24"	3'7"

New to Fletcher, Burrows and Co Ltd
Possibly No 5 in Fletcher, Burrow's stock
Transferred to Gin Pit between 1939 and 1943

COLONEL	0-6-0STIC	HE	1459	1927	15"x20"	3'7"

New to Fletcher, Burrows and Co Ltd
No 4 in Fletcher, Burrows' stock
At Gin Pit for repairs mid 1938
Transferred to Gin Pit betwen 1943 and 1947

GOWER	0-6-0STIC	SS	3090	1882	17"x24"	4'0"

Transferred from Walkden to Chanters, 25-7-1930
Transferred to Bedford Colliery probably in early 1930s, and before June 1938

CERBERUS	0-6-0STIC	SS	2909	1880	17"x24"	4'0"

Transferred from Walkden to Chanters 10-3-1937
Transferred from Chanters to Gin Pit by January 1938
Taken out of service February 1938 and scrapped at Gin Pit at end of 1938

MADGE	0-6-0STIC	NW	782	1906	17"x24"	4'1"

Transferred to Chanters from Walkden via Gin Pit 28-3-1938
At Gin Pit for repairs end of 1938, early 1939 and returned to Chanters
Scrapped at Gin Pit early 1946

EDITH	0-6-0STIC	HE	436	1887	14"x18"	3'1"

Transferred from Shakerley Colliery to Howe Bridge, late 1938 or early 1939
To NCB at Gibfield 1-1-1947

SHAKERLEY	0-6-0STIC	HE	736	1901	14"x18"	3'2½"

Transferred from Shakerley Colliery to Howe Bridge, late 1938 or early 1939
To NCB at Chanters 1-1-1947

VIOLET	0-6-0STIC	NW	852	1908	17"x24"	4'1"

Transferred from Gin Pit to Chanters in 1943 or 1944
To NCB at Chanters 1-1-1947

T.B.WOOD	0-6-0T IC	LE	233	1899	16"x24"	3'10"

Temporarily at Chanters from Gin Pit late 1938, early 1939, and returned to Gin Pit

GORDON	0-6-0STIC	RSH	7288	1945	18"x26"	4'3"

Originally WD 71479 and purchased by Manchester Collieries Ltd
Delivered to Walkden Yard and sent on to Chanters 18-4-1946
To NCB at Chanters 1-1-1947

National Coal Board

1861	0-4-0WTOC	H(L)	244	1861	12"x18"	3'6½"

Ex Manchester Collieries Ltd at Howe Bridge 1-1-1947
Repairs at Gin Pit early 1951
Sold to a consortium of railway societies and despatched to Leith 18-9-1957

	0-4-0WTOC	H(L)	340	1867	12"x18"	3'6½"

Ex Manchester Collieries Ltd at Howe Bridge 1-1-1947
Temporarily at Ashton Moss Colliery, 1947
Scrapped July 1952 at Gibfield

ATLAS 0-6-0STIC P 1177 1909 16"x22" 3′10"
Ex Manchester Collieries Ltd at Chanters 1-1-1947
Transferred to Gin Pit by 8-1948
Returned to Chanters by 5-1951
Temporarily at Bedford Colliery mid 1953
At Howe Bridge and Gibfield in 1957 and 1958
Transferred to Bedford Colliery between 11-1958 and 3-1959

EDITH 0-6-0STIC HE 436 1887 14"x18" 3′1"
Ex Manchester Collieries Ltd at Gibfield 1-1-1947
Taken out of service at Howe Bridge by 12-1956 and scrapped there 5-1959

SHAKERLEY 0-6-0STIC HE 736 1901 14"x18" 3′2H"
Ex Manchester Collieries Ltd at Chanters 1-1-1947
Transferred to Cleworth Hall between 7-47 and 12-1949

VIOLET 0-6-0STIC NW 852 1908 17"x24" 4′1"
Ex Manchester Collieries Ltd at Chanters 1-1-1947
Sent to Walkden Yard mid 1962 for repairs, but laid aside and dismantled by 3-1963. Remains scrapped in 9 or 10-1965.

GORDON 0-6-0STIC RSH 7288 1945 18"x26" 4′3"
Ex Manchester Collieries Ltd at Chanters 1-1-1947
At Gin Pit 1950 to 1951
Sent from Chanters to Parsonage for repairs about 9-1954 and then sent on to Kirkless 2-1-1955
Transferred to other Wigan Area Collieries on completion of repairs about 4-1955
Returned to Chanters from Low Hall about 6-1959
Transferred to Bickershaw end of 1960 or early 1961
Scrapped at Bickershaw 10-1966

HUMPHREY 0-6-0STIC RSH 7293 1945 18"x26" 4′3"
Transferred from Astley Green to Chanters 31-12-1948
Sent from Chanters to Parsonage for repairs from about 5-1954 to 8-1954 and returned to Chanters
Sent from Chanters to Kirkless for repairs early in 1956 and returned to Chanters 3-9-1956
Sent from Chanters to Walkden Yard for repairs 11-1961 to 6-1962 and returned to Chanters
Sent from Chanters to Walkden Yard for repairs 5-1965 to 11-1965 and returned to Chanters
Transferred from Chanters to Gin Pit 7-1966 after Chanters closed

LINDSAY 0-6-0STIC WCI 1887 16"x20" 4′3"
Transferred to Howe Bridge after overhaul at Kirkless 29-1-1957
Transferred from Howe Bridge to John Pit 18-4-1957

CRAWFORD 0-6-0STIC WCI 1883 16"x20" 4′3"
Transferred to Gibfield after overhaul at Kirkless 3-1957
Taken out of service at Gibfield late 1963 when colliery closed and scrapped there 5-1964

ACHILLES 0-6-0STIC HCR 217 1880 14"x20" 3′10½"
Transferred from John Pit to Howe Bridge about 4-1957
Out of use at Howe Bridge from 2-1960 to 5-1960 and then sent to Chanters
Out of use at Chanters from 5-1960 until scrapped there by Central Wagon Company early in 1962

STANLEY 0-6-0STIC HE 3302 1945 18"x26" 4′3"
Temporarily at Chanters circa 11-61 to 7-62 to replace HUMPHREY in shops

WITCH 0-6-0STIC HE 3842 1946 18"x26" 4′3"
Transferred from Walkden to Chanters about 7-1962 to replace VIOLET
Transferred from Chanters to Walkden late 1964 or early 1965

RENOWN 0-6-0STIC HE 3697 1950 18"x26" 4′3"
Temporarily at Chanters from about 3-1965 to late 1965 to replace HUMPHREY in shops

John Speakman's Bedford Colliery

John Speakman from about 1874 until about 1893
John Speakman and Sons from about 1893 to 30-7-1914
John Speakman and Sons Ltd 1-8-1914 to 3-3-1929
Manchester Collieries Ltd 4-3-1929 to 31-12-1946
National Coal Board 1-1-1947 to 1966
No 1 (Manchester) Area 1-1-1947 to 31-12-1951
No 2 (Wigan) Area 1-1-1952 to 31-12-1960
East Lancashire, Burnley and Cumberland Area 1-1-1961 to 25-3-1967
North Western Area from 26-3-1967

Colliery closed October 1967

John Speakman; John Speakman and Sons; John Speakman and Sons Ltd; Manchester Collieries Ltd

	0-6-0ST	AB or Bys			10"x18"	2′9

Possibly named BEDFORD
Sold to Thomas Mitchell and Sons Ltd, dealers, Bolton, about 1899

THE SIRDAR	0-4-0T OC	VF	1540	1897	15"x20"	3′7"

New to John Speakman and Sons
Transferred to Robin Hood early 1930s, possibly via Agecroft Colliery, and scrapped at Robin Hood early 1946. See Chapter 6

BEDFORD	0-6-0T IC	MW		1865	15¼"x22½"	3′10½"

Either Manning Wardle 151 or 167 (see text)
Possibly ex Norton Cannock Colly Co Ltd, Walsall 1910
Transferred to Astley Green, probably in 1933 or 1934. See Chapter 10

GOWER	0-6-0STIC	SS	3090	1882	17"x24"	4′0"

Transferred from Chanters mid 1930s
Sent to Gin Pit between 3-1943 and early 1945 and scrapped there 4-1945

JAMES LORD	0-6-0T IC	LE	243	1903	16"x24"	3′10"

Transferred from Gin Pit between 3-1943 and early 1945
To NCB at Bedford 1-1-1947

National Coal Board

JAMES LORD	0-6-0T IC	LE	243	1903	16"x24"	3′10"

From Manchester Collieries Ltd at Bedford 1-1-1947
At Gin Pit for repairs in July 1947
Taken out of service early 1959 and scrapped at Bedford 12-1960

ATLAS	0-6-0STIC	P	1177	1909	16"x22"	3′10"

Temporarily at Bedford Summer 1953
Transferred to Bedford between 11-1958 and 3-1959 to replace JAMES LORD
At Walkden Yard for repairs 4-1962 to 12-1962
Sent to Walkden Yard 11-1966, laid aside and scrapped there 9 or 10-1968

KIRKLESS	0-6-0STIC	NW	442	1892	16"x20"	4′3"

Temporarily at Bedford in 1956

COLONEL	0-6-0STIC	HE	1459	1927	15"x20"	3′7"

Transferred to Bedford 1-1962
Taken out of service by 3-1963 and scrapped at Bedford 8-1966

RENOWN 0-6-0STIC HE 3697 1950 18"x26" 4'3"
Temporarily at Bedford mid 1962 to 2-63 to replace ATLAS under repairs
Transferred to Bedford 3-1967 after overhaul at Walkden Yard to replace RODNEY
Transferred to Gin Pit 21-10-1967 and then in 12-1967 to Walkden

RODNEY 0-6-0STIC HE 3695 1950 18"x26" 4'3"
Transferred to Bedford 3-1966 after overhaul at Walkden Yard to replace ATLAS. Previously at Bickershaw
Transferred to Walkden by 5-67 or earlier

Astley and Tyldesley Collieries

John Darlington from mid 1840s to about 1842
Samuel Jackson and Company from about 1842 to about 1864
Astley and Tyldesley Coal and Salt Company from about 1864 to about 1871
Astley and Tyldesley Coal and Salt Co Ltd from about 1871 to 1900
Astley and Tyldesley Collieries Co Ltd from 1900 to 3-3-1929
Manchester Collieries Ltd from 4-3-1929 to 31-12-1946
National Coal Board
No 1 (Manchester) Area 1-1-1947 to 31-12-1960
East Lancashire, Burnley and Cumberland Area 1-1-1961 to 25-3-1967
North Western Area from 26-3-1967

Railway system closed October 1967

Astley and Tyldesley Coal and Salt Company; Astley and Tyldesley Coal and Salt Co Ltd; Astley and Tyldesley Collieries Co Ltd; Manchester Collieries Ltd

In addition to the standard gauge locomotives listed below, the Astley and Tyldesley Coal and Salt Company operated at least one narrow gauge locomotive - see text. This may have been named GORDON.

TYLDESLEY 0-6-0STIC MW 252 1868 12"x17" 3'1³⁄₈"
New to Astley and Tyldesley Coal and Salt Co. Class K. Ex works 27-3-1868
Renamed JACKSON by 3-1872
Sold to Peckett and Sons Ltd about 1895
Resold to Sussex Portland Cement Co Ltd, Heighton, Sussex by 3-1896, where renamed EDITH

LADY CORNWALL 2-2-0WTOC BCK 1846 13"x16" 5'0"
Built as tender loco for Preston and Wyre Railway, to L&YR as No 8, later No 214.
Purchased by George Peace of the Astley and Tyldesley Coal and Salt Co Ltd, 25-11-1874
Stated scrapped around 1895 to 1900

MADEN 0-6-0STIC MW 570 1875 15"x22" 3'9"
New to Astley and Tyldesley Coal and Salt Co Ltd. Class O
Ordered by Logan and Hemingway butorder cancelled
Presumed scrapped or sold about 1910

ASTLEY 0-6-0T IC SS 3355 1886
New to Astley and Tyldesley Coal and Salt Co Ltd.
Stated scrapped or sold in 1920s

TYLDESLEY 0-6-0T IC P 603 1894 16"x22"
New to Astley and Tyldesley Coal and Salt Co Ltd. Class X
Stated scrapped or sold around 1920

T.B.WOOD 0-6-0T IC LE 233 1899 16"x24" 3'10"
New to Astley and Tyldesley Coal and Salt Co Ltd. Class H
Temporarily at Chanters Colliery late 1938, early 1939
To NCB at Tyldesley 1-1-1947

JAMES LORD	0-6-0T IC	LE	243	1903	16"x24"	3'10"

New to Astley and Tyldesley Collieries Co Ltd. Class H
Transferred to Bedford Colliery between 3-1943 and early 1945 to replace GOWER

GEORGE PEACE	0-6-0T IC	LE	245	1906	16"x24"	3'10"

New to Astley and Tyldesley Collieries Co Ltd. Class D
To NCB at Tyldesley 1-1-1947

MADEN	0-8-0T OC	NW	918	1910	16"x24"	3'9"

New to Astley and Tyldesley Collieries Co Ltd
To NCB at Tyldesley 1-1-1947

EMANUEL CLEGG	0-8-0T OC	NW	1419	1924	17"x24"	3'9"

New to Astley and Tylsesley Collieries Co Ltd
Repairs at Gin Pit late 1938, early 1939
To NCB at Tyldesley 1-1-1947

CERBERUS	0-6-0STIC	SS	2909	1880	17"x24"	4'0"

Transferred from Chanters to Gin Pit by 1-1938
Taken out of service February 1938 and scrapped at Gin Pit end of 1938 or early 1939

GOWER	0-6-0STIC	SS	3090	1882	17"x24"	4'0"

Transferred from Bedford Coliery between 3-1943 and early 1945
Scrapped at Gin Pit, 4-1945

CHOWBENT	0-6-0STOC	AB	1802	1923	16"x24"	3'7"

Transferred from Atherton Collieries between 1939 and 1943
To NCB at Tyldesley 1-1-1947

COLONEL	0-6-0STIC	HE	1459	1927	15"x20"	3'7"

Transferred from Atherton Collieries between 1943 and 1947
To NCB at Tyldesley 1-1-1947

Engines from other collieries noted at Gin Pit up to the end of 1946 include:

COLONEL from Howe Bridge for repairs, mid 1938
MADGE from Chanters Colliery for repairs, late 1938, early 1939
ATHERTON from Howe Bridge for repairs, early 1940
ATLAS from Chanters for repairs, mid 1946
LILFORD sent from Howe Bridge to to Gin Pit between April and June 1938 and remained out of use. Dismantled by December 1938 and scrapped early in 1939
MADGE from Chanters Colliery in 1946 and scrapped

National Coal Board

T.B.WOOD	0-6-0T IC	LE	233	1899	16"x24"	3'10"

Ex Manchester Collieries Ltd at Tyldesley, 1-1-1947
Repairs at Gin Pit 1946 to 1947
Sent to Walkden Yard for repairs 1957 and broken up there mid 1958

GEORGE PEACE	0-6-0T IC	LE	245	1906	16"x24"	3'10"

Ex Manchester Collieries Ltd at Tyldesley, 1-1-1947
Repairs at Gin Pit 1951/2
Temporarily working at Astley Green in 1952
Scrapped at Gin Pit by Stone and Hutchinson, of Bolton, end of 1957

MADEN	0-8-0T OC	NW	918	1910	16"x24"	3'9"

Ex Manchester Collieries Ltd at Tyldesley, 1-1-1947
Repairs at Gin Pit 1951/2, 1953 and 1959
Scrapped at Gin Pit early 1962

EMANUEL CLEGG 0-8-0T OC NW 1419 1924 17"x24" 3'9"
Ex Manchester Collieries Ltd at Tyldesley, 1-1-1947
Repairs at Gin Pit 1952
Withdrawn from service 1958
Scrapped at Gin Pit by Stone and Hutchinson, of Bolton, mid 1965

CHOWBENT 0-6-0STOC AB 1802 1923 16"x24" 3'7"
Ex Manchester Collieries Ltd at Tyldesley, 1-1-1947
Transferred to Parsonage Colliery between 1947 and 1950

COLONEL 0-6-0STIC HE 1459 1927 15"x20" 3'7"
Ex Manchester Collieries Ltd at Tyldesley, 1-1-1947
Transferred to Howe Bridge early 1947

W.H.R. 0-6-0STIC RSH 7174 1944 18"x26" 4'3"
Purchased from War Department, received at Walkden 18-6-1947 and sent on to Gin Pit 30-7-1947
Repairs at Gin Pit mid 1953
At Walkden Yard for repairs 1957, 12-1961 to 3-1962, 2-1964 to 5-1964
Transferred to Central Railways system about 7-1964

GORDON 0-6-0STIC RSH 7288 1945 18"x26" 4'3"
Transferred from Chanters about 1950 and returned to Chanters in 1951

RENOWN 0-6-0STIC HE 3697 1950 18"x26" 4'3"
Transferred from Parsonage Colliery by 8-1951
At Walkden Yard for repairs 1956, returned to Gin Pit 31-11-1956
At Walkden Yard for repairs 12-1960 to 5-1961 and used temporarily at Astley Green
Temporarily transferred to Bedford Colliery mid 1962 to 2-63 to replace ATLAS under repairs
Sent to Walkden Yard for repairs 1965 and subsequently transferred to Chanters and later Bedford
Stored at Gin Pit from 21-10-1961 after closure of Bedford and sent to Walkden Yard, coupled to HUMPHREY 12-1967

WEASEL 0-6-0STIC HE 3844 1957 18"x26" 4'3"
Transferred from Central Railways system 5-1958
At Walkden Yard for repairs in 1961 and 1963
Sent to Walkden Yard late 1965 and transferred to Ladysmith Colliery, Cumberland, by 3-1967

WASP 0-6-0STIC HE 3808 1954 18"x26" 4'3"
Temporarily at Gin Pit 8-1959 to 5-1960, MADEN under repair

HARRY 0-6-0STIC HC 1776 1944 18"x26" 4'3"
Sent from Peel Hall Opencast Disposal Point for storage mid 1964 as WD 71499 and later same year sent to Walkden Yard for overhaul
Transferred from Opencast Executive to East Lancashire Area stock and named HARRY
Returned from Walkden Yard to Gin Pit end of 1965
Sent to Walkden Yard for repairs 3 or 4-1966 and subsequently used on Central Railways system

HUMPHREY 0-6-0STIC RSH 7293 1945 18"x26" 4'3"
Transferred from Chanters 7-1966
Sent to Walkden Yard 12-1967, following closure of Gin Pit railway system

Engines from other collieries noted at Gin Pit from 1-1-1947 onwards include:

JAMES LORD from Bedford Colliery, overhauled summer 1947
ATLAS from Chanters Colliery, overhauled in summer 1948
JESSIE from Cleworth Hall Colliery in summer 1951
COLONEL From Parsonage Colliery for repairs in summer of 1951. Sent to Central Railways on completion
SHAKERLEY from Cleworth Hall Colliery in sumer of 1952

References to Chapter 9

1 *"The Coal Pits of Chowbent"* - Kenneth Wood - Publ Kenneth Wood, Leigh - 2nd edn, 1985
2 *"Carbon"* February 1923
3 *"The Industrial Railways of the Wigan Coalfield - Part Two"* - Townley, Smith and Peden - Runpast Publishing, Cheltenham, 1992
4 *"Collieries in the Manchester Coalfields"* - GoffreyHayes - De Archaeologische Pers, Eindhoven, nd
5 BC 30-7-1831
6 LRO PDR 131
7 LRO DRM 1/9
8 BMB ZJA 153/16
9 LC 14-2-1857
10 LC 11-4-1857
11 LC 26-9-1857
12 LC 6-2-1858
13 BC1-6-1861
14 LC 20-2-1858
15 LRO PDR 717
16 23 & 24 Vic cap cxiii; 3rd July 1860
17 LC 29-9-60
18 LC 1-6-1861
19 BJ 15-3-1862
20 BC 27-2-1864
21 LG 6-7-1875
22 BC 25-4-1892
23 LC 6-12-1862
24 *"Carbon"* Sept 1933
25 LRO PDR 1491
26 Letter from Clement Fletcher to C A Appleton, 19-9-1957
27 Information from Industrial Locomotive Society lists
28 *"Carbon"* Feb 1926
29 *"Carbon"* May 1928
30 *"Carbon"* June 1925
31 *"Colliery Year Book"* 1923
32 Photograph in *"Carbon"* May1928
33 *"The Bridgewater Heritage"* - Christopher Grayling - Bridgewater Estates plc, Manchester, 1983
34 *"Carbon"* Jan 1932
35 LRO NCMc 3/14
36 Observations by authors and their colleagues
37 *"From Walkden Yard Records - Part One"* - C A Appleton - in *"Industrial Locomotive"* No 62, 1991
38 *"List of Locomotives in No 1 (Manchester) Area"* - NCB document, copy in authors' posssession
39 LC 25-1-1952
40 Newsletter of Manchester Collieries Ltd, June 1943
41 Newsletter of Manchester Collieries Ltd, September 1943
42 Newsletter of Manchester Collieries Ltd, November 1944
43 LC 8-3-1952
44 Information from Industrial Railway Society Lists
45 Correspondence in Industrial Railway Record No 138, September 1994
46 *"The Standish Collieries Railway"* - Steve Oakden - *"Industrial Railway Record"* No 127, December 1991
47 Correspondence in *"Industrial Railway Record"* No 133, June 1993
48 *"Industrial Locomotive Society Journal"* Vol XVIII No 1, March 1964
49 Line Plan of Bedford Leigh Branch - BR, 1965 - At BRPB, Manchester Office
50 Probate Records
51 SMM U263/11
52 *"Working on the Gin Pit Railway"* - Steven Oakden - *"Industrial Railway Record"*, No 114, September 1988
53 BLN 120A
54 BC 13-7-1839
55 MC 4-4-1841
56 LRO DRM 1/11
57 LG 25-12-1846
58 *"Royal National Commercial Directory and Topography of the County of Lancaster"* - Isaac Slater, Manchester, 1848
59 *"Royal National Commercial Directory and Topography of the County of Lancaster"* - Isaac Slater, Manchester, 1851
60 LC February 1853
61 LRO DRM 1/8
62 LRO PDR 539
63 10 &11 Vic cap ccxxii; 22nd July 1847
64 SAO Bridgewater Trustees Agreement Book No 1, p 447
65 LRONCBw 19/1
66 Line Plan of Eccles, Tyldesley and Wigan Railway - LNWR, Rugby, 1868 - 2 chains to 1 inch - at GMRO
67 *"British Locomotive Catalogue, Part 3B"* B Baxter - Moorland Publishing Co, Ashbourne, 1982
68 BC25-12-1875
69 LRO NCAt 3/8
70 SMM U263/E11
71 LNWR Sdgs Diag 152, 12-1916
72 *"More Memories of the Gin Pit Railway"* in *"Industrial Railway Record"*, No 120, March 1990
73 Newsletter of Manchester Collieries Ltd, March 1944

CHAPTER 10

TYLDESLEY, LITTLE HULTON AND ASTLEY GREEN

We continue our exploration of the area around Tyldesley and now move to the north and east of the town, where several collieries were opened out in the 1840s and 1850s. Expansion followed the opening of the LNWR's Eccles, Tyldesley and Wigan line in 1864. One colliery survived to be taken over by the National Coal Board and did not close until 1963.

From Tyldesley we move north to the Little Hulton district. Here mining was well established by the 1840s. Much of the coal was worked by the Trustees of the Duke of Bridgewater. Their mines here, as elsewhere, were connected to the underground canal system, which we describe in Chapter 11.

The independent collieries had to rely entirely on road transport until the 1870s, although there had been a number of projected railways which would have opened up the district. In 1830, the Manchester and Preston Railway had proposed a line from Clifton to Peel Hall [1]. The Manchester and Southport Railway's branch from Tyldesley terminating north of Manchester Road had been authorised in 1846 [2], but not built. A further project in 1860 by the Lancashire and Yorkshire Railway, which included a branch from Tyldesley to a point near Wharton Hall Colliery [3], did not obtain Parliamentary approval. It was not until 1870 that the most easterly of the collieries were connected to the London and North Western's Little Hulton Branch. The remainder had to wait until the completion of the Little Hulton Extension Railway and the Little Hulton Mineral Branch in 1874.

To conclude the chapter we move south again, to Astley Green. The colliery here was a much later development, which tapped the deep seams at the southern edge of the coalfield. It was sunk in the early years of the present century by a subsidiary of the Clifton and Kersley Coal Company and had a productive life of nearly sixty years. When it closed in April 1970 a trust was set up to preserve one of the steam winding engines and create a mining museum.

TYLDESLEY

The Tyldesley Coal Company up to 1947

Land to the east of Tyldesley was leased to George and William Green. The partnership, which traded as the Tyldesley Coal Company, sank the Yew Tree Pits on the north side of the main road to Worsley. John Holland, the railway contractor, joined the partnership around 1860 and the firm subsequently traded as Green, Holland and Company. A limited liability company, with the title of the Tyldesley Coal Co Ltd, was formed in November 1870 [4].

According to Hayes [5] work started in 1835 at Yew Tree and the first coal was raised in 1845. This is open to doubt, however, as the colliery is not marked on the first edition of the 6" map, surveyed in 1845 and 1846 [6].

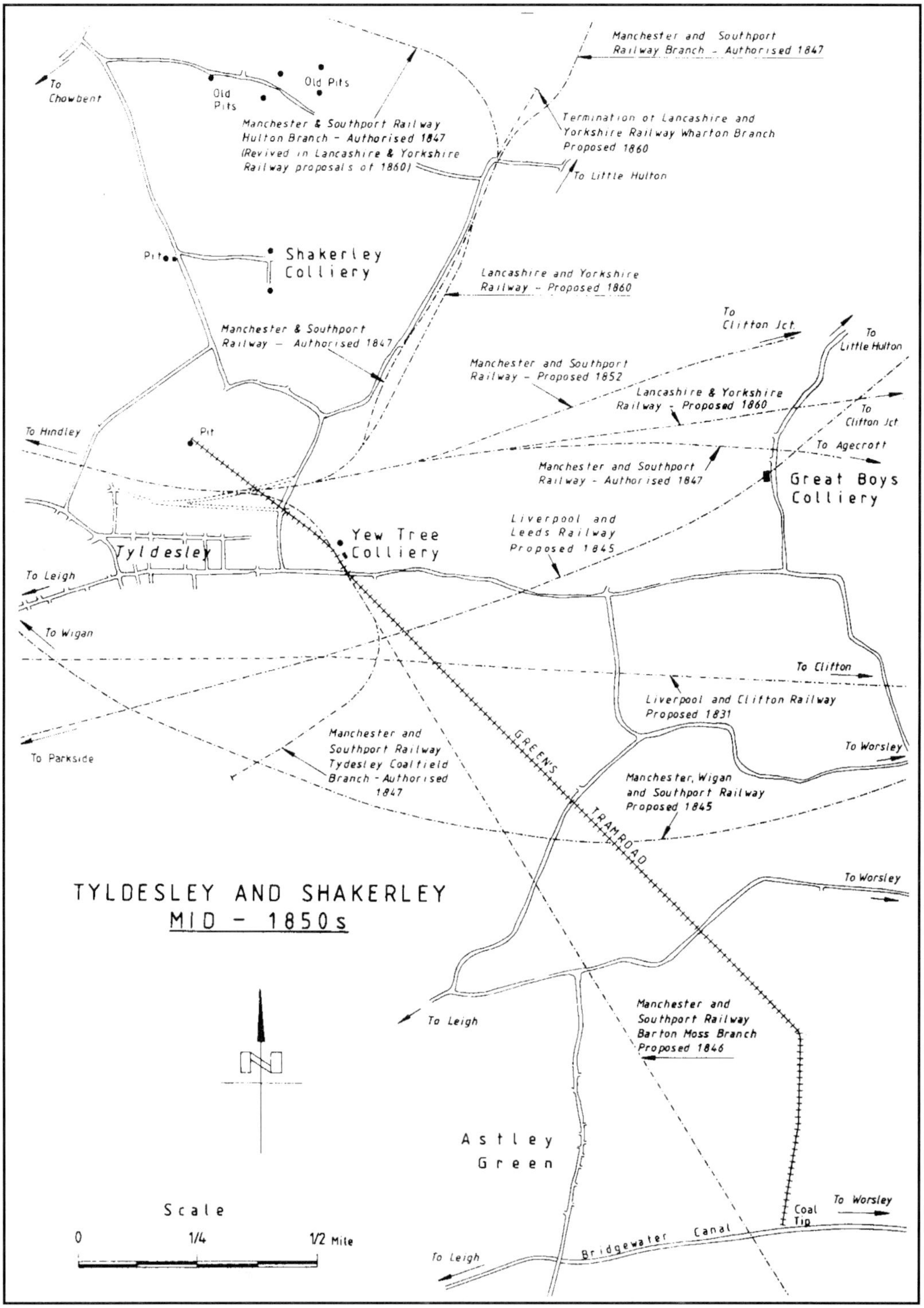
Manchester and Southport Railway Branch - Authorised 1847
To Chowbent
Old Pits
Old Pits
Manchester & Southport Railway Hulton Branch - Authorised 1847 (Revived in Lancashire & Yorkshire Railway proposals of 1860)
Termination of Lancashire and Yorkshire Railway Wharton Branch Proposed 1860
To Little Hulton
Pit
Shakerley Colliery
Lancashire and Yorkshire Railway - Proposed 1860
Manchester & Southport Railway - Authorised 1847
To Clifton Jct.
To Little Hulton
Manchester and Southport Railway - Proposed 1852
Lancashire & Yorkshire Railway - Proposed 1860
To Clifton Jct
To Hindley
Pit
To Agecroft
Manchester and Southport Railway - Authorised 1847
Great Boys Colliery
Liverpool and Leeds Railway Proposed 1845
Yew Tree Colliery
Tyldesley
To Leigh
To Wigan
To Clifton
Liverpool and Clifton Railway Proposed 1831
Manchester and Southport Railway Tydesley Coalfield Branch - Authorised 1847
To Parkside
GREEN'S TRAMROAD
To Worsley
Manchester, Wigan and Southport Railway Proposed 1845
TYLDESLEY AND SHAKERLEY
MID - 1850s
To Worsley
To Leigh
Manchester and Southport Railway Barton Moss Branch Proposed 1846
N
Astley Green
Scale
0
1/4
1/2 Mile
To Worsley
Coal Tip
Bridgewater Canal
To Leigh

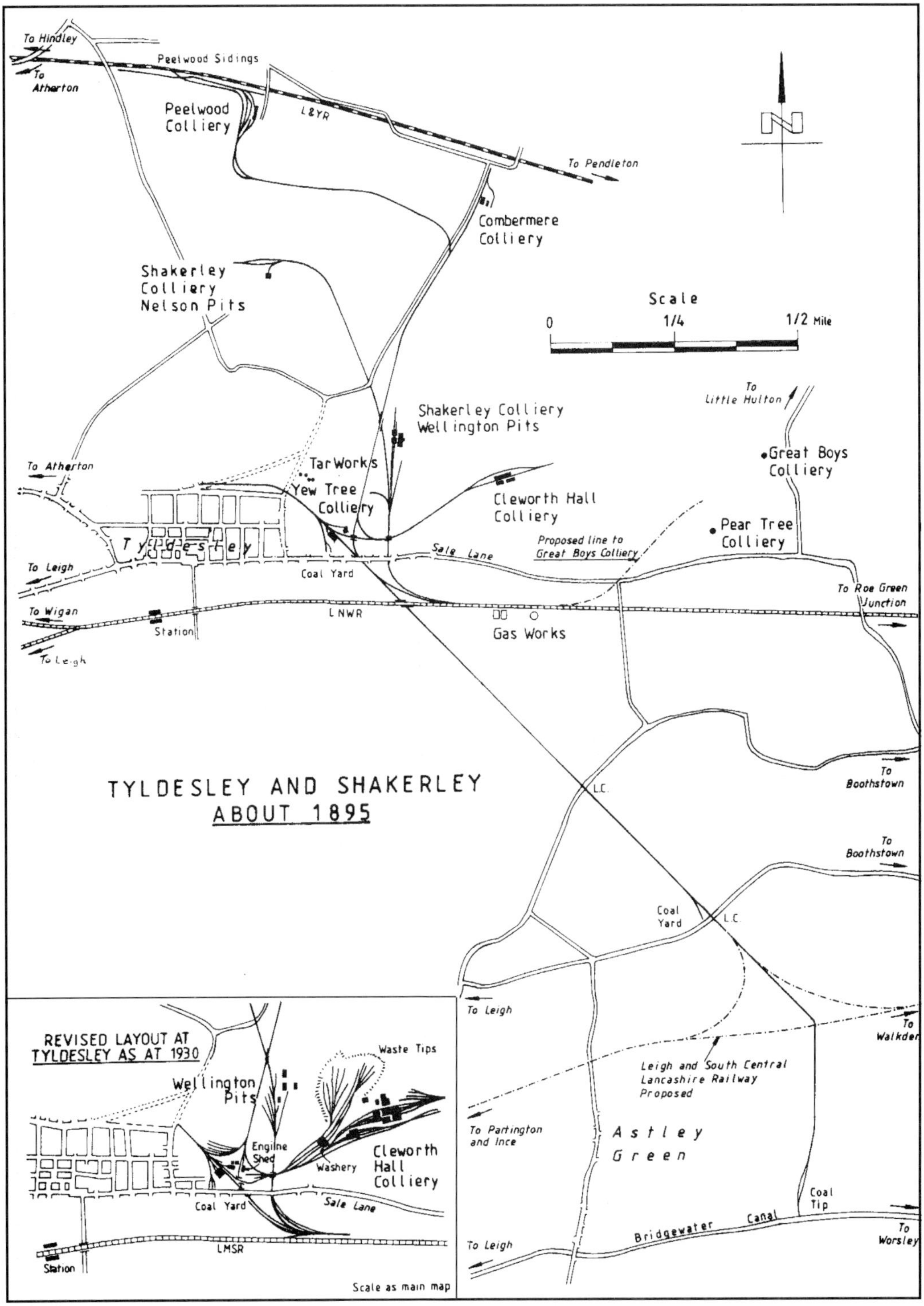
To Hindley
To Atherton
Peelwood Sidings
Peelwood Colliery
L&YR
To Pendleton
Combermere Colliery
Shakerley Colliery Nelson Pits
Scale
0
1/4
1/2 Mile
To Little Hulton
Shakerley Colliery Wellington Pits
Great Boys Colliery
To Atherton
Tar Works
Yew Tree Colliery
Cleworth Hall Colliery
Proposed line to Great Boys Colliery
Pear Tree Colliery
Tyldesley
Sale Lane
To Leigh
Coal Yard
To Roe Green Junction
To Wigan
LNWR
Station
Gas Works
To Leigh
To Boothstown
TYLDESLEY AND SHAKERLEY
ABOUT 1895
L.C.
To Boothstown
Coal Yard
L.C.
REVISED LAYOUT AT TYLDESLEY AS AT 1930
Waste Tips
Wellington Pits
Engine Shed
Washery
Cleworth Hall Colliery
Coal Yard
Sale Lane
LMSR
Station
Scale as main map
To Leigh
To Walkden
Leigh and South Central Lancashire Railway Proposed
To Partington and Ince
Astley Green
Coal Tip
To Leigh
Bridgewater Canal
To Worsley

A date of around 1850 seems more likely for the opening of the mine. George Green first appears as a colliery proprietor in a directory for 1851 [7]. The Mines Lists for 1853/4 record the Tyldesley Coal Company in occupation. There is also a revision of the 6" map, probably published in the early 1850s [8], which does show Yew Tree Colliery and another pit some 700 yards to the north east. The revised map also marks a tramroad which started at this pit and ran past Yew Tree Colliery to the Bridgewater Canal near Astley Green. Significantly, the tramroad and the pits do not not appear on either the Astley Tithe Map [9] or the Tyldesley Tithe Map [10], both dated 1847.

Following the opening of the Eccles, Tyldesley and Wigan line of the London and North Western in 1864, standard gauge sidings were provided to serve Green, Holland and Company's Colliery. The layout is shown on a Line Plan of 1868 [11], which also indicates that the line to the canal was standard gauge by this date.

During the next twenty years there were considerable additions to the firm's private railway system as new pits were opened out. Immediately to the north of the main road to Worsley a complex network of lines developed, with the tracks of the Tyldesley Coal Company crossing and recrossing those of the neighbouring colliery proprietor, William Ramsden.

The first extension of the Tyldesley Coal Company's railway was to serve Combermere Colliery. The line must have been completed around 1867, the first year that the new colliery appears in the Mines Lists.

Shakerley Colliery, not to be confused with Ramsden's pits with the same name, is first shown in the Mines List for 1869. We have not been able to find its precise location. We think that it was near Little Shakerley Common and that the line shown on the second edition of the 6" map terminating here was built to serve it.

Cleworth Hall Colliery was sunk in the early 1870s on a site to the east of the Yew Tree Pits. It was reached by a branch line which crossed Ramsden's railway by a bridge.

The final development was Peelwood Colliery, which required an extension of the railway beyond Combermere Colliery. Peelwood was opened in the 1880s, possibly in the 1883 as stated by Hayes [5] or possibly a little later as suggested by the entries in the Mines Lists.

Peelwood was located alongside the route of the Lancashire and Yorkshire's new direct line from Pendleton to Hindley, which was completed in 1888. A siding connection was put in which provided an alternative outlet for the Tyldesley Coal Company's rail traffic, hitherto handled only by the London and North Western Railway.

The earliest locomotive which we have been able to trace was named TYLDESLEY. We were told by old employees whom we interviewed in the 1940s that it was a four coupled saddle tank with inside cylinders, built by the Haigh Foundry Company of Wigan in 1867. These details are confirmed in the records of the Hunslet Engine Company of Leeds, which carried out repairs to the boiler in 1917 [12].

In March 1873 the firm advertised that it needed a tank locomotive with cylinders about 14" diameter [13], no doubt to cope with the increased traffic from the new collieries. We do not know whether some short term stop gap was obtained, but two new engines were purchased shortly afterwards.

BEATRICE, a four coupled saddle tank, was delivered by the Vulcan Foundry of Newton-le-Willows in 1877. According an old employee, the saddle tanks were replaced by side tanks in the early years of the present century. At about the same time the firm ordered a six coupled saddle tank from Walker Brothers of Wigan. Named JESSIE, it was stated by our informants to have had flangless centre wheels to negotiate the sharply curved tracks.

Shakerley Colliery closed in the late 1880s, being last shown in the Mines List for 1886, while Combermere Colliery ceased work towards the end of 1893 [14]. Yew Tree Colliery was redeveloped during the period from 1890 to 1893, when the shafts were deepened.

To cater for the increased coal production, two further locomotives were purchased around the turn of the century, bringing the total stock to five.

VICTORIA, a four coupled saddle tank similar to BEATRICE, but with larger cylinders came from the Vulcan Foundry in 1897. LOUISA, a six coupled side tank, was supplied by the Hunslet Engine Company in 1902. Like the older engines, they were built to a reduced loading gauge because of the restricted headroom at the bridge under Manchester Road.

The railway to the canal ceased to be used in the early years of the twentieth century. It was still in operation in February 1911, when a governess cart and pony ran into a train at Henfold Level Crossing [15]. By March 1913 the company had decided that it would be more economical to send traffic by rail instead of by canal and that notice would be given to the Earl of Ellesmere that the lease of land occupied by the line would not be renewed [16].

This was followed by an enquiry from Jesse Wallwork, the Earl of Ellesmere's agent, about a possible purchase of the line. He was told that £1,920 was being asked for the track and £120 for the turntable and weighing machine at the canal basin [17]. The deal must have fallen through as, in October 1913, the Tyldesley Coal Company accepted an offer of £600 from the Clifton and Kersley Coal Company for the tipping plant and the sidings at Astley [18]. As to be described later, these were taken over for use by the new Astley Green Colliery, which was then under construction.

Cleworth Hall Colliery was modernised during the period before the first world war and the Arley Pit there was equipped with new steel headgear supplied by the Lilleshall Company [19]. As a result the original pits at Yew Tree were taken out of production and are shown as "discontinued" in the Mines Lists for 1914. A washery and coal preparation plant were later erected on the Cleworth Hall site. In 1915 sinking started at Bank House, but the pit there was abandoned in 1922.

With the closure of Peel Wood Colliery in 1929, where the Mines List show that the Nos 1 and 2 pits were abandoned on 4th January, only Cleworth Hall Colliery remained in production. A brickworks had been built on the site of Combermere Colliery and the railway northwards from the Yew Tree site was kept in operation to serve the works and, until the mid 1930s, to give access to the exchange sidings on the Pendleton to Hindley line.

In 1927 a new four coupled side tank was delivered by the Hunslet Engine Company of Leeds. Named JESSIE, it replaced the Walker Brothers engine of the same name, which was taken out of service. Also taken out of service at the same period was TYLDESLEY, the Haigh Foundry engine of 1867.

Cleworth Hall Colliery 1947 to 1963

The Tyldesley Coal Co Ltd remained as an independent concern until the industry was nationalised on 1st January 1947. Cleworth Hall Colliery was absorbed into the No 1 (Manchester) Area of the North Western Division. It became part of the East Lancashire, Burnley and West Cumberland Area on 1st January 1961.

Four of the Tyldesley Coal Company's locomotives were taken over by the National Coal Board - BEATRICE, VICTORIA, LOUISA and JESSIE. Only two were in working order.

BEATRICE, built by the Vulcan Foundry in 1877, photographed at Cleworth Hall in 1938. Alex Appleton

VICTORIA photographed at Cleworth Hall Colliery in August 1950. Like all the former Tyldesley Coal Company's engines, VICTORIA had a cut down chimney and boiler mountings to pass under the low bridges on the railway. Frank Jones

LOUISA at Cleworth Hall in August 1950. Note that the centre wheels have no flanges to enable the engine to negotiate sharp curves in the track. Frank Jones

JESSIE, the last engine to be delivered to the Tyldesley Coal Company in 1927, to a modern design with outside valve gear and other up-to-date features. Photographed here with Cleworth Hall washery in the background in May 1955. David Chatfield

The boiler and firebox of BEATRICE had been condemned in 1944 but repairs had not been started. The new management decided that the work would be too costly and the engine was broken up a year or two later.

LOUISA was undergoing repairs to the firebox and engine work on vesting day. It was later returned to traffic. By 1953 it had been laid aside and was scrapped at Cleworth Hall in February 1955.

VICTORIA was broken up in April 1953, but JESSIE remained at Cleworth Hall until it was withdrawn from service in March 1961. During this time it was sent to Gin Pit for overhaul in 1951, to Walkden Yard in 1955 and again to Walkden at the end of 1958.

To supplement JESSIE, two locomotives, CARBON and SHAKERLEY, were transferred to Cleworth Hall from other locations in the Manchester Area.

CARBON, a four coupled saddle tank, arrived from Astley Green Colliery early in 1947. By August 1948 it had been sent to Walkden Yard where the boiler was condemned. Delays in obtaining a replacement meant that the overhaul was not complete until autumn 1950. It returned from Walkden Yard on 7th September [20] and, apart from two short spells elsewhere, it worked at Cleworth Hall until rail traffic ceased.

On 28th February 1955 CARBON travelled under its own steam to Robin Hood Sidings, where it deputised for KEARSLEY, which was under repair. It returned under its own steam to Cleworth Hall on 25th April. CARBON was also away at Walkden Yard for repairs in 1956, being sent there on 13th September and returning on 4th December [20].

SHAKERLEY was transferred from Chanters Colliery about 1949 and was one of the regular engines at Cleworth Hall until it was taken out of service late in 1960 or early in 1961. It was overhauled at Gin Pit during the summer and autumn of 1952 and afterwards seems to have spent a few weeks working at Astley Green. It was also overhauled at Walkden in 1956.

The Tyldesley Coal Company's locomotive shed near the site of the old Yew Tree Colliery, photographed in August 1959. CARBON stands outside, with JESSIE just visible in the lower level shed. The line to the ex-LNWR exchange sidings passes to the right of the shed and under the low bridge. Alex Appleton

The colliery ceased production on 25th January 1963 [21], but the washery continued in operation for some time after that, processing coal brought in from other pits. Latterly road transport was used, rail traffic having finished on Friday 5th May 1961 [21].

During the final month of railway operation two working locomotives were still required. With only CARBON available after JESSIE was laid aside in March, WESTWOOD was sent from Walkden Yard in April 1961 [22], having previously been employed at Astley Green.

By the end of May the track was being lifted and all four locomotives were out of use in the shed [22]. The first to leave was WESTWOOD, which was sent to Peel Hall Opencast Disposal Point in July [22].

SHAKERLEY was moved into the open and stood on a short length of track until it was cut up for scrap at the end of the year [22].

JESSIE and CARBON were despatched together in September 1961 to Walkden Yard [22]. JESSIE remained out of use there until it was sold for scrap to Maudland Metals Ltd in February 1967. CARBON was overhauled, fitted with a Giesl ejector and repainted in the Walkden maroon livery. It was then sent to Bank Hall Colliery at Burnley, where it was eventually broken up in November 1968.

Ramsden's Shakerley Colliery

In the area north of Shakerley Hall coal had been mined from the end of the eighteenth century [5] and probably much earlier. Numerous disused pits are shown in the area around Guest Fold on the first edition of the 6" map, surveyed in 1845 and 1846. These were on land owned by the Trustees of the late Ellis Fletcher [10] and had probably been worked by the Fletcher family.

The map also marks Shakerley Colliery, a more extensive establishment, a little further south. This was probably sunk in the late 1830s or early 1840s under a lease from the Trustees of Ellis Fletcher [10]. Shakerley Colliery appears in directories for 1848 [23] and 1851 [7], when it was being worked by Nathaniel Eckersley. According to the Mines Lists it remained in his possession until 1857, when it was taken over by his representatives. In 1861 it passed to William Ramsden.

Very little information has come to light about the subsequent development of the collieries. The Mines Lists refer to Shakerley Colliery until 1869, when Meshing Trees is shown in addition, under Ramsden's name. We assume that this was the colliery located not far from the Manchester road, which from the 1880s became known as the Wellington Pit. The original Shakerley Colliery took the name of Nelson Pit at the same time. William Ramsden and Sons Ltd, was registered on 30th June 1898 to take over the property [24].

Until the opening of the Eccles, Tyldesley and Wigan line, Shakerley Colliery relied entirely on road transport. By 1868, William Ramsden had constructed a standard gauge railway system leading to exchange sidings with the LNWR to the east of those of the Tyldesley Coal Company [11].

The second edition of the 6" map, surveyed in 1888 to 1892, shows Ramsden's private line curving northwards from the LNWR and passing under the Manchester road and the Tyldesley Coal Company's branch to Cleworth Hall Colliery to reach the Wellington Pits, where the engine shed was situated. North of there, the line continued under the Tyldesley Coal Company's line to Combermere Colliery and terminated at the Nelson Pits.

The first engine which we have on record was a four coupled saddle tank, purchased from the Manning Wardle and Company of Leeds in 1874, and named SHAKERLEY. It was followed by EDITH, a six coupled saddle tank, from the Hunslet Engine Company, also of Leeds, in 1887.

In January 1901, SHAKERLEY was sold to Thomas Mitchell and Sons Ltd, of Bolton, who resold it to the Ince Waggon and Ironworks Co Ltd, of Wigan. It was replaced by a new engine, identical to EDITH, purchased from the Hunslet Engine Company in 1901 and also named SHAKERLEY.

The Hunslet Engine Company's records also show that a locomotive was hired in December 1902, and again in May 1905, to William Ramsden and Sons, presumably while one or other of the firm's own engines was under repair. On both occasions, the engine sent to Shakerley was a four coupled saddle tank which had been built in 1877 and had been repurchased by the Hunslet Engine Company at the end of 1898.

Shakerley Colliery remained outside the merger which led to the formation of Manchester Collieries Ltd in 1929. Then, in 1935, it was decided to sell out. Manchester Collieries Ltd was deemed to have taken over on 31st March, although the deal was not actually concluded until 24th June [25]. An inventory of plant, prepared in connection with the sale, included the two locomotives and 268 railway wagons.

Coal production was run down by the new owners. According to the Mines Lists the Wellington Pits were abandoned in May 1935 and the Nelson Pits in October 1938. The two locomotives, EDITH and SHAKERLEY, remained until the private railway system was taken out of use towards the end of 1938. They were then transferred to the Atherton collieries, formerly owned by Fletcher, Burrows and Co Ltd. We have dealt with their later history in Chapter 9

EDITH, the Hunslet of 1887, taken when still in the ownership of William Ramsden and Sons Ltd.
Frank Smith collection

Great Boys Colliery

Great Boys Colliery is shown on the first edition of the 6" map alongside Mort Lane, leading from Tyldesley to Little Hulton. It was offered for sale by the executors of William Atkin on 24th May 1855 [26]. It was purchased by John Fletcher and Samuel Scowcroft, who had extensive mining interests in the neighbourhood of Bolton. The partnership was dissolved on 13th December 1869 [27], leaving John Fletcher in sole possession of the property at Tyldesley. The firm became John Fletcher and Sons in 1877. In the mid 1860s new pits were sunk on the north side of Sale Lane, the Tyldesley to Manchester road. Originally known as Pear Tree House, from the name of the nearby farm, they first appear in the Mines Lists for 1867. They are not shown separately after 1872, and subsequently they appear to have been considered as part of the Great Boys Colliery.

In connection with these developments, Thomas Fletcher and Samuel Scowcroft were given permission by the Bridgewater Trustees, who owned the land, to build a private railway from the LNWR Eccles, Tyldesley and Wigan line across Sale Lane towards Great Boys Colliery and the new pits at Pear Tree House. The lease of the ground which was needed was signed on 2nd October 1868 and covered a 20 year period from 25th October 1868 [28]. We do not know if the line was ever constructed, as we have found no other reference to it.

Great Boys Colliery closed in the mid 1880s and is not shown in the Mines Lists after 1885.

LITTLE HULTON AND MIDDLE HULTON

Smithfold Colliery

We start our exploration of the Little Hulton area at Smithfold Colliery, the first to have a rail connection. Only a single isolated shaft is marked here on the first edition of the 6" map, surveyed in 1844 to 1846. We think that the colliery must have been developed shortly afterwards by George Gibson, who is recorded a working a mine at Little Hulton in directories for 1848 [23] and 1851 [7]. The Mines Lists from 1853/4 through to 1881 show John Gibson and Company as the occupiers. The firm is recorded as experimenting around 1859 with a steam road tractor, built by Charles Burrell and Sons of Thetford, for hauling coal to Manchester. The train it drew consisted of six wagons, weighing in all some 40 tons [29].

Smithfold Colliery was without rail connection until the Little Hulton Branch of the LNWR was opened for goods and mineral traffic in July 1870 [30]. It seems that for several months coal was carted from the colliery to a tipping stage alongside the main line. By August 1870, it was reported that the colliery company owned 20 standard gauge wagons and that the tipping stage and siding was also being used by the Charlton and Bank Collieries and by the Bridgewater Trustees [31].

In August of the same year, work was in progress to lay a short private branch to the colliery to permit the railway wagons to be loaded at the pit head [32]. The new arrangements are shown on the 1876 Line Plan [33].

The colliery went out of production around 1880 and it is not shown in the Mines Lists after 1881. Its closure was perhaps precipitated by the bankruptcy in 1878 of Samuel Wild, one of the partners [34]. The main line connection at Gibson's Sidings was subsequently removed.

Bank Colliery

The first edition of the 6" map marks Bank Colliery alongside what later became Highfield Road, north of Manchester Road. On 16th March 1854 it was put up for sale by ticket by the owner, Thomas Wright [35]. It appears in the Mines Lists from 1855 to 1867 as being worked by John Wright and from 1868 to 1872 by his executors. It then passed to the Bank Colliery Company, in which John Chadwick seems to have been the principal partner.

Following the opening of the Little Hulton Mineral Railway at the end of 1874, a siding was provided which joined the LNWR line to the north of Manchester Road bridge. We have no record of any locomotive being employed by the firm and we think it likely that horses were used to haul the coal wagons between the colliery and the exchange sidings.

Bank Colliery was for sale on 23rd April 1884, on expiry of the lease, and 82 railway wagons were included [36,37]. It was never reopened although in 1900 the leases were acquired by James Roscoe and Sons [38]. In November 1901 it was reported that this firm was sinking new shafts at their Peel Hall Colliery and was driving a tunnel to the Bank collieries, nearly a mile away [39].

E Bennis and Co Ltd

The firm of E Bennis and Co Ltd acquired a site adjacent to the closed Bank colliery and moved its factory here from Bolton in 1904. As long ago as 1883 the company had been making marine stoking systems and now expanded into the manufacture of water tube boilers, travelling stokers, elevators and conveyors. The works which had occupied 2 acres in 1904 had expanded to cover about 30 acres by 1939. The founder, Edward Bennis, died on 29th October 1918 and his son Alfred Bennis succeed him as chairman and Managing Director. In 1935 the original firm went into voluntary liquidation to form a public company, Bennis Combustion Ltd [40,41].

The connection originally provided for Bank Colliery was relaid to serve the factory, under an agreement between E Bennis and Co Ltd and the LNWR, dated 21st December 1904 [33,42]. Additional sidings were constructed in 1939, presumably associated with extensions of the factory [40,41]. It is unlikely that the firm ever employed a locomotive of its own.

In the 1960s [43,44] the firm amalgamated with James Hodgkinson (Salford) Ltd . The works passed to a subsidiary, Hodgkinson Bennis Ltd and was still in production in 1977 [45] . It closed a few years later, rail traffic having already ceased. The site is now occupied by warehouses and light industry.

Bank House and Wharton Collieries

Bank House and Wharton Collieries are shown on the first edition of the 6" map on the south side of Manchester Road. We associate both with the the Charlton family. As early as 1823 there was an accident at one of Robert Charlton's pits at Little Hulton [46] and there is record of a lease to Francis Charlton on 15th July 1839 [47]. Francis Charlton appears in directories for 1848 [23] and 1851 [7] as a coal proprietor at Little Hulton. He is shown as working Bank House Colliery in the Mines Lists for 1853/4.

Wharton Colliery first appears in the Mines Lists for 1858 and we think this entry relates to new pits which were sunk by Francis Charlton on a site nearer Manchester Road than the old ones. Bank House Colliery seems to have closed in 1861 and is not shown in the Mines Lists after that date.

After the opening of the Little Hulton Mineral Railway of the LNWR in 1874 a connection was put in near the end of the branch to serve Wharton Colliery [33], although we have no record of a locomotive being used here.

Wharton Colliery was taken over by the Bridgewater Trustees about 1879 and the siding connection was transferred to them under an agreement with the LNWR of 20th September 1887 [48].

The colliery was worked by the new owners for a further ten years without much alteration [5]. It closed towards the end of the century and is shown in the Mines Lists as being discontinued on 11th September 1901. It was retained for pumping purposes. The main line connection was apparently still in use in 1916, as it is shown on a siding diagram of that date [48].

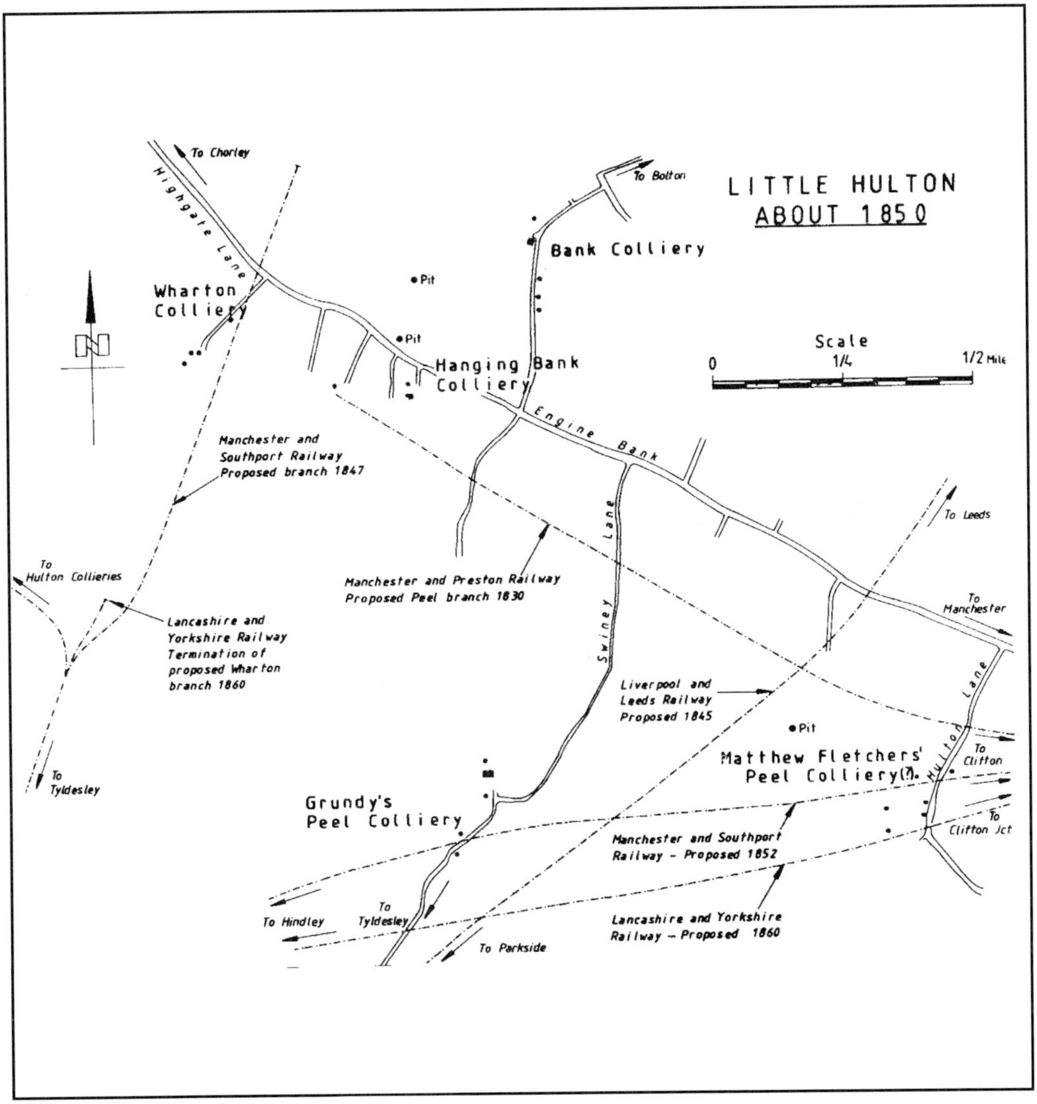

Hanging Bank Colliery

Hanging Bank Colliery is shown on the first edition of the 6" map to the south of Manchester Road. It was apparently the same as the New Guinea Pit, which by 1847 was being worked by James Bennett in partnership with James and Ralph Kay [49].

Hanging Bank is shown in the Mines Lists for 1853/4 until 1857 in the occupation of James Kay and Company. By 1859, the coal was exhausted and the partnership was dissolved [49]. A few years earlier the proprietors had decided to give up their coal delivery business and sold off their horses and carts in May 1854 [50].

Matthew Fletcher's Peel Colliery

We have traced three separate Peel Collieries in the area south of Manchester Road. The earliest appears to date from the first decade of the nineteenth century and some facts about it appear in an advertisement announcing that is was to be sold by auction as a going concern on 19th May 1824 [51]. It had lately been in the possession of Matthew Fletcher (1729-1808) and the mining leases had been granted on 2nd November 1803. The colliery was then at full work and there were four excellent steam engines.

We believe that this Peel Colliery was situated on Hilton Lane, later Hulton Lane, a little to the south of Engine Fold. The Deposited Plans for the Manchester and Southport Railway, drawn up in 1852 [52] show old pits here, on land owned by Jacob Fletcher.

The colliery was evidently purchased by the Trustees of the Duke of Bridgewater, possibly at the 1824 sale. It was latterly known as the Hilton Lane Pit. A list of the Trustees' steam engines, dated December 1842 [53] shows what is called a "double winding and pumping engine" here, with a note which says purchased with Peel Colliery in 1832. Hilton Lane Pit seems to have closed a few years later and is not shown in the Mines Lists for 1858.

Grundy's Peel Colliery

The Mines Lists for the period 1853/4 to 1860 show a Peel Colliery in Tyldesley worked by Thomas Grundy. We presume that the entry relates to the pits which are shown on the Tyldesley Tithe Map of 1847 alongside Swiney Lane, just to the south of the Little Hulton boundary. The land was owned by Lord Kenyon and the pits were then in the occupation of George Grundy and Brothers [10].

Bennett's Peel or Streetgate Colliery

James Bennett, whom we have earlier in connection with Hanging Bank, was also partner in another colliery concern with the title of Matthew Bennett and Brothers. In 1853 the firm was reported to be sinking a new pit at Streetgate, Little Hulton [54].

The first note of the colliery in the Mines Lists is in 1857, when it is referred to as Bennett's, presumably to avoid confusion with Thomas Grundy's Peel Colliery. Between 1861 and 1864 the name is given as Peel Colliery and from 1865 onwards it is Streetgate.

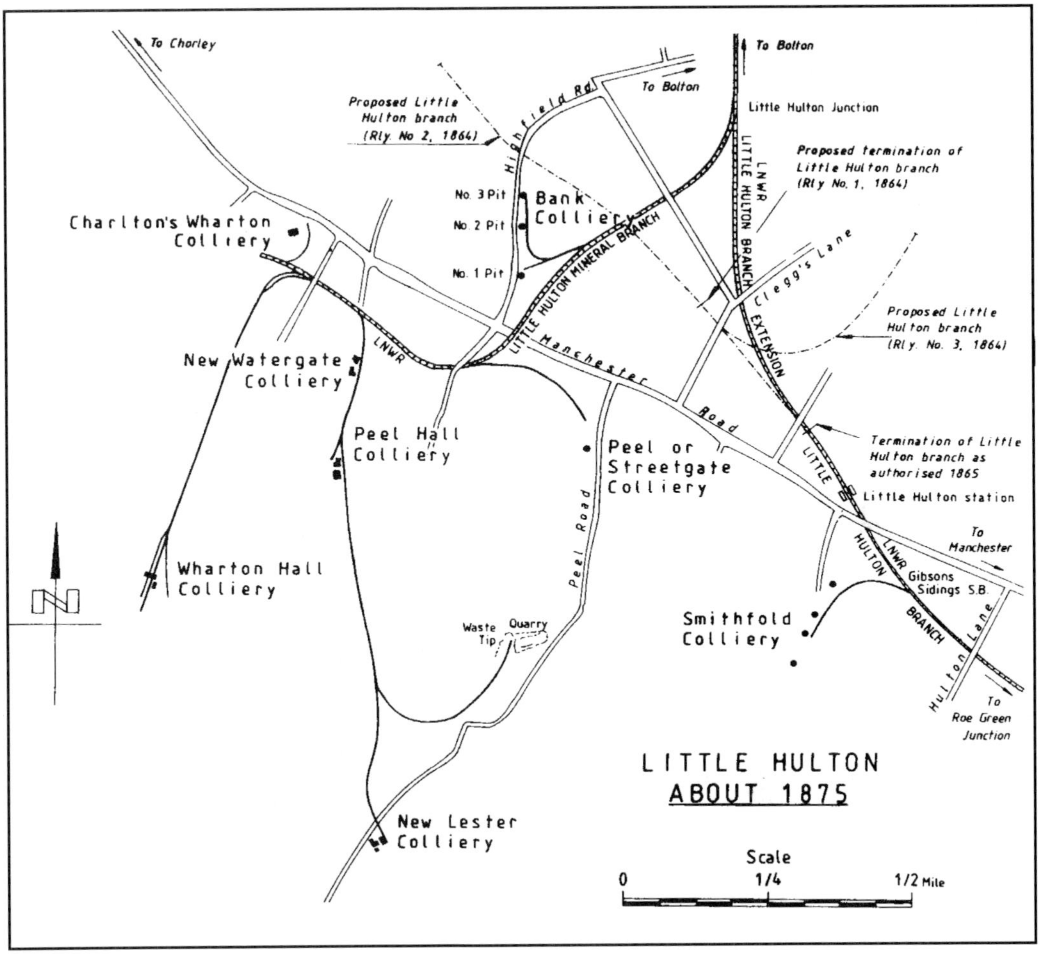

On 28th February 1859, James Bennett retired, leaving his brothers Matthew, Samuel and John to carry on the partnership which worked the colliery [55]. He retired from a second partnership which ran a coal merchants business on 22nd August 1860 [56].

In 1870, when John Gibson connected his Smithfold Colliery with the Little Hulton Branch, the Bennett Brothers were invited to use his line [57]. However, we have no evidence to suggest that this offer was taken up. It seems that Streetgate Colliery was without rail access until after the opening of the Little Hulton Mineral Railway. A connection was then put in from a point just to the south of where the branch crossed over Manchester Road.

Matthew Bennett died on 4th March 1875 [58,59] and his only son, Matthew Henry, died in September two years later [60]. The colliery was put up for sale as a going concern on 14th November 1877 [61,62].

The sale must have fallen through as the Streetgate Colliery continues to appear in the Mines Lists under the firm of Matthew Bennett and Brothers until 1881. By that date the coal had been exhausted and the plant was auctioned on 19th April 1883 [63,64].

A locomotive was included with the plant offered for sale in November 1877. It was presumably the same one, now identified as built by Sharp, Stewart and Company, which appeared in the closure sale in April 1883. We have been unable to discover any further information about it.

Peel Hall, New Lester and associated collieries

The New Watergate Colliery, on the south side of Manchester Road, was sunk towards the end of the 1840s or in the early 1850s. It is not marked on the first edition of the 6" map, surveyed in 1844 to 1846, but is shown in the occupation of James and William Roscoe in the Mines Lists for 1853/4. As we mention in Appendix 5, James Roscoe had previously been associated with George Grundy's colliery near the Fishpool Workhouse in Farnworth.

The Peel Hall Pits, to the south of New Watergate, date from the same period, being first shown in the Mines Lists for 1856. New Lester Colliery, over the Tyldesley boundary, alongside Mort Lane, was sunk in the late 1860s, first appearing in the Mines Lists for 1867.

As with the other collieries in the district, New Watergate, Peel Hall and New Lester relied on horse drawn transport to send away their coal. The Deposited Plans for the Little Hulton Mineral Branch of the London and North Western Railway, dated 1868, [65] show a cart road from New Watergate Colliery to the Manchester Road. There is also a tramroad leading southwards from New Watergate in the direction of the Peel Hall pits. It may also have served New Lester Colliery, but we have no firm evidence to support this.

Following the opening of the Little Hulton Mineral Branch, a main line railway connection was provided under an agreement with the LNWR dated 4th February 1874 [33,66] and a private line was constructed which ran past New Watergate Colliery to New Lester.

In the early days, the management of the collieries seems to have been left to James Roscoe, as William became a locomotive driver on the Midland Railway, eventually being promoted to a more senior position [67]. The partnership was dissolved in the 1870s, when William Roscoe returned to Little Hulton to take sole charge of the mining activities.

The construction of the Lancashire and Yorkshire's line from Pendleton to Hindley provided a second main line outlet. Section 25 of the L&YR Act 1885 [68] introduced to protect the interests of the landowner, Lord Kenyon, specified the size of bridge to be built over Roscoe's line from New Lester to Peel Hall. It also required the L&YR to provide a connection with the private line, the arrangements being agreed between Lord Kenyon and the railway company on 2nd July 1888 [69].

James Roscoe died on 1st August 1890 [67] and the property was managed by his executors until 1892, when the firm of James Roscoe and Sons was formed. At the time of Roscoe's death major redevelopment of the mines was under way. The Watergate and Peel Hall pits were reorganised under the title of Peel Hall Colliery. A new Arley Pit was sunk on the Watergate site, which seems to have come into production in 1892. The adjacent No 2 pit was closed on 5th April 1894 [70], while the Nos 3 and 4 Pits, presumably the old Peel Hall Pits, were abandoned in 1896 and 1894 respectively. The New Lester Colliery was also modernised. The Mines Lists for 1894 and 1896 recorded the Nos 1 and 2 Pits here as sinking.

The first locomotive that we have on record was a six coupled saddle tank which came second hand at an unknown date. It had been built by Manning, Wardle and Company of Leeds in 1863. It was followed by another six coupled saddle tank, named LORD KENYON, which was purchased new from the Hunslet Engine Company of Leeds in 1884.

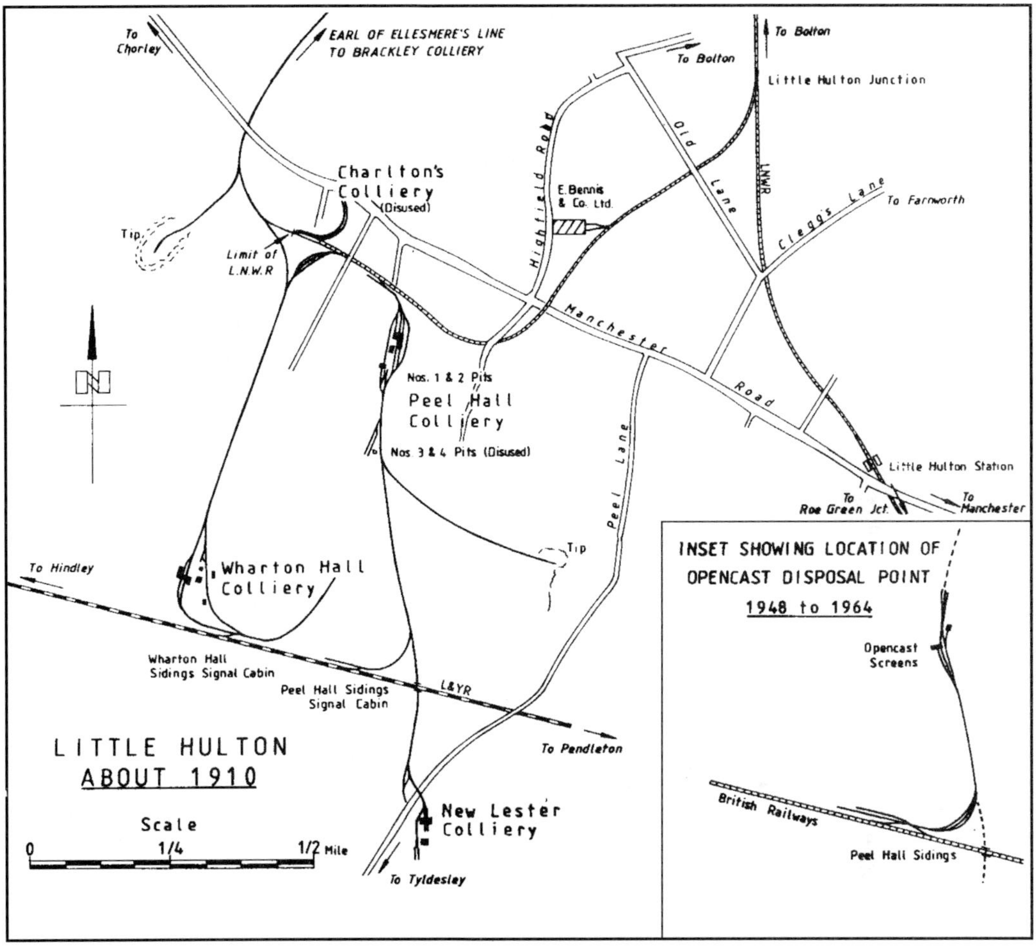

In 1900, MARY, a six coupled side tank was delivered by the Hunslet Engine Company. It was similar in design to those supplied at the same period to the Manchester Ship Canal Company. Like the Ship Canal engines, side play in the bearings of the centre axle and jointed coupling rods provided flexibility when negotiating sharp curves. Two identical locomotives followed, KING EDWARD VII in 1907 and KING GEORGE V in 1914.

Little seems to have taken place in the way of colliery development in the twentieth century and the picture is one of a static establishment. The property remained in the hands of the partnership until 1938, when Peel Collieries Ltd was formed to take over.

Peel Hall Colliery had already closed, the Mines Lists showing that it was abandoned in December 1931. However, the winding engine houses and chimneys were not demolished until April 1960 [5].

Output from New Lester Colliery was run down in the early years of the second world war. The Colliery Year Book for 1943 records that 480 men were employed underground and in 1944 only 13. There were a few employees on the surface during 1945 and 1946, engaged in clearing up. The colliery was not taken over by the National Coal Board.

An early photograph of James Roscoe and Sons' LORD KENYON at one of the Peel Hall Collieries.
Lancashire Mining Museum

Peel Hall Colliery Company's KING GEORGE V at New Lester Colliery in 1943 in its declining days.
Harry Townley

The railway from New Lester to the former LNWR Little Hulton Mineral Branch and the spur to the former L&YR line fell into disuse. The agreement relating to the connection at Little Hulton was cancelled as from September 1947 [33].

The locomotives remained in a disused state in the engine shed at Peel Hall Colliery until 1947. According to an old employee, Lever Brothers Ltd had made an offer to buy KING EDWARD VII and KING GEORGE V for use on their railway system at Port Sunlight but the deal had fallen through because the wheelbase was too long.

MARY was partly cut up by May 1947, while the other two engines were still intact in November. According to our informant KING EDWARD VII was taken away by Thompson and Company of Ince, while KING GEORGE V was broken up on site by the same firm.

Peel Hall Opencast Disposal Point

The connection between Roscoe's collieries and the Pendleton to Hindley line was relaid to serve a disposal point, where coal from neighbouring opencast workings came in by road and was loaded into railway trucks. Traffic commenced during the middle of 1948, although the agreement between British Railways, the National Coal Board and the Ministry of Works relating to the sidings was not signed until 12th February 1951 [69].

The disposal point was operated by Sir Alfred McAlpine and Son Ltd, on behalf of the Ministry of Fuel and Power until 1st April 1952 and afterwards on behalf of the Opencast Executive of the National Coal Board. Sir Alfred McAlpine and Son Ltd were responsible for the construction of the sidings and possibly the loading bunkers.

The regular locomotive was a six coupled austerity saddle tank, built by Hudswell. Clarke and Company of Leeds in 1944, which had been purchased by the Ministry of Fuel and Power in 1945 from the War Department. It had previously been used at an opencast disposal point at Wentworth near Barnsley and arrived at Peel Hall during the first half of 1948 still carrying its War Department number - 71499.

It became the property of the Opencast Executive of the National Coal Board in 1952. Apart from the occasions when it was sent away for overhaul, 71499 remained at Peel Hall until June 1964, by which time the disposal point had been closed. As we have recounted in Chapter 9, it was then sent to Gin Pit and was later taken into the stock of the East Lancashire Area of the NCB where it was named HARRY.

Several locomotives owned by Sir Alfred McAlpine and Son Ltd also worked at Peel Hall at various times. They were all six coupled saddle tanks built by Hudswell, Clarke and had been used on several public works contracts.

No 200 arrived from McAlpine's Plant Yard at Ellesmere Port in late 1949 or early 1950 to act as spare engine to 71499. It had returned to Ellesmere Port by September 1950. 71499 was sent away for repairs in February 1952, reputedly to a firm in Barnoldswick, and had returned to Peel Hall by September. McAlpine's No 40 came from Ellesmere Port to take its place and stayed until late 1952 or early 1953. No 40 was back at Peel Hall again from the middle of 1956 to the middle of 1957, while 71499 was undergoing overhaul at Walkden Yard.

There is a record in the Industrial Railway Society lists that McAlpine's No 47 was at Peel Hall for a time. Possibly this was when 71499 was under repairs in 1955.

In July 1961, when 71499 paid another visit to Walkden Yard, WESTWOOD, the four coupled Hudswell Clarke saddle tank, was sent from Cleworth Hall Colliery. By January 1962, it had moved on to the Opencast Disposal Point at Pemberton, near Wigan.

The opencast screens at Peel Hall in August 1956, with WD 71499 in the foreground, out of use and waiting to go to Walkden for overhaul. Housing is already beginning to encroach on the site. David Chatfield

A 1952 photograph of the locomotive shed at Peel Hall Opencast Disposal Point, with Sir Alfred McAlpine's No 42 outside. The derelict winding engine houses and chimney of Peel Hall Colliery can be seen in the background. Roscoe's locomotive shed, long since disused, is on the left of the winding engine house.
Bernard Roberts

Wharton Hall Colliery

The firm of Potter and Graham, trading as the Wharton Hall Colliery Company, acquired the mining rights of the Wharton Hall Estate in April 1872. Their Wharton Hall Colliery was sunk soon afterwards and a siding connection was provided to the Little Hulton Mineral Railway of the LNWR under an agreement of 18th January 1873 [33].

A small four coupled saddle tank was ordered from Walker Brothers of Wigan in about 1873. Named GRAHAM, it was presumably delivered in time for the start of coal production. A second locomotive, a six coupled saddle tank named WHARTON HALL, came in 1876 from Manning, Wardle and Company of Leeds.

GRAHAM was severely damaged in an accident which occurred in the early hours of Thursday, 13th May 1875. While an LNWR train on the Little Hulton Mineral line was engaged in shunting operations at Wharton Hall sidings nine wagons ran away down the 1 in 20 gradient towards the colliery. After travelling for a distance of 1100 yards at speeds reputedly up to 70 or 80 miles an hour, three wagons left the rails in the pit yard and ran into the engine shed in which GRAHAM was standing. The building was reduced to a mass of rubble and the engine was pushed some distance, finishing up on its side [71,72,73]. No doubt the railway company, whose shunters were responsible for the accident, paid for the repairs to GRAHAM and perhaps provided a temporary replacement.

In 1879 the Bridgewater Trustees purchased the Wharton Hall Estate and Potter and Graham's lease was terminated. The Trustees took over the colliery and most of the plant, including the two locomotives. The Wharton Hall Colliery Company was left to dispose of surplus material. 80 8-ton wagons were advertised for sale in July 1879 [74]. A final sale of effects was held on 15th June 1881, which included a further 152 8-ton wagons and a lease of the company's coal depot at Cook St, Bolton [75].

We shall follow the later history of Wharton Hall Colliery and its railways and locomotives under the ownership of the Bridgewater Trustees in Chapter 11.

ASTLEY GREEN COLLIERY

The Pilkington Colliery Co Ltd and Manchester Collieries Ltd

To conclude the chapter we move south to Astley Green. In 1908 the Pilkington Colliery Co Ltd, a subsidiary of the Clifton and Kersley Coal Co Ltd, commenced sinking two shafts here, on a site on the north side of the Bridgewater Canal [5]. In March 1913 it was reported that sinking operations had been completed and that the current year would be occupied in erecting screens, making railway connections and developing the mines [76].

As mentioned earlier, in October 1913 the firm purchased the canal basin formerly used by the Tyldesley Coal Company, located at the east end of the site.

To provide a rail outlet, a private line some $1^1/_2$ miles in length was built from the colliery across Astley Moss to join the London and North Western Railway east of Astley Station. During construction it was necessary to adopt methods very similar to those used by George Stephenson on the Liverpool and Manchester Railway. Tree trunks and large branches of wood were placed on the peat to give a floating foundation for the trackbed, with pit waste laid on top to support the sleepers and the rails.

The construction of the line from Astley Green Colliery across the moss to the London and North Western Railway, with the locomotive ASTLEY in the background. Note the tree trunks laid on top of the peat to form a foundation for the permanent way. Lancashire Mining Museum

The new Peckett locomotive ASTLEY photographed in August 1908. Note the dumb buffers for shunting contractors type tip wagons. Also note the newly installed Lancashire boilers and the temporary head frame used for sinking the second shaft. Lancashire Mining Museum

Construction of the railway sidings at Astley Green. Note the Clifton and Kersley Company's wagons, presumably indicating that some coal was already being wound. It will be seen that the majority of the wagons were of a type fitted with dumb buffers which was not phased out for main line traffic until 1913.
Lancashire Mining Museum

WINNIE, a typical contractor's locomotive, built in 1883 for J P Edwards, who used it on railway construction work. It was purchased by the Pilkington Colliery Co Ltd to assist in the building of Astley Green Colliery, where the photgraph was taken. Note the temporary engine shed in the background.
Wigan Metropolitan Borough Heritage Centre

The first locomotive which we have on record at Astley Green was a four coupled saddle tank, carrying the name ASTLEY. It was purchased in 1908 from Peckett and Sons of Bristol and was used on the construction of the railway across the moss.

In 1911, a small four coupled saddle tank named WINNIE came from Thomas Mitchell and Sons, the Bolton machinery merchants. It had been built by Manning, Wardle and Company of Leeds in 1883 and had passed through the hands of a number of public works contractors. It appears to have been used on construction work and tracklaying around the colliery yard at Astley Green and was sold back to Mitchells in 1916. As we have mentioned in Chapter 5, WINNIE had been hired from the colliery company for a short period during 1914 by Mitchells, who had rehired it to the Bury Papermaking Co Ltd.

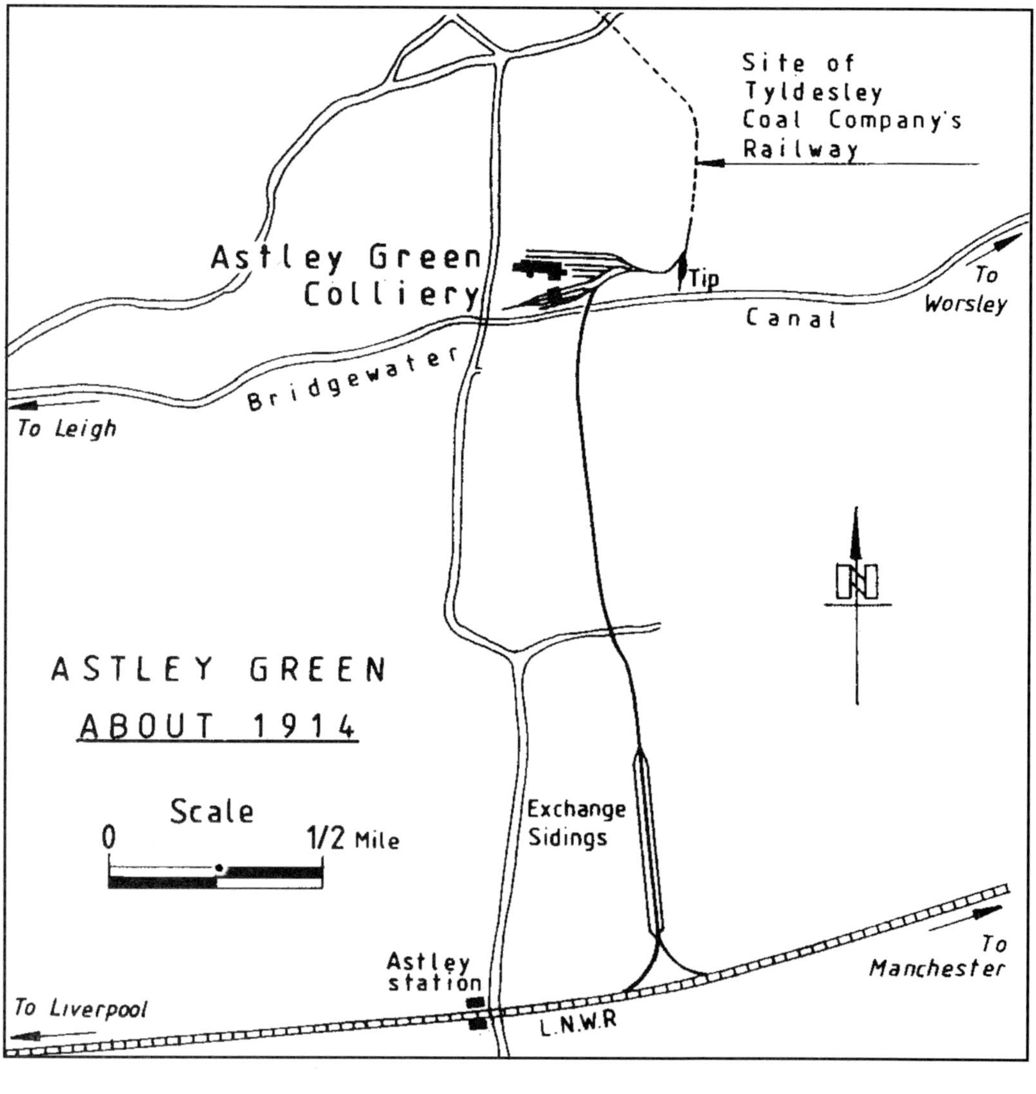

With production about to start more powerful locomotives were needed. The four coupled Peckett locomotive, OUTWOOD No 2, taken over by Outwood Collieries Ltd from Thomas Fletcher and Sons Ltd, was transferred to Astley Green in 1912 [77].

A year or two later another engine came second hand, this time from J F Wake and Co Ltd, of Darlington. A six coupled saddle tank, built by Andrew Barclay Sons and Company of Kilmarnock in 1880, it had been delivered to the Llanelly and Mynnydd Mawr Railway, where it had been named JOHN WADDELL. It had been rebuilt by the Avonside Engine Company in 1901 or 1902 and the railway company had decided to dispose of it in 1908 [78]. After its arrival in Lancashire it was renamed ASTLEY GREEN.

In 1916, a six coupled saddle tank, carrying the name EDWARD, was purchased from R and W Hawthorn, Leslie and Company of Newcastle on Tyne. Rather larger than its predecessors, it was presumably intended for working the traffic to the LNWR exchange sidings.

After the first world war, there were further transfers of engines from associated companies. The surviving records of the Clifton and Kersley Coal Company and its subsidiaries are mainly of a financial nature and are difficult to follow. What seems to have happened is that OUTWOOD No 2 was taken out of service, probably at some date between 1916 and 1919, as it shown as "extinct stock" in the 1919 stock returns [79]. BLACK DIAMOND, the four coupled saddle tank built by Sharp, Stewart and Company in 1878, was transferred from the Clifton and Kersley Coal Co Ltd in 1922 [80] as a replacement.

Finally, NEWTOWN, the four coupled saddle tank built by Hawthorn, Leslie and Company of Newcastle in 1904, was transferred to Astley Green during the financial year ending 31st March 1928 [79]. As we have mentioned in Chapter 6, it may have returned to Spindle Point Colliery for a short period later in 1928 when there was a shortage of workable locomotives at Clifton. It was back at Astley Green towards the end of the year or possibly early in 1929.

Astley Green Colliery was taken over by Manchester Collieries Ltd in March 1929. Following the merger a great deal of development work was carried out. A modern washery was completed in 1932 [81]. The siding layout around the pit yard was brought up to date and a new section of railway constructed to connect with the Bridgewater Collieries system at Boothsbank was opened in 1931 [81]. The canal tip, taken over from the Tyldesley Coal Company, was swept away and replaced by a new installation [81].

Five locomotives were taken over by the new company - EDWARD, BLACK DIAMOND, NEWTOWN, ASTLEY, ASTLEY GREEN. The last named, according to old employees was out of use. However, it was not cut up immediately. It was sent to Walkden Yard, where it remained until 1936, when it was sold to Harry Stephenson and Sons Ltd, of Hindley, for scrap.

ASTLEY was taken out service in the mid 1930s and sold to Craven Bros (Manchester) Ltd, Reddish, in 1937. The other three engines remained at Astley Green until after the second world war. NEWTOWN was broken up there at the end of 1945 or early in 1946, as a result, we were told, of a misunderstanding between the engineering staff at Astley Green and Walkden Yard. BLACK DIAMOND was broken up at Walkden Yard in October 1949, while EDWARD lasted until 1968.

BEDFORD, CERBERUS and STANLEY were brought in from other collieries in the early and middle 1930s to replace ASTLEY and ASTLEY GREEN. All were quite old stagers although no doubt in good repair.

ASTLEY GREEN, the engine built by Andrew Barclay and Co of Kilmarnock in 1880 for use on the Llanelly and Mynydd Mawr Railway. It was at Astley Green from about 1914 to the mid 1930s

Lancashire Mining Museum

EDWARD, the large Hawthorn Leslie engine, which was purchased in 1916 for hauling heavy trains between Astley Green Colliery and the LNWR exchange sidings. Photographed at Astley Green in August 1938

Alex Appleton

BEDFORD, formerly the property of John Speakman and Sons Ltd, was a six coupled side tank built by Manning Wardle and Company in 1865. We have already met the locomotive in Chapter 9. It remained at Astley Green for the remainder of its life, apart from three short visits to Walkden Yard for repairs, at the end of 1938, at the end of 1939 and between 18th March and 27th August 1940. It was out of service when the National Coal Board took over on 1st January 1947 and was in need of extensive repair [82]. It was sent to Walkden Yard, but it was decided that was not practible to proceed with the work. BEDFORD was officially withdrawn from service in 1947 [20] but was not actually broken up at Walkden until August 1950.

CERBERUS, a six coupled saddle tank, had been supplied by Sharp, Stewart and Company to the Bridgewater Trustees in 1880. After a short spell at Astley Green, it was sent to Walkden Yard for overhaul on 9th April 1936. It was back at Astley Green between 7th December 1936 and 12th January 1937 when it returned to Walkden Yard. As we have described in Chapter 9, it was subsequently used at Chanters Colliery and Bedford Colliery.

STANLEY was one of the original six coupled saddle tank built by Manning, Wardle and Company for the Bridgewater Trustees in 1871. It returned to Walkden during the early years of the war and stood out of use for some time before it was broken up in 1943 or early 1944.

A view of the locomotive shed at Astley Green taken in August 1938. The front engine is BLACK DIAMOND, which had come from the Clifton and Kersley Collieries in 1922. Behind this is STANLEY, the 1871 Manning Wardle, which had been transferred from the Bridgewater system after the formation of Manchester Collieries Ltd. Alex Appleton

Later, further engines were drafted in.

CARBON, the six coupled saddle tank built by Andrew Barclay, Sons and Company in 1920 for Fletcher, Burrows and Co Ltd, was transferred from Chanters Colliery early in 1938, presumably as a replacement for CERBERUS. It was away at Walkden Yard for repairs between 12th February and 5th June 1941 and was working on the Bridgewater railway system during 1944, returning to Astley Green on 14th January 1945 [20]. It was at Astley Green on vesting day [82], but, as we have seen earlier in the chapter, it was transferred to Cleworth Hall Colliery shortly afterwards.

Walkden records [83] show that FRANCIS, the ex ROD six coupled side tank, was sent to Astley Green on 16th July 1945, after an overhaul at Walkden Yard. It may have seen some service at Astley Green before that date, although it was noted working on the Bridgewater system in 1943.

Towards the middle of 1946, HUMPHREY, an austerity saddle tank arrived at Astley Green. Built by Robert Stephenson and Hawthorn in 1945, as War Department 71484, it had been purchased by Manchester Collieries Ltd. It was delivered to Walkden in March 1946 and, according to Walkden Yard records, was sent to Astley Green on 3rd May.

Astley Green Colliery was taken over by the National Coal Board on 1st January 1947 and it is more convenient to describe subsequent events when we deal with the post NCB history of the Bridgewater collieries railway system in Chapter 13.

LOCOMOTIVE SUMMARY

Tyldesley, Peel Wood and Cleworth Hall Collieries

Tyldesley Coal Company from about 1840 to about 1860
Green, Holland and Company from about 1860 to November 1870
Tyldesley Coal Co Ltd from November 1870 to 31-12-1946
National Coal Board
No1 (Manchester) Area from 1-1-1947 to 31-12-1960
Manchester, Burnley and Cumberland Area from 1-1-1961
Cleworth Hall Colliery closed January 1963, no rail traffic after 5th May 1961

Green, Holland and Company; Tyldesley Coal Co Ltd.

TYLDESLEY	0-4-0STIC	HF		1867	10"x20"	
Probably new Green, Holland and Co Boiler repaired by Hunslet Engine Co in 1917 Stated to be scrapped about 1930, perhaps earlier						
JESSIE	0-6-0STIC	WKB	1544	c'1877	13"	
New to Tyldesley Coal Co Ltd Stated to be scrapped about 1930						
BEATRICE	0-4-0T OC	VF	809	1877	14"x20"	3'3"
New to Tyldesley Coal Co Ltd Stated to have been rebuilt from saddle tank about 1905 Withdrawn from service 1944 To NCB on 1-1-1947 at Cleworth Hall						
VICTORIA	0-4-0STOC	VF	1539	1897	15"x20	3'5"
New to Tyldesley Coal Co Ltd To NCB on 1-1-1947 at Cleworth Hall						

LOUISA 0-6-0T IC HE 792 1902 15½"x20" 3'4"
New to Tyldesley Coal Co Ltd
To NCB on 1-1-1947 at Cleworth Hall

JESSIE 0-4-0T OC HE 1557 1927 16"x24" 3'9"
New to Tyldesley Coal Co Ltd
To NCB on 1-1-1947 at Cleworth Hall

National Coal Board

BEATRICE 0-4-0T OC VF 809 1877 14"x20" 3'3"
Ex Tyldesley Coal Co Ltd on 1-1-1947 at Cleworth Hall, withdrawn from service
Scrapped at Cleworth Hall about 1948

VICTORIA 0-4-0STOC VF 1539 1897 15"x20 3'5"
Ex Tyldesley Coal Co Ltd on 1-1-1947 at Cleworth Hall
Scrapped at Cleworth Hall 4-1953

LOUISA 0-6-0T IC HE 792 1902 15½"x20" 3'4"
Ex Tyldesley Coal Co Ltd on 1-1-1947 at Cleworth Hall
Withdrawn from service by 8-1953 and scrapped February 1955 at Cleworth Hall, by Stone and Hutchinson

JESSIE 0-4-0T OC HE 1557 1927 16"x24" 3'9"
Ex Tyldesley Coal Co Ltd on 1-1-1947 at Cleworth Hall
At Gin Pit for repairs, mid 1951
At Walkden Yard for repairs 1955-1956 and 1958
Withdrawn from service March 1961
Sent to Walkden Yard September 1961 and then to Maudland Metals, Preston, for scrap February 1967

CARBON 0-4-0STOC AB 1704 1920 14"x22" 3'5"
Transferred from Astley Green early 1947
At Walkden Yard for repairs mid 1948 to 7-9-1950 (New boiler from Andrew Barclay Sons and Co)
Temporarily at Robin Hood 28-2-1955 to 25-4-1955
At Walkden Yard for repairs 13-9-1956 to 4-12-1956
Sent to Walkden Yard 9-1961 and transferred to Bank Hall Colliery, Burnley by 2-1962

WESTWOOD 0-4-0STOC HC 1036 1913 16"x24" 3'8"
Transferred from Astley Green 4-1961 to replace JESSIE
Transferred to Peel Hall Opencast Disposal Point 7-1961

SHAKERLEY 0-6-0STIC HE 736 1901 14"x18" 3'2½"
Transferred from Chanters Colliery 1949
At Gin Pit for repairs in 1952 and temporarily in use there afterwards
At Walkden Yard for repairs 12-1952 and temporarily used at Astley Green
At Walkden Yard for repairs in 1956
Scrapped at Cleworth Hall late 1961 or early 1962

Shakerley Colliery

Nathaniel Eckersley and executors from about 1840 to about 1861
William Ramsden from about 1861 to June 1898
William Ramsden and Sons Ltd from June 1898 to March 1935
Manchester Collieries Ltd from March 1935

Colliery closed October 1938

SHAKERLEY 0-4-0STOC MW 469 1873 12"x18"
New to William Ramsden. Class H
Sold to Thomas Mitchell and Sons Ltd, Bolton, 1-1901
Resold 1-1901 to Ince Waggon and Ironworks Co Ltd

EDITH 0-6-0STIC HE 436 1887 14"x18" 3′1"
New to William Ramsden
To Manchester Collieries Ltd, March 1935
Transferred to Howe Bridge Colliery in 1939, after closure of Shakerley Colliery

SHAKERLEY 0-6-0STIC HE 736 1901 14"x18" 3′2½"
New to William Ramsden and Sons Ltd
To Manchester Collieries Ltd, March 1935
Transferred to Howe Bridge Colliery late 1938, after closure of Shakerley Colliery

0-4-0STOC HE 177 1877 12"x18" 3′1"
Hired from Hunslet Engine Co Ltd in December 1902, while HE 736 under repairs at Hunslet and in May 1905, when EDITH HE 436 under repair at Hunslet. HE 177 was new to James Muspratt and Sons, Widnes, as NESSIE. Sold back to HE when under repair, 10-98 and used as hire loco.

Streetgate Colliery

Matthew Bennett and Brothers 1853 to 1883

Colliery closed 1883

Locomotive advertised for sale on 14th Nov 1877 (BC 13-10-1877, MG 3-11-1877)
Locomotive built by Sharp, Stewart and Co offered for sale on 19th April 1883 (CG 13-4-1883, BC 17-3-1883)

Peel Hall, New Lester and associated collieries

James and William Roscoe from about 1850 to 1870s
William Roscoe and executors from 1870s to 1892
James Roscoe and Sons from 1892 to about 1938
Peel Collieries Ltd from about 1938

Peel Hall Colliery abandoned December 1931
New Lester Colliery closed about 1944

0-6-0STIC MW 76 1863 12"x17" 3′1⅜"
Class Old I, new to George Thomson and Co, Liverpool - No 6 LIVERPOOL
With Henry Parkinson, Bolton, by 12-1872

LORD KENYON 0-6-0STIC HE 289 1884 13"x18" 3′1"
New to James Roscoe and Sons
Believed scrapped about 1910

MARY	0-6-0T IC	HE	720	1900	15½"x20"	3'4"

New to James Roscoe and Sons
Scrapped at Peel Hall Colliery, November 1947

KING EDWARDVII	0-6-0T IC	HE	953	1907	15½"x20"	3'4"

New to James Roscoe and Sons
Scrapped about December 1947 by Thompson and Co of Ince. Possibly removed from site intact - see text.

KING GEORGE V	0-6-0T IC	HE	1151	1914	15½"x20"	3'4"

New to James Roscoe and Sons
Scrapped at Peel Hall Colliery, about December 1947 by Thompson and Co of Ince

Peel Hall Opencast Disposal Point

Ministry of Fuel and Power from mid 1948 to 31-3-1952
National Coal Board Opencast Executive from 1-4-1952 to mid 1964

Operated by Sir Alfred McAlpine and Son Ltd under contract

Disposal Point closed mid 1964

71499	0-6-0STIC	HC	1776	1944	18"x26"	4'3"

Transferred from Wentworth Disposal Point, South Yorkshire, mid 1948
At Green and Palmer, Barnoldswick, for repairs, February 1952 to about September 1952.
At Walkden Yard for repairs late 1955, returned to Peel Hall November 1955
At Walkden Yard for repairs November 1956 to April 1957
At Walkden Yard for repairs July and August 1961
At Walkden Yard for repairs in 1962 and returned to Peel Hall July 1962
To NCB Gin Pit for storage, circa 6-1964

No 200	0-6-0STIC	HC	1749	1946	13"x20"	3'3½"

From Sir Alfred McAlpine and Son Ltd's Ellesmere Port Plant Yard, temporarily at Peel Hall in 1950

No 40	0-6-0STIC	HC	1525	1924	12"x18"	3'1½"

From Sir Alfred McAlpine and Son Ltd's Ellesmere Port Plant Yard, temporarily at Peel Hall in 1952, WD 71499 away for repairs
From Sir Alfred McAlpine and Son Ltd's Ellesmere Port Plant Yard, temporarily at Peel Hall late 1956 to early 1957, WD 71499 away for repairs

WESTWOOD	0-4-0STOC	HC	1036	1913	16"x24	3'8"

Temporarily at Peel Hall. Came from Cleworth Hall July 1961 and returned to Walkden Yard December 1961

No 47	0-6-0STIC	HC	1511	1923	12"x18"	3'1"

Here according to Industrial Railway Society List, perhaps in 1955

Wharton Hall Colliery

Wharton Hall Colliery Company 1872 to 1879
Bridgewater Trustees from 1879 - see Chapter 11

GRAHAM	0-4-0STIC	WKB	412	c1873	14"	

New to Wharton Hall Colliery Co
Taken over by Bridgewater Trustees in 1879
Sold to Thomas Mitchell and Sons Ltd, Bolton, October 1907 and resold February 1908 to George Watkinson, Buckley

WHARTON HALL	0-6-0STIC	MW	638	1876	14"x20"	3'6"

New to Wharton Hall Colliery Co. Class N
Taken over by Bridgewater Trustees in 1879
Sold to Thomas Mitchell and Sons Ltd, Bolton, April 1911 and scrapped by them.

Astley Green Colliery

Pilkington Colliery Co Ltd
Manchester Collieries Ltd from 4-3-1929 to 31-12-1946
National Coal Board from 1-1-1947 - see Chapter 13

Pilkington Colliery Co Ltd and Manchester Collieries Ltd

ASTLEY	0-4-0STOC	P	1164	1908	9"	

New to Astley Green Colliery. Class M5
Sold to Craven Brothers (Manchester) Ltd, Reddish, 1936 or 1937

WINNIE	0-4-0STOC	MW	880	1883	9"x14"	2'6"

From Thomas Mitchell and Sons Ltd in 1911
Hired from Thomas Mitchell and Sons Ltd for use at Gigg Mills, Bury, March 1914
Sold back to Thomas Mitchell and Sons Ltd May 1916 and scrapped by them February 1917

OUTWOOD	0-4-0STOC	P	935	1902	10"x14"	

Transferred from Outwood Collieries Ltd September 1912
Scrapped or sold by 1922

ASTLEY GREEN	0-6-0STOC	AB	221	1880	14"x21"	3'6"

New to Llanelly and Mynydd Mawr Railway as JOHN WADDELL
Purchased from J F Wake and Co Ltd, Darlington about 1914
Sent to Walkden Yard and sold to H Stephenson and Sons Ltd, Hindley, for scrap, May 1936

EDWARD	0-6-0STOC	HL	3184	1916	17"x24"	3'10"

New to Astley Green Colliery
At Walkden Yard for repairs 17-5-1938 to 18-7-1938
To N C B on 1-1-1947 at Astley Green

BLACK DIAMOND	0-4-0STOC	SS	2742	1878	16"x20"	4'0"

Transferred from Clifton and Kersley Coal Co Ltd in 1922
To N C B on 1-1-1947 at Astley Green

NEWTOWN	0-4-0STOC	HL	2580	1904	15"x22"	3'9"

Transferred from Collieries (Clifton and Kersley) Ltd in 1928
Scrapped at Astley Green, late 1945 or early 1946

CERBERUS	0-6-0STIC	SS	2909	1880	17"x14"	4'0"

Transferred from Central Railways system before 1936
At Walkden Yard for repairs 9-4-1936 to 15-5-1936 and returned to Astley Green 7-12-1936, presumably after working on Central Railways system
Sent to Walkden Yard for repairs 12-1-1937 and transferred to Chanters Colliery 10-3-1937

STANLEY	0-6-0STIC	MW	366	1871	15"x22"	4'0"

Transferred from Central Railways system in 1930s, possibly July 1933
At Walkden Yard for repairs 28-3-1933 to 17-7-1933
Sent to Walkden Yard between 1940 and 1943 and scrapped there

BEDFORD	0-6-0T IC	MW		1875	15¼"x22½"	3'10½"

Transferred from Bedford Colliery, probably in 1933 or 1934
At Walkden Yard for repairs October 1938, November 1939 and 18-3-1940 to 27-8-1940
To N C B on 1-1-1947 at Astley Green, out of use

CARBON 0-4-0STOC AB 1704 1920 14"x22" 3'5"
Transferred from Atherton Collieries between January and April 1938
Transferred to Central Railways system between February 1943 and March 1944 and returned to Astley Green 14-1-1945
To N C B on 1-1-1947 at Astley Green

FRANCIS 0-6-0TOC KS 3068 1917 17"x24" 3'11"
Transferred from Central Railways system, probably in 1945
To N C B on 1-1-1947 at Astley Green

HUMPHREY 0-6-0STIC RSH 7293 1945 18"x26" 4'3"
Originally WD 71484, purchased by Manchester Collieries Ltd March 1946
To N C B on 1-1-1947 at Astley Green

For locomotives at Astley Green after 1-1-1947 see Chapter 13

References to Chapter 10

1 LRO PDR 195
2 LRO PDR 539
3 LRO PDR 707
4 Minute Books of Tyldesley Coal Co Ltd - SMM U258
5 *"Collieries in the Manchester Coalfields"* Geoff Hayes - De Archaeoligische Pers, Eindhoven, nd
6 At LRO
7 *"Royal National Commercial Directory and Topography of the County of Lancaster"* - Isaac Slater, Manchester, 1851
8 At Cambridge University Library
9 LRO DRM 1/8
10 LRO DRM 1/100
11 Line Plan of Eccles, Tyldesley and Wigan Railway - LNWR, Rugby, 1868 - 2 chains to 1 inch - at GMRO
12 Hunslet Engine Company Repair Order dated 28th June 1917 - copy supplied by Mr Ken Plant
13 CG 14-3-1873
14 BC 20-10-1893
15 Tyldesley Coal Co Ltd Minute of 20-2-1911 SMM U258
16 Idem 31-3-1913
17 Idem 28-4-1913
18 Idem13-10-1913
19 Idem 17-2-1913
20 *"From Walkden Yard Records - Part Two"* - Alex Appleton - *"Industrial Locomotive"*, Vol 6, No 63, 1991
21 *"Industrial Locomotive Society Journal"*, Vol XVIII, No 1, March 1964
22 *"Industrial Locomotive Society Journal"*, Vol XVIII, No 2, June 1964
23 *"Royal National Commercial Directory and Topography of the County of Lancaster"* - Isaac Slater, Manchester, 1848
24 Bridgewater Archives at Salford Mining Museum
25 LRO NCMc 33/17
26 BC 5-5-1855
27 LG 17-12-1869
28 SAO Bridgewater Trustees Agreement Book No 1, p 313
29 *"The Story of St Nicholas Works"* - Michael R Lane - Unicorn Press, Stowmarket, 1994
30 *"Chronology of the Railways of Lancashire and Cheshire"* - M D Greville Railway and Canal Historical Society, 2nd edition, 1981
31 BC 20-8-1870
32 BC 15-10-1870
33 Line Plan of Little Hulton Branch, etc - LNWR Rugby 1876 - 2 chains to 1 inch - GMRO A19/4/143
34 BC 24-8-1878
35 BC 25-2-1854
36 BC 29-3-1884
37 FJ 29-3-1884
38 BC22-11-1900
39 FJ15-11-1901
40 FJ 19-1-1939
41 FJ 8-9-1939
42 LNW Sdgs Diag No147,12.1916
43 *"Chambers' Trades Register of Manchester, Liverpool and Districts"* - Chambers Registers and Directories Ltd, London, 1959
44 *"County Borough of Bolton Directory"* -Blair Publications Ltd, St Annes on Sea, 1971
45 *"Manchester Chamber of Commerce and Industry Regional Directory"* - Kemps Group (Printers and Publishers) Ltd, Birmingham, 1977
46 *"Bolton Express"* 20-12-1823
47 WRO DDX/Ta 29/4

48 LNW Sdgs Diag No149,12.1916
49 BC 7-5-1881
50 BC 22-4-1854
51 *"Bolton Express"* 1-5-1824
52 LRO PDR 592
53 LRO NCBw 19/1
54 BC 16-7-1853
55 BC 5-3-1859
56 LG 24-8-1860
57 BC 23-4-1870
58 BC 6-3-1875
59 Probate Records
60 BC 29-9-1877
61 BC 13-10-1877
62 MG 3-11-1877
63 BC 17-3-1883
64 CG13-4-1883
65 LRO PDR 869
66 LNW Sdgs Diag No 148, 12.1916
67 BC 2-8-1890
68 48 & 49 Vic cap xciv; 16th July 1885
69 Line Plan of Wigan to Manchester Line, 14½ mp to 3½ mp - 2 chains to 1inch BR, Euston, 1956 - At BRPB, Manchester
70 BC 5-5-1894
71 FJ 15-5-1875
72 WO 22-5-1875
73 *"Accident at Wharton Hall"* - Alex Appleton - in *"Industrial Locomotive"* No 66, 1992
74 BC 12-7-1879
75 BC 28-5-1881
76 Clifton and Kersley Coal Co Ltd Minutes, 4-3-1913 - SMM U64
77 Pilkington Colliery Co Ltd, Additions to Stock, 1912 to 1916 - SMM U64
78 *"The Locomotives of the Great Western Railway"* - Part Ten - Railway Correspondence and Travel Society, 1966
79 Pilkington Colliery Co Ltd, Stock Returns, 1912 to 1922 - SMM U64
80 Pilkington Colliery Co Ltd, Stock Returns, 1926 to 1928 - SMM U64
81 Carbon, April 1932
82 *"List of Locomotives in No 1 (Manchester) Area"* - NCB document - copy in authors'possession
83 *"From Walkden Yard Records - Part One"* Alex Appleton - in *"Industrial Locomotive"*, No 62, 1991

CHAPTER 11

THE BRIDGEWATER COLLIERIES UP TO 1929

In our three final chapters we turn our attention to the Bridgewater Collieries, which have a history extending from the middle of the eighteenth century through to the 1970s. The mines were opened up by the third Duke of Bridgewater and were worked by his trustees after his death in 1803. The third Earl of Ellesmere inherited the property in 1903 and Bridgewater Collieries Ltd was formed by the fourth Earl in 1921. In 1929, the Bridgewater collieries came under the control of Manchester Collieries Ltd, which was created through an amalgamation of the leading mining firms in the area.

For the first ninety years or so, the Bridgewater collieries relied for transport on a unique system of underground canals. Two horse worked tramroads were built in the 1830s and 1840s, but a proper railway system, operated by locomotives, did not start to be developed until the 1870s. Eventually there more than 12 miles of main route, served by some 20 steam locomotives, making it one of the most extensive private railways in Lancashire.

In the present chapter we describe the history of the collieries and the railway system up to 1929, leaving subsequent events under Manchester Collieries and NCB ownership to Chapters 12 and 13 respectively.

Mining up to 1803 and the Duke of Bridgewater's Underground Canals

Coal had been mined on a small scale in and around Worsley for several centuries before Francis Egerton, the third Duke of Bridgewater, succeeded to the title in 1748. He soon decided on a policy of exploiting the commercial potential of his estates, but there were two factors inhibiting the expansion of the mining industry - the lack of adequate means of transport to the developing towns and the need to provide a cheap and effective means of draining the coal workings.

The construction of the Bridgewater canal, mentioned in Chapter 2, solved the transport problem. To provide drainage, an underground level was driven northwards from the canal at Worsley Delph to intersect the coal seams and from this developed a canal system which was unique in the British Isles.

Branches from the main level gave access to the working faces, where coal was loaded into small boats. These were legged through the tunnel by gangs of men, assisted in the outward direction by the water flow.

Pits were sunk at intervals along the main tunnel and the branches, principally to provide access for men and materials and to provide ventilation. Some, such as those at Walkden and Dixon Green, were also used for winding coal for local sale.

Spoil from the underground workings was used in the reclamation of Worsley Moss and was boated along an extension of the canal westwards from Worsley Delph. This extension was in use by 1764 as it is shown on an estate plan of that date [1]. There was also a branch canal, perhaps of a slightly later date, which ran southwards across the Moss in the direction of the later Botany Bay Wood, which was planted in 1790 [2].

On the moss itself, a series of horse worked tramroads conveyed the spoil to where it was needed. Again, it has not proved possible to discover when they were laid down, but they were in use by 1845, when the surveys were carried out for the first edition of the 6" map. They had disappeared by 1891, when the second edition was surveyed. At the turn of the century, as shown on the third edition of the map, a narrow gauge railway had been laid down from the head of the canal branch across the moss. By 1929, when the map was revised, this had disappeared. The branch canal itself was disused and had probably been filled in.

Much of the land owned by the Duke was used for agricultural purposes and there was also a certain amount of residential property. The main workshops, which were set up alongside the canal at Worsley, dealt with general estate maintenance as well as undertaking the more specialised work needed by the mines. A boatyard was established nearby to build and repair the special boats used on the main navigable level as well as the conventional barges for the Bridgewater Canal.

The underground canal system has received comprehensive treatment in several publications [3,4] where those interested can find further information. Here we shall provide only an outline of the developments which took place.

By 1770 the main water level had reached Parr Fold, south of Walkden, and about 1½ miles from the entrance at Worsley. North of here an upper navigable level was driven, 35 yards above the main level, making use of Massey's Walkden Moor drainage sough, which dated from an earlier phase of mining operations. By the 1780s the upper navigable level had reached Plodder Lane, some 1¾ miles from Walkden. As has been described in Chapter 4, branches were subsequently constructed in the Cannel and Dean Moor seams to reach coal owned by the Duke in an area south west of Bolton, previously worked by shafts.

Workshops were established at Walkden for the construction and maintenance of the boats used on the upper level. Here an inclined shaft was sunk from the surface and the boats were hauled up on a cradle running on rails. Materials could also be taken down this way, but coal conveyed on the upper level and destined for the Bridgewater Canal had to be wound to the main level down the shaft at Barlow Fold or one of the neighbouring pits.

To overcome the expense of transhipment and to enable boats to be transferred between the two levels, an underground inclined plane was constructed in the late 1790s at Ashton's Field. The boats were floated on to cradles running on rails. The cradles were joined together by a rope which passed over a brake wheel at the top of the incline, the weight of a loaded boat going down being used draw up the empty boat.

As the shallower coal became worked out, the main navigable level was pushed northwards. It had reached Buckley Lane by the end of the century and eventually extended as far as Farnworth and the pits south west of Bolton. Branches were driven eastwards from Walkden to Linnyshaw and westwards from a point near the entrance at Worsley in the direction of Chaddock Pit.

A series of deep navigable levels was introduced before the end of the century and these were extended and developed up to the 1840s as many of the earlier pits were sunk to greater depths. These deeper levels were self contained and served to transport coal locally to the pit bottom, where it was wound up to the main navigable level, or to the surface for local sale.

1803 to 1850: the Trustees and the first tramroads

The Duke of Bridgewater died on 8th March 1803. Under the terms of his will, the Worsley estate, the collieries and the canals, together with the Cheshire estates and the Brackley estate in Northamptonshire, were placed in trust for the benefit of his nephew George Granville Leveson-Gower, Marquis of Stafford and later first Duke of Sutherland. He was to receive the revenue from the estate during his life time and, on his death, it would pass to his second son, Francis, on condition that he changed his name to Egerton, the Bridgewater family name. The trust was to last until twenty years after the deaths of all of the peers of the realm living in 1803 and their eldest sons. It eventually came to an end in 1903 [5].

Management of the estates rested in the hands of three trustees, one of whom was to be Resident Superintendent, enjoying virtually dictatorial powers. The post was first filled by Robert Haldane Bradshaw, who has been criticised for having a conservative outlook but who was hampered by the arrangements under the Duke's will, which left inadequate finance for maintenance and development. Bradshaw retired in 1833, when James Southern took over. Southern left in 1837, to be succeeded by James Loch. Following Loch's death in 1855, Lord Ellesmere's youngest son, the Hon Algernon Egerton, was appointed.

The subsequent colliery developments have been described by Glen Atkinson [3]. To the west of the previous workings, the Chaddock and Queen Anne Pits were sunk around 1820. They were provided with a separate navigable level which joined the Leigh Branch of the Bridgewater Canal near Booothstown Bridge. They were also served by westward extensions of the Wood Pit and Inglis Pit deep levels, the latter eventually being continued to pits at Henfold, north of Astley [3].

The series of small pits alongside the Manchester Road at Wardley also date from this period. They were not connected to the underground canal system and remained as landsale pits until redeveloped many years later.

The scale of the mining operations at this time can be judged by an estimate that no less than 300 shallow shafts had been sunk, although many were short-lived [6]. By 1836 coal output had risen to 283,700 tons per annum compared with 165,000 tons in 1830 [3] and the navigable levels were being worked to near full capacity. It was during this period that the first surface tramroad was constructed to transport coal from Burgess Land Pits, which were sunk north of Ellenbrook in the 1830s, to the Bridgewater Canal near Boothstown.

Atkinson's suggestion that a tramroad had been built as early as 1764 to link pits at Abbot's Fold with the canal at Boothstown seems to be incorrect. The canal terminated at Keepers Lodge, on Worsley Moss, well short of Boothstown, until the branch to Leigh was opened in 1799 [7]. That the canal did not extend beyond Keepers Lodge at an earlier date is confirmed by Deposited Plans [8,9], prepared in 1793 and 1794, neither of which show a tramroad in the neighbourhood of Abbots Fold.

Work started on the Boothsbank tramroad in 1833 and was completed by 1835 [3], the date being confirmed by the fact that it is shown on the Deposited Plans, dated November 1834, for a proposed railway from Agecroft to Liverpool [10]. It was about a mile in length and was reputed to have been to a gauge of 4ft [3]. Horses provided the motive power.

We have been unable to confirm Atkinson's statement that the line was extended to Tynesbank Pit. Evidence, for example from the 2" drawings and from the first edition of the 6" map, points to the contrary.

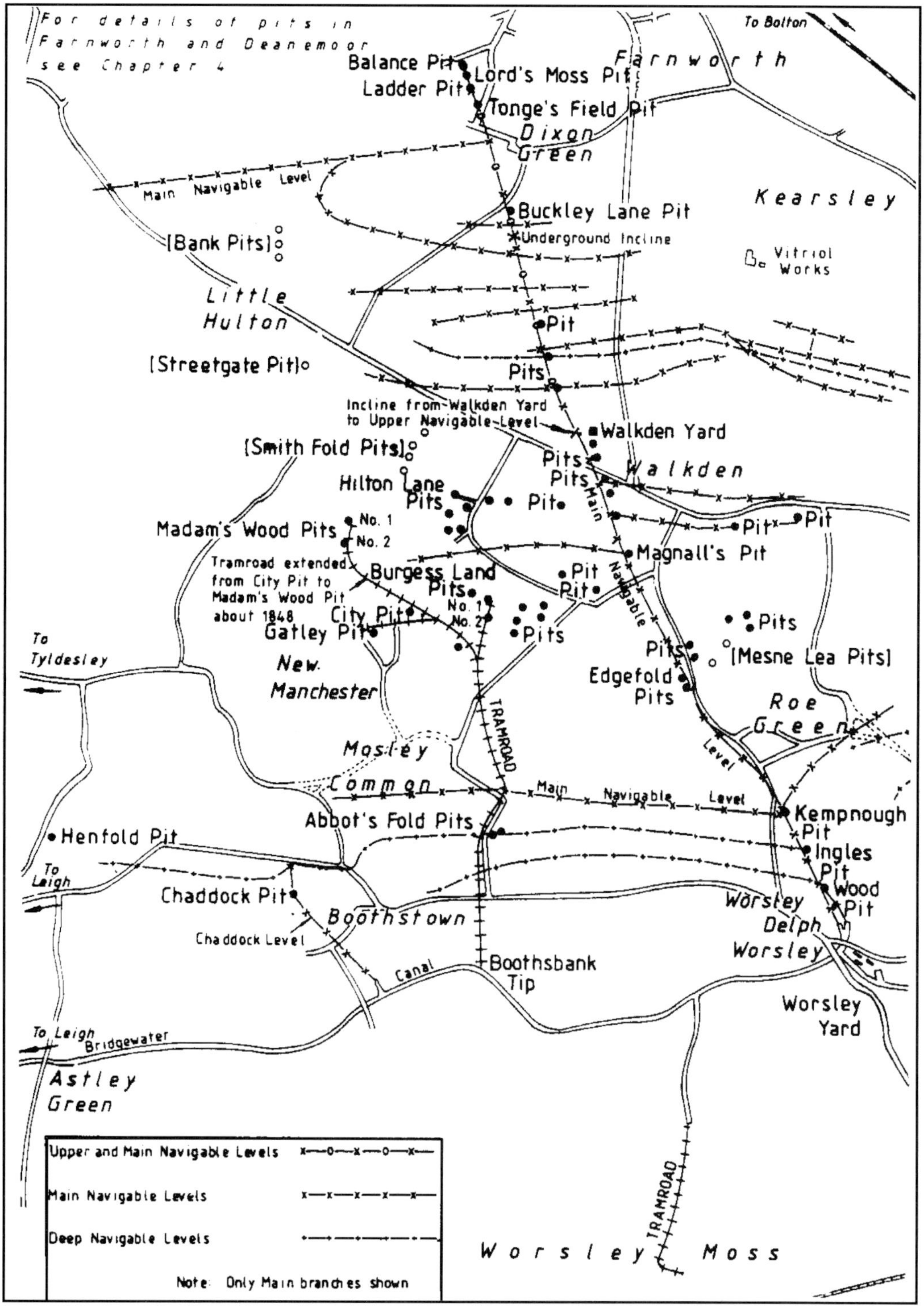
For details of pits in Farnworth and Deanemoor see Chapter 4
To Bolton
Farnworth
Balance Pit
Lord's Moss Pit
Ladder Pit
Tonge's Field Pit
Dixon Green
Main Navigable Level
Kearsley
Buckley Lane Pit
Underground Incline
[Bank Pits]
Vitriol Works
Little Hulton
Pit
[Streetgate Pit]
Pits
Incline from Walkden Yard to Upper Navigable Level
Walkden Yard
[Smith Fold Pits]
Pits
Pits
Walkden
Hilton Lane Pits
Pit
Pit
Pit
Madam's Wood Pits
No. 1
No. 2
Magnall's Pit
Tramroad extended from City Pit to Madam's Wood Pit about 1848
Burgess Land Pits
No. 1
No. 2
Pit
Pit
Main Navigable Level
City Pit
Gatley Pit
Pits
Pits
Pits
[Mesne Lea Pits]
To Tyldesley
New Manchester
Edgefold Pits
TRAMROAD
Roe Green
Mosley Common
Main Navigable Level
Abbot's Fold Pits
Kempnough Pit
Henfold Pit
Ingles Pit
To Leigh
Chaddock Pit
Wood Pit
Worsley Delph
Boothstown
Chaddock Level
Worsley
Canal
Boothsbank Tip
Worsley Yard
To Leigh
Bridgewater
Astley Green
Upper and Main Navigable Levels
Main Navigable Levels
Deep Navigable Levels
Note: Only Main branches shown
TRAMROAD
Worsley Moss

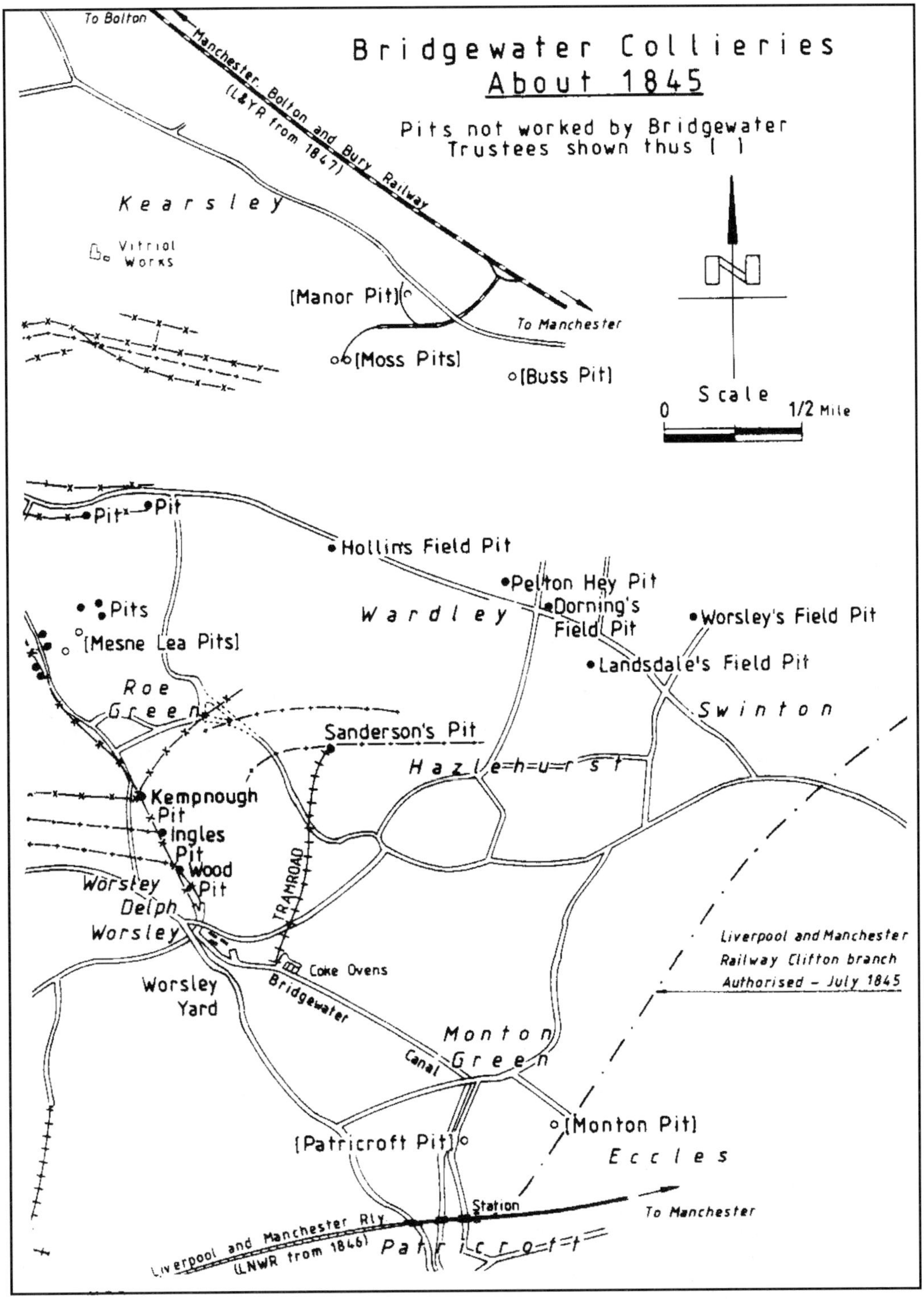
Bridgewater Collieries
About 1845
Pits not worked by Bridgewater Trustees shown thus [ ]
To Bolton
Manchester, Bolton and Bury Railway
(L&YR from 1847)
Kearsley
Vitriol Works
[Manor Pit]
[Moss Pits]
[Buss Pit]
To Manchester
Scale
0
1/2 Mile
Pit
Pit
Hollins Field Pit
Pelton Hey Pit
Dorning's Field Pit
Wardley
Worsley's Field Pit
Landsdale's Field Pit
Pits
[Mesne Lea Pits]
Roe Green
Swinton
Sanderson's Pit
Hazlehurst
Kempnough Pit
Ingles Pit
Wood Pit
Worsley Delph
Worsley
TRAMROAD
Coke Ovens
Worsley Yard
Bridgewater Canal
Liverpool and Manchester Railway Clifton branch Authorised – July 1845
Monton Green
[Monton Pit]
[Patricroft Pit]
Eccles
Station
To Manchester
Liverpool and Manchester Rly
(LNWR from 1846)
Patricroft

The City and Gatley Pits were developed in the 1840s and, although they were connected to the navigable levels, a branch tramroad was built from Mather's Fold. This line was extended to Madam's Wood, where sinking of two shafts was started in 1847. The colliery came into full production in 1848 [3] and the tramroad extension cannot be of an earlier date, as it is not shown on the Tyldesley Tithe Map of 1847 [11]. The final addition to the tramroad was made in the 1860s when a branch was constructed from the Madam's Wood line to serve the new Ellenbrook Colliery. Sinking of No 1 shaft started in 1864 and of No 2 shaft in 1865. The colliery was in full production by September 1867 [3] and with this extra traffic the tramroad must have been working at near capacity. There were four loops, or pass-byes, on the section south of Ellenbrook Church and a signal was installed in 1862 to control the movement of trains at the level crossing at Newearth Road [12].

On the eastern side of the Trustees' territory, a second tramroad was built to link the newly opened Sanderson's Pit, at Roe Green, with the Bridgewater canal near Worsley Yard. Construction is said to have started in 1835 [3] and cannot have been any earlier as the line is not shown on the Deposited Plans of November 1834, referred to above [10]. Sanderson's No 2 Pit was sunk in the late 1840s [3]. Although the colliery was connected to the deep navigable levels, it appears that most of the coal was raised up the shafts.

Like that to the canal at Boothsbank, the tramroad was stated to have been 4ft gauge and horse worked. Atkinson and other writers have reproduced a drawing showing a horse riding the incline towards the canal in a dandy cart, but we have been unable to verify whether or not this system was actually used on either tramroad.

Atkinson refers to third and much shorter tramroad which he says was planned much later. Delph Pit at Over Hulton was sunk in 1848 in order to supply coals to the Bolton market. Proposals were made for a line from Delph to Watergate Pit at this time, but were apparently dropped.

By 1853, when returns were prepared for the newly formed Government Inspectorate of Mines [13], the Trustees had 25 working pits or drifts. There were a further 37 old pits, all stated to be fenced off. The total work force at the pits was around 1100 men and boys, although this figure does not appear to have included those employed at Worsley and Walkden Yards, at the coke ovens and on the tramroads and the canal. 274,380 tons of coal had been raised in the previous year, little changed from the 1836 total. Indeed output remained virtually steady between 1835 and 1855 [3] and it was only after the the new deep pits had been sunk in the late 1850s and 1860s that production showed a marked increase. Two schedules were drawn up for the Mines Inspectorate which differ in some details. From these it can be seen that the Trustees had twelve high pressure engines, either for pumping or winding, along with a seven condensing beam engines. Two atmospheric engines were still in use, at Watergate and Burgess Land, and a horse gin at Howarth's Field. The Dixon Green Cannel Pit and the Lime Stone Pit had water balance engines.

Along the main line of the navigable level Edge Fold Nos 1 and 2 Pits, Mangnall's Nos 1 and 2 Pits and the Causeway Side, Barracks and Buckley Lane Pits were all at work, together with the Cannel Pit and the Lords Moss Field and Tonge's Field Pits at Dixon Green. Ashton's Field Pit was still under development.

In the Dean Moor area there were the Watergate, Sappling Field, Fray's Horse Field, Eckersley's Field and Delph Pits. West of the main navigable level there were the Burgess Land, Gatley and Madam's Wood pits. To the east there were two pits at Sanderson's and Cinder Field, Hollin's Field and the two Coppice Field Pits at Wardley.

Coke ovens were located at Dixon Green, Walkden and Worsley. Those at Dixon Green and Walkden had been extended during the period 1834 to 1836 [13].

Comparison of the 1853 lists with those prepared in 1842 and 1845 [13] recording the condition of the pumping and winding engines, shows that several pits had closed down in the intervening period. These included the two Chaddock Pits, Dorning's Field, Lansdale's Field, Copy Field, Hilton Lane, Mather's Field, Atkinscroft and Burton's Garden.

The Trustees First Standard Gauge Railway

Around 1850 the Bridgewater Trustees began to consider the possibility of connecting their collieries with the main line railway system. A number of different schemes were drawn up which are documented in surviving material at the Lancashire Record Office and at the Salford City Archives Office.

The promotion of the Manchester and Southport Railway seems to have been a major factor influencing them. The main line, authorised in 1847 [14], was intended to run through New Manchester, Edge Fold, Roe Green and Hazlehurst, passing a little to the north of Sanderson's Pit [15,16].

The Trustee's tramroad to Boothsbank would have been crossed in the vicinity of Mather's Fold and plans were drawn up to build several standard gauge connecting lines [17]. Between Boothsbank and a point north of Abbot's Farm the tramroad was to be relaid and beyond here a new line was to be built through Mather's Ford to terminate on the north side of the Manchester to Chorley road at Tynesbank. There was to be spur to the Manchester and Southport Railway at Mather's Fold and a branch serving the Gatley and Madam's Wood Pits was also included.

The Manchester and Southport Act of 1847 also authorised the Wardley Branch. Starting from a junction facing Manchester, a spur ran in a south westerly direction to connect with the Sanderson's Pit tramroad, where, after a reversal, the branch continued northwards to terminate beyond the Manchester to Chorley road [15,16].

Alterations to the Wardley Branch were considered by the railway company soon after it obtained its Act. In November 1847 [18], it was proposed to alter the junction with the main line at Roe Green and to build spurs to the Coppice Field, Cinder Field and Hollin's Field Pits. The Branch was to be extended to Fletcher's Manor Pit, near where there was to be a junction with the Lancashire and Yorkshire's Clifton Branch. There was also to have been a triangular junction, near Harrison Blair's vitriol works, with the Lancashire and Yorkshire's Clifton Branch Extension which had been authorised earlier in 1847 [19]. In 1848 various alternative connections with the Clifton Branch were contemplated and there were to be alterations in the route of the lines to the Coppice Field, Cinder Field and Hollin's Field Pits, by now known as Wardley Nos 1 to 4 Pits [20,21].

Unfortunately for the Bridgewater Trustees, the Manchester and Southport failed to raise sufficient capital to build any of its lines east of Hindley. Before this became apparent, the Trustees had already committed themselves to the reconstruction of their tramroad from Sanderson's pit to Worsley.

A contract was let on 4th January 1851 to James Jennings of Frodsham for the conversion of the tramroad from Sanderson's Pit to Worsley to a standard gauge single track railway suitable for wagons loaded with 5 tons of coal [13]. The line in the vicinity of Worsley appears to have been relevelled as part of this work. Replacement of the crossing over the Worsley to Swinton road by a bridge seems to date from this period, as does the provision of a cable worked incline down to the canal through the grounds of Drywood Hall, now Bridgewater School. The stationary engine which lowered the loaded wagons to the coal tip and drew back the empties is believed to have been installed about 1850 [6].

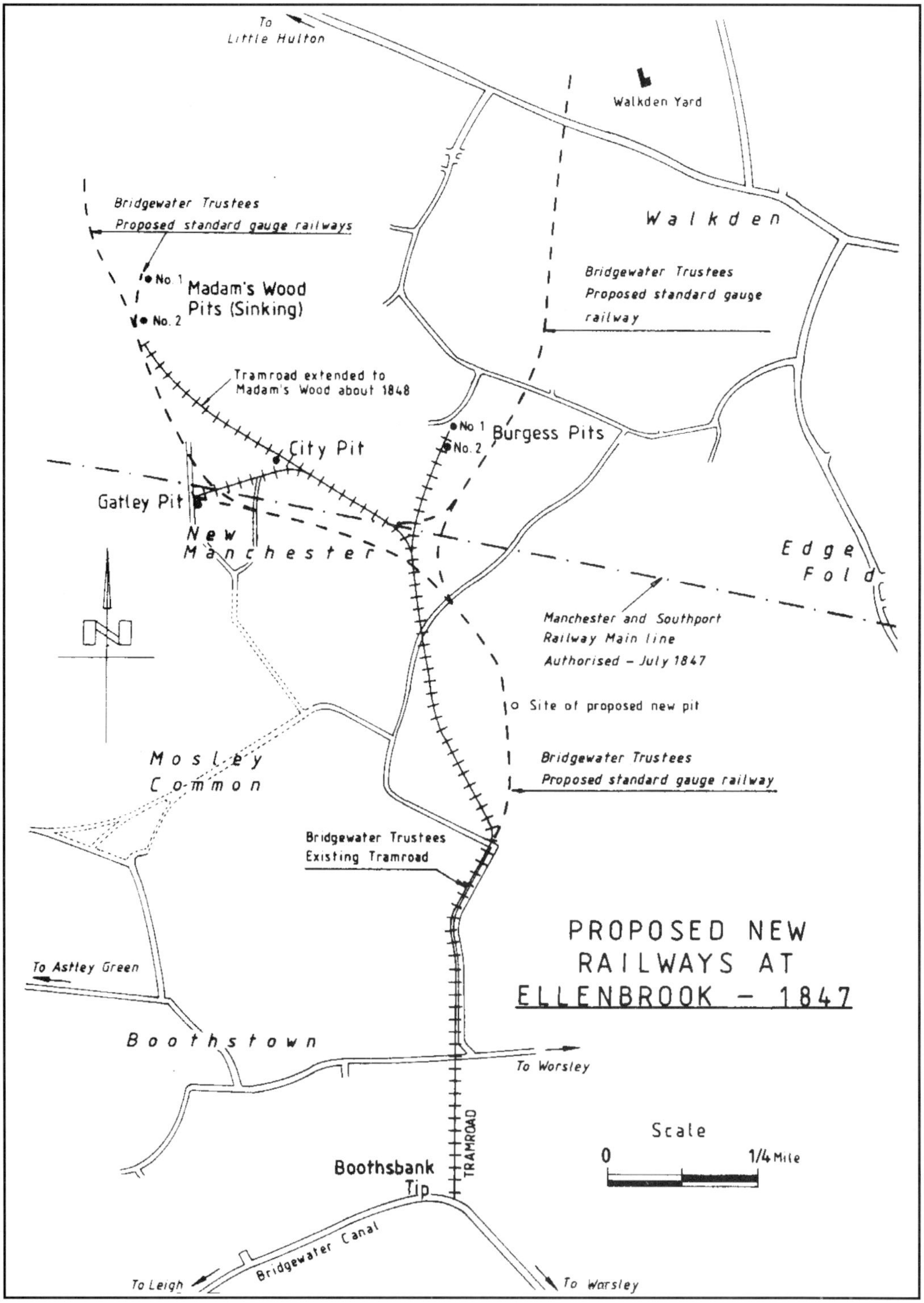
To Little Hulton
Walkden Yard
Walkden
Bridgewater Trustees Proposed standard gauge railways
No. 1
No. 2
Madam's Wood Pits (Sinking)
Bridgewater Trustees Proposed standard gauge railway
Tramroad extended to Madam's Wood about 1848
No 1
No. 2
Burgess Pits
City Pit
Gatley Pit
New Manchester
Edge Fold
Manchester and Southport Railway Main line Authorised – July 1847
Site of proposed new pit
Bridgewater Trustees Proposed standard gauge railway
Mosley Common
Bridgewater Trustees Existing Tramroad
PROPOSED NEW RAILWAYS AT ELLENBROOK – 1847
To Astley Green
Boothstown
To Worsley
TRAMROAD
Scale
0
1/4 Mile
Boothsbank Tip
Bridgewater Canal
To Leigh
To Worsley

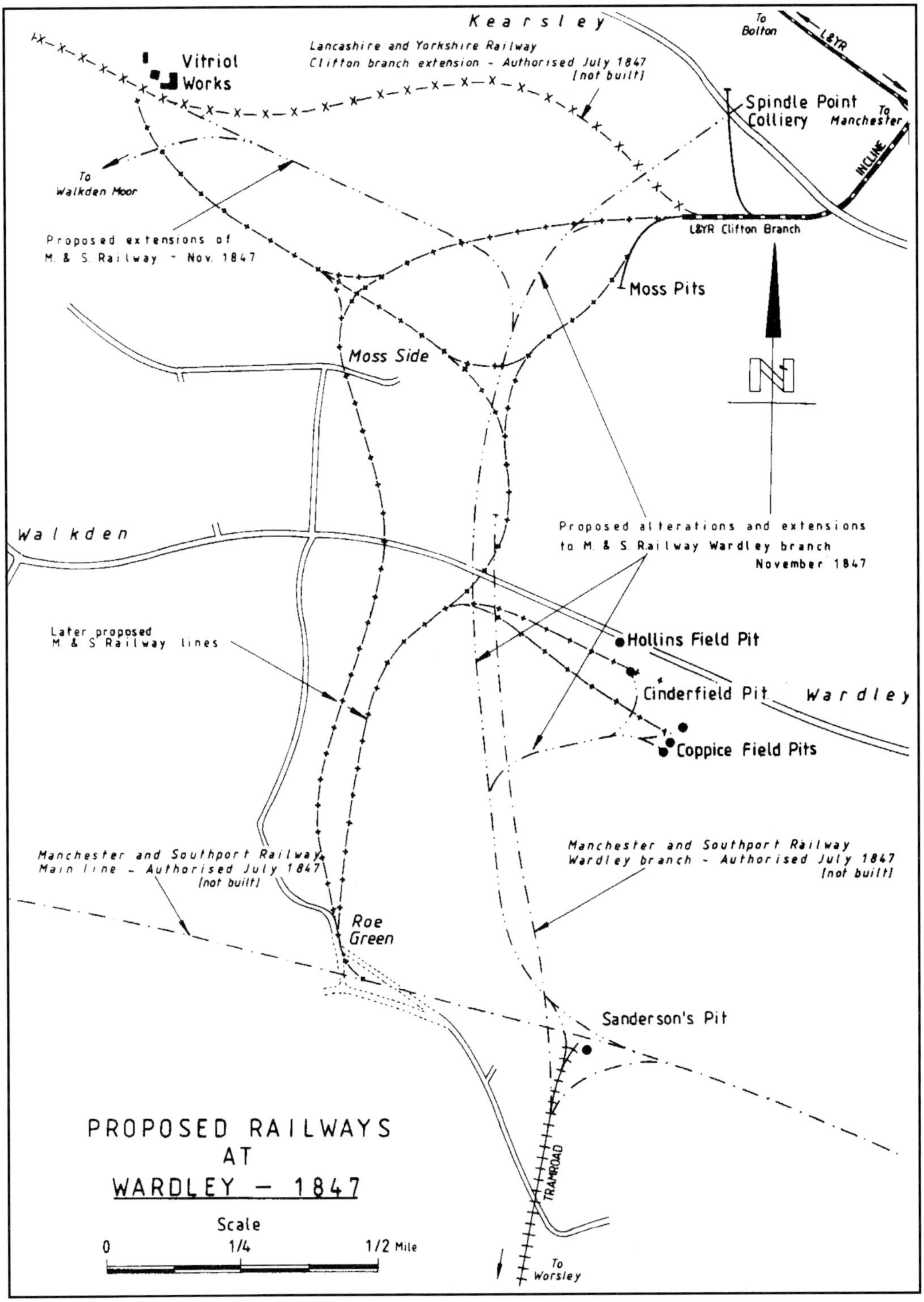
Kearsley
To Bolton
L&YR
To Manchester
INCLINE
Lancashire and Yorkshire Railway
Clifton branch extension - Authorised July 1847
(not built)
Vitriol Works
Spindle Point Colliery
To Walkden Moor
Proposed extensions of
M. & S. Railway - Nov. 1847
L&YR Clifton Branch
Moss Pits
Moss Side
N
Walkden
Proposed alterations and extensions
to M. & S. Railway Wardley branch
November 1847
Hollins Field Pit
Later proposed
M. & S. Railway lines
Cinderfield Pit
Wardley
Coppice Field Pits
Manchester and Southport Railway
Main line - Authorised July 1847
(not built)
Manchester and Southport Railway
Wardley branch - Authorised July 1847
(not built)
Roe Green
Sanderson's Pit
TRAMROAD
PROPOSED RAILWAYS
AT
WARDLEY - 1847
Scale
0
1/4
1/2 Mile
To Worsley

An extension of the standard gauge line northwards to the Wardley Pits, previously not served by rail, was undertaken shortly afterwards. A number of alternative alignments were surveyed in 1850 [22,23], a route east of Wardley Hall finally being chosen. A cross section, dated March 1851 [24], infers that the line was then either complete or under construction. Another, dated 6th April 1852 [25], shows it as "existing railway"

A proposal, for which estimates were drawn up on 4th April 1850 [13], was to carry carts on flat wagons on the reconstructed Wardley Railway. However, this does not seem to have been implemented. The idea had been to convey the cart bodies, loaded with coal, to the canal at Worsley, where they would be transferred by crane on to barges. At Manchester, they would be taken from the barges by another crane and lowered on to their wheels, ready to be hauled to their destination by horses.

More Railway Proposals in the 1850s

In 1850, surveys [26] were made for three alternative routes for a line from the Wardley Railway to join the LNWR's Worsley Branch. One left the Trustees' line near the top of the incline leading to the canal at Worsley. The other two took a more direct course from Sanderson's Colliery. The Worsley Branch had been included in the Liverpool and Manchester Railway's proposals for its Patricroft and Clifton line in 1845 [27] and the subsequent Act [28] permitted its sale to either the Bridgewater Trustees or the Earl of Ellesmere.

The Patricroft and Clifton line was opened by the London and North Western Railway, successor to the Liverpool and Manchester, on 2nd February 1850 [29], but no construction took place on the Worsley Branch, apart from a short length near the junction at Monton.

With the Worsley Branch unlikely to be completed, the Trustees turned their attention to a connection with the Patricroft and Clifton line. For the most part the plans have been lost and only the cross sections [24], dated March 1851, have survived, but from these it is possible to deduce the route which it was intended to follow.

The proposed line started at Ashton's Field, where it was intended to sink new pits to the Trencherbone Seam, and ran across Linnyshaw Moss to join the Wardley Railway near Coppice Field. South of Coppice Field the proposed line left the Wardley Railway and ran through Moorside to join the LNWR south of Pendlebury Tunnel. There was a branch from a point north of the Manchester to Chorley road to Linnyshaw Colliery, where sinking was about to start. Various alternative routes were surveyed [30] and costed [13], some involving a level crossing over the main road and others an underbridge, .

There is some evidence that a westward extension from Ashton's Field may have been planned, possibly to link up with the Dean Moor Mines, or perhaps the Delph Pit, which had been sunk in 1848 [3]. There are no plans or estimates, but there was an agreement dated 24th June 1851 [31] under which the Trustees were permitted to build a line across land belonging to Francis Charlton to the north west of Rothwell's Farm at Little Hulton.

Nothing was done and in 1852 the Trustees sought advice from Edward Woods of Liverpool. In his report of 21st April 1852 to James Loch [32] he put forward four options - to connect only with the canal, to connect with the L&YR and the canal, to connect with the LNWR and the canal, to connect with the L&YR, the LNWR and the canal. Production at the Coppice Field pits was estimated to be 150 tons per week, at the the Linnyshaw Pits 500 tons and at the Buckley Lane and Ashton's Field Pits 500 tons. This was sufficient to fill around 40 5-ton wagons per day.

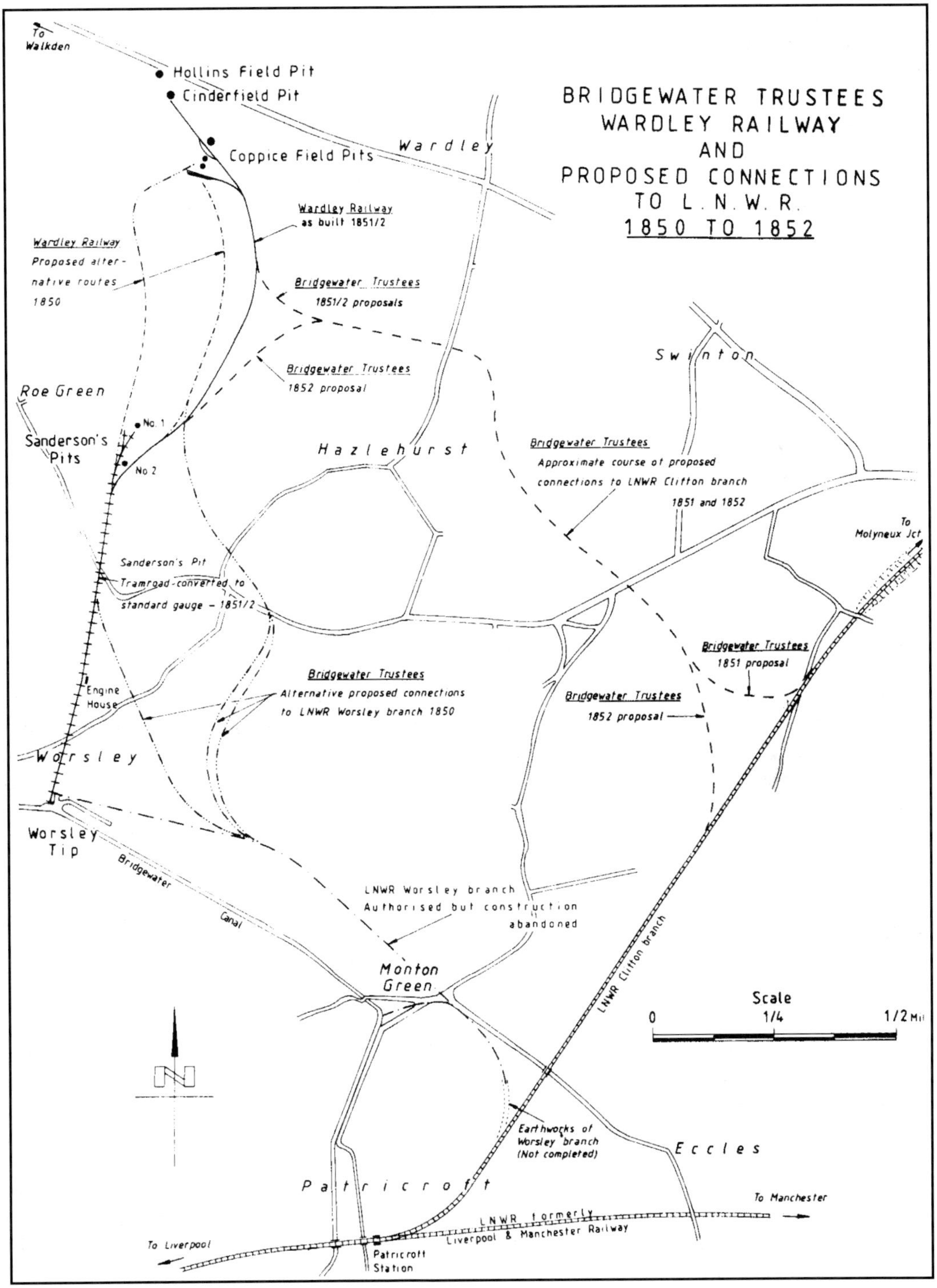
BRIDGEWATER TRUSTEES
WARDLEY RAILWAY
AND
PROPOSED CONNECTIONS
TO L.N.W.R.
1850 TO 1852
To Walkden
Hollins Field Pit
Cinderfield Pit
Coppice Field Pits
Wardley
Wardley Railway as built 1851/2
Wardley Railway Proposed alternative routes 1850
Bridgewater Trustees 1851/2 proposals
Bridgewater Trustees 1852 proposal
Swinton
Roe Green
No. 1
Sanderson's Pits
No 2
Hazlehurst
Bridgewater Trustees Approximate course of proposed connections to LNWR Clifton branch 1851 and 1852
To Molyneux Jct
Sanderson's Pit Tramroad-converted to standard gauge – 1851/2
Bridgewater Trustees 1851 proposal
Engine House
Bridgewater Trustees Alternative proposed connections to LNWR Worsley branch 1850
Bridgewater Trustees 1852 proposal
Worsley
Worsley Tip
Bridgewater Canal
LNWR Worsley branch Authorised but construction abandoned
LNWR Clifton branch
Monton Green
Scale
0
1/4
1/2 Mi
Earthworks of Worsley branch (Not completed)
Eccles
Patricroft
To Manchester
LNWR formerly Liverpool & Manchester Railway
To Liverpool
Patricroft Station

His recommended line from Ashton's Field to the LNWR Patricroft and Clifton Branch took a course very similar to that of the 1851 scheme. Again no plans exist, but sections dated 6th April 1852 [25] apparently to refer to this line.

It started at Ashton's Field and ran past Linnyshaw Colliery to join the Wardley Railway at Coppice Pits. There were alternative routes across the Bolton to Worsley Turnpike and there was a branch to Buckley Lane Pit. South of Coppice Field, there was a triangular junction with the Wardley Railway and the proposed line then followed much the same course as the 1851 scheme, but with a junction with the Clifton Branch facing towards Patricroft. There is an estimate, dated 13th March 1852, of the cost of construction of this line, stated to be suitable for locomotive working [13].

The lines to the Lancashire and Yorkshire proposed by Woods in 1852 were intended to connect with one of the many schemes put forward by the railway company to serve the district south of Farnworth. In 1849 [33] the L&YR had been authorised to build the Clifton and Wardley Branches. The Clifton Branch was essentially an extension of the earlier branch of the same name, completed to the Moss Pits in 1840 [18]. It replaced the Clifton Branch extension authorised in 1847, on which no work had been carried out. The Wardley Branch turned south from a triangular junction with the Clifton Branch to form an end on junction with the Manchester and Southport's Wardley Branch [18] for which powers had been obtained under that company's 1847 Act.

No plans or sections have been identified with these proposals. However, from Woods' report, we know that he recommended two lines. One, from Ashton's Field, descended in a straight line on a 1 in 120 gradient across the Bolton and Worsley Turnpike to join the L&YR, presumably near the vitriol works. The second, from Linnyshaw Colliery descended a 1 in 60 gradient to join the L & YR, presumably on that company's Wardley Branch.

Woods went on to recommend that if the connections were built to the LNWR and the L&Y, the railway companies should be approached with a view to working the traffic from the pits to the main line. If the Trustees only opted to build the portion of their line to the canal, or if they failed to persuade the main line companies to work as far as the collieries, they could either use locomotives or horses.

With one exception, the gradient was downhill for the loaded wagons. Only traffic from Wardley bound for the L&Y had to go uphill on a 1 in 50 gradient. If horses were to be used on the rest of the system, a stationary engine would be needed here. He recommended laying all the lines with 63 lbs per yard bridge rail on longitudinal sleepers so that the horse path could be made easily. At the same time the proposed lines were to be constructed so that they were suitable for locomotives.

The Lancashire and Yorkshire Railway failed to build its Clifton and Wardley Branches. A later proposal was put forward by the Manchester and Southport Railway in 1853. East of Tyldesley the revised route was to pass through the centre of Walkden and then across the moss and down the valley of the Unity Brook to join the Manchester and Bolton line at Clifton. The Wardley Branch was now to leave the main line on the moss, pass to the east of Linnyshaw Colliery and terminate near the Manchester and Chorley road [34]. As mentioned earlier, the whole of the project fell through.

With a connection on the moss no longer a possibility, the Trustees turned their attention to a junction with the Lancashire and Yorkshire's Manchester to Bolton line to the north of Moses Gate. The surviving plans [13], dated June and July 1853, only show the course of the line southwards as far as Dixon Green, but it seems likely that it was intended to continue as far as Buckley Lane or Ashton's Field Pits.

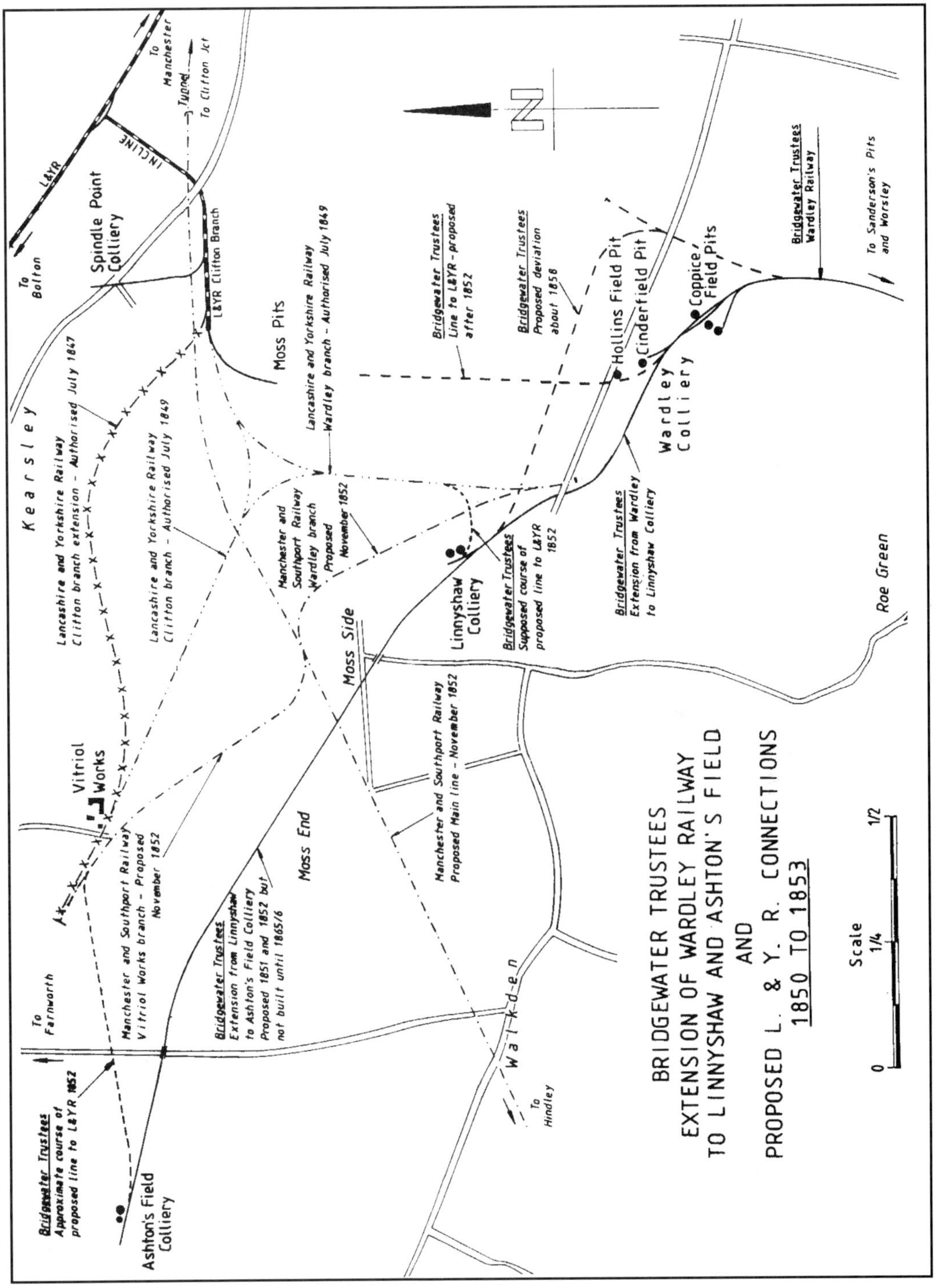
BRIDGEWATER TRUSTEES
EXTENSION OF WARDLEY RAILWAY
TO LINNYSHAW AND ASHTON'S FIELD
AND
PROPOSED L. & Y. R. CONNECTIONS
1850 TO 1853
Scale
0
1/4
1/2
To Bolton
L&YR
INCLINE
To Manchester
Tunnel
To Clifton Jct
Spindle Point Colliery
L&YR Clifton Branch
Moss Pits
Kearsley
Lancashire and Yorkshire Railway Clifton branch extension - Authorised July 1847
Lancashire and Yorkshire Railway Clifton branch - Authorised July 1849
Lancashire and Yorkshire Railway Wardley branch - Authorised July 1849
Manchester and Southport Railway Wardley branch Proposed November 1852
Bridgewater Trustees Line to L&YR - proposed after 1852
Bridgewater Trustees Proposed deviation about 1858
Hollins Field Pit
Cinderfield Pit
Coppice Field Pits
Bridgewater Trustees Wardley Railway
To Sanderson's Pits and Worsley
Wardley Colliery
Bridgewater Trustees Extension from Wardley to Linnyshaw Colliery
Bridgewater Trustees Supposed course of proposed line to L&YR 1852
Linnyshaw Colliery
Roe Green
Moss Side
Vitriol Works
Manchester and Southport Railway Vitriol Works branch - Proposed November 1852
Moss End
Manchester and Southport Railway Proposed Main line - November 1852
Bridgewater Trustees Extension from Linnyshaw to Ashton's Field Colliery Proposed 1851 and 1852 but not built until 1865/6
To Farnworth
Walkden
To Hindley
Bridgewater Trustees Approximate course of proposed line to L&YR 1852
Ashton's Field Colliery

There is also an undated plan [35] which shows a proposed extension of the Wardley Railway northwards from Cinder Field Pit across the main road in the direction of the Moss Pits, on the completed portion of the Clifton Branch. Presumably this was drawn up when it became clear that the various Lancashire and Yorkshire and Manchester and Southport Railway lines to Wardley and the vitriol works were unlikely to be built.

For reasons which are not now apparent none of these connections with the main line railways was ever built. The Bridgewater Trustees were left with an isolated standard gauge line running from Wardley Colliery, past Sanderson's Pits, to the canal at Worsley. The railway was later extended to Linnyshaw Colliery [13,30,36,37] and this involved alterations to the original line in the vicinity of the Wardley Pits [13,37,38]. Sinking at Linnyshaw started about 1850 or 1851, although the pits did not come into production until some years later [3]. The extension appears to have been completed before 1858, as plans [38,39], believed to have been prepared in that year, were drawn up but not implemented for a new route north of the Manchester to Chorley road.

The lack of a main line outlet was clearly embarrassing when coke had to be despatched by rail to the London and North Western Railway and other customers. The Trustees were granted permission, in the winter of 1854-5, to use James Nasmyth and Company's private siding at Patricroft [12], the coke presumably coming by barge from Worsley.

1865 to 1875 : Completion of the first phase of theTrustees' railway system

In 1861, the Lancashire and Yorkshire Railway submitted a Bill to Parliament for a line pasing through Walkden which closely followed the route proposed by the Manchester and Southport eight years earlier. A Wardley Branch was included, leaving the main line on Linnyshaw Moss and terminating at Linnyshaw Colliery [40].

Parliamentary approval was not forthcoming but, in the same year, the London and North Western's Eccles, Tyldesley and Wigan line was authorised [41]. This crossed under the Trustees' Wardley Railway near Roe Green and over their tramroad to Boothsbank near Ellenbrook. It was opened for traffic on 1st September 1864 [29] and provided the first main line outlet for the Bridgewater collieries. A junction was made with the Wardley Railway at Sanderson's Siding, under an agreement dated 21st February 1861 [42]. The connection was probably built to coincide with the opening of the LNWR line; it had certainly been completed by 1868 [43].

The Eccles, Tyldesley and Wigan Railway was followed by other LNWR lines which penetrated the districts in which the Trustees' collieries were situated. The Little Hulton Branch was authorised from Roe Green Junction on the Eccles, Tyldesley and Wigan line to just north of the Manchester and Chorley road in 1865 [44]. It was opened for goods traffic on 1st July 1870 [29]. It had originally been intended to continue the line to a point near the site of the later Brackley Colliery and there was to have been a branch from the crossing over Clegg's Lane to Ashton's Field [45]. The Little Hulton Extension Railway, continuing the Little Hulton Branch to Bolton, and the Little Hulton Mineral Railway were authorised in 1869 [46] and opened for goods traffic on 16th November 1874 [29].

By now the Bridgewater Trustees were committed to a policy of extending their own railway system to serve their deep collieries, where the workings were well below the level of the underground canal. The advantages of distribution of coal by rail as well as by canal were now becoming clear. Production had risen from 279,000 tons per year in 1855 to 371,400 tons by 1860, more than the navigable levels, supplemented by the horse worked Wardley Railway and the tramroad to Boothsbank, could reasonably transport.

A massive programme of new colliery developments was in hand. The pits at Ashton's Field and Linnyshaw had already come into production by the late 1850s. Work was now under way at four further sites. At Mosley Common the winding engines, supplied by E J Timmins of the Bridgewater Foundry, Runcorn, were commissioned at the end of 1862 to assist with the development [47]. Sinking started at Ellenbrook Colliery in 1864 and at Bridgewater and Ellesmere Collieries in 1865 [3]. All were in operation by the early 1870s and their technical features were described in an article in the Mining Journal [48]. There were other improvements as well. Plans were agreed in 1869 for a new head office at Walkden. New offices had already been completed at the New Dock, Runcorn, and at Prince's Dock, Liverpool, to look after the steadily growing trade in shipment coal [49].

It is of interest to note that the last two collieries to be developed at this period broke with the long tradition where the name of the pit reflected its location. Bridgewater and Ellesmere were family estates in Somerset and Shropshire, while the later Brackley Colliery took is name from an estate in Northamptonshire. Bridgewater, Ellesmere and Brackley soon became very much part of the scene in the Walkden and Worsley districts, with not only collieries and locomotives being so named, but streets and public houses as well.

The new railway system was planned in the form of an inverted "V". The eastern arm was to run from Ashton's Field past Linnyshaw Colliery and Bridgewater Colliery to the canal at Worsley, utilising part of the existing standard gauge Wardley Railway and the connection with the LNWR at Sanderson's Siding. The western arm was to be built from Ashton's Field past Ellesmere Colliery and the new sinkings at Mosley Common to the canal basin at Boothsbank. A connection with the London and North Western Railway at Ellenbrook was to be provided under an agreement of 21st February 1861, negotiated before the Eccles, Tyldesley and Wigan Act was passed [50]. Later agreements of 21st April 1871 and 13th May 1875 covered the connection with the Little Hulton Branch at Walkden [51].

Most of the constructional work was undertaken by John Claridge of Swinton, to whom the Trustees let contracts between 1865 and 1873. Material preserved in the Lancashire Record Office [13] includes many of Claridge's tenders and time sheets, as well as estimates of expenditure prepared by Bridgewater Trustees' officials. Although the records are not complete, it is possible to build up a reasonably comprehensive picture of the development of the railway system.

The eastern arm of the railway system was taken in hand initially. The first agreement between the Trustees and Claridge was dated 20th February 1865 and covered the section from Linnyshaw Colliery to the Ashton's Field and Buckley Lane Pits. The route followed that of the earlier projects of the 1850s and entailed the provision of an embankment across the Trustees' Black Leach reservoir. A letter accompanying the agreement recommended that this should be sufficiently wide that a double line of rails could be laid at any future time. The agreement specified that the the Trustees would provide wagons, rails, sleepers, barrows, tressels (sic) and wheeling planks and this arrangement appears to have applied in all the later contracts.

Surviving records show that William Barningham of the Pendleton Ironworks supplied chairs, fishplates, crossings and switches, while the rails came from the Bolton Iron and Steel Company and Thomas Walmsley and Son of the Atlas Forge, Bolton. James Bland and Company of Canada Dock, Liverpool, supplied sleepers, which were placed on board the Trustees' flats at the dock. There is no evidence that Claridge used locomotives; as with his later contracts, his time sheets all refer to the number of men and horses employed.

Correspondence between the Bridgewater Trustees and Harrison Blair and Company during the period from August 1863 to February 1864 [32] suggests that some thought had been given to providing a branch across Linnyshaw Moss to serve the vitriol works. However, nothing came of the idea.

The opening of the new Bridgewater Colliery, where coal was first won in 1871 [6], led to significant alterations to the eastern arm of the Trustees' railway system. Tenders submitted by Claridge on 16th February 1871 and 26th December 1872 cover work on a new line which took a direct route from a point north of the Manchester and Chorley road to rejoin the original Wardley Railway near Sanderson's No 2 Pit. The work seems to have been completed during 1873.

The greater part of the original alignment between Sanderson's Colliery and Linnyshaw Colliery was subsequently abandoned. A spur was constructed from a point on the new line north of the Manchester and Chorley road to Linnyshaw Colliery. A second spur, which left the new line just north of Bridgewater Colliery, provided access to Wardley Colliery until its closure about 1881 [52]. A third spur also seems to have been planned, as there is an estimate dated 21st October 1872 for a railway, 1300 yards in length, going north of Linnyshaw to a proposed new sinking at Morton Moss. Evidently the scheme for a pit here was not pursued and this part of the railway was never built.

At Worsley, estimates were prepared on 6th December 1872 for a branch into Worsley Yard from the line to the canal tip. The cable operated incline down to the canal was reconstructed, presumably to make it suitable for working by locomotives. Claridge's time-sheets of 14th October and 27th October 1873 refer to work at the Gig Brow, including pulling out the old incline.

On the western arm of the railway system some work had also been carried out in the 1860s. Presumably as part of the negotiations about land to be taken for the Little Hulton Branch, agreements were signed on 29th March 1865 and 19th July 1866 by representatives of the LNWR and by Mr Fereday Smith on behalf of the Trustees [53]. These required the LNWR to construct the earthworks of what is called the Barracks Tramway.

The Trustees were to supply 320,000 cubic yards of spoil and the work had to be completed by 1st September 1868. The agreement seems to have covered the section of line from the neighbourhood of the Ellesmere Pits to Mosley Common and included the earthworks for the two spurs, to the Eccles, Tyldesley and Wigan line at Ellenbrook and to the Little Hulton Branch at Walkden. Between the bridge over the Little Hulton Branch and the Eccles, Tyldesley and Wigan line, the formation had to be wide enough for double track.

According to Atkinson [3], the Trustees' railway from the Ellesmere Pits to the exchange sidings at Ellenbrook was opened in October 1871, when it was inspected by officials. The colliery had come into production the previous year and coal had been despatched by boat along the navigable level.

There may also have been some temporary arrangements to transport coal from Mosley Common Colliery to the canal at Boothsbank. An LNWR Line Plan of 1868 [43], as well as marking the 1835 tramroad on its original alignment, shows a single line of rails on the new formation where it ran under the main line at Ellenbrook. The earthworks of the spur to the exchange sidings are finished, but no track is shown. Ellenbrook Colliery, where full production had started in September 1867 [3], was served by a short spur from the tramroad which ran to the Gatley and Madam's Wood Pits.

Construction of the link between the eastern and western arms of the railway system was taken in hand in 1871. This was followed by conversion to standard gauge of the tramroad serving the Gatley and Ellenbrook pits, the completion of the spur to the LNWR at Walkden and laying permanent track in the vicinity of the Ellesmere and Mosley Common pits.

The railway northwards from Ellesmere Colliery to Ashton's Field was built in two parts. An estimate drawn up on 7th March 1871, based on Claridge's tenders of 16th February and 4th March 1871, covered excavations on a 34 chain section from a point near the bridge over the Little Hulton Branch, south of the Ellesmere Pits, to a point near Pipe Hall. There was also to be an 8 chain branch into the old Walkden Yard and the main road at Walkden was to be crossed on the level. Work started in March 1871 [54]. It is not known whether a bridge under the road was substituted for the level crossing when the line was built or whether this was a later development.

Claridge submitted a tender for the continuation from Pipe Hall to Ashton's Field on 23rd July 1872 and the contract was let on 1st August. Construction proceeded during the rest of 1872, throughout 1873 and into early 1874. An account submitted by Claridge at the end of 1872 relates to work on the branch from Ashton's Field to Buckley Lane Colliery. The last account for work on the Ellesmere railway was dated 4th March 1874.

The contract for ballasting and laying rails from Ellesmere Colliery to Hilton Lane and to the connection with the LNWR's Little Hulton branch was let on 1st August 1872, based on Claridge's tender of 23rd July. Work continued until early 1873.

Between June and September 1873 Claridge carried out work at Mosley Common and on the Mosley Common Railway. This seems to have involved laying new sidings at the colliery and improvement of the line to the canal at Boothsbank. There is mention of excavation and ballasting at Boothsbank and from the junction with the old line at Mosley Common to the canal, laying the permanent way and pulling out the old road.

The new line to Boothsbank replaced the 1835 tramroad, which was abandoned except for the portion from Mather's Fold to the Gatley and Ellenbrook Pits, which was converted to standard gauge. Tenders were submitted by Claridge on 29th August 1873 covering excavating, ballasting, laying the new track and and pulling out the old road on these sections. The work seems to have been completed by the end of the year.

The Burgess Land and Madam's Wood Pits were on the point of closure and the tramroad branches were never altered to standard gauge. Accounts sent in by Claridge 11th and 20th November 1873 relate respectively to pulling up the road on the Burgess Branch and to levelling the ground at the site of the Madam's Wood Pits.

There had been some discussion about building a direct line to the Ellenbrook Pits, leaving the old line 740 yards from the canal and then running over Mosley Common and past the Gatley Pit. A comparison of the distances and gradients with those of the old line is contained in an undated document [13]. It seems that the advantages did not justify the cost and the scheme did not proceed. However, an underbridge was provided when the Eccles, Tyldesley and Wigan was built and this was later used by a new road to New Manchester.

The first locomotives

As described earlier, horse traction had been employed on the two narrow gauge tramroads. This had continued after the conversion of the Wardley Railway to standard gauge in the 1850s. The haulage work was evidently contracted out, for in April 1869 a horse belonging to John Partington, a contractor for the conveyance of coal from the colliery to Worsley basin, was killed by runaway wagons at Coppice Field [55].

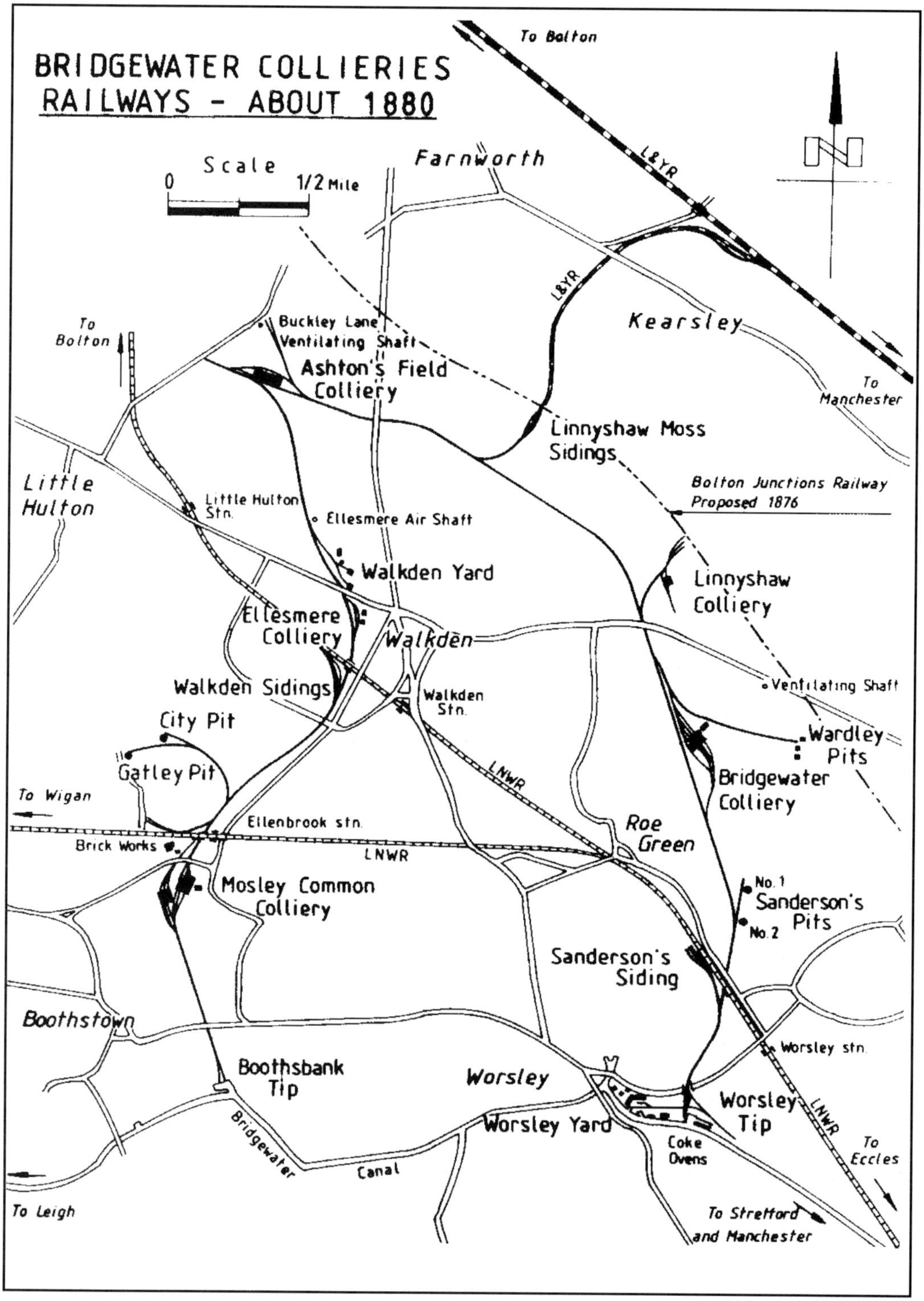
BRIDGEWATER COLLIERIES
RAILWAYS - ABOUT 1880
Scale
0
1/2 Mile
To Bolton
L&YR
Farnworth
Kearsley
To Manchester
To Bolton
Buckley Lane Ventilating Shaft
Ashton's Field Colliery
Linnyshaw Moss Sidings
Little Hulton
Little Hulton Stn.
Ellesmere Air Shaft
Bolton Junctions Railway Proposed 1876
Walkden Yard
Linnyshaw Colliery
Ellesmere Colliery
Walkden
Walkden Sidings
Walkden Stn.
Ventilating Shaft
City Pit
Wardley Pits
Gatley Pit
LNWR
Bridgewater Colliery
To Wigan
Ellenbrook stn.
Roe Green
Brick Works
LNWR
Mosley Common Colliery
No. 1
Sanderson's Pits
No. 2
Sanderson's Siding
Boothstown
Worsley stn.
Boothsbank Tip
Worsley
Worsley Tip
Worsley Yard
Coke Ovens
Bridgewater
Canal
To Eccles
To Leigh
To Stretford and Manchester

Locomotives did not make their appearance until 1870, after the Trustees had decided on a major expansion of their railway network. The *"Eccles Advertiser"* of 14th May reported the arrival of the first. We have been unable to trace any other information about this engine, which we think may have been hired.

The same paper on 17th September reported the arrival of a second locomotive and said that it was hauled by a team of horses to Sandhole Colliery, where a new shed, capable of holding two engines, had been built. From the records of Manning, Wardle and Company of Leeds we can identify this as FRANCIS, a small six coupled K class saddle tank with 12"x19" cylinders. It was undergoing steam trials at the maker's works on 8th June 1870.

In 1871, the Trustees purchased a somewhat larger six coupled saddle tank from the same makers. This was of the firm's class O design with 15"x22" cylinders. It was named STANLEY and we think that, like FRANCIS, it was initially used on the eastern arm of the railway system.

Towards the end of 1873 a small locomotive was purchased from Alexander Chaplin and Company of Glasgow [56], apparently for shunting duties at the coke works and the workshops at Worsley. Like all Chaplin's products, the engine had a vertical boiler and vertical cylinders driving the wheels through gears. It seems to have been called TOW, perhaps a nickname only. It was referred to by old employees we interviewed in the 1950s as "th' owd tater roaster", no doubt from its unconventional design. By all accounts it was a difficult engine to work satisfactorily and was said to have been in collision with GOWER on one occasion.

An estimate of extraordinary expenditure for 1873 [13] includes the completion of the Mosley Common Railway, together with a sufficiently powerful locomotive engine and an engine house, at a total cost of £7,000. Provision was made for spending £1000 on new railway wagons in addition to £5,000 allocated in the previous year. The 1873 estimates also include £4000 for fifty "locomotive coal wagons".

A rough note dated 13th June 1873 [13] shows that the Trustees' Engineer was deliberating about the best type of engine for future use. As well as the Manning Wardle designs already in service, he was considering an 18"x24" six coupled engine and 14"x20" four coupled saddle tanks working in pairs.

The decision was made to keep to the larger Manning Wardle design. Two further Class O locomotives were purchased, presumably to work on the western portion of the railway. These were GRAND DUCHESS and ADMIRAL which arrived in 1874 and 1875 respectively.

1875 to 1903 Colliery and railway developments

With the new collieries sunk in the late 1860s coming into operation, many of the older and smaller pits were closed down. Causeway Side is last shown in the Mines Lists in 1864, Barracks in 1881 and Mangnall's in 1885. Buckley Lane and Edge Fold, which ceased production in 1873 and 1883 respectively, were retained for pumping purposes, the latter until 1968.

South of Walkden, the Burgess Land and Madam's Wood Pits closed in 1871, followed by Gatley Pit in 1881 and the short lived Ellenbrook Pits in 1885. At Wardley, the Coppice Field Pits had all closed by 1881, followed by Hollin's Field in 1885.

At Farnworth Howarth's Field closed in 1872, followed by Tonge's Field in 1880 and Lord's Moss and the Machine Pit, both in 1883. The Machine Pit and Tonge's Field Pit continued in use for pumping until 1908 and 1909 respectively.

An early photograph of GRAND DUCHESS, one of the larger Manning, Wardle locomotives, purchased in 1874.
Alex Appleton collection

The vertical boiler locomotive supplied by Alexander Chaplin and Company of Glasgow in 1873. Nicknamed TOW, it was used for shunting at Worsley Yard.
Alex Appleton collection

In the Dean Moor area, Sapling Field closed in 1879, Delph in 1881 and Watergate, after several periods of idleness, finally ceased working in 1885.

In 1878, the Trustees started work at their Brackley Colliery, near Little Hulton and in 1879 took over the nearby Wharton and Wharton Hall Collieries.

There were also developments at Mosley Common at this period, where sinking of the Nos 4 and 5 pits started in 1881 [57]. The canal basin at Boothsbank was enlarged, probably at this time, and a second tippler installed. The first edition of the 25" map, surveyed in 1891, shows that a tubway was constructed, parallel to the railway, from the pit head to the basin. By 1904, when the second edition of the map was surveyed, the tubway had been removed and extra railway sidings provided at the basin.

By 1886 more than 1,300,000 tons of coal were being raised and output remained at around that level until the end of the century, only falling below 1,000,000 tons in 1893, 1896 and 1897 [3].

The amount transported on the underground canal system had fallen off considerably, ceasing completely in 1887. Much of the output was taken by rail to the tips at Worsley and Boothsbank to be loaded on to barges but an increasing amount of coal was now sent away over the main line railways. As well as the three interchange points with the London and North Western Railway, two connections were made with the Lancashire and Yorkshire Railway. Having all these outlets enabled the Trustees to select the least costly routing for their outgoing traffic.

The Lancashire and Yorkshire Railway had finally reached Linnyshaw Moss and Harrison Blair's vitriol works when the Kearsley No 1 Branch was opened on 1st March 1879 [58]. The long awaited outlet to that company's lines was provided by a short spur which the Trustees built from their Ashton's Field to Worsley line to exchange sidings at the end of the branch.

The second junction with the L&YR was put in following the opening of the direct line from Pendleton to Hindley in 1888 [58]. The connection, at Walkden, was covered by agreements dated 17th April 1883 and 28th May 1885 [59].

Meanwhile, the possibility of access to a third main line railway had arisen when the Bolton Junctions Railway Bill was submitted to Parliament in the 1876 Session. The proposed route from the Cheshire Lines Railway in Manchester to an independent terminus in Bolton ran through Moorside and then passed to the east of Linnyshaw Colliery, to the west of Farnworth and to the north of Moses Gate [60]. Although the Bill was rejected, the Trustees had previously reached an agreement with the railway company, on 24th February 1876, which protected their interests [61].

As well as providing for occupation bridges at specified locations and a station where the line was to cross the Manchester to Chorley road at Wardley Lane, provision was made for junctions with the Trustees' railways. One of these was to be where the Bolton Junctions line crossed the short branch which led to the L&YR at Linnyshaw Moss. The other two were at points near to Dixon Green Colliery and near to the LNWR Patricroft to Clifton line, where the Trustees might wish to build a railway in the future. The Trustees were clearly still keeping their options open to build a line to connect with the LNWR Clifton Branch, as the Bolton Junctions company was required to build a double track overbridge, suitable to carry locomotives over the route of the Trustees' proposed line near Red Cat Lane.

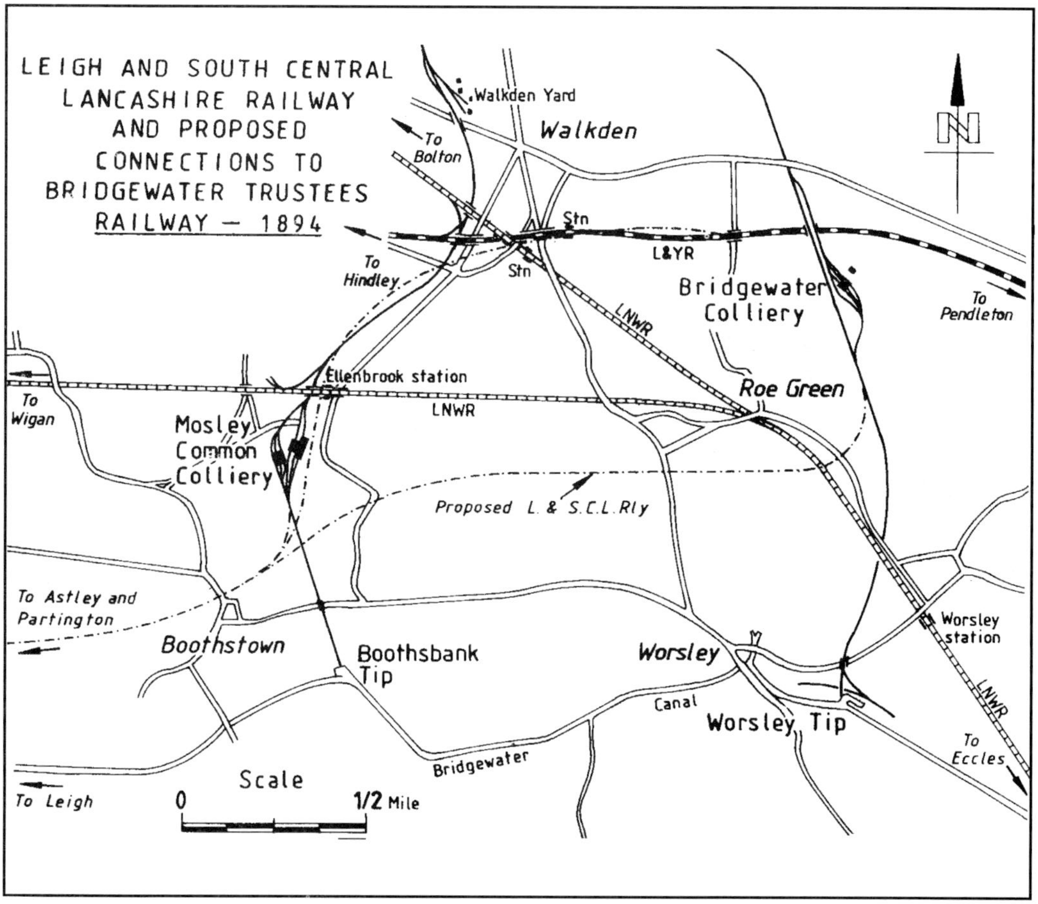

In 1894 proposals were made for a Leigh and South Central Lancashire Railway [62]. The intention was to provide direct access to the facilities which had been installed on the Manchester Ship Canal at Partington North for the export of coal and the supply of bunker fuel. Connections were to have been made with the western arm of the Trustees' system at Mosley Common and with the eastern arm near Roe Green, north of Sanderson's Siding. Had the scheme been completed it would no doubt have had a considerable influence on the traffic patterns on the Trustees' railway. However, the Bill was rejected by Parliament in 1895 and the project was never revived.

The increasing amount of traffic carried by the Trustees' railway system needed more and larger locomotives and five six coupled saddle tanks, with 17"x24" cylinders, were purchased from Sharp, Stewart and Company. The first, SULTAN, was delivered in 1875, followed by ALERT in 1877, ATLAS in 1880, GOWER in 1882 and WARDLEY in 1888. The last was notable in that it was the last locomotive built by the firm in Manchester before it moved its business to Glasgow.

SULTAN, one of the long boiler locomotives supplied by Sharp, Stewart and Company, then based in Manchester, photographed at Walkden near the junction with the branch leading to the L&YR exchange sidings
Cyril Golding collection

The hub of the Bridgewater railway system was at Ashton's Field, where the lines from Worsley and Boothsbank met in a series of dead end sidings. Northbound trains had to face steep gradients on both lines, but particularly coming up from Boothsbank, which overall was about 1 in 50 with stretches at 1 in 30. It seems certain that the working of trains over the steeply graded main line would have been entrusted to the Sharp, Stewart locomotives, with the smaller Manning Wardle engines being employed on shunting duties at the collieries.

The principal locomotive shed was Walkden, near Ellesmere Colliery, and others were provided at Bridgewater Colliery and at Mosley Common. Old employees have told us that in 1900 ADMIRAL and GOWER were based at Mosley Common, with GRAND DUCHESS and WARDLEY at Ellesmere Shed and ALERT and ATLAS at Bridgewater Colliery.

We presume that major overhaul of the locomotives was originally carried out at Worsley Yard, where the Trustees' main workshops had been established. In 1900 [63], a new works was built at Walkden, which included a locomotive repair shop, a machine shop, fitting and blacksmith shops, a wagon repair shop and a sawmill and joiner's shop [3].

The boatyard at Worsley was retained, but the rest of the workshop site was cleared in about 1905 and is now known as "The Green". The base of one of the old chimneys was made into a memorial to the Canal Duke [64].

The original Walkden Yard had been established in the 1770s or 1780s on the north side of the main Manchester Road. Its principal purpose was to maintain the boats used on the upper navigable level although its activities also included repairs to all kinds of colliery equipment. Following the opening of the new workshops, which were located to the south of the main road, on the opposite side of the railway, the earlier buildings were demolished and the site used for a landsale depot.

A view in Worsley Yard, probably around the turn of the century. Note the then modern spring buffer wagons in the current Bridgewater Trustees livery. Lancashire Mining Museum

Boothsbank Basin, photographed in March 1959, when it was still in use. The basin was originally built in the 1830s to serve the horse worked tramroad from the pits south of Walkden. The line to Boothsbank was converted to standard gauge in the 1870s. Alterations were made to the coal tips and the basin on many occasions afterwards.The basin has recently been turned into a marina. Peter Norton

Worsley Tip in 1957, showing a barge being loaded with coal. This was the terminus of the tramroad from Sanderson's Pit, later altered to standard gauge. Harry Townley

The sidings at Worsley, looking from the canal tip, photographed in 1955. Loaded wagons ran by gravity from the higher level on the left, and, after the coal had been discharged, ran down again by gravity to the sidings on the right. Note the unusual pointwork where the loaded and empty wagon lines meet. Harry Townley

Developments at Little Hulton 1875 to 1903

Towards the end of the 1870s, the Bridgewater Trustees turned their attention to the area around Little Hulton. Sinking of their Brackley Colliery started, according to the Mines Lists, in 1878. In 1879, the Trustees purchased the Wharton Estate and, as a result, took over the Wharton Hall Colliery of Potter and Graham and the Wharton Colliery of Francis Charlton. The previous history of both these concerns has been described in Chapter 10.

The Little Hulton operations remained isolated from the main railway system of the Trustees until about 1908. Wharton Hall Colliery and Charlton's Wharton Colliery were already linked to the LNWR Little Hulton Mineral Branch and a new private railway was built by the Trustees from Brackley Colliery to the same line, the connection to the LNWR being provided under an agreement dated 12th October 1880 [65]. A short curve was also laid in between the Trustee's railway to Brackley and the Wharton Hall sidings to enable through running between the two collieries without having to pass over LNWR property.

Following the opening of the Lancashire and Yorkshire Railway's direct line from Pendleton to Hindley in 1888, the Trustees' line was extended from Wharton Hall Colliery to sidings on the new line. These were laid in under agreements dated 17th April 1883 and 28th May 1885, the former negotiated before the L&Y line was authorised by Parliament [66].

Coke production was centralised at Brackley Colliery, where work started in 1898 on the construction of a new plant to replace the earlier coke ovens at Dixon Green, Walkden and Worsley. Originally consisting of 25 Semet Solvay ovens with tar and by-product extraction [67], the works was extended in 1900 [68].

A view of the coke works at Brackley, with the colliery in the distance on the right. Looking north, showing the railway from the LNWR exchange sidings at Little Hulton in the foreground.
Lancashire Mining Museum

Charlton's Wharton Colliery continued to work the cannel seam without any major alteration [3] for an number of years. The Mines Lists show that coal production was discontinued on 11th September 1901, but the pit was subsequently used for pumping.

The two locomotives mentioned in Chapter 10 and which were the property of Potter and Graham were taken over by the Bridgewater Trustees when Wharton Hall Colliery was acquired in 1879. Based at the shed at Wharton Hall, they worked the traffic from Brackley, Wharton Hall and Wharton Collieries until after the turn of the century. No doubt they were supplemented from time to time by engines transferred from the main Bridgewater Collieries railway system.

The Earl of Ellesmere's Collieries 1903 to 1921

In 1903 the conditions laid down in the Duke of Bridgewater's will were met and, on 19th October, all assets were turned over to the Third Earl of Ellesmere as owner and not merely as sole beneficiary. The earl played little part in the administration of his estates and industrial operations and a new trust was created to look after affairs [5].

The post of Resident Superintendent was abolished and Walter Longley Bourke, who had succeeded Algernon Egerton in 1891, retired. Henry Hart Davies was appointed to the virtually equivalent position of Chief Agent. The collieries continued under the direction of Mr Jesse Wallwork, a gentleman who was to exert a considerable influence for many years [3,5].

Plans had already been drawn up to modernise Wharton Hall Colliery [69]. The work was sanctioned at the beginning of 1904 [70,71], when it was reported that No 1 Pit was gradually being worked out. No 2 Pit, which had practically been closed in the Spring of the previous year, was sunk down the Arley seam and a new winding engine and new headgear were to be installed. The work was probably completed in 1905.

Concurrently with these developments, moves were made to join Brackley and Wharton Hall Collieries with the main Bridgewater Collieries railway system. The new line took a rather circuitous route, starting at Ashton's Field and passing under the LNWR's Little Hulton Extension line near Plodder Lane Station. There was also a short spur to a landsale coal yard in Farnworth, on the site of the old Dixon Green Colliery, replacing the existing yard at Plodder Lane.

For part of its length the railway ran through land belonging to the Earl of Bradford and discussions about access started in October 1904 [72]. There were other negotiations about rent for land in 1905 [73] and plans and sections of the line were submitted in July 1907 to the Earl of Bradford's agent by Jesse Wallwork [74].

Construction was undertaken by the Manchester based contractors Etheridge and Clarke [73]. According to old Bridgewater Collieries employees two narrow gauge locomotives were used on the work. One was named FLEETWOOD, which has been identified as the product of the German firm of Orenstein and Koppel.

We have been unable to find the precise date that the new line was opened for traffic. Work seems to have been well advanced, at least on some sections, in August 1907 [75] and we think that the line was probably completed during 1908. Documents at the Salford Archive Office [76] show that the final certificate for the contract covered work carried out in 1907 and 1908, at a cost of a little over £12,300. The final measurement was not agreed until July 1911. There is also a note that rent for land occupied by the Dixon Green Coke Ovens ceased on 25th March 1908 and that the new landsale yard was opened in December on the site [73].

Shortly after the completion of the line to Brackley Colliery, there was a further extension of the railway system, from Linnyshaw Colliery to a landsale coal yard in Moss Lane, Newtown. As well as providing easy access to customers in Pendlebury and Swinton, in competition with the Clifton and Kersley Coal Company, there was probably another reason for building the line.

Consideration was being given to opening a new colliery on the site of Andrew Knowles and Sons' Clifton Moss pits, which had closed in the early 1890s. According to the Mines Lists exploratory work was in progress between 1910 and 1921, but had been abandoned by 1922. As we shall see later, Newtown Colliery was purchased from the Clifton and Kersley Company in 1925 in order to work the deep seams in the north of the Earl of Ellesmere's estate.

The contract for building the Pendlebury line was let to Etheridge and Clarke, although some of the excavation at the coal yard was undertaken by J Rawlinson and Company and by Dean and Gorton Ltd. Construction started on 7th June 1912 and ballasting was under way in March 1913 [76]. The railway was probably completed later that year.

One further scheme which did not come to fruition was for a line from Boothsbank across Barton Moss to a wharf on the Manchester Ship Canal. The proposal was put forward by Jesse Wallwork in 1913, but the first world war caused it to be put into abeyance. In 1918 land on the course of the line was bought from Manchester Corporation Cleansing Department. Foundations were laid for the bridge which would have spanned Liverpool Road near the Ship Canal, but the project was then suddenly dropped [77,78].

The third Earl of Ellesmere died on 13th July 1914 and was succeeded as fourth Earl by his son John [79]. Valuation of all the assets, including those elsewhere in the country, for inheritance tax purposes was to occupy the next seven years. The inventory [80] provides a useful list of the more significant assets in 1914. The collieries were at Ashton's Field, Ellesmere, Linnyshaw, Brackley, Wharton Hall, Bridgewater and Mosley Common. Mosley Common was by far the largest and Bridgewater next [6]. There were pumping pits at Edge Fold, Walkden and Clifton Moss and ventilating shafts at Hollin's Field for Bridgewater Colliery and at Buckley Lane for Ashton's Field. There was a large brickworks at Ellenbrook, opened in 1907 or 1908 to replace the earlier one which had been located at Mosley Common, closed in 1903. Coal output for 1913 was 1,196,288 tons.

There were 1,742 railway wagons in general use and a further 142 for internal use only, details of which can be found in Appendix 6. All the rails on the through route of the main line and at the connections with the LNWR and L&YR had been renewed during the period 1902 to 1914. The coal tip fixtures at Boothsbank had been replaced in 1914 following damage caused by a runaway train.

On the canal there was one steam tug, ELLESMERE, purchased in 1912 and a large number of other craft of various types. The inventory lists 43 lighters, with a capacity of 40 to 58 tons, 2 Liverpool flats capable of carrying 64 tons, 2 "bastard" boats loading between 42 and 45 tons, 23 box boats each taking 10 coal boxes of 2 tons capacity, 56 16-ton "B" boats, 20 10-ton "M" boats and a further five small boats used for maintenance of the underground canal.

There had been a number of changes to the locomotive stock.

GRAHAM, which had been taken over with Wharton Hall Colliery, was sold on 15th October 1907 to Thomas Mitchell and Sons Ltd, the Bolton machinery merchants, for £125. It was resold by Mitchells to George Watkinson and Company of Buckley in February 1908 for £250.

The other engine which had been taken over, WHARTON HALL, was sold to Mitchells on 10th April 1911 for £130 and was subsequently scrapped by them.

The vertical boilered engine, TOW, was taken out of use, possibly after the closure of the coke ovens at Worsley around 1910, and is not shown in the inventory. ADMIRAL, the Manning, Wardle of 1875, likewise does not appear and must have been disposed of before 1914.

Five new engines had been purchased. The first pair, built by Nasmyth, Wilson and Company were six coupled saddle tanks with 17"x24" cylinders. Named MADGE and VIOLET, they were delivered in 1906 and 1908 respectively. A second pair of larger locomotives, with 18"x26" cylinders, came from the same makers in 1910 and 1912 and were named BRACKLEY and ELLESMERE.

In 1914 Manning, Wardle and Company of Leeds supplied a unique eight coupled side tank with inside cylinders 18"x26", named KATHARINE. The specification was said to have been drawn up by a Mr Greenhalgh, an engineer with the Earl of Ellesmere.

After the first world war a further locomotive was acquired, a six coupled side tank which had been built by Kerr, Stuart and Company of Stoke on Trent in 1917. It was of the firm's "Victory" class and had originally been delivered to the war-time Inland Waterways and Docks organisation as their No 12. It had subsequently passed to the Railway Operating Division of the Royal Engineers, where it had been given the number 603. It arrived on the Bridgewater railway system in 1919 and was named FRANCIS [81].

The earlier FRANCIS, built by Manning, Wardle and Company in 1870, was sold in March 1920 to T W Ward Ltd of Sheffield for £200 [80]. Wards replaced the boiler, tanks and other a parts with those from a sister engine they had purchased from the Lewes Portland Cement and Lime Co Ltd. FRANCIS was then hired out to a number of firms before Wards sold it, in June 1926, to Charles Walmesley and Co Ltd, of Bury, for use on a contract at Gravesend [82].

VIOLET, one of a handsome pair of locomotives supplied by Nasmyth, Wilson and Co.
Lancashire Mining Museum

The inventory of 1914 [80] lists locomotive sheds at Bridgewater Colliery, Mosley Common, Ellesmere Colliery, Wharton Hall and Worsley.

Presumably the eight wheeler, KATHARINE, and some of the more powerful of the six coupled engines were stationed at Ellesmere Colliery and Mosley Common for hauling trains over the steep gradients up to Ashton's Field. Lighter duties would include shunting at the collieries, at Boothsbank basin and at the LNWR and L&YR sidings at Ellenbrook and Walkden.

The Bridgewater Colliery engines were responsible for working the traffic over the eastern section of the line from the colliery to Ashton's Field and Worsley, as well as on the branch to Pendlebury coal yard. There was also shunting work at Bridgewater Colliery and its associated washery and at the main line exchange points at Linnyshaw Moss and Sanderson's Sidings.

The line from Ashton's Field to Brackley seems to have been the preserve of the Wharton Hall engines, which also worked to Dixon Green coal yard. Shunting duties included Brackley Colliery and coke works, Wharton Hall Colliery, the LNWR exchange sidings at Little Hulton and the L&YR exchange sidings on the Pendleton to Hindley line. STANLEY, the Manning Wardle of 1871, was working here in 1910. It was involved in a near miss with the District Manager's saloon on 28th November of that year, while running without the single line staff over LNWR tracks at the end of the Little Hulton Mineral Branch [73,83].

The engine shed at Worsley was, we have been told by an old employee, built under one of the arches of the viaduct leading to the coal tip. TOW was presumably kept here until it was broken up. We have been told that after that the Manning, Wardle FRANCIS was stationed here for a time, presumably for shunting at the canal tip and the boatyard.

A feature of railway operations at this time was the workmen's train service. According to information gathered from old employees, an engine left Bridgewater shed at 5.0 am for Pendlebury coal yard, where it picked up a set of coaches which conveyed miners to Bridgewater Colliery and then ran on to Ashton's Field. There was a connecting train which ran from Ashton's Field taking miners to Mosley Common. Corresponding trains ran in the reverse direction at the end of the shift.

Bridgewater Collieries Ltd 1921- 1929

In the years immediately after the first world war, the fourth Earl turned his attention to reducing future liability for inheritance tax, which had already fallen heavily on the estates after the death of the third Earl. There was also concern about recommendations to nationalise the mining industry made by the Royal Commission set up in 1919.

Two private companies were formed. Bridgewater Collieries Ltd, registered on 4th March 1921, took over the collieries and their railway system. Bridgewater Wharves Ltd, registered on 4th August 1921, took over the 26 coal depots located either on the canal or on the main line railways [5]. The coke works at Brackley also became the property of the latter company. The Earl was appointed Governing Director with a salary and revenue from the shares and debentures. He also received a payment of £2,000,000 for the assets which were handed over. Jesse Wallwork became General Manager [5].

In 1922, the Earl of Ellesmere decided to sell all his holdings in the Worsley area. Jesse Wallwork set about the formation of a syndicate to buy the estate and the collieries. In this he secured the assistance of Joseph Ramsden, son of the proprietor of Shakerley Colliery [5]. A number of other neighbouring colliery proprietors also participated, some influenced by the fact that they mined coal under lease from the Earl [5].

One of the workmen's trains in Bridgewater Colliery Company's days. FRANCIS, the Manning, Wardle of 1870 and two four wheeled coaches, presumably second hand from one of the main line companies.
Alex Appleton collection

In January 1923 the Earl accepted an offer of £3,353,000, of which a little over £1 million was in cash and the remainder in debentures. In so doing, he ended the family's direct interest in affairs at Worsley. Bridgewater Estates Ltd, was registered on 24th March 1923 to take over the property, with Bridgewater Collieries Ltd and Bridgewater Wharves Ltd as wholly owned subsidiaries. Jesse Wallwork was appointed managing director of all three companies. Joseph Ramsden became chairman of the Estates Company, with Emanuel Clegg, chairman of Astley and Tyldesley Collieries Ltd, as vice chairman [5].

Demand for coal in 1923 was high and output was about 1½ million tons. Thereafter circumstances both nationally and abroad reduced demand, whilst a series of coal strikes culminating in the general strike of 1926 caused markets overseas to be lost [5].

The Mines List show that Linnyshaw and Ellesmere Collieries ceased working on 31st March 1921. Both were subsequently used for pumping purposes and Linnyshaw Colliery was not dismantled until the financial year ending 31st March 1937 [84]. The reason given for the closure of Ellesmere Colliery was that the workings had extended to the point where it was cheaper to continue them from Mosley Common [85]. Similarly, the Linnyshaw coal was later worked from Bridgewater Colliery.

Ashton's Field Colliery closed on 22nd May 1925, throwing about 800 men out of work [86]. It reopened in 1926 [5], but, according to the Mines Lists, was abandoned in November 1929.

The Mines Lists show that production at Wharton Hall was suspended on 23 December 1927, although the surface buildings were not demolished until 1936 [87]. No 2 Pit remained in use as a pumping station and the headgear was not dismantled until 1964 [6].

On a more positive note, Newtown Colliery was purchased from the Clifton and Kersley Coal Co Ltd in September 1925 and was developed to reach coal which could not be worked satisfactorily from Bridgewater Colliery. Although the line from Linnyshaw to the landsale yard at Pendlebury ran within a quarter of a mile of Newtown Colliery, a connection would have been difficult as it would have involved crossing the main Manchester to Bolton road on the level. Instead, as we have described in Chapter 6, the existing arrangements were retained, coal being taken down an inclined tubway to the Robin Hood screening plant, alongside the Manchester to Bolton line of what was now the London, Midland and Scottish Railway.

As far the railway system was concerned there were few developments during the period that Bridgewater Collieries Ltd was in control.

There was evidently a temporary shortage of locomotives soon after the new company took over and it was necessary to seek help from outside. The Wigan Coal and Iron Company's six coupled saddle tank KIRKLESS was hired in March 1922, while in May and June the six coupled saddle tank SHAKERLEY was hired from W Ramsden and Sons Ltd for twelve weeks [88].

In 1924 a pair of six coupled side tanks, JOSEPH and BRIDGEWATER, were purchased from the Hunslet Engine Company of Leeds. Both were painted olive green, lined with yellow and vermilion. Curiously the manufacturers charged £3060 for the former, but £3160 for the latter [89]. With outside cylinders 18"x24" and Walschaert valve gear, they proved to be good strong locomotives, although in later years they were considered to have wheels a bit too small for the longer hauls on the line. The hard work necessitated them eventually being fitted with stiffeners between the frames [6].

This four wheeled Atkinson Walker locomotive was demonstrated on the Bridgewater Collieries railway in 1928. It is photographed here arriving at Sanderson's Siding on a long train from Nanny Lane.
Alex Appleton Collection

Also in 1924, GRAND DUCHESS, built for the Bridgewater Trustees in 1874 by Manning, Wardle and Company, was sold, presumably for scrap [89].The final locomotive to be purchased was a four coupled saddle tank to work at the Robin Hood Sidings, which served Newtown Colliery. The engine came second hand from George Cohen, Sons and Co Ltd in 1926 for £825 [90]. It had been built in 1918 by Kerr, Stuart and Co Ltd, of Stoke on Trent, for the Government's Inland Waterways and Docks organisation and was one of the firm's "Moss Bay" class with outside cylinders 15"x20". Named KEARSLEY by Bridgewater Collieries Ltd, it is said to have come from a Government Factory at Wednesbury.

In 1928, a locomotive built by Atkinson, Walker and Company of Preston arrived for a few days on trial. The firm had recently developed a novel design of shunting engine, with a vertical boiler and high speed steam engine [91] and were trying to interest potential customers. There is a photograph showing the engine at work at Sanderson's Sidings, but it was evidently not considered suitable as no purchase was made.

The independent life of Bridgewater Collieries Ltd ended in 1929. The first move towards an amalgamation with neighbouring firms came in September 1927, when R A Burrows, of Fletcher, Burrows and Co Ltd convened a meeting to discuss the possibility. As a result of further negotiations, Manchester Collieries Ltd was formed on 4th March 1929 [5] and we continue the history of the collieries and their railway system under their new owners in the next chapter.

LOCOMOTIVE SUMMARY

Bridgewater Collieries

Trustees of the Duke of Bridgewater until 1903
Third Earl of Ellesmere 1903 to 1914
Fourth Earl of Ellesmere 1914 to 1921
Bridgewater Collieries Ltd 1921 to 1929

Locomotive delivered in May 1870. See text and Eccles Advertiser 14-5-1870

FRANCIS	0-6-0STIC	MW	311	1870	12"x17"	

New to Bridgewater Trustees. Class K
Named after Francis Egerton, 1st Earl of Ellesmere
Sold to T W Ward Ltd, 3-1920

STANLEY	0-6-0STIC	MW	366	1871	15"x22"	4'0"

New to Bridgewater Trustees. Class O
Possibly named after Edward Henry Stanley, 15th Earl of Derby
Overhauled at Walkden Yard 1922, new cylinders
To Manchester Collieries Ltd, 3-1929

TOW	0-4-0VBVC	Chap	1643	1873	15 HP	

New to Bridgewater Trustees
Perhaps only a nickname
Scrapped or sold before 7-1914

GRAND DUCHESS	0-6-0STIC	MW	484	1874	15"x22"	4'0"

New to Bridgewater Trustees. Class O
Overhauled at Walkden Yard 1912, new boiler
Sold in 1924, presumably for scrap

ADMIRAL	0-6-0STIC	MW	518	1875	15"x22"	4'0"

New to Bridgewater Trustees. Class O
Named after Francis Egerton, second son of 1st Earl of Ellesmere, who was appointed a Vice Admiral
Scrapped or sold before 7-1914

SULTAN	0-6-0STIC	SS	2490	1875	17"x24"	4'0"

New to Bridgewater Trustees
Overhauled at Walkden Yard 1907, new boiler
Overhauled at Walkden Yard 1921, new boiler
To Manchester Collieries Ltd, 3-1929

ALERT	0-6-0STIC	SS	2714	1877	17"x24"	4'0"

New to Bridgewater Trustees
Overhauled at Walkden Yard 1906, new boiler
Overhauled at Walkden Yard 1923 and 1924, new cylinders and new firebox
To Manchester Collieries Ltd, 3-1929

GRAHAM	0-4-0STIC	WkB	412	c1873	14"	3'6"

Ex Wharton Hall Colliery Co, 1879
Sold to Thos Mitchell and Sons Ltd, Bolton, 10-1907 and resold to George Watkinson and Sons Ltd, Buckley, North Wales, 2-1908

WHARTON HALL	0-6-0STIC	MW	638	1876	14"x20"	3'6"

Ex Wharton Hall Colliery Co, 1879
Sold to Thos Mitchell and Sons Ltd, Bolton, 4-1911 and scrapped by them

ATLAS	0-6-0STIC	SS	2909	1880	17"x24"	4'0"

New to Bridgewater Trustees
Overhauled at Walkden Yard 1912, new boiler
Overhauled by Nasmyth, Wilson and Co Ltd, 1922
Overhauled at Walkden Yard 1924, new cylinders
To Manchester Collieries Ltd, 3-1929

GOWER	0-6-0STIC	SS	3090	1882	17"x24"	4'0"

New to Bridgewater Trustees
Overhauled at Walkden Yard 1907, new boiler
Overhauled at Walkden Yard 1922 and 1923, new cylinders and new firebox
To Manchester Collieries Ltd, 3-1929

WARDLEY	0-6-0STIC	SS	3423	1888	17"x24"	4'0"

New to Bridgewater Trustees
Overhauled at Walkden Yard 1911, new boiler
Overhauled at Walkden Yard 1922, new cylinders
To Manchester Collieries Ltd, 3-1929

MADGE	0-6-0STIC	NW	782	1906	17"x24"	4'1"

New to 3rd Earl of Ellesmere
Probably named after a daughter of John Egerton, Viscount Brackley, later 4th Earl of Elllesmere
Overhauled at Walkden Yard 1923, new cylinders, and 1924, new boiler
To Manchester Collieries Ltd, 3-1929

VIOLET	0-6-0STIC	NW	852	1908	17"x24"	4'1"

New to 3rd Earl of Ellesmere
Probably named after Violet Lambton, wife of John Egerton, Viscount Brackley, later 4th Earl of Elllesmere
Overhauled at Walkden Yard 1923, new boiler
To Manchester Collieries Ltd, 3-1929

BRACKLEY	0-6-0STIC	NW	912	1910	18"x26"	4'3"

New to 3rd Earl of Ellesmere
Overhauled at Walkden Yard 1922, new boiler and 1925, new cylinders
To Manchester Collieries Ltd, 3-1929

ELLESMERE	0-6-0STIC	NW	976	1912	18"x26"	4'3"

New to 3rd Earl of Ellesmere
Overhauled at Walkden Yard, 1922, new firebox, and 1928, new cylinders
To Manchester Collieries Ltd, 3-1929

KATHARINE	0-8-0T IC	MW	1853	1914	18"x26"	4'2"
New to 3rd Earl of Ellesmere Named after Katharine, wife of 3rd Earl of Ellesmere Overhauled at Walkden Yard 1926, new firebox To Manchester Collieries Ltd, 3-1929						
KIRKLESS	0-6-0STIC	NW	442	1892	16"x20"	4'3"
Hired 3-1922 from Wigan Coal and Iron Co Ltd						
SHAKERLEY	0-6-0STIC	HE	736	1901	14"x18"	3'2½"
Hired 5 and 6-1922 from William Ramsden and Sons, Ltd						
FRANCIS	0-6-0T OC	KS	3068	1917	17"x24"	3'11"
Purchased in 1919, by 4th Earl of Ellesmere. Previously ROD 603 Overhauled at Walkden Yard 1923, new copper firebox To Manchester Collieries Ltd, 3-1929						
JOSEPH	0-6-0T OC	HE	1456	1924	18"x24"	3'9"
New to Bridgewater Collieries Ltd To Manchester Collieries Ltd, 3-1929						
BRIDGEWATER	0-6-0T OC	HE	1475	1924	18"x24"	3'9"
New to Bridgewater Collieries Ltd To Manchester Collieries Ltd, 3-1929						
KEARSLEY	0-4-0STOC	KS	3123	1918	15"x20"	3'2"
Purchased by Bridgewater Collieries Ltd from Geo Cohen and Sons Ltd, 25-1-1926, for use at Robin Hood Sidings. See Chapter 6 To Manchester Collieries Ltd, 3-1929						
	4wl VBVC	AtW				
On trial 1928						

References to Chapter 11

1 *"Map of the Manor of Worsley in the County of Lancaster belonging to his Grace the Duke of Bridgewater Surveyed in 1764"* - reproduced in ref 2

2 *"Worsley in the Eighteenth Century"* - Helen Wickham - 1984

3 *"The Canal Duke's Collieries"* - Glen Atkinson - publ Neil Richardson, Swinton, nd

4 *"The Duke of Bridgewater's Underground Canal at Worsley"* - Frank Mullineux - Transactions of Lancashire and Cheshire Antiquarian Society, Vol 71, 1961

5 *"The Bridgewater Heritage* - Christopher Grayling - Bridgewater Estates plc, Manchester, 1983.

6 *"Collieries in the Manchester Coalfields"* Geoff Hayes - De Archaeologische Pers, Eindoven, nd

7 *"The Canals of North West England"* - Charles Hadfield and Gordon Biddle - David and Charles, Newton Abbot, 1970

8 LRO PDC 17

9 LRO PDC 25

10 LRO PDR 236

11 LRO DRM 1/100

12 *"After the Canal Duke"* - F P Mather - Oxford University Press, Oxford, 1970

13 LRO NCBw 19/1

14 10 &11 Vic cap ccxxi; 22nd July 1847

15 LRO PDR 503

16 LRO PDR 539

17 SAO CO 312

18 SAO CO 315

19 10 & 11Vic cap clxiii; 9th July 1847

20 SAO CO 323

21 SAO CO 326

22 SAO CO 313

23 SAO CA 83

24 SAO CO 319

25 SAO CO 320

26 SAO CO 314

27 LRO PDR 390

28 8 & 9 Vic cap cxxiii; 21st July 1845

29 *"Chronology of the Railways of Lancashire and Cheshire"* - M D Greville Railway and Canal Historical Society, 2nd edn, 1981

30 SAO CO 324

31 SAO Bridgewater Archives - Agreement Book No 1, p 94
32 SAO CO 329
33 12 &13 Vic cap l; 13th July 1849
34 LRO PDR 592
35 SAO CO 328
36 SAO CO 316
37 SAO CO 317
38 SAO CO 322
39 SAO CO 327
40 LRO PDR 707
41 24 & 25 Vic cap cxxx; 11th July 1861
42 LNW Sdgs Diag 156, 12-1916
43 Line Plan of Eccles, Tyldesley and Wigan Railway - LNWR Rugby, 1868 - 2 chains to 1 inch - GMRO A19/2/24
44 28 &29 Vic cap cccxxiii; 5th July 1865
45 LRO PDR 799
46 32 & 33 Vic cap cxv; 12th July 1869
47 BC 8-11-1862
48 MJ 21-5-1870
49 BJ 13-2-1869
50 LNWR Sdgs Diag 155, 12-1916
51 LNWR Sdgs Diag 150, 12-1916
52 SAO E3 - Estate Plan dated 1841, but with later additions
53 SAO Bridgewater Archives - Agreement Book No 2, p 675
54 BC11-3-1871
55 BC 17-4-1869
56 LeiRO28 D 69/95
57 BC 23-7-1881
58 *"The Lancashire and Yorkshire Railway"* John Marshall - David and Charles, Newton Abbot, 1961
59 L&YR Sdgs Diag 114,22nd Jan 1897
60 BMB ABPP/15/1
61 SAO Bridgewater Archives - Agreement Book 1, p 531
62 LRO PDR 1491
63 FJ 14-7-1900
64 *"Old Worsley and Little Hulton"* - publ Worsley Urban District Council, 1973
65 LNWR Sdgs Diag 149, 12-1916
66 L&YR Sdgs Diag 115, 22nd Jan 1898
67 FJ 15-10-1898
68 FJ 21-7-1900
69 FJ 18-5-1901
70 BJ 23-1-1904
71 FJ 22-1-1904
72 BMB ZBR/5/65/554
73 Bridgewater Estate Records at Salford University
74 BMB ZBR/5/68/438
75 BMB ZBR/5/68/543
76 SAO CO 62
77 Information provided by Lancashire Mining Museum
78 *"The Railways of the Manchester Ship Canal"* - Don Thorpe - Oxford Publishing Co, 1984
79 *"Burke's Peerage and Baronetage"* - Burke's Publishing Co Ltd, London, 1924
80 LRO NCBw 11/1-6
81 *"Industrial Steam. Kerr Stuart Victory Class 0-6-0T"* - Don Townsley - *"Railway Modeller"*, September 1966
82 Information from T W Ward Ltd records, supplied by Mr Ken Plant
83 *"Another Adventure at Wharton Hall"* - Alex Appleton - *"The Industrial Locomotive"*, No 72, 1994
84 LRO NCMc 4/4
85 FJ 9-3-1923
86 FJ22-5-1925
87 LRO NCMc 4/5
88 LRO NCBw 20/15 89 LRO NCBw 20/1
90 Records formerly held at Walkden Yard
91 *"The Industrial Railways of the Wigan Coalfield - Part Two"* - Townley, Smith and Peden - Runpast Publishing, Cheltenham, 1992

CHAPTER 12

THE BRIDGEWATER COLLIERIES 1929 to 1947

The formation of Manchester Collieries Ltd and developments from 1929 to 1940

With the depressed state of the coal industry after the first world war, legislation was passed by Parliament, under the Mining Industries Act of 1925 [1], to encourage the amalgamation of existing firms. The larger companies thus created would be better able to survive the current economic conditions and would be sufficiently well capitalised to undertake modernisation and improvement of the most productive pits.

As long ago as 1923 there had been preliminary discussions about a merger between Bridgewater Collieries Ltd, the Astley and Tyldesley Collieries Co Ltd and the Clifton and Kersley Coal Co Ltd. These had fallen through, partly because the Clifton and Kersley company did not find the proposals attractive financially [2].

The next attempt in 1927, led by Robert Burrows of the firm of Fletcher, Burrows and Co Ltd, was more successful [3]. By July 1928, for example, the Board of the Clifton and Kersley Coal Company recommended the amalgamation to their shareholders [4]. By October it was announced that all the firms concerned had agreed to the merger [5].

Manchester Collieries Ltd was registered on 4th March 1929 [3], with Joseph Ramsden, a director of William Ramsden and Sons Ltd as chairman. R A Burrows and Henry Speakman were Deputy Chairmen and Jesse Wallwork a member of the board [6]. The new company brought together nearly all the major coal producers in the area west of Manchester, taking over the assets of :

Astley and Tyldesley Collieries Co Ltd
Clifton and Kersley Coal Co Ltd and its subsidiaries, Collieries (Clifton and Kearsley) Ltd, Outwood Collieries Ltd and Pilkington Colliery Co Ltd
Fletcher, Burrows and Co Ltd
Andrew Knowles and Sons Ltd
John Speakman and Sons Ltd

Bridgewater Collieries Ltd and Bridgewater Wharves Ltd retained their separate identities until 1934, although Manchester Collieries Ltd had a controlling interest and for all practical purposes the two companies were part of the new organisation [3].

Initially, the collieries were divided into three Groups, although there were changes later. The Central Group comprised those formerly owned by Bridgewater Collieries Ltd and the railway system based on Walkden became known as the Central Group Railways, often abbreviated to Central Railways in National Coal Board times.

Bridgewater Estates Ltd continued as a separate company. Although its affairs do not concern us directly, there was a close working relationship with Manchester Collieries Ltd, facilitated by Ramsden being chairman of the estates company from 1923 to 1946, succeeded by Wallwork from 1946 to 1951 [3]. Until 1st July 1942, when the Government acquired the mineral rights under the Coal Act of 1938 [7], Manchester Collieries Ltd paid royalties to the Estates Company on coal mined on the land previously owned by the Earl of Ellesmere.

The Estates Company was in existence until 1984. It was then bought by Peel Holdings Ltd, but retained its separate identity until 1987. By 1992 Peel Holdings Ltd had become Peel Investments (North) Ltd [8].

The principal firms that did not join the merger were William Ramsden and Sons Ltd, the Tyldesley Coal Co Ltd, Peel Collieries Ltd, the Ladyshore Coal Co (1930) Ltd and Thomas Brocklehurst and Co Ltd at Deane, near Bolton.

Of these, the Shakerley Colliery at Tyldesley, owned by William Ramsden and Sons Ltd, was taken over as from 31st March 1935 [9]. We have already dealt with the history of the firm in Chapter 10 and, as mentioned there, the last remaining pits had been closed by October 1938.

Another acquisition in 1935 was Bradford Colliery, in east Manchester, which was purchased from the Bradford Colliery Co Ltd, a subsidiary of Fine Cotton Spinners Ltd. This colliery had a long history, going back to 1740, when mineral rights had been granted by Sir Oswald Mosley of Ancoats Hall to John Seddon for 200 years [10]. In the 1840s it had been worked by Clegg and Livesey [11] and by Thomas Livesey subsequently. The Bradford Colliery Co Ltd took over in 1899 and undertook a programme of development. Sinking of Deep Pit to tap domestic coal commenced in 1903, reaching coal in 1906 [10].

The railway connection to the nearby Beswick Branch of the Lancashire and Yorkshire Railway was put in around this time. Previously most of the coal had been sold locally, much of it to the local ironworks. Some had also gone away by boat, the colliery being served by a branch from the Ashton Canal. The site was very cramped, surrounded by factories and domestic property property and vertical winders had been installed to save space. Much of the shale from the pit supplied a brickworks on the site capable of producing 5,000,000 engineering bricks per annum [10].

During the depression years of the 1930s output from the Manchester Collieries pits was strictly regulated under the Lancashire and Cheshire (Coal Mines) Scheme of 1931. In July 1935, Lancashire Associated Collieries Ltd was formed to market all the coal produced in Lancashire and Cheshire and, amongst its other functions, took over the running of the landsale yards and sales offices previously operated by Manchester Collieries Ltd.

At least two collieries which were on the point of closure were bought out at this period. There was no intention of reopening them, but the production quotas which they were allocated could be added to the amount which it was permissible to mine at pits operated by Manchester Collieries Ltd. The West Leigh Colliery Co Ltd was purchased on 30th July 1937 for £4,670, the vendors being allowed retain the loose plant, including such items as the boilers and railways. They were also permitted to use the railways up to 30th June 1938 for dismantling purposes [12]. The Coppull Coal Co Ltd was purchased on 30th June 1939 [12]. The history of both these concerns appears in *"Industrial Railways of the Wigan Coalfield, Part Two"* [13].

Plans had already been made to close some of the less profitable operations before the merger took place. Ashton's Field Colliery finally closed in November 1929, the workings being taken over by Brackley Colliery.

It was announced that Brackley Coke Works was to close on 31st December 1929, but there was a delay until 31st March of the following year [14]. This followed objections from the local council, which had to make alternative arrangements for gas supplies from Salford Corporation, at a higher price. The coke works was sold for demolition during the year ending 31st March 1932 [9].

To offset these closures, developments were undertaken elsewhere. New screens at Mosley Common No 4 Pit were put to work in November 1932 [15,16]. There were extensions to Sandhole No 3 Pit [17], Sandhole being the name given locally to Bridgewater Colliery and adopted officially in Manchester Collieries days. Work started in 1934 on replacing old wooden headgear at Sandhole No 2 Pit with reinforced concrete headgear [18]. A new washery was commissioned at Astley Green in 1931 [15,17] and during the summer of 1932 the washery at Sandhole was reconstructed [19].

The Ellenbrook Brick Works, owned by Bridgewater Estates Ltd, but rail connected to the colliery system, was extended during 1932 and 1933 [3]. Wartime conditions forced its closure in 1941, although it reopened after hostilities ceased.

Railways and locomotives 1929 to 1936

On the railway side, an important addition to the network was made when a new line was opened for traffic, probably in 1931, connecting Astley Green Colliery with the Bridgewater system at Boothsbank. It has been said that the scheme envisaged a continuation beyond Astley Green to connect with the former Astley and Tyldesley Collieries Ltd's railway south of Tyldesley, but that the proposed East Lancashire Road (A 580) caused the plan to be abandoned. It would have been necessary to cross the new road by an expensive bridge with steep approach gradients.

A report for the year ending 31st March 1932 [9] said that over 200,000 tons of coal had passed over the line from Astley Green, giving savings by reducing the use of the LMSR sidings at Astley Moss. Observations by one of the authors in the late 1930s indicated that most of the traffic over the line was taking coal north rather than the reverse. The locomotives based at Astley Green shed worked the trains as far as Boothsbank, where engines from Ellesmere shed took over.

The line was formally opened on 30th May 1932, when a party of directors and other officials made a tour of inspection to Walkden Yard, Mosley Common and Astley Green [20]. Joe Cunliffe, formerly Workshop Superintendent at Walkden, told us more about the celebrations. Some wagons were thoroughly cleaned out, lined with white material and fitted with seats. Screw couplings were borrowed from the LMS Railway Company, to replace the three link couplings normally used. The locomotive MADGE, recently turned out from the repair shops, was specially cleaned for the occasion and hauled the train from Walkden to the exchange sidings at Astley and back, breaking a tape over new line.

In 1934 the line from the connection with the former London and North Western Railway at Little Hulton to Wharton Hall Colliery was taken out of use. The pits here had ceased production in December 1927, but, as the locomotives used at Brackley Colliery were kept there, the railway had remained in use for light engine movements. A small amount of coal was also worked over the line to the pumping engines and the emergency winding engine at Wharton Hall No 2 Pit.

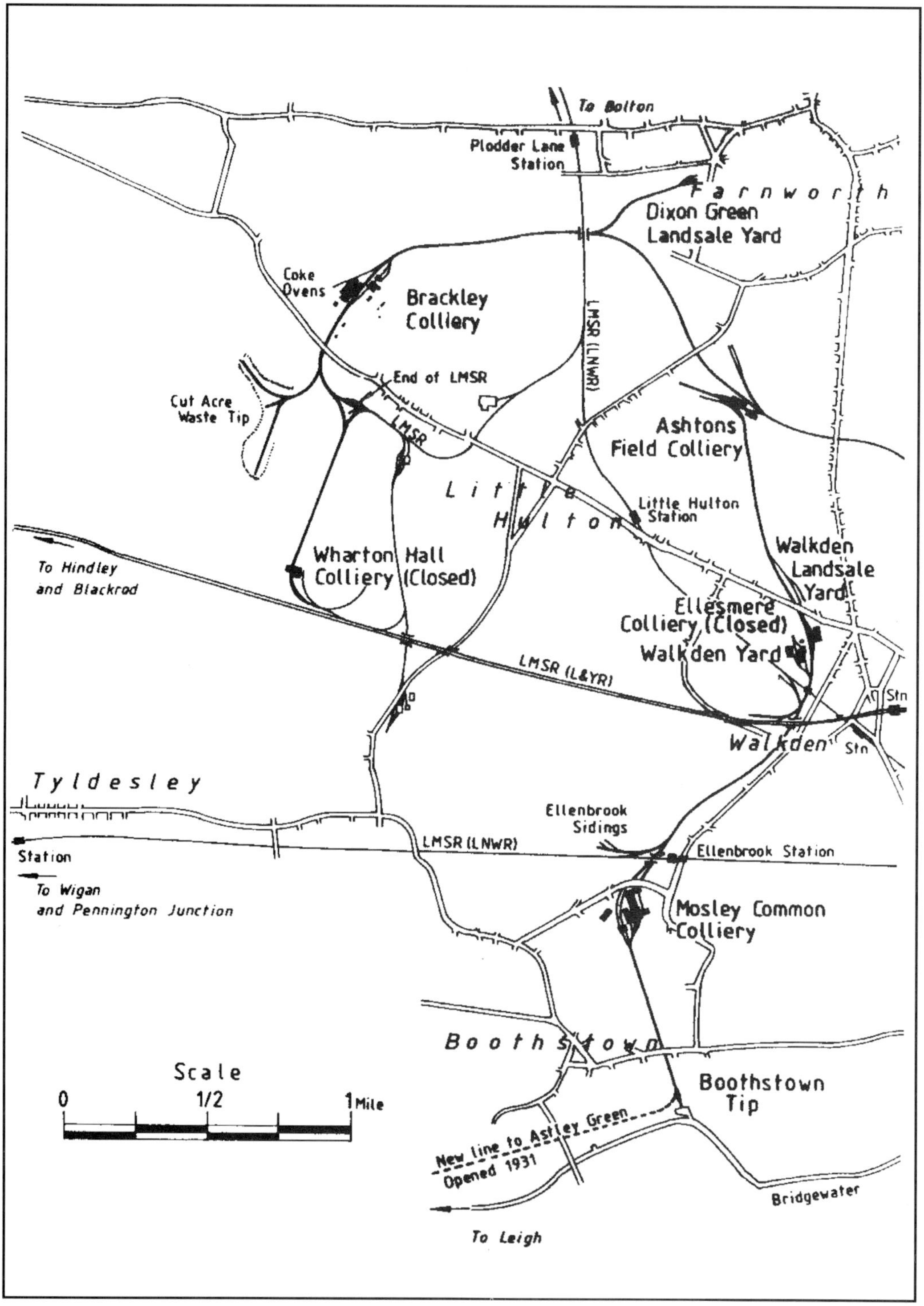
To Bolton
Plodder Lane Station
Farnworth
Dixon Green Landsale Yard
Coke Ovens
Brackley Colliery
LMSR (LNWR)
End of LMSR
Cut Acre Waste Tip
LMSR
Ashtons Field Colliery
Little Hulton
Little Hulton Station
Walkden Landsale Yard
To Hindley and Blackrod
Wharton Hall Colliery (Closed)
Ellesmere Colliery (Closed)
Walkden Yard
LMSR (L&YR)
Stn
Walkden
Stn
Tyldesley
Ellenbrook Sidings
LMSR (LNWR)
Ellenbrook Station
Station
To Wigan and Pennington Junction
Mosley Common Colliery
Boothstown
Scale
0
1/2
1 Mile
Boothstown Tip
New line to Astley Green Opened 1931
Bridgewater
To Leigh

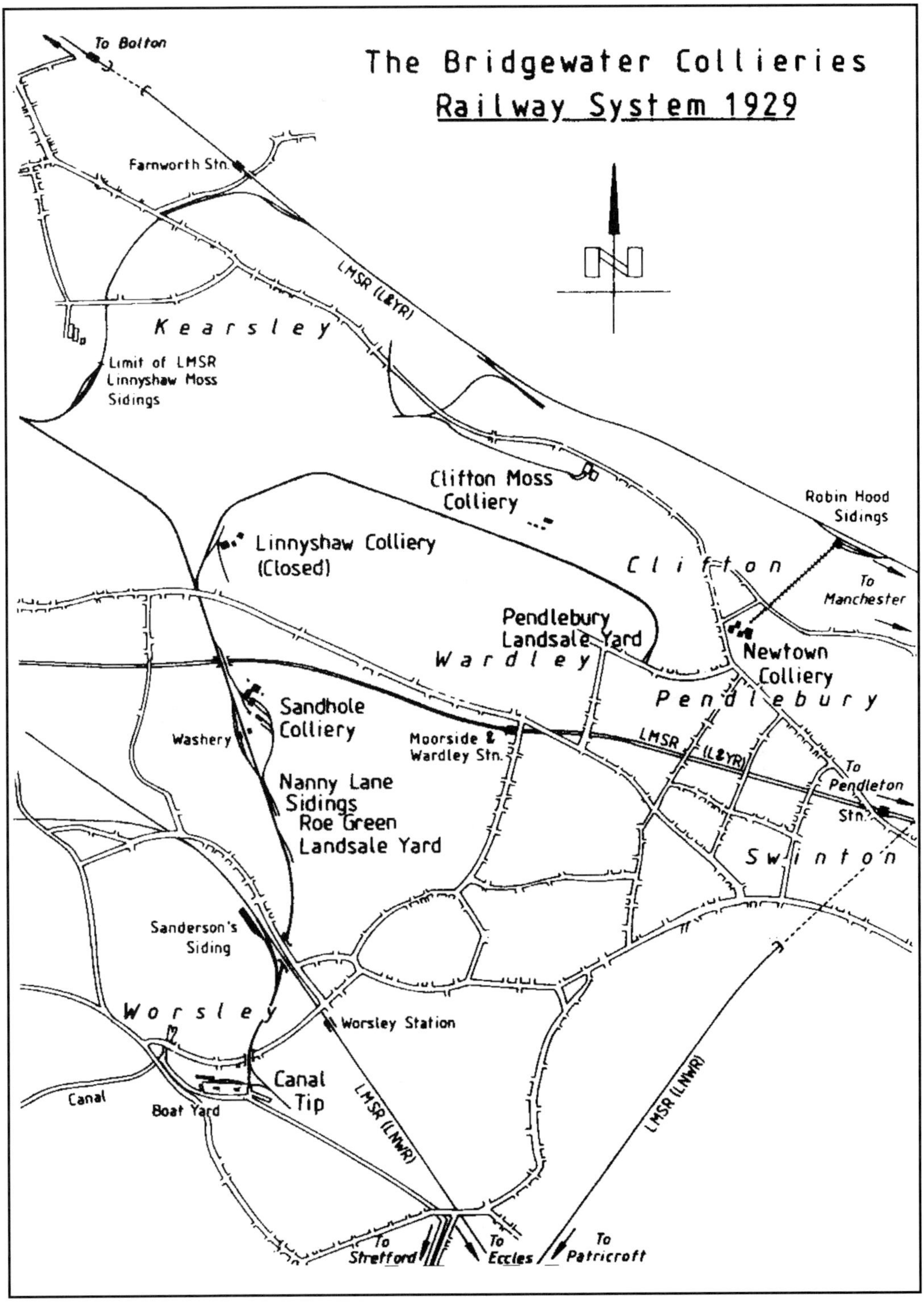
The Bridgewater Collieries
Railway System 1929
To Bolton
Farnworth Stn.
LMSR (L&YR)
Kearsley
Limit of LMSR
Linnyshaw Moss
Sidings
Clifton Moss
Colliery
Robin Hood
Sidings
Linnyshaw Colliery
(Closed)
Clifton
To
Manchester
Pendlebury
Landsale Yard
Wardley
Newtown
Colliery
Pendlebury
Sandhole
Colliery
Washery
Moorside &
Wardley Stn.
LMSR (L&YR)
To
Pendleton
Stn.
Nanny Lane
Sidings
Roe Green
Landsale Yard
Swinton
Sanderson's
Siding
Worsley
Worsley Station
Canal
Tip
Canal
Boat Yard
LMSR (LNWR)
LMSR (LNWR)
To
Stretford
To
Eccles
To
Patricroft

The pumps and the winding engine were converted to electric operation in 1934, the electric winder being the first to be used by Manchester Collieries Ltd [21]. A new locomotive shed was completed at Brackley during the financial year ending 31st March 1935 [21] and the line to Wharton Hall was lifted, releasing 1000 yards of railway track for use elsewhere [21]. The agreement in respect of the connection with the former L&YR Pendleton and Hindley line was cancelled on 28th March and the railway company's sidings removed [23].

Repairs to Manchester Collieries wagons was centralised at Walkden and by December 1932 the extensions which were required to the wagon shops had been completed [17,19]. Manufacture and repair of all the firm's pit tubs were transferred to the workshop at Ashton's Field, set up in the days of the Bridgewater Trustees [17]. During the financial year ending 31st March 1932, 6032 wagons passed through the wagon shops [9]. The total stock of wagons for main line traffic owned by Manchester Collieries Ltd rose from 8619 in 1934 to 10,966 in 1936 [9]. In addition there were many internal user wagons, which were confined to the various colliery railway systems.

A number of different colour schemes and designs of lettering were tried out for the wagons, but it was found that red with white letters was the most effective [24]. There is photographic evidence [25] that some wagons had already been repainted with this style of lettering by the end of 1929, but the colour cannot be ascertained. By the mid 1930s most had been dealt with. The basic colour was a medium red, with the title MANCHESTER COLLIERIES in white on the sides and a white M on the ends. A new batch of wagons obtained in 1939 was painted black, with the letters M C in white. Some of the existing stock was repainted in a similar style, but the majority remained in the original red livery until requisitioned during the war.

By January 1932 [17] the repair of mechanical equipment, including locomotives, had been centralised at the workshops at Walkden and Gin Pit. The shops at Gin Pit, as has been mentioned earlier, became responsible for locomotives from the former Fletcher, Burrows collieries as well as those working on the Astley and Tyldesley system. Walkden Yard continued to maintain the fleet of locomotives used on the Bridgewater railway system. Locomotives also came here from other collieries such as Astley Green, Outwood and Wheatsheaf. The scope of the activity at Walkden can be judged by the fact that, in the year ending 31st March 1935, 15 steam locomotives were overhauled [9]. Several engines which came in for repairs were found to be in bad state and were broken up.

The livery adopted for the locomotives after the amalgamation was black with red lining, although some ran in unlined black.

Fifteen locomotives were taken over by Manchester Collieries Ltd from Bridgewater Collieries Ltd :

The last survivor of the Manning, Wardle engines of the 1870s, STANLEY

The five Sharp, Stewart engines built between 1875 and 1888, SULTAN, ALERT, ATLAS, GOWER and WARDLEY

The four Nasmyth, Wilson engines of the early 1900s, MADGE, VIOLET, BRACKLEY and ELLESMERE

The eight coupled engine, KATHARINE

The ex ROD side tank, FRANCIS

The two Hunslet side tanks, built post war, JOSEPH and BRIDGEWATER

The Kerr, Stuart four wheeler, used at Robin Hood, KEARSLEY

Of the five Sharp Stewart engines, GOWER was transferred to Chanters Colliery in 1930. ATLAS, renamed CERBERUS to avoid confusion with the Fletcher, Burrows locomotive of the same name, was sent to Astley Green Colliery in the 1930s and moved on to Chanters Colliery in March 1937. We have dealt with the subsequent history of both CERBERUS and GOWER in Chapters 9 and 10.

According to old employees, STANLEY was based at Ellesmere shed in the early 1930s. Its duties were to shunt wagons into and out of the former LNWR and L&YR exchange sidings at Walkden and also to provide banking assistance for trains going up the hill to Ashton's Field. It was transferred to Astley Green Colliery, probably in 1933.

The other two Sharp, Stewarts remained on the Bridgewater system and were presumably also used on light duties. SULTAN is said to have been based at Sandhole and was used for shunting at Sanderson's Siding.

Brackley engine shed in 1943, with the pit head in the background. The two Hunslet six coupled side tanks were the regular engines here for many years. BRIDGEWATER stands outside the shed, with JOSEPH inside.
Harry Townley

In 1935, an interesting exchange of eight coupled engines took place, presumably to test the relative merits of the two different types. KATHARINE went to Gin Pit on 16th March and, on the same day, EMANUEL CLEGG came from there to Walkden. Both returned home on 8th August.

KATHARINE subsequently disgraced herself by leaving the track and turning over into a field near Mosley Common, being rescued by an LMSR breakdown crane. We have no date for the accident, but it must have been shortly before the locomotive's stay in the shops at Walkden, from 4th September to 25th November 1936. Included in the work carried out was the straightening of the frames and the fitting of new and shorter side tanks. The name plates were shortened and fitted to the cabsides instead of the tanks.

KATHARINE at Ellesmere shed at Walkden in pre war days, in its modified form after its accident.
Jack Ellison

Railways and locomotives 1936 to 1940

By the mid 1930s, many of the locomotives used on the Bridgewater railways system were quite old and needed to be replaced by something larger and more powerful. The decision was taken to purchase five 0-6-2 tanks from the London and Midland Scottish Railway and it is probably no coincidence that Sir Robert Burrows was a director of both Manchester Collieries Ltd and the railway company. The engines, all of the New L Class, had been built at the Stoke works of the North Staffordshire Railway. The last two to be acquired by Manchester Collieries were not completed until 1923, after the North Staffordshire Railway had been taken over.

The first, LMSR No 2257, arrived at Walkden on 12th June 1936. On the next day it was named KENNETH, after Kenneth Burrows, a director of the colliery company.

No 2262 came on 4th February 1937 and was named SIR ROBERT, after Sir Robert Burrows, at a ceremony shortly afterwards. No 2257 followed in May 1937 and was given the name KING GEORGE VI.

The final pair, Nos 2270 and 2271, arrived together on 8th October 1937. 2270 was named QUEEN ELIZABETH early in 1938 and 2271 was named PRINCESS in either May or June of the same year. Unlike the earlier engines, these two were fitted with superheaters which they retained until the boilers were replaced after the war.

Although some of the engines were still in their LMSR livery when put into traffic, most were repainted soon afterwards. However, some were still carrying their LMSR number plates on the smokebox several years later, as well as their Stoke (5D) shed plates.

KENNETH, the ex North Staffordshire Railway 0-6-2 tank, in the repair shop at Walkden Yard in February 1938. The smokebox door still has the LMSR numberplate 2264 and the shed plate 5D in place
Jim Peden collection

QUEEN ELIZABETH, formerly LMSR No 2270, photographed at Walkden Yard in 1943 Harry Townley

Another 0-6-2 Tank arrived at Walkden on 29th August 1939, this time from the Great Western Railway. It was bought through the intermediary of J F Wake and Company of Darlington, but came to Walkden direct from the GWR works at Swindon. It had been built for the Barry Railway by Sharp, Stewart and Company of Glasgow in 1890. Numbered 46 on the Barry Railway, it had become GWR No 244 in 1923. It was put into traffic on the Bridgewater collieries system on 4th September 1939, the day after war was declared, and was given the name WILLIAM, after William Green, the Traffic Manager.

It was now possible to dispose of some of the earlier engines.

SULTAN was scrapped at Walkden in 1937, all good parts being kept for use on the other Sharp, Stewart locomotives. The cab and saddle tank, with nameplate attached were seen at Walkden yard in August 1938 and it is thought that the tank was later fitted to WARDLEY.

The older pair of Nasmyth, Wilson locomotives left the Bridgewater system. VIOLET was sent to Gin Pit in June 1937 and MADGE was despatched to the same destination "for Chanters" in March 1938.

Visits to the system during the period 1937 to 1940 enable us to give some impression of the operations. With the main lines only single track, some form of control was necessary. Telephones were strategically placed in weighbridge cabins and elsewhere which enabled the engine drivers to enquire about conflicting train movements before they proceeded. Despite the lack of conventional signalling, no serious accidents were recorded, although one former driver is on record as saying that he always kept a look out for WILLIAM, which wouldn't stop for anything !

A feature of the traffic pattern was that a high proportion of the loaded wagons were routed via Ashton's Field and hence had to be hauled against quite severe gradients. The dead end layout at Ashton's Field enabled all the locomotives to work chimney first when proceeding uphill. The acquisition of the 0-6-2 tanks was timely for the improvement in demand for coal during the late 1930s led to a significant increase in traffic. Even these engines sometimes required the assistance of pilot engine or a banker when hauling heavy trains through Walkden or past Sandhole Colliery.

One major customer was the Lancashire Electric Power Company's generating station at Kearsley. Raw coal coming from Astley Green, Mosley Common and Brackley had first to worked to the blending plant at Ashton's Field, which came into operation in the financial year ending 31st March 1937[26]. The blended coal was then hauled to Linnyshaw Moss Sidings where it was handed over to the LMSR.

In 1935, Manchester Collieries Ltd challenged the high rate charged by the main line company for the short haul between the Linnyshaw Moss and the power station sidings. The Engineering Report for the year ending 31st March 1936 [9] notes that to assist the negotiations a scheme had been prepared for an overhead ropeway from a point on Linnyshaw Moss direct to the power station. Nothing further is heard about the project so the railway company's rates presumably were reduced to an acceptable level.

There was a considerable exchange of outgoing loaded wagons and incoming empties with the London Midland and Scottish Railway at Astley Moss, Ellenbrook, Walkden, Little Hulton and Sanderson's Siding. Which of these five points was used depended on the most favourable rates to the destination. On the Bridgewater system itself there were the landsale yards at Dixon Green, Pendlebury, Walkden and Roe Green where coal was sold directly to merchants. The Pendlebury yard seems to have been particularly busy at this period, with as many as three trains in and out each day.

There was still a significant amount of coal being sent away by canal; a new diesel tug, PHYLLIS, had been commissioned in the financial year ending 31st March 1935 and preparations had also been made to fit a diesel engine to the steam tug ELLESMERE [9,21].

By this date the workmen's passenger service had finished. We were told that the Pendlebury to Sandhole train ceased to operate in 1930 or 1931 and the Ashton's Field to Mosley Common train in 1932. Many of the coach bodies remained in existence and could be seen in use as mess huts at various points along the railway.

The principal locomotive depot was the Ellesmere shed at Walkden and it was usual for four of the ex LMSR engines and WILLIAM to be based there. These mainly worked the section of line from Boothsbank to Ashton's Field, but engines from here were also supplied to the other sheds when the need arose.

Locomotives based at Ellesmere shed were coaled at Mosley Common from tubs on an overhead gantry. There was also an engine shed here which was in use until early in the war, when the duties were transferred to Ellesmere to save manpower. Regular engines kept at Mosley Common in the late 1930s were MADGE and FRANCIS, the latter having been earlier at Sandhole according to what we were told. Both subsequently moved, MADGE to Chanters Colliery and FRANCIS to Astley Green.

The shed at Sandhole handled the traffic on the section between Ashton's Field and Worsley and its engines rarely worked elsewhere. It had been extended in the financial year ending 31st March 1938 [22], so that all locomotives could be kept under cover when not in use. One of the North Staffordshire engines, usually SIR ROBERT, worked the heavier trains between Sandhole Colliery, and Ashton's Field. The Sharp, Stewart WARDLEY generally worked at Sanderson's Sidings and the canal tip at Worsley. The other remaining Sharp Stewart, ALERT, was kept as a spare to WARDLEY.

WARDLEY shunting at Sanderson's Siding in June 1938. Compare with the picture of SULTAN in Chapter 11 and note how the appearance has changed with succesive rebuildings. Alex Appleton

FRANCIS, the ex-ROD Kerr, Stuart side tank shunting at Mosley Common Colliery in 1938
Alex Appleton

SIR ROBERT outside the engine shed at Sandhole in January 1958, with the pit yard in the background. It had been based here almost continuously since it arrived in 1937. Jim Peden

The ex-Barry Railway locomotive WILLIAM photographed at Astley Green about 1950, little changed in appearance from its main line days apart from the livery and the nameplate. Bob Fysh

Nanny Lane Sidings with a train hauled by BRACKLEY leaving for Linnyshaw Moss, photographed from the East Lancashire Road bridge in May 1954. Although the photograph was taken afer the formation of the National Coal Board the scene was typical of the Manchester Collieries era, except perhaps for the steel wagons. Alex Appleton

The two regular engines at Brackley were JOSEPH and BRIDGEWATER. They worked from Brackley to Ashton's Field, to Dixon Green landsale yard, to Cutacre Tip and to the LMS exchange sidings on the Little Hulton Mineral Branch.

What might be termed second string engines KATHARINE, BRACKLEY and ELLESMERE moved about, generally between the sheds at Ellesmere and Sandhole. KATHARINE, although powerful, was plagued with frequent defects and was slow on the longer hauls. During one footplate run from Nanny Lane sidings, south of the A580 road, to Ashton's Field, the slow progress, accompanied by a not unpleasant rolling motion was apparent. "Rock you to sleep" the driver said to one of the authors.

Railways and locomotives 1940 to 1947

During the war years, the Bridgewater railway system had to make do and mend and there was no question of any further additions to the locomotive stock. The company was probably hard pressed to maintain the engines which it had, as the workshops at Walkden Yard were required to undertake work for the Ministry of Supply, such as the machining of tank turrets. Presumably to meet blackout requirements, spark arrestors were fitted to the five North Staffordshire locomotives in 1940.

The wagon shops were also enlisted to help with the war effort and the shortage of internal user wagons had become so acute that by 1944 there had been a change over to motor lorries for the disposal of pit waste. They were first introduced at Astley Green and their use spread quickly to other collieries, including Mosley Common [27].

Two of the older locomotives were broken up during the war. As we have already mentioned, ALERT, the Sharp Stewart of 1877, had been put into store as a spare engine "for the duration". However, the war lasted so long that it was scrapped in 1943. STANLEY, the Manning Wardle of 1871, which had been transferred to Astley Green, was brought back to Walkden and scrapped in 1943 or early 1944.

The last remaining Sharp Stewart, WARDLEY, was overhauled at Walkden Yard at the end of 1944, when it was fitted with the cylinders from ALERT [28]. With ALERT no longer available to deputise for shunting at Sanderson's Sidings and at the Worsley Tip, the four coupled saddle tank CARBON, which was normally at Astley Green, was sent to Sandhole shed for a short period. It was returned to Astley Green on 14th January 1945 [29].

Towards the end of the war, ambitious plans were made to modernise the collieries, with skip winding to be introduced at Mosley Common, Sandhole and Newtown. Mosley Common was to be effectively rebuilt, with a new coal preparation plant [30]. These schemes, said to cost £4,500,000, were not completed until after nationalisation.

In connection with the Mosley Common project, consideration was once again given to the construction of a railway to the Manchester Ship Canal, this time to include a connection to the Liverpool and Manchester line at Barton Moss [31]. The proposed route is shown on plans dated 1947, now at the Salford City Archives Office [32], but no work was undertaken.

At end of 1944 a number of the austerity saddle tanks which had been ordered by the War Department were found to be surplus to requirements and could be put to good use helping out industries, such as coal mining, which were essential to the war effort. Manchester Collieries Ltd was allocated two of the engines.

The first to arrive at Walkden, on 29th December 1944, was WD 71501 which came from the Longmoor Military Railway in Hampshire. It was put to work in January 1945. WD 71500, also from Longmoor, which arrived on 19th April 1945, was put to work on 24th April.

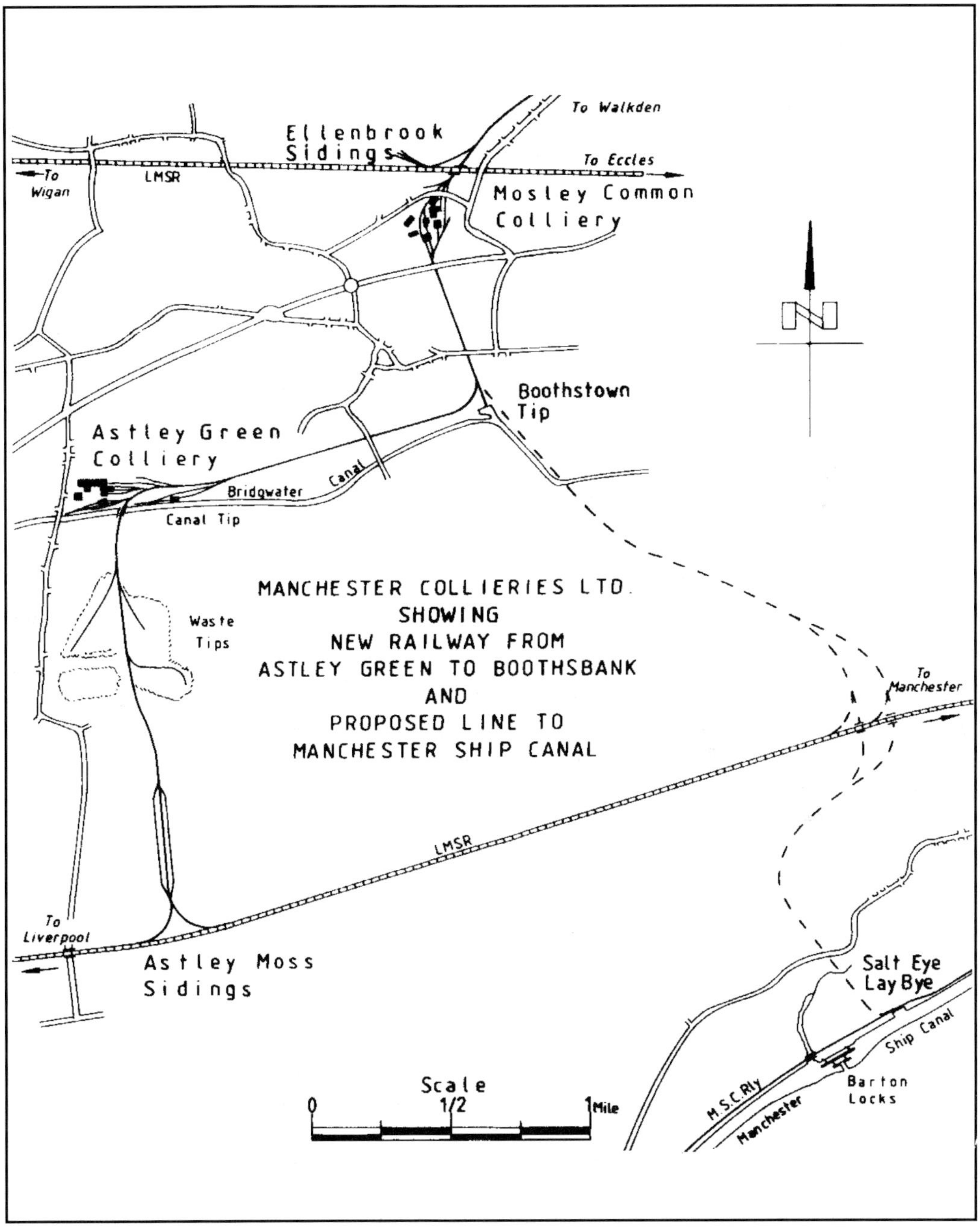

Both these locomotives were initially on hire and retained their War Department lettering and numbers. However, they were purchased in July 1946. They were subsequently repainted in black livery with red lining and given the names CHARLES and ALLEN, after Charles Fish, the traffic manager and Allen Beaumont, one of the firm's engineers

Manchester Collieries Ltd was fortunate to be able to buy a new locomotive of the same type from the Hunslet Engine Company, being only the second private firm to do so during war time. The engine had originally been ordered by the Garswood Hall Collieries Ltd but the order had been cancelled [13]. It arrived at Walkden on 4th August 1945 and was given the name STANLEY after Stanley Greenhaulgh, another of the colliery engineers.

71500, the second of the War Department austerity saddle tanks to be hired to Manchester Collieries Ltd, photographed at Walkden in June 1945. The engine was purchased in 1946 and named ALLEN. J D Darby

After the end of hostilities, many of the austerity engines in War Department stock were put up for sale. Manchester Collieries Ltd purchased three which were in store at Longmoor. WD 71479 arrived at Walkden on 8th April 1946, was named GORDON and was sent to Chanters Colliery. WD 71484 arrived on 17th April 1946, was named HUMPHREY, after Humphrey Browne, General Manager of the company, and was sent to Astley Green. WD 71480 arrived on 24th April 1946 and was retained for use on the Bridgewater system, entering traffic on 3rd May 1946 with the name FRED, after Fred Hilton, the Manager at Walkden Yard.

Immediately after the end of the war, new boilers for the North Staffordshire locomotives were ordered from the Hunslet Engine Company. The first engine to be dealt with was KENNETH, which re-entered traffic in October 1945. This was followed by PRINCESS in November 1946 and QUEEN ELIZABETH in January 1947. The latter had been out of service since December 1945.

The remaining engines were rebuilt after nationalisation. Indicative of the scale of the work carried out at Walkden Yard was that done on PRINCESS. In addition to reboilering, new side and back water tanks, a new bunker, new cylinders and new slide valves were fitted.

The post war period saw the demise of KATHARINE, the eight coupled engine built in 1914 for the Earl of Ellesmere. It was broken up at Walkden in October 1945. FRANCIS, the ex ROD Kerr Stuart was transferred to Astley Green Colliery in July 1945.

The Manchester Collieries' wagons which had been requisitioned during the war and absorbed into the national pool were returned in 1945. During that year and in 1946, there were negotiations with the Central Wagon Co Ltd to purchase the whole of the fleet and hire it back under a leasing agreement. Documents of April 1945 refer to 8398 owned by the company, with a further 1150 on hire, while documents of April and June 1946 refer respectively to 9530 and 9515 wagons owned [12].

LOCOMOTIVE SUMMARY

Bridgewater Collieries – Manchester Collieries Ltd 4-3-1929 to 31-12-1946

Locomotives taken over from Bridgewater Collieries Ltd, March 1929

STANLEY	0-6-0STIC	MW	366	1871	15"x22"	4'0"

Transferred to Astley Green Colliery in early 1930s. See Shapter 10
Scrapped at Walkden Yard 1943 or 1944

SULTAN	0-6-0STIC	SS	2490	1875	17"x24"	4'0"

Scrapped at Walkden Yard, 1937

ALERT	0-6-0STIC	SS	2714	1877	17"x24"	4'0"

In store at Walkden Yard, 2-1940
Scrapped at Walkden Yard, 1943

CERBERUS	0-6-0STIC	SS	2909	1880	17"x24"	4'0"

Originally named ATLAS. Renamed CERBERUS by Manchester Collieries Ltd
Transferred to Astley Green Colliery in 1930s and later at Chanters Colliery. See Chapters 9 and 10
Repairs at Walkden Yard 9-4-1936 to 15-5-1936 and 12-1-1937 to 15-2-1937
Scrapped at Gin Pit early 1939

GOWER	0-6-0STIC	SS	3090	1882	17"x24"	4'0"

Transferred to Chanters Colliery 25-7-1930, later worked at Bedford Colliery. See Chapter 9
Scrapped at Gin Pit 4-1945

WARDLEY	0-6-0STIC	SS	3423	1888	17"x24"	4'0"

Repairs at Walkden Yard 1932, 1935, late 1938 / early 1939 and 1944
To NCB 1-1-1947, on Central Rlys

MADGE	0-6-0STIC	NW	782	1906	17"x24"	4'1"

Transferred to Chanters Colliery 3-1938. See Chapter 9
Scrapped at Gin Pit, 1946

VIOLET	0-6-0STIC	NW	852	1908	17"x24"	4'1"

Transferred to Gin Pit 6-1937, later worked at Chanters Colliery. See Chapter 9
To NCB 1-1-1947 at Chanters Colliery

BRACKLEY	0-6-0STIC	NW	912	1910	18"x26"	4'3"

To NCB 1-1-1947, on Central Rlys

ELLESMERE	0-6-0STIC	NW	976	1912	18"x26"	4'3"

To NCB 1-1-1947, on Central Rlys

KATHARINE	0-8-0T IC	MW	1853	1914	18"x26"	4'2"

Scrapped at Walkden Yard late 1945 or early 1946

KEARSLEY 0-4-0STOC KS 3123 1918 15"x20" 3′2"
Used at Robin Hood Sidings. See Chapter 6
To NCB 1-1-1947, at Robin Hood

FRANCIS 0-6-0T OC KS 3068 1917 17"x24" 3′11"
Transferred to Astley Green Colliery, probably in 1945. See Chapter 10
To NCB 1-1-1947, at Astley Green

JOSEPH 0-6-0T OC HE 1456 1924 18"x24" 3′9"
To NCB 1-1-1947, on Central Rlys

BRIDGEWATER 0-6-0T OC HE 1475 1924 18"x24" 3′9"
To NCB 1-1-1947, on Central Rlys

The 0-6-2 Tanks purchased 1936 to 1939

KENNETH 0-6-2T IC Stoke 1921 18½"x26" 5′0"
Ex LMSR 2264, 6-1936
To NCB 1-1-1947 on Central Rlys

SIR ROBERT 0-6-2T IC Stoke 1920 18½"x26" 5′0"
Ex LMSR 2262, 1-1937
To NCB 1-1-1947 on Central Rlys

KING GEORGE VI 0-6-2T IC Stoke 1913 18½"x26" 5′0"
Ex LMSR 2257, 5-1937
To NCB 1-1-1947 on Central Rlys

QUEEN ELIZABETH 0-6-2T IC Stoke 1923 18½"x26" 5′0"
Ex LMSR 2270, 10-1937
To NCB 1-1-1947 on Central Rlys

PRINCESS 0-6-2T IC Stoke 1923 18½"x26" 5′0"
Ex LMSR 2271, 10-1937
To NCB 1-1-1947 on Central Rlys

WILLIAM 0-6-2T IC SS 3606 1890 17½"x26" 4′3"
Ex GWR 244, 7-39
To NCB 1-1-1947 on Central Rlys

Locomotive temporarily transferred

CARBON 0-4-0STOC AB 1704 1920 14"x22" 3′5"
Temporarily transferred from Astley Green to Central Railways at Sandhole at end of 1944 when WARDLEY under repair. Returned to Astley Green 14-1-1945
To NCB 1-1-1947 at Astley Green

The austerity saddle tanks

71501 0-6-0STIC HC 1778 1944 18"x26" 4′3"
Arrived at Walkden 29-12-1944 on hire
Purchased by Manchester Collieries Ltd 7-1946 and named CHARLES
To NCB 1-1-1947 on Central Rlys

71500 0-6-0STIC HC 1777 1944 18"x26" 4′3"
Arrived at Walkden 19-4-1945 on hire
Purchased by Manchester Collieries Ltd 7-1946 and named ALLEN
To NCB 1-1-1947 on Central Rlys

STANLEY 0-6-0STIC HE 3302 1945 18"x26" 4′3"
New, arrived Walkden 4-8-1945
To NCB Central Rlys Walkden List
To NCB 1-1-1947 on Central Rlys

GORDON 0-6-0STIC RSH 7288 1945 18"x26" 4'3"
Ex WD 71479, arrived Walkden 8-4-1946 and sent to Chanters Colliery. See Chapter 9
To NCB 1-1-1947 at Chanters

HUMPHREY 0-6-0STIC RSH 7293 1945 18"x26" 4'3"
Ex WD 71484, arrived Walkden 17-4-1946 and sent to Astley Green. See Chapter 10
To NCB 1-1-1947 at Astley Green

FRED 0-6-0STIC RSH 7289 1945 18"x26" 4'3"
Ex WD 71480, arrived Walkden 3-5-1946 and retained on Central Railways
To NCB 1-1-1947 on Central Rlys

Locomotives known to the authors to have been brought into Walkden Yard from other collieries for overhaul or disposal

AGECROFT 0-6-0STIC MW 1120 1889
Overhaul from 19-9-1933 to 21-2-1934 (Ref 29)
From Agecroft Colliery or Wheatsheaf Screens and returned probably to Wheatsheaf

OUTWOOD 0-6-0STOC P 923 1901
Overhaul 22-10-1934 to 14-2-1935 (Ref 29)
From Outwood Washery and returned to Outwood

CERBERUS 0-6-0STIC SS 2909 1880
Overhaul from 9-4-1936 to 15-5-1936 (Ref 28)
From Astley Green Colliery and then probably used on Central railways system before return to Astley Green on 7-12-1936
Overhaul from 12-1-1937 to 15-2-1937 (Ref 28)
From Astley Green Colliery. Sent from Walkden to Chanters Colliery on 10-3-1937

KNOWLES 0-6-0STIC MW 1520 1901
Probably from Agecroft Colliery. Scrapped at Walkden Yard in 1936

ASTLEY GREEN 0-6-0STOC AB 221 1880
From Astley Green Colliery. Sold to Harry Stephenson and Sons Ltd, Hindley, for scrap 5-1936

VICTORIA 0-4-0STOC BH 896 1887
From Robin Hood Sidings. Sold to Harry Stephenson and Sons Ltd, Hindley, for scrap 5-1936

NEWTOWN 0-4-0STOC HL 2580 1904
Overhaul 30-5-1937 to 23-7-1937 (Ref 29)
From Astley Green Colliery and returned to Astley Green

EDWARD 0-6-0STOC HL 3184 1916
Overhaul from 27-5-1938 to 18-7-1938 (Ref 28)
From Astley Green Colliery and returned to Astley Green

ROBIN HOOD 0-4-0STOC CF 1200 1901
Overhauled 1940
From Outwood Washery and returned to Outwood

CARBON 0-4-0STOC AB 1704 1920
Overhaul from 12-2-1941 to 5-6-1941 (Ref 29)
From Astley Green Colliery and returned to Astley Green

References to Chapter 12

1 16&17 Geo 5 cap 28; 4th August 1926
2 Clifton and Kersley Coal Co Ltd Minutes, 3-1-1923 - SMM U64
3 *"The Bridgewater Heritage"* - Christopher Grayling - Bridgewater Estates plc, Manchester, 1983
4 Clifton and Kersley Coal Co Ltd Minutes, 19-7-1928 - SMM U64
5 BEN 1-10-1928
6 *"Colliery Year Book"* - The Louis Cassier Co Ltd, London, 1930
7 1&2 Geo 6 cap 52; 29th July 1938
8 Chronology in SMM catalogue of Bridgewater archives
9 LRO NCMc 33/17
10 *"Carbon"*, December 1935

11 *"Collieries in the Manchester Coalfields"* Geoff Hayes - De Archaeologische Pers, Eindhoven, nd
12 LRO NCMc 3/14
13 *"The Industrial Railways of the Wigan Coalfield - Part Two"* -Townley, Smith and Peden - Runpast Publishing, Cheltenham, 1992
14 FJ 10-1-1930
15 *"Carbon"*, April 1932
16 *"Carbon"*, April 1933
17 *"Carbon"*, Jan 1932
18 *"Carbon"*, Sept 1934
19 *"Carbon"*, Dec 1932
20 LRO NCMc 33/16
21 *"Carbon"*, April 1934
22 LRO NCMc 4/5
23 Endorsement on L&YR Sdgs Diag No 115, 22nd Jan 1897 at BRPB, Manchester Office
24 *"Carbon"*, Sept 1933
25 *"Carbon"*, Oct 1929
26 LRO NCMc 4/4
27 Manchester Collieries Newsletter, 9-4-1944
28 *"From Walkden Records - Part One"* - Alex Appleton - in *"Industrial Locomotive"*, Vol 6, No 62, 1991
29 *"From Walkden Records - Part Two"* - Alex Appleton - in *"Industrial Locomotive"*, Vol 6, No 63, 1991
30 Manchester Collieries Newsletter, 16-3-1945
31 *"The Railways of the Manchester Ship Canal"* - Don Thorpe - Oxford Publishing Co, 1984
32 SAO E1202/35

CHAPTER 13

THE BRIDGEWATER COLLIERIES AND ASTLEY GREEN COLLIERY FROM 1947

From 1947 to 1961 - The No 1 Area of the National Coal Board

In 1947, when the National Coal Board was formed, all the collieries still at work around Manchester and in the eastern part of South Lancashire came under the control of the No 1 (Manchester) Area of the North Western Division. In all 22 collieries, some outside the geographical area of the present book, were taken over. Previously the property of eight different firms, they comprised :

- Bickershaw Collieries Ltd
  - Bickershaw Colliery, Leigh
- Thomas Brocklehurst and Co Ltd
  - Victoria Colliery, Deane
- The Chamber Colliery Co Ltd
  - Ashton Moss Colliery, Audenshaw
  - Oak and Victoria Pits, Hollinwood
  - Woodpark Colliery, Bardsley
- Ladyshore Coal Co (1930) Ltd
  - Ladyshore Colliery
- Manchester Collieries Ltd
  - Astley Green Colliery
  - Bedford Colliery
  - Brackley Colliery
  - Bradford Colliery
  - Chanters Colliery
  - Gibfield Colliery
  - Gin Colliery
  - Howe Bridge Colliery
  - Mosley Common Colliery
  - Newtown Colliery
  - Nook Colliery
  - Sandhole Colliery
  - Wheatsheaf Colliery
- Platt Bros and Co (Holdings) Ltd
  - Moston Colliery
- Tyldesley Coal Co Ltd
  - Cleworth Hall Colliery
- Wigan Coal Corporation Ltd
  - Parsonage Colliery, Westleigh

We have already dealt with the history of Manchester Collieries Ltd, the Tyldesley Coal Company and the Ladyshore Coal Company. The Victoria Colliery at Deane appears in Appendix 5. Bickershaw Colliery and Parsonage Colliery are described in *"The Industrial Railways of the Wigan Coalfield"* [1].

The remaining collieries lie outside our present geographical boundary and we shall deal with them only briefly before continuing our story of the Bridgewater collieries railway system. Only two, Ashton Moss and Moston, were large enough to employ their own locomotives, details of which will be found in Appendix 4.

Woodpark Colliery, at Bardsley, and Hollinwood Colliery, comprising the Oak and Victoria Pits, were of relatively minor importance. Woodpark closed in March 1955 and Hollinwood in July 1956. They were too small to need a rail connection and all the coal was sold locally at the pit head, although Woodpark at one time had a tramroad to the Ashton Canal. The Chamber Colliery Company had been existence since the mid 1850s, with a number of landsale collieries in the neighbourhood of Oldham, Chadderton and Ashton under Lyne.

Ashton Moss Colliery was much larger. It had been sunk in the early 1870s by the Ashton Moss Colliery Company and taken over by the New Moss Colliery Co Ltd around the turn of the century. It was acquired by the Chamber Colliery Co Ltd in the 1920s. It had a quite extensive system which gave access to the former London and North Western Railway.

Moston Colliery, which had a connection with the nearby Lancashire and Yorkshire Railway, was probably sunk in the 1850s. After being worked by various members of the Stanley family and the Moston Coal Co Ltd, it was acquired by Platt Bros and Company, the Oldham textile machinery manufacturers, in 1875 or 1876. The firm worked a number of other small pits at Crompton and Milnrow in the latter part of the nineteenth century, of which the Jubilee Colliery at Milnrow survived until the 1930s.

As already mentioned in Chapter 10, there was a reorganisation on 1st January 1952, when Bickershaw, Parsonage, Bedford and the Atherton Collieries were transferred to the No 2 (Wigan) Area. The locomotives employed at these collieries then came under the jurisdiction of Kirkless Workshops instead of Walkden Yard, but, as far as the Bridgewater railway system was concerned, the reorganisation had little, if any, effect.

Colliery Developments 1947 to 1961

The National Coal Board inherited the modernisation projects which had been initiated by Manchester Collieries Ltd at Mosley Common, Astley Green and Bradford.

The coal preparation plant at Mosley Common, expected to be completed by December 1948, was brought into operation in 1950, the first half of the plant being handed over by the contractors on 13th January [2]. Widening of the main winding shaft from 12 ft diameter to 22 ft diameter and installation of the new electric winding engine, said then to be the largest in the world, was completed in July 1954. The skip winding system had a potential capacity of 8,000 tons per day working two shifts and the intention was to bring up the coal previously wound at Newtown and Sandhole [3]. In the 12 months to 7th December 1957 a there was a record output of 828,123 tons, over 1/5th of the total raised in the Manchester Area of the NCB [4]. Although the colliery had a possible future life of 100 years [3], its potential was never realised and it was closed ten years later.

At Astley Green, No 2 shaft was modernised and a skip winding system was introduced early in 1953; a scheme was then put in hand to modernise No 1 Pit [5] . In 1956, 692,941 tons of coal were raised. During 1959 and 1960, a new coal preparation plant was erected, replacing the existing screens and washery [6].

The work which had been started in 1944 to deepen the shafts at Bradford Colliery was completed in 1948. Skip winding was introduced and a new coal preparation plant was built on the old brickworks site [6]. A tunnel was built so that coal could be supplied by conveyor to the new power station at Stuart Street, which opened in December 1949.

At the same, a coal loading bunker was built on the west side of Forge Lane, fed by an overhead conveyor from the preparation plant, thus eliminating the need for a level crossing over what had now become a busy road. The Avonside locomotive, which had been at the colliery all its working life, left on 7th February 1956 for Robin Hood Sidings. Rail traffic may have continued after this, with the shunting performed by British Railways engines. Coal production continued until 6th September 1968 [7,8].

The Locomotives on the Bridgewater system - 1947 to 1961

The Austerity Saddle Tanks

The first engines to be purchased by the National Coal Board were two further austerity saddle tanks, which came second hand from the War Department in 1947. They were named W.H.R. and JAMES, the former after W H Richards, the manager at Astley Green Colliery.

A further five austerity saddle tanks, all named after ships of the second world war, came new from the Hunslet Engine Company at the end of 1950. Finally, six more, all with names beginning with W, were delivered between 1952 and 1957.

The majority were retained for use either at Astley Green or on the Central Railways, but a few were sent to other collieries in the NCB's No 1 Area. The thirteen locomotives comprised

W.H.R.	Delivered 18th June 1947 and sent to Gin Pit on 30th July 1947
JAMES	Delivered 16th August 1947 and retained for use on Central Railways and at Astley Green
RODNEY	Delivered 20th October 1950 and sent to Bickershaw Colliery; absorbed into stock of No 2 (Wigan) Area 1st January 1952
RESPITE	Delivered 28th October 1950 and retained for use at Astley Green and on Central Railways
RENOWN	Delivered 4th November 1950 and sent to Parsonage Colliery; later at Gin Pit and retained in No 1 (Manchester) Area stock on 1st January 1952
REPULSE	Delivered 16th November 1950 and retained for use on Central Railways
REVENGE	Delivered 23rd November 1950 and retained for use on Central Railways
WARSPITE	Delivered November 1952 and retained for use on Central Railways
WASP	Delivered 20th January 1954 and retained for use on Central Railways
WARRIOR	Delivered 2nd September 1954 and retained for use on Central Railways
WITCH	Delivered 14th April 1956 and retained for use on Central Railways and at Astley Green
WIZARD	Delivered 21st September 1956 and retained for use on Central Railways
WEASEL	Delivered March 1957 and sent to Gin Pit

The No 1 Area of the NCB inherited a further five engines of the same type from Manchester Collieries Ltd - ALLEN, CHARLES, STANLEY, FRED and HUMPHREY. FRED was transferred from Walkden to Bickershaw Colliery on 7th December 1948 and HUMPHREY from Astley Green to Chanters Colliery on 21st December 1948.

The 0-6-2Ts

Reboilering of the ex North Staffordshire Railway engines was completed shortly after nationalisation. KING GEORGE VI was dealt with in 1948 and SIR ROBERT in 1949 to 1950.

WILLIAM, the ex Great Western engine, was transferred to Astley Green Colliery on 1st March 1949 [9], but by May 1951 it was back at Walkden, out of use. It was broken up there later that year or early in 1952.

In 1952 QUEEN ELIZABETH needed expensive replacement parts. By August of that year it had been taken out of service and was gradually cannibalised to provide a source of spares for the other four ex NSR locomotives. It had been largely dismantled by May 1957, but the frames were not cut up until 1963.

In 1960 it was decided that one of the Walkden locomotives would take part in the celebration of the centenary of the North Staffordshire Railway. PRINCESS was repainted in full NSR livery and emerged from Walkden shops as North Staffordshire Railway No 2. The only incongruous note was that it carried a plate, taken from KING GEORGE VI, stating that it had been built at Stoke in 1913, presumably because the correct plates, dated 1923, had been lost.

PRINCESS, in its new guise, appeared at the exhibition at Stoke on Trent and afterwards carried a plaque bearing the city coat of arms on the left hand cabside. During its absence British Railways made available one of its six coupled side tanks, 47669, for use at Walkden.

PRINCESS as repainted for the North Staffordshire Railway Centenary. The plaque bearing the coat of arms of the City of Stoke on Trent can be seen on the cabside. The photograph was taken on 3rd August 1964, on the occasion of a rail tour of the Bridgewater Collieries railway system. The engine had recently been overhauled at Walkden Yard, where it had been fitted with the frames, cylinders and wheels from SIR ROBERT, but still retained the incorrect plate giving the building date as 1913. Note the small hole in the frame above the front buffer beam, mentioned in the text. Harry Townley

The Older Locomotives

The influx of new motive power from 1947 onwards meant that, in addition to QUEEN ELIZABETH and WILLIAM, many of the other older engines were taken out of service.

BEDFORD, which had been lying out of use at Astley Green on vesting day, waiting to be repaired, was taken to Walkden soon afterwards. It lay there derelict until the end of 1950, when it was broken up.

BLACK DIAMOND, another of the Astley Green veterans, was sent to Walkden in the middle of 1948 and was scrapped there in October 1949.

WARDLEY, the last of the Bridgewater Trustees' Sharp Stewart's went into the workshops for repairs in November 1950. It was found to have a broken frame and was considered not worth repairing and was laid aside. It was broken up in June 1953

The two Nasmyth, Wilson engines, BRACKLEY and ELLESMERE, were taken out of service in 1955 or 1956. BRACKLEY was cut up at Walkden in February 1957. ELLESMERE was partly dismantled and the frames, complete with cylinders and wheels were put out to grass. The remains were eventually cut up for scrap in November 1963.

JOSEPH, the Hunslet side tank, which had latterly worked at Astley Green, went into the shops at Walkden for overhaul at the end of 1958. The repairs were stopped in May 1959 and the engine, stripped of its boiler, tanks and cab was placed alongside Ellesmere shed, where they stayed until broken up in April 1963.

The Hunslet locomotive JOSEPH climbing the bank from Mosley Common to Ashton's Field. The photograph was taken in 1952 near Mather's Fold. The Ellenbrook Brickworks can be seen in the background. The wooden poles were a prominent feature of the Bridgewater Collieries railway in Manchester Collieries and early National Coal Board days and provided the means of distributing electricity to the pits and other installations.
John Snell

CARR the only four coupled saddle tank to come new in NCB times, photographed at Astley Green in October 1948, soon after arrival. Alex Appleton

CARR, WESTWOOD and COLONEL

In 1948 Hudswell Clarke and Company completed four identical four coupled saddle tanks ordered by the Ministry of Fuel and Power two years earlier. Only one of these was allocated to the No 1 Area, despite the need to replace the ageing fleet of small locomotives. Named CARR and painted dark blue with yellow lining, it was sent to Astley Green Colliery, where it replaced BLACK DIAMOND. It remained at Astley Green, apart from visits to Walkden Yard for repairs, until 1965, when it was transferred to Cumberland.

When WARDLEY, the veteran Sharp, Stewart of 1888 was withdrawn from service in 1950, WESTWOOD from Moston Colliery took over its shunting duties at Sanderson's Siding and Worsley Canal tip.

WESTWOOD had a short spell at Wheatsheaf Screens early in 1952 and was under repair at Walkden Yard during the summer of 1953. During these absences its duties were taken over by COLONEL, the six coupled engine which had originally been at Fletcher, Burrows' Atherton Collieries. WESTWOOD left the Bridgewater system on 6th January 1955, when it was sent to Ashton Moss Colliery. Its place was taken once again by COLONEL, which was recorded here between 1955 and 1957.

WESTWOOD seems to have been regarded subsequently as the stand-by engine for the Area. It was sent to a number of locations where only the smaller locomotives could be used, deputising for engines which were out of service. It was at Astley Green for a short period during the summer of 1959.

Diesel locomotives

There were several attempts by locomotive manufacturers to interest the authorities at Walkden in diesel traction. The first was in 1954 when the Hunslet Engine Company provided one of their six coupled engines for tests. It arrived on 30th March and, after two weeks at Walkden, left under its own power for the steel works at Hawarden Bridge.

In 1956 a six coupled locomotive built by the Yorkshire Engine Company was tried out. It arrived on 24th August, having travelled from Irlam over the Manchester Ship Canal Railway and thence over the ex-L&YR route from New Barns Junction to Walkden.

Two further demonstrations machines followed - a 440 HP diesel hydraulic locomotive from the North British Locomotive Company in 1957 and a six wheeler from Sentinel in November 1961.

The management, however, was very pro-steam and, as they did not wish to change over to diesel, no large scale change emerged from these demonstrations. Only one diesel locomotive, built by the Yorkshire Engine Company in 1957, was allocated to the Bridgewater railway system at this period. It seems likely that it was intended for the new Agecroft Colliery, but that it was delivered to Walkden instead, as developments at Agecroft were behind schedule. It saw little use on the Bridgewater system and seems to have mainly been employed around the workshops, although it was noted on one occasion in 1961 at Sandhole Colliery. It was transferred from Walkden to Agecroft Colliery early in 1962

Walkden Yard 1947 to 1961

The National Coal Board established what was officially its Central Workshops for the No 1 Area at Walkden, although the complex continued to be known as Walkden Yard by all concerned.

The ex Great Western Railway engine, WILLIAM, was the first locomotives to be turned out of the shops after vesting day. The local management was under instructions to make sure that all Coal Board property was made to look smart and, taking this to apply to the locomotives as much as anything else, WILLIAM was repainted in green livery, lined out in yellow, black and red.

Unfortunately the new paint scheme proved too expensive and was not perpetuated. Until about 1950, most of the locomotives repaired at Walkden continued to be turned out in the old Manchester Collieries livery of black with red lining. The austerity saddle tanks delivered in 1950 were painted black lined with yellow and this was gradually adopted for other locomotives in the Manchester Area. The one exception seems to have been KEARSLEY, which was noted in 1955 painted light blue with single yellow lining, similar to CARR which had this livery when new.

The austerity tanks delivered in 1950 and later had brass nameplates. The previous engines had only their names painted on the tanks, but all those working on the Bridgewater system and at Astley Green were subsequently fitted with plates of Hunslet style cast by Lancaster and Tonge Ltd of Pendleton.

The existing locomotive shop at Walkden was rather cramped and, with the impending closure of the facilities at Gin Pit, modernisation was put in hand. A new building was opened in August 1953 and we have been told that the first engine to be overhauled in it was FAILSWORTH, the six coupled saddle, then working at Wheatsheaf Screens.

The interior of the new locomotive repair shop at Walkden which was opened in 1953.
Alex Appleton collection

This photograph of ELLESMERE, one of the larger Nasmyth, Wilson saddle tanks, was taken at Walkden in March 1952. The engine had recently been repainted in the black livery lined in yellow adopted from 1950 for the locomotives based on the Bridgewater system.
J D Darby

Ellesmere shed at Walkden in May 1960. The austerity tanks are in prominence, with REPULSE in the foreground, but one ex North Staffordshire Railway engine, SIR ROBERT, is still in evidence on the right. The British Railways locomotive, 47669, is here temporarily to replace the 0-6-2 tank which was sent to the NSR centenary celebrations. Alan Tyson

Railway Operation 1947 to 1961

In the 1950s four engines were normally allocated to Astley Green. The larger engines, EDWARD, FRANCIS and HUMPHREY were the mainstay on the long hauls to the exchange sidings on the Liverpool and Manchester line and to Boothstown, where trains destined for Ashton's Field and beyond were handed over to engines working from Ellesmere shed. HUMPHREY was replaced by ALLEN in 1950. When ALLEN was not available, JAMES and RESPITE were brought in temporarily. The ex Great Western Railway 0-6-2 tank, WILLIAM, was also here from 1949 to 1951.

The smaller engines were normally used for shunting in the colliery yard. BLACK DIAMOND and CARBON were so employed at the time of nationalisation, but CARBON was transferred to Cleworth Hall Colliery shortly afterwards. BRIDGEWATER, the six coupled Hunslet side tank came to replace it and stayed until 1949. It then worked for about ten years from Sandhole, Brackley and Ellesmere sheds before returning to Astley Green.

CARR, the new Hudswell Clark four wheeler, took over from BLACK DIAMOND in 1948 and stayed at Astley Green until 1965. As mentioned earlier, GEORGE PEACE was temporarily here in 1952 and WESTWOOD in 1959.

Normally there were seven active locomotives allocated to Ellesmere shed at Walkden but there were always others to be seen, spare, awaiting attention in the shops or being run in after repairs. The shed was home to four of the five North Staffordshire Railway 0-6-2 tanks and was responsible for working most of the heavy trains over the western leg of the system to Ashton's Field. WILLIAM, the ex Great Western Railway 0-6-2 tank, was usually to be found here as well.

The first Austerity tanks which arrived in 1946 were allocated to Ellesmere shed and as more engines of the same type arrived they increasingly took over the longer and heavier duties. Although they were well suited to the work, it was, however, still necessary to bank or to double-head on the steepest sections of line

Sandhole shed, with an allocation of five locomotives, was responsible for traffic on the eastern leg of the railway, from Ashton's Field past Bridgewater Colliery to Sanderson's Siding and the canal tip at Worsley. The fifth ex North Staffordshire Railway locomotive, usually SIR ROBERT, was stationed here for the heaviest work, supported by either BRACKLEY or ELLESMERE, sometimes both. These two were replaced by Austerity tanks, which do not seem to have made an appearance at Sandhole until the mid 1950s.

One of the Sandhole duties was shunting at Sanderson's Siding and the canal tip at Worsley; in turn WARDLEY, WESTWOOD, COLONEL and BRIDGEWATER were used. WESTWOOD was particularly popular with the crews as it was a left hand drive engine and much of the work at the sidings was round a left hand curve. Another Sandhole duty was shunting at Linnyshaw Moss and working trips to Pendlebury Landsale Yard.

Two locomotives were stationed at Brackley Colliery, one for working trains to Ashton's Field and Dixon Green Landsale Yard, the other for shunting in the colliery yard and taking wagons of pit waste to Cutacre Tip. STANLEY was used on the former duty in the early years of nationalisation and JOSEPH on the latter. JOSEPH was later replaced by the Austerity tank JAMES.

At this time, the drivers on the Bridgewater railway system retained the same locomotive for long periods, which meant that the engines were generally well cared for. The locomotives were normally manned by a driver, brakesman and fireman, in that order of seniority, the fireman being required to assist the brakesman when necessary.

1961 to 1967 The East Lancashire Area of the National Coal Board

There were further changes to the National Coal Board organisation on 1st January 1961. As we have mentioned in previously, an East Lancashire, Burnley and Cumberland Area was created to take over the collieries in the No 1 (Manchester) Area which were still at work as well as those around Burnley and in West Cumberland. The Atherton Collieries and Bedford Colliery, which had been transferred to the No 2 (Wigan) Area on 1st January 1953, were included in the new East Lancashire Area. Bickershaw and Parsonage Collieries, which had also been transferred to the No 2 Area in 1953, were taken into the new West Lancashire Area, which included the collieries in and around Wigan and St Helens.

Walkden Yard 1961 to 1967

The workshops at Walkden took over the responsibility for major overhauls to all the locomotives in the North Western Division, including those from the North Wales Area. Locomotive work ceased at the workshops at Kirkless in November 1962 [10] and Haydock in March 1963 [11]. To cater for the increased workload there were extensions in 1963 at Walkden Yard which included a 50ft addition to the locomotive shop [12].

Personnel from Walkden, including a number of former drivers who had been redeployed as fitter's mates, were sent to outlying parts of the Division to carry out minor repair work. Maintenance facilities in Cumberland seem to have been particularly poor and at Ladysmith Colliery there was an unusually high number of accidents to locomotives. Walkden had frequently to supply engines to replace those made unserviceable.

A feature of the Walkden scene at this period was the long row of locomotives, brought in as a result of colliery closures, which were stored out of use, awaiting disposal. Such details as we have of these engines as well as those overhauled at the workshops are given in the Locomotive Summary.

In March 1962 REVENGE appeared in a new colour scheme of maroon lined out in yellow, with the National Coal Board crest on the cabside, and this was adopted for locomotives working in the East Lancashire Area. The new livery was eventually applied to all the austerity tanks, with the exception of JAMES and WARSPITE. and to some of the older locomotives, including BRIDGEWATER, FRANCIS, SIR ROBERT and ATLAS. It was not, however used on engines which were repaired at Walkden from other Areas of the National Coal Board, which were usually repainted in their original colours.

The Locomotives 1961 to 1967

By 1961, the greater part of the stock consisted of austerity tanks. CHARLES, JAMES, REPULSE, RESPITE, REVENGE, STANLEY, WARRIOR, WARSPITE, WASP, WITCH, WIZARD were normally employed on the former Bridgewater Collieries section. ALLEN was usually to be found at Astley Green.

Four of the ex-North Staffordshire Railway locomotives were still in existence at the beginning of 1961. KENNETH was retired later in that year or early in 1962, but was not broken up until early in 1967.

There was a certain amount of cannibalisation and exchange of identities which at this time which kept the other three running. No official records of the period survive, so our account of events is to a certain extent surmise and deduction.

During the summer of 1964, the boiler, cab, bunker and tanks from the former PRINCESS, were fitted to the frames, cylinders and wheels of SIR ROBERT. The rebuilt NSR No 2, still painted in North Staffordshire livery, came out of the workshops at the end of July 1964. The boiler was subsequently condemned and the engine had been withdrawn from service by August 1965. It was donated to the Staffordshire County Museum at Shugborough in 1967 or 1968, later going to the Chatterley Whitfield Mining Museum.

The original SIR ROBERT had a round hole in the left hand frame above the front buffer beam, a unique feature which distinguished it from the other engines of the class. In August 1964 NSR No 2 displayed the same feature. There is also a story that when SIR ROBERT was in Walkden shops after coming from the LMSR in 1937, a fitter welded his initials on the inside of the frames. The initials are said to visible today on NSR No 2 [13].

SIR ROBERT, now fitted with the chassis from PRINCESS and with the bunker and some other fittings from KING GEORGE VI, emerged in August 1965. It was repainted in the No 1 Area maroon livery, the only one of the ex-NSR engines to be so treated. It lasted until 1967, when it was taken out of service. After lying derelict at Walkden, it was cut up in September 1969.

KING GEORGE VI, which had gone into the workshops in 1965, never returned to service and was broken up in May 1966.

One further austerity saddle tank was taken into stock late in 1964 or early in 1965. As we have already described in Chapters 9 and 10, WD 71499 had been employed at the Peel Hall Opencast Disposal Point until it was sent to Gin Pit for storage. It was overhauled at Walkden, repainted in the maroon livery and named HARRY, after Harry Tweedy, the Foreman of Control on the Central Railways system. It was sent from Walkden Yard to Gin Pit, but returned in March 1966 and, after further repairs, was then used at Astley Green.

Railway operation 1961 to 1967

The progressive closure of the collieries from the early 1960s onwards resulted in a contraction of railway operations. Sandhole Colliery ceased work in September 1962, the workings having been connected underground to Mosley Common. The washery was retained for a few more years but the engine shed there closed at the same time as the colliery. The remaining work on the eastern leg of the railway was transferred to Ellesmere shed at Walkden.

At this time there was a significant amount of inwards coal traffic from other collieries, including Bedford [14], which had to be hauled to the washery at Sandhole and the coal blending plant at Ashton's Field. The eastern leg of the system also handled coal for the landsale yard at Roe Green, which remained open until at least 1965.

Traffic south of Sandhole appears to have ceased in 1966 and the connection with British Railways at Sanderson's Siding was taken out of use at the end of the year [15]. By May 1970 the track had been lifted. The section of line northwards from Sandhole to Linnyshaw Moss remained in use until September 1968, when the washery closed.

At this period eight of the locomotives stabled at Ellesmere shed were in use on the morning shift on weekdays, seven on Saturday mornings and three on Sunday mornings [14, 16]. At least one locomotive was employed on the afternoon shift, finishing at 11.0 pm and another on nights between 11.0 pm and 7.0 am. Except on Sundays two engines were employed on the heavy traffic between Sandhole Washery, Linnyshaw Moss and Ashton's Field [14].

NSR No 2 double heading CHARLES on a loaded coal train passing Sandhole Washery. The photograph was taken in November 1964 and dismantling is well underway at Sandhole Colliery which can be seen in the background. H D Bowtell

Two locomotives, normally WARSPITE and JAMES, were stabled at Brackley until the colliery closed on 22nd May 1964. JAMES was then transferred to Astley Green. WARSPITE remained there for working Cutacre Tip, returning to Walkden about once a month for washouts and minor repairs [14]. Cutacre Tip had been developed to dispose of the dirt from all the collieries and washeries connected to the railway system. It was popularly believed to have become the largest waste tip in Europe and its southern end covered the site of the old Wharton Hall Colliery. In 1965 around 120 wagons a day were being dealt with [14].

The dirt trains were normally worked to Ashton's Field by locomotives based at Astley Green, Ellesmere and Sandhole as appropriate and then taken on by one the Brackley locomotives. However, on occasions the Brackley engines ran through to Astley Green on this traffic. JAMES was noted passing Walkden, bunker first up the incline, in September 1962. WITCH, which had taken over from WARSPITE by May 1967, was seen on several occasions at Astley Green at the end of that year and in 1968.

Five locomotives were in daily use at Astley Green in August 1964 [17] , which was still very much the preserve of the older engines, EDWARD, FRANCIS and BRIDGEWATER, together with the Hudswell Clarke four wheeler, CARR, until it was transferred to William Pit at Whitehaven in 1965.

ALLEN was the only austerity permanently based here although no doubt others were transferred temporarily from Walkden if the need arose. Occasionally engines sent to Walkden from other collieries for overhaul were used; this was the case with RENOWN which was sent from Gin Pit to Walkden at the end of 1963 and was noted at Astley Green in October and November before being taken into the shops later in November. The permanent allocation of austerities at Astley Green was increased when JAMES arrived towards the end of 1964, followed by HARRY and W.H.R. in 1966.

The Smoke Problem

The use of steam locomotives at such a late date gave rise to numerous complaints about smoke nuisance. Houses backed on to the steeply graded sections on the eastern and western legs of the railway and in Walkden the line passed close to the town centre and the District Council is said to have posted men on the bridges to monitor the smoke. Various measures were tried by the N C B authorities in an attempt to solve the problem.

The first was to burn a mixture of coal and coke, the earliest observations of this alteration being in September 1959. The Austerity tanks needed a rearward extension of the bunker to accommodate the extra bulk of the coke and the buffers and drawgear were lengthened. Longitudinal dividing plates were fitted in the bunker to separate the coal and the coke. Six of the austerity tanks were dealt with - CHARLES, RESPITE, REVENGE, WARSPITE, WASP and WARRIOR. In the case of the former North Staffordshire engines the bunkers did not need an extension and we can only be sure that KENNETH and PRINCESS were fitted with dividing plates.

The experiment was not a success and the use of coke ceased. It was found that the extended bunkers when full of coal made the engines "back end heavy", so the bunkers, buffers and drawgear were reduced to the original length, starting in 1963. The exceptions were WARSPITE, which retained the lengthened bunker to accommodate a mechanical stoker, and CHARLES, which retained the long buffers and drawgear when transferred to Cumberland.

REVENGE, showing the extended bunker to hold coke and coal, very smart in the new maroon livery, probably recently ex shops in 1962. Industrial Railway Society, Ken Cooper collection

SIR ROBERT in the maroon livery adopted in 1962, with the National Coal Board North Western Division emblem on the cabside. The photograph is believed to have been taken in 1965. By this time steam jets had been fitted to the chimney. The row of holes along the side of the smokebox show that the engine was also equipped with a secondary air system . Industrial Railway Society, Ken Cooper collection

CHARLES photographed in May 1965 near Sandhole. The extended bunker, originlly fitted to permit the engines to burn a coal and coke mixture, is well ilustrated in this rear end view, as are the extensions to the buffers and the drawgear. The conventional chimney has been replaced by a Giesl ejector, fitted with steam jets.

Cooper's Railway Photographs

HARRY working hard at Astley Green in December 1968. Notice how the steam from the jets in the chimney give the impression of white smoke !

Philip Hindley

The earliest observation of a locomotive fitted with a Giesl ejector, in place of the conventional blast pipe and chimney, was CHARLES, in May 1961. This device was adopted on many locomotives owned by the National Coal Board in an attempt to reduce fuel consumption. At Walkden it was also hoped that it would reduce smoke emission.

Giesl ejectors were subsequently fitted to FRANCIS, STANLEY, REPULSE, RESPITE, REVENGE, RODNEY, WARRIOR, WARSPITE, WASP and WIZARD as well as some locomotives working elsewhere that were overhauled at Walkden Yard.

In 1961 WARSPITE was fitted with a Hill-Bigwood mechanical stoker driven by a diesel engine. The diesel engine also operated a fan which introduced air into the firebox. When the mechanical stoker was first fitted, WARSPITE had a conventional chimney, but was later fitted with a Giesl ejector.

In 1963 and 1964 WASP from the Bridgewater railway system and FRED and HURRICANE from Bickershaw Colliery, were fitted with the Hunslet complete combustion system, incorporating a steam driven mechanical stoker and a Kylpor blast pipe. The alterations were carried out at Walkden Yard, with Hunslet personnel in attendance. WASP lost its Giesl ejector as a result. The modification to the Bickershaw engines seems suprising as there is no evidence that smoke was a problem there. It has been suggested that one or two other locomotives, including REVENGE, were also fitted with mechanical stokers, without the refinement of Kylpor blast pipes, but no proof has been forthcoming.

A relatively inexpensive idea that was adopted was the fitting of a ring of steam jets around the top of the chimney. Steam was fed through a pipe along the tank and was controlled by a valve in the cab. Officially the steam jets were intended to act as a blower to aid combustion. Unofficially it was hoped that white "smoke" would be more acceptable than black. The device was first noted in August 1963, fitted to REPULSE. Almost all the locomotives of whatever type that remained in service were fitted subsequently. The exceptions were some of those which had Giesl ejectors, but others which had Giesl ejectors, for example FRANCIS and CHARLES, had the steam jets fitted.

Yet another scheme made its appearance in 1964 known as the Secondary Air System. Additional air was introduced into the firebox through tubes which connected with holes in the smokebox. These tubes , which passed through the boiler tubes, were made of a special grade of steel, imported from East Germany, and had a life of 9 to 12 months. REVENGE was the first locomotive to be noted with this modification, in July 1964. Subsequently all active locomotives on the system were so equipped, KING GEORGE VI and SIR ROBERT having the inlet pipes on the side of the smokebox, while the austerity tanks had them on the front.

It has been said that some Austerity tanks had steam jets fitted in the firebox and others in the smokebox. This has been identified only on REPULSE. That engine, and WARRIOR, had a small sliding door in the back of the bunker, the purpose of which has not been ascertained. It has been suggested that it was to give access to a mechanical stoker, but there is no evidence that one was fitted to these engines,

The complexity of all these modifications is illustrated by WASP. In June 1960 it had an extended bunker, but was otherwise unaltered. By March 1963 it had a Giesl ejector and retained the long bunker. By May 1964 it had been fitted with a Hunslet mechanical stoker, the Giesl ejector had been removed and the bunker had reverted to normal length.

The final years - The North Western Area of the National Coal Board 1967 to 1971

There was yet another reorganisation of the National Coal Board structure, which took effect from 26th March 1967. The North Western Division was done away with and its three Areas were merged into what was then known as the North Western Area. By this time, the coal industry in South Lancashire was in a state of terminal decline and the last two collieries connected to the Walkden railway system closed within the next three years.

The organisational changes also affected the workshops at Walkden, which now came directly under the control of the N C B Headquarters instead of the Division. In addition to those from the new North Western Area, several locomotives came in for overhaul from as far afield as South Wales. More locomotives also joined the lines of those in store and awaiting disposal. Despite the reduced requirements in Lancashire, a shortage of austerity tanks developed and, in July 1970, it was necessary to purchase another second hand from the Hunslet Engine Company. It was in poor condition and needed to be overhauled at Walkden before being sent to work at Gresford Colliery in North Wales, where it was named ALISON.

As far as the Bridgewater locomotive stock was concerned, there were many changes as engines were withdrawn from service and replaced by others, sometimes only on a temporary basis, from collieries where production had already ceased. The full story, as far as it is known, can be found in the locomotive summary at the end of the chapter.

By August 1967, there were now only four locomotives in daily use at Ellesmere shed out of a total of six on the working roster, which comprised STANLEY, RESPITE, REPULSE, REVENGE, WARRIOR and WIZARD.

At Astley Green there was an almost complete change in the locomotive stock in 1967 and 1968. All the veterans which had survived from pre-NCB days were broken up. BRIDGEWATER, EDWARD and FRANCIS were still at Astley Green in August 1967, but were later sent to Walkden Yard, where they were broken up in October 1968.

JAMES was sent from Astley Green to Walkden Yard in August 1967 and was broken up there in November of the following year. W.H.R. followed in August 1967 and ALLEN by March 1968.

Other austerities replaced them. HARRY, the former Opencast Executive engine which had been taken into East Lancashire Area stock in 1965, arrived in 1966 and remained at Astley Green until the end. HUMPHREY was here from late 1967 to the middle of 1968. RESPITE and REPULSE were here in 1968 and 1969, but towards the end of 1969 or early 1970 both were out of use at Walkden. STANLEY arrived towards the end 1969 and was here until 1970. RENOWN was temporarily here in September 1968

Mosley Common, one of the two remaining collieries connected with the railway system, closed with effect from 10th February 1968 [18]. Cutacre Tip closed at the same time and as a result the section of line to here from Ashton's Field was taken out of use. The last trip was on 6th February to collect empty wagons [19] and WITCH, the last locomotive to be stabled at Brackley, was transferred to Astley Green. By May 1970, the track between Ashton's Field and Cutacre had been lifted.

If Mosley Common Colliery had remained open, as was originally intended, it had been proposed to divert the trains to Cutacre Tip over the former London and North Western Railway between Walkden and Brackley as a motorway was to cut across the site of the NCB line [20]. Although the main line had been closed some years previously, the track had been left in situ on the sections between Walkden and Little Hulton Junction and on the Little Hulton Mineral Branch. The impending closure of Mosley Common caused the scheme to be abandoned and the track from Little Hulton Junction to Brackley was lifted early in 1967 [19].

Astley Green Colliery in April 1970, shortly before closure. Philip Hindley

RESPITE shunting at the east end of the colliery yard at Astley Green in April 1970. Note the egg ended boiler serving as a water tank for the locomotives, which has survived the modernisation of the colliery. Philip Hindley

WARRIOR, fitted with a Giesel ejector, on a coal train from Astley Green Colliery. The photograph was taken at the level crossing south of Ashton's Field in September1969. Philip Hindley

The Yorkshire Engine Company's 0-6-0 Diesel electric loco with a train at Ashton's Field blending plant in April 1970. Philip Hindley

Sandhole Washery closed in September 1968 and, as a result, the line northwards to Linnyshaw Moss ceased to be used. On the Eastern leg of the railway system, only the short portion between Linnyshaw and Ashton's Field still carried traffic.

The western leg remained in use to serve Astley Green Colliery and it associated coal preparation plant, which also processed coal brought in by road from other collieries, such as Bedford [21]. The connections with British Railways at Ellenbrook and Walkden had been taken out of use by this time and all traffic was exchanged at Astley Moss or Linnyshaw Moss.

In April 1969 about 40 wagons per day were being despatched via Astley Moss for destinations such as Hartshead Power Station. A further 40 wagons a day went to Ashton's Field, involving two N C B trains daily, each of about 20 wagons. At Ashton's Field the coal was blended with other coal brought in by road from Agecroft Colliery and then conveyed by N C B train to Linnyshaw Moss, where the wagons were handed over to British Railways for transfer to Kearsley Power Station sidings [21].

Two working locomotives were needed at Astley Green, running traffic to Astley Moss exchange sidings and shunting at the colliery and the washery. It was usual to keep a third engine there as a spare. The three austerity saddle tanks HARRY, RESPITE and REPULSE were often to be found there at this period.

One engine based at Walkden, usually WARRIOR, was employed on the trains between Astley Green, Ashton's Field and Linnyshaw Moss until January 1970, when a six coupled diesel electric locomotive of Yorkshire Engine Company manufacture arrived from Parsonage Colliery. Subsequently the steam engine was usually confined to the heavy haul from Astley Green to Ashton's Field, while the diesel worked the relatively level section from Ashton's Field to Linnyshaw Moss.

Coal production at Astley Green Colliery ceased with effect from 3rd April 1970 [22], with many years supply of coal still unworked. The coal preparation plant remained in use until October. REPULSE was returned to Walkden soon after the colliery closed. In September 1970, HARRY and RESPITE were still at work.

One locomotive finished at 2 pm, while the second, which shunted at the washery, finished at 4.30 pm [22]. One of the locomotives based at Ellesmere shed, still usually WARRIOR, worked as far as Ashton's Field. while the diesel engine, also based at Ellesmere shed, was employed between Ashton's Field and Linnyshaw Moss [22].

The end came on Friday, 2nd October, when coal traffic finally ceased on the Bridgewater railways system and the last wagons were exchanged with British Railways at Linnyshaw Moss [22,23]. Although the exchange sidings, along with the branch to Kearsley Junction, were formally closed by British Rail with effect from 5th October, the line was actually used on 12th October to transfer a diesel locomotive, which had been overhauled at Walkden, to Agecroft Colliery under its own power [23].

The Bridgewater railway north of Walkden was not used again after the passage of the diesel engine, but there was some activity on the line between Walkden and Astley Moss. One locomotive, reputedly a diesel engine which had been sent from Agecroft Colliery, was put to use at Walkden before it was overhauled. Until 11th October it ran light to Astley Green each day to marshal wagons and return with those that were fit for further use [23,24].

After repairs at Walkden, 200 steel wagons were despatched to Bold and Bickershaw Collieries. They travelled from Walkden via Astley Green and were handed over to British Railways at Astley Moss. The last train ran on or about 22nd April 1971, one of the Walkden locomotives being specially steamed to haul it [25].

It is also recorded [24] that a diesel locomotive built by the Yorkshire Engine Company, presumably the one previously used on the Ashton's Field to Linnyshaw trains, was sent from Walkden to Parkside Colliery, late in 1970. It travelled on its own wheels and was handed over to British Railways at Astley Moss.

The portion of line between Walkden and Astley Green was retained briefly for the movement of engines sent by road transport for repairs at the Central Workshops. Until facilities had been provided there, the engines were loaded and unloaded at Astley Green [23,24,26].

A November 1970 photograph showing a locomotive being loaded on to a road vehicle at Astley Green for despatch to Gresford Colliery, near Wrexham, where it was subsequently named ALISON. The diesel locomotive has brought the austerity tank from Walkden Yard, where it has just been overhauled. Note the conical chimney to accommodate the Kylpor blast pipe. Alex Appleton collection

Most of the railway system was lifted during 1971. On 25th August it was observed that the track at Ashton's Field was being taken up by Metallic Salvage and Supply Co Ltd of Chester, using road transport. By that date track north and south of Ashton's Field had gone as had some of the main line in the Walkden area. Track at Astley Green and from there to the exchange sidings at Astley Moss was still in place, but eastwards towards Mosley Common it had been lifted.

A few hundred yards at Walkden, between Manchester Road and the bridge under the ex-L&YR line, was retained for testing locomotives overhauled at the workshops [24,25]. The engines made redundant by the closure of the railway system were brought here where they joined HUMPHREY which had been out of use since arriving from Gin Pit in 1967. REPULSE, RESPITE, REVENGE and STANLEY were later overhauled and sent to collieries in West Cumberland, while HARRY and HUMPHREY were eventually sold for scrap. WARRIOR was used as the works shunter, but was only steamed occasionally when engines needed moving in or out of the shops. It had been transferred to Bickershaw Colliery by August 1977.

Repairs to steam locomotives continued until the beginning of 1980, when JOSEPH was despatched to Bold Colliery. Increasingly the works turned over to the repair of diesel locomotives, including a number of narrow gauge engines used underground. The last standard gauge engine to be repaired was a 650 HP Sentinel diesel which was sent to Sutton Manor Colliery in October 1983 [27].

The workshops finally closed in 1986, thus bringing to an end a link with mining which had existed in Walkden for upwards of three centuries.

Today, very little remains to remind us of the industrial past. Large parts of the railway system have disappeared under new motorways. Surpisingly in view of recent redevelopment, much of the branch to the coal yard at Pendlebury is still in situ and large parts of the line from Ashton's Field to Boothsbank and from Boothsbank through Astley Green to the British Railways line at Astley Moss can still be traced. The bridge under Manchester Road at Walkden is still in situ and a road has been built on the railway formation to provide access to the car park at the Ellesmere shopping centre.

The collieries at Brackley, Sandhole, Mosley Common and the coal blending plant at Ashton's Field have all been razed to the ground and landscaped. The workshops at Walkden, after standing idle for a few years, were demolished and replaced by a housing estate.

Only at Astley Green is there anything significant to be seen. A steam winding engine and some of the buildings have been preserved as part of a Mining Museum which is being developed. Two standard gauge locomotives, one steam, the other diesel, have been brought to the site under the auspices of the Red Rose Steam Society. A number of narrow gauge diesel locomotives have also been here from time to time.

LOCOMOTIVE SUMMARY

National Coal Board – Central Railways System and Astley Green

WARDLEY 0-6-0STIC SS 3423 1888 17"x24" 4'0"

Ex Manchester Collieries Ltd, 1-1-1947, on Central Railways system
At Walkden Yard for repairs 1947, completed 27-4-1947
Normally based at Sandhole shed
Laid aside at Walkden Yard 11-1950 and scrapped there 6-1953

BRACKLEY 0-6-0STIC NW 912 1910 18"x26" 4'3"

Ex Manchester Collieries Ltd, 1-1-1947, on Central Railways system
Normally based at Sandhole shed
At Walkden Yard for repairs 4-1947 to 10-1947 (new cylinders fitted), and late 1953
Laid aside at Walkden Yard by 9-1956 and scrapped there by Stone and Hutchinson 2-1957

ELLESMERE 0-6-0STIC NW 976 1912 18"x26" 4'3"

Ex Manchester Collieries Ltd, 1-1-1947, on Central Railways system
Normally based at Sandhole shed
At Walkden Yard for repairs late 1947, mid 1951 to early 1952, mid 1952, late 1953, mid 1954.
Partly cut up at Walkden Yard 9-1956, chassis cut up 11-1963

JOSEPH	0-6-0T OC	HE	1456	1924	18"x24"	3'9"

Ex Manchester Collieries Ltd, 1-1-1947, on Central Railways system
Normally based at Brackley Colliery
At Walkden Yard for repairs 17-2-1948 to 25-11-1948 (Side tanks renewed), mid 1952 to early 1953, mid 1956 to early 1957
Withdrawn from service by 11-1958
Dismantled at Walkden Yard 5-1959, chassis cut up 3-1963

BRIDGEWATER	0-6-0T OC	HE	1475	1924	18"x24"	3'9"

Ex Manchester Collieries Ltd, 1-1-1947, on Central Railways system
Sent to Astley Green 21-5-1947 and used there to 2-1948
At Walkden Yard for repairs mid 1948 and returned to traffic early 1951 (New boiler from Hunslet Engine Co)
At various locations on Central railway system 1952 to 1959
At Walkden Yard for repairs, early 1953, 1955, early 1957, late 1963 to early 1964, mid 1965
Sent to Astley Green 1958 and remained there until late 1967 or early 1968
Laid aside at Walkden Yard by 3-1968 and cut up there 10-1968

BEDFORD	0-6-0T IC	MW		1865	15¼"x22½"	3'10½"

Ex Manchester Collieries Ltd, 1-1-1947, at Astley Green, out of use
Laid aside at Walkden Yard by 4-1947 and broken up late 1950

BLACK DIAMOND	0-4-0STOC	SS	2742	1878	16"x20"	4'0"

Ex Manchester Collieries Ltd, 1-1-1947, at Astley Green
Based at Astley Green until sent to Walkden Yard in 1948
Laid aside at Walkden Yard by 8-1948 and broken up there 10-1949

EDWARD	0-6-0STOC	HL	3184	1916	17"x24"	3'10"

Ex Manchester Collieries Ltd, 1-1-1947, at Astley Green
Based at Astley Green until late 1967 or early 1968
At Walkden Yard for repairs 1955, 1956, late 1958, 1960, 1963, 1964
Sent to Walkden Yard late 1967 or early 1968 and scrapped there 10-1968

FRANCIS	0-6-0 TOC	KS	3068	1917	17"x24"	3'11"

Ex Manchester Collieries Ltd, 1-1-1947, at Astley Green
Based at Astley Green until late 1967 or early 1968
At Walkden Yard for repairs late 1947 to early 1948, 24-4-1950 to 18-1-1951 (new boiler from Hunslet Engine Co), 1954, late 1956 and early 1957, 1965, 1967
Sent to Walkden Yard late 1967 or early 1968 and scrapped there 10-1968

CARBON	0-4-0STOC	AB	1704	1920	14"x22"	3'5"

Ex Manchester Collieries Ltd, 1-1-1947, at Astley Green
Based at Astley Green until transferred to Cleworth Hall Colliery by 5-1947, see Chapter 10
Later at Bank Hall Colliery, Burnley, and scrapped there 11-1968

CARR	0-4-0STOC	HC	1812	1948	16"x24"	3'9"

New, delivered to Walkden 4-6-1948 and sent to Astley Green on 15-6-1948
Based at Astley Green until 1965
At Walkden Yard for repairs 3-1955 to 8-1955, 1960, late 1963 to early 1964 mid 1965
Transferred to William Pit, Whitehaven, late 1965 and scrapped at Ladysmith Colliery 11-1972

WESTWOOD	0-4-0STOC	HC	1036	1913	16"x24"	3'8"

From Moston Colliery to Walkden Yard for repairs on 8-8-1948
Repairs completed 8-7-1949 and transferred to Central Railways. Based at Sandhole shed until 1955
At Walkden yard for repairs mid 1953
Transferred to Ashton Moss Colliery 6-1-1955 and then at other locations. See Chapters 7 and 10 and Appendix 4
Temporarily at Astley Green late 1959

COLONEL 0-6-0STIC HE 1459 1927 15"x20" 3'0"
Temporarily on Central Railways late 1952 to 1953 and again in 1957. For earlier and later history, see Chapters 7 and 9

GEORGE PEACE 0-6-0 TIC LE 245 1906 16"x24" 3'10"
Temporarily transferred from Gin Pit to Astley Green mid 1952
For full history see Chapter 10

KENNETH 0-6-2T IC Stoke 1921 18½"x26" 5'0"
Ex Manchester Collieries Ltd, 1-1-1947, on Central Railways system
Normally based at Ellesmere shed
At Walkden Yard for repairs 1951, 1952, 1954, 1955, 1956, late 1958 to mid 1959.
Laid aside at Walkden Yard by 5-1962, scrapped 4 -1967

SIR ROBERT 0-6-2T IC Stoke 1920 18½"x26" 5'0"
Ex Manchester Collieries Ltd, 1-1-1947, on Central Railways system
Normally based at Sandhole shed
At Walkden Yard for repairs 8-1-1947 to 23-4-1947 (new cylinders), 1-8-1949 to 18-5-1950 (new boiler from Hunslet Engine Co), late 1952, 1954, 1957, 1960, 1961
Laid aside by 5-1962 and boiler condemned 3-1963
Taken into Walkden Yard 1964 and fitted with frames from PRINCESS. Ex shops by 10-1965
Out of use at Walkden Yard by early 1968 and scrapped there 9-1969

KING GEORGE VI 0-6-2T IC Stoke 1913 18½"x26" 5'0"
Ex Manchester Collieries Ltd, 1-1-1947, on Central Railways system
Normally based at Ellesmere shed, but noted at Sandhole in 1957
At Walkden Yard for repairs 1948 (New boiler from Hunslet Engine Co), 1951, 1956, 1959, 1961, late 1962
Dismantled at Walkden Yard by 8-1965 and scrapped 5-1966

QUEEN ELIZABETH 0-6-2T IC Stoke 1923 18½"x26" 5'0"
Ex Manchester Collieries Ltd, 1-1-1947, on Central Railways system
Normally based at Ellesmere shed
At Walkden Yard for repairs 6-12-1945 to 14-1-1947 (New boiler)
Laid aside at Walkden Yard by 8-1952
Dismantled by 5-1957, chassis broken up 5-1963

PRINCESS 0-6-2T IC Stoke 1923 18½"x26" 5'0"
Ex Manchester Collieries Ltd, 1-1-1947, on Central Railways system
Normally based at Ellesmere shed
At Walkden Yard for repairs 1950, 1951, late 1953, late 1958, 1960
Repainted in North Staffordshire Railway Livery as NSR No 2 in 4-1960 and sent to Crewe for North Staffordhsire Railway Centenary celebration, Returned by 31-5-1960
At Walkden Yard for repairs 1964 and fitted with frames from SIR ROBERT
Withdrawn from service by 8-1965
To Shugborough Museum 1967 or 1968

WILLIAM 0-6-2T IC SS 3606 1890 17½"x26" 4'3"
Ex Manchester Collieries Ltd, 1-1-1947, on Central Railways system
Normally based at Ellesmere shed until 1949
At Walkden Yard for repairs 1948 and returned to traffic 1-3-1949
Sent to Astley Green 1-3-1949 and remained there until 1951
Laid aside at Walkden Yard by 5-1951, officially withdrawn 15-10-1951 and broken up 6-1952

47669 0-6-0T IC Hor 1931 18"x26" 4'7"
Loaned by British Railways in 1960 while NSR No 2 at centenary celebrations
Based at Ellesmere shed

ALLEN 0-6-0STIC HC 1777 1944 18"x26" 4'3"
Ex Manchester Collieries Ltd, 1-1-1947, on Central Railways system
On Central railways until 12-5-1950, based at Ellesmere shed, and then based at Astley Green until withdrawn from service in 1968
At Walkden Yard for repairs 1950, 8-1-1951 to 30-4-1951, 23-5-1953 to 23-3-1954, 1956, 2-1960 to 6-1960, 1-1963 to 3-1963, early 1965, mid 1966, mid 1967
Sent from Astley Green to Walkden by 3-1968 and remained out of use there until scrapped there 9-1968

CHARLES 0-6-0STIC HC 1778 1944 18"x26" 4'3"
Ex Manchester Collieries Ltd, 1-1-1947, on Central Railways system
Normally based at Ellesmere shed until 1967
At Walkden Yard for repairs 15-5-1950 to 20-7-1950, 28-1-1953 to 3-3-1953, early 1954, 1956, early 1958, mid 1959, late 1963 to early 1964 (boiler off WASP, tank off WARSPITE)
Transferred to Ladysmith Colliery, Cumberland, 8-1967 and scrapped there 8-1973

STANLEY 0-6-0STIC HE 3302 1945 18"x26" 4'3"
Ex Manchester Collieries Ltd, 1-1-1947, on Central Railways system
Normally based at Brackley from 1947 to 1961.
Temporarily at Chanters from about 11-1961 to 7-1962
Based at Sandhole in 1962 for a short period, then Ellesmere shed. At Brackley in 1963 Normally based at Ellesmere shed from 1964 until late 1969 and then at Astley Green.
At Walkden Yard for repairs late 1949, mid 1952, 1954, late 1957 to early 1958, mid 1961, 1966, late 1967 to early 1968, mid 1969
Transferred to Ladysmith Colliery, Cumberland, late 1970 or early 1971 and scrapped there 6-1975

FRED 0-6-0STIC RSH 7289 1945 18"x26" 4'3"
Ex Manchester Collieries Ltd, 1-1-1947, on Central Railways system
Normally based at Ellesmere shed until transferred to Bickershaw Colliery 7-12-1948
At Walken Yard for repairs mid 1949, 6-11-1950 to 18-1-1951
Possibly used temporarily on Central railways system from 18-1-1951 until returned to Bickershaw 12-3-1951
Became part of No 2 Area stock on 11-1952
At Walkden Yard for repairs, from Bickershaw, 11-1961 to 5-1962, 1963, aabout 8-1966 to 10-1966
Sent from Bickershaw to Walkden Yard about 7-1967 and remained out of use there until sold to Keighley and Worth Valley Railway 12-1968.
Moved to Keighley 4-1969

HUMPHREY 0-6-0STIC RSH 7293 1945 18"x26" 4'3"
Ex Manchester Collieries Ltd, 1-1-1947, on Central Railways system
Based at Astley Green until 1948, but at Brackley in 8 and 9-1948
At Walkden Yard for repairs 12-9-1947 to 19-9-1947 and at Ellesmere shed for repairs late 1948
Transferred to Chanters Colliery 31-12-1948 and became part of No 2 (Wigan) Area stock on 1-1-1952; see Chapter 9
Transferred from Gin Pit to Walkden Yard 11-1967 and based at Astley Green until mid/late 1968
Withdrawn from service and laid aside at Walkden Yard by 12-1968 and sold Jose K Holt Gordon Ltd for scrap 2-1976

W.H.R. 0-6-0STIC RSH 7174 1944 18"x26" 4'3"
Purchased second hand, originally WD 71520
Arrived at Walkden 18-6-1947 and transferred to Gin Pit in 7-1947. See Chapter 9
Transferred from Gin Pit late 1964. Based at Astley Green in 1964, at Ellesmere shed in 1965 and at Astley Green in 1966 and 1967
Laid aside at Walkden Yard by 8-1967 and broken up 10-1968

JAMES 0-6-0STIC RSH 7175 1944 18"x26" 4'3"

Purchased second hand, originally WD 71521

Arrived at Walkden 16-6-1947

Normally based at Ellesmere shed until 1954 Temporarily at Astley Green August 1947 to late 1947 or early 1948, 6 to 12-12-1949, mid 1950,

At Brackley from 1957 to 1962 and at Astley Green from 10-1964 until withdrawn at end of 1967.

At Walkden Yard for repairs 6-9-1952 to 16-1-1953 (new boiler), 1-6-1954 to 24-6-1954, 11-5-1956 to 29-5-1956 (boiler off RESPITE fitted), mid 1961, mid 1964, late 1966

Laid aside at Walkden Yard by 8-1967 and scrapped there 11-1968

RODNEY 0-6-0STIC HE 3695 1950 18"x26" 4'3"

Delivered to Walkden 20th Oct 1950, sent to Bickershaw Colliery and absorbed into stock of No 2 (Wigan) Area on 1st January 1952

Never returned to Walkden railway system and was scrapped at Bickershaw 4-1976

RESPITE 0-6-0STIC HE 3696 1950 18"x26" 4'3"

Delivered to Walkden 28th Oct 1950

Based at Astley Green 1950 to mid 1952.

Based at Ellesmere shed mid 1952 to 12-1968, with temporary transfer to Astley Green mid 1960.

At Walkden Yard for repairs mid 1955, late 1965 to early 1966, late 1967

Normally based at Astley Green from 12-1968 to late 1970 or mid 1971

Laid aside at Walkden Yard by mid 1971, but taken into shops in 1972

Transferred to Ladysmith Colliery, Cumberland, 11-1972 and later at Bickershaw Colliery, from where sold to Resco (Railways) Ltd in 1981

To National Railway Museum 2-1985

RENOWN 0-6-0STIC HE 3697 1950 18"x26" 4'3"

Delivered to Walkden 4th Nov 1950 and sent to Parsonage Colliery, later at Gin Pit and retained in No 1 (Manchester) Area stock on 1st January 1952. See Chapter 9

Temporarily at Astley Green late 1963, before going for repair at Walkden Yard in November 1963 and then returned to Gin Pit early 1964

Transferred from Gin Pit in 11-1967, and put into store at Walkden Yard until August 1968

Used at Astley Green temporarily in 9-1968

Scrapped at Walkden Yard 10-1968

REPULSE 0-6-0STIC HE 3698 1950 18"x26" 4'3"

Delivered to Walkden 16th Nov 1950

Normally based at Ellesmere shed until early 1968, with a period in 1952 at Brackley and at Sandhole in 1957 and 1958. Used at Astley Green 1968 and 1969

At Walkden Yard for repairs mid 1954, early 1957, late 1960 to early 1961

Put into store at Walkden Yard early 1970, but taken into shops in 1973 overhauled early 1973

Transferred to Ladysmith Colliery, Cumberland, 5-1973 and sold to Lakeside and Haverthwaite Railway 9-1976

REVENGE 0-6-0STIC HE 3699 1950 18"x26" 4'3"

Delivered to Walkden 23rd Nov 1950

Normally based at Ellesmere shed until 1967

At Walkden Yard for repairs mid 1954, 1957, early 1962, late 1967

Transferred to Ladysmith Colliery, Cumberland, 2-1968 and scrapped there about 10-1976

WARSPITE 0-6-0STIC HE 3778 1950 18"x26" 4'3"

Delivered to Walkden Nov 1952

Based at Ellesmere shed until early 1961, with temporary transfer to Astley Green in 1960

Based at Brackley from early 1961 until late 1965 or early 1966, then based at Ellesmere shed until early 1967

At Walkden Yard for repairs late 1958, late 1961, early 1963

Put into store at Walkden Yard by 5-1967 and overhauled 1968

Transferred to Harrington Colliery, Cumberland, 11-1968 and scrapped at Ladysmith Colliery in 1976

WASP 0-6-0STIC HE 3808 1954 18"x26" 4'3"
Delivered to Walkden 20th Jan 1954
Normally based at Ellesmere shed until 1967, with temporary transfer to Gin Pit, 8-1959 to 5-1960
At Walkden Yard for repairs mid 1960, 1963
Laid aside at Walkden Yard by 8-1967 and scrapped by Maudland Metals Ltd 10-1969

WARRIOR 0-6-0STIC HE 3823 1954 18"x26" 4'3"
Delivered to Walkden 2nd Sept 1954
Normally based at Ellesmere shed until 1970
At Walkden Yard for repairs mid 1959, early 1963
Used as works shunter at Walkden 1970 to 1977
Transferred to Bickershaw Colliery before 8-1977, where renamed FRED
Sold to Dean Forest Railway and arrived at their Norchard site 3-9-1984

WITCH 0-6-0STIC HE 3842 1956 18"x26" 4'3"
Delivered to Walkden 14th April 1956
Normally based at Sandhole shed until 1962.
Transferred to Chanters Colliery in 1962. See Chapter 9
Returned to Central Railways late 1964 or early 1965
Based at Ellesmere shed 1965 to mid 1967, at Brackley mid 1967 to early 1968 and at Astley Green mid 1968
At Walkden Yard for repairs mid 1960, mid 1967
Laid aside at Walkden Yard by 8-1968 and sold to Maudland Metals Ltd for scrap 4-1969

WIZARD 0-6-0STIC HE 3843 1956 18"x26" 4'3"
Delivered to Walkden 21st Sept 1956
Normally based at Sandhole shed until 1962 and then at Ellesmere shed until withdrawn from service in 1968
At Walkden Yard for repairs mid 1961
Laid aside at Walkden Yard by 12-1968 and sold to Maudland Metals Ltd for scrap 4-1969

WEASEL 0-6-0STIC HE 3844 1957 18"x26" 4'3"
Delivered to Walkden 3-1957 and sent to Gin Pit 5-1958.
From Gin Pit to Walkden Yard for repairs late 1965 and used temprorarily Astley Green 11-1965, before going into shops
To Ladysmith Washery, Cumberland, 2-1967
Laid aside at Walkden Yard by 7-1970 and sold to Jose K Holt Gordon Ltd for scrap 2-1976

HARRY 0-6-0STIC HC 1776 1944 18"x26" 4'3"
Transferred from Gin Pit early 1966 and, after overhaul at Walkden Yard, normally based at Astley Green until late 1973 or early 1974
Laid aside at Walkden Yard late 1973 or early 1974
Sold to Jose K Holt Gordon Ltd 14-12-1976 and sent to their yard at Chequerbent. Resold early 1992 to Shropshire Railway Preservation Society

0-6-0DE YE 2660 1957 200HP
New
Transferred to Agecroft Colliery 4-1962

0-6-0DE YE 2712 1958 400HP
Transferred from Parsonage Colliery, 1-1970
Transferred to Parkside Colliery, 1971

Diesel locomotives on trial on Central Railway System

0-6-0D HE 4003 1954 500HP
At Walkden from 30-3-1954 to 14-4-1954

0-6-0D YE 2595 1956
At Walkden 8-1956

0-6-0D NBL 440HP
At Walkden about 10-1957

0-6-0D S 10072
At Walkden 11-1961

Locomotives sent to Walkden Yard for overhaul or disposal

The list covers the period from 1947 to 1983 and is drawn from personal observations of the authors and their colleagues, supplemented by information in the publications of the Industrial Locomotive Society and the Industrial Railway Society. As it does not come from official records it may be incomplete.

The list excludes locomotives coming to Walkden from locations formerly owned by Manchester Collieries Ltd, Overhauls to these engines are given, as far as they are known, in the Locomotive Summaries at the end of the relevant chapters.

The list also excludes underground diesel locomotives. For details of those overhauled at Walkden the reader is referred to the Bulletins of the Industrial Railway Society.

1947 EMPEROR 0-6-0STIC WCI 1893
From Parsonage Colliery. Being dismantled 6-3-1947. Some parts still extant in 10-1949

1949 FRED 0-6-0STIC RSH 7289 1945
From Bickershaw Colliery by 1-6-1949. To Bickershaw 24-8-1949

KIRKLESS 0-6-0STIC NW 442 1892
From Parsonage Colliery 29-1-1949. To Parsonage 14-10-1949

1950 FRED 0-6-0STIC RSH 7289 1945
From Bickershaw Colliery. In shops 6-11-1950. Reps complete by 18-1-1951 New cyls

1955 0-6-0STIC RSH 7096 1943
From Hafod Opencast DP 30-4-1955. Consigned by rail to Llanharan 19-12-1955

1956 71507 0-6-0STIC RSH 7161 1944
From Watnall Opencast DP 21-12-1955. To Pemberton Opencast DP 16-3-1956

71508 0-6-0STIC RSH 7162 1944
From Pemberton Opencast DP 22-3-1956. Ex shops 2-1957 to Pemberton Opencast DP

71499 0-6-0STIC
From Peel Hall Opencast DP 11-1956. To Peel Hall Opencast DP 4-1957

1961 FRED 0-6-0STIC RSH 7289 1945
From Kirkless 11-1961. To Bickershaw Colliery 5-1962

WESTWOOD 0-4-0STOC HC 1036 1913
From Peel Hall Opencast DP 12-1961 and put into store at Walkden Yard. Sent to Pemberton Opencast DP in 1-1962

1962 BILL 0-6-0STIC HE 1901 1938
From Bickershaw Colliery. Noted in shops 19-5-1962

WESTWOOD 0-4-0STOC HC 1036 1913
From Pemberton Opencast DP 7-1962 and laid aside at Walkden Yard until 1965

1963 AMAZON 0-6-0STIC VF 5297 1945
From Haydock 3-1963. To Haydock 7-1963

HURRICANE 0-6-0STIC HE 3830 1955
From Parsonage Colliery (?) 10-11-1963. To Bickershaw Colliery, where arrived 23-3-1964

LO 61 0-6-0DE YE 2660 1957
From Agecroft Colliery 3-1963. To Agecroft 8-1963

FRED 0-6-0STIC RSH 7289 1945
From Bickershaw Colliery 10-1963. To Bickershaw Colliery 12-1963. Fitted withmechanical stoker

No 1 0-6-0STIC RS 2880 1900
From Ince Moss Colliery early 1963. Scrapped 3-1963

HURRICANE 0-6-0STIC HE 3830 1955
From Parsonage Colliery 11-1963. To Bickershaw 6-1964

1964 0-6-0DE YE 2717 1958
From Parsonage Colliery. Noted in shops 3-8-1964

No 6 0-6-0STIC HC 449 1895
From Chisnall Hall Colliery 5-1964. Not worth repairing. Scrapped 11-1964

ROBIN HILL 0-6-0STIC HE 3779 1952
From Standish Collieries 30-10-1964. Noted in shops 6-8-1965 To Cronton Colliery ???

SPITFIRE 0-6-0STIC HE 3831 1955
From Bickershaw Colliery. Noted in shops 11-1964 and dates to 20-3-1966. To Bickershaw

1965 BOLD 0-4-0STOC P 1737 1927
Arrived from Ravenhead Colliery by road 1-8-1965. Ex shops 10-1966 to Ravenhead

WESTWOOD 0-4-0STOC HC 1036 1913
Into shops from store after 8-1965. Ex shops to Ravenhead Colliery 11-1965

1966 FRED 0-6-0STIC RSH 7289 1945
From Bickershaw Colliery about 8-1966. To Bickershaw 10-1966

RODNEY 0-6-0STIC HE 3695 1950
From Bickershaw Colliery early 1966. To Bedford Colliery

HURRICANE 0-6-0STIC HE 3830 1955
From Bickershaw Colliery by 12-1966. To Bickershaw 6-1967

1967 FAIRFIELD 0-4-0STOC KS 4025 1919
From Ravenhead Colliery 9-1967. Not repaired and scrapped 9-1968

FRED 0-6-0STIC RSH 7289 1945
From Bickershaw about 7-1967 and laid aside. Sold to Keighley and Worth Valley Railway 12-1968 and moved there 4-1969

REVENGE 0-6-0STIC HE 3699 1950
To Ladysmith Colliery 2-1968

RODNEY 0-6-0STIC HE 3695 1950
From Bedford Colliery. Ex shops by 21-10-1967 To Bickershaw Colliery

0-6-0STOC RSH 7739 1952
From Ladysmith by 26-3-1967. Repairs suspended 8-1967. Scrapped 11-1968

1968 LO 52 0-6-0DE YE 2745 1960
From Agecroft Colliery 12-1968. To Agecroft in 1969

GORDON 0-6-0STIC
From Bickershaw Colliery. Scrapped 1968

WEASEL 0-6-0STIC
From Ladysmith Washery. Noted in shops 12-1968. To Ladysmith Washery

1970 0-6-0STIC HE 3163 1944
Rbt HE 3885 1965
From Hunslet Engine Co 22-7-1970. Ex shops to Gresford arriving 20-11-1970 where named ALISON 22-11-1970

LO 52 0-6-0DE YE 2745 1960
From Agecroft Colliery about 7-1970. To Agecroft Colliery 1971

WEASEL 0-6-0STIC HE 3844 1957
From Ladysmith. Laid aside by 18-7-1970. Sold to Jose K Holt Gordon Ltd for scrap 2-1976

1971 KING 0-4-0STOC AB 1448 1919
From Bank Hall Colliery about 8-1971. To Ladysmith Colliery 5-1972

LLANTARNAM ABBEY 0-6-0STOC AB 2074 1939
From East Wales Area. Noted in shops 8-1971. To East Wales Area

1972 No 8 0-4-0STOC AB 1974 1930
From Ladysmith Colliery 11-11-1972. Repainted black livery and ready for despatch to Ladysmith 24-10-1973

SIR GOMER 0-6-0STOC P 1859 1932
From East Wales Area. Noted in shops 1-1972. Replacement blr fitted. Steam tested 7-12-1972. To Mountain Ash Colliery 12-1972

1973 HURRICANE 0-6-0STIC HE 3830 1955
From Bickershaw Colliery 8-6-1973. To Bickershaw on 14-3-1974

MERLIN 0-4-0DH NB 27729 1957
From Huncoat Colliery 1-1973. Laid aside. Scrapped 1978

1974 GWYNETH 0-6-0STIC RSH 7135 1944
From Gresford Colliery about 3-1974. To Bickershaw Colliery 14-1-1975

RESPITE 0-6-0STIC
From Ladysmith Washery 11-1974. To Bickershaw Colliery 6-1975

1975 D 5 0-4-0DH NBL 27876 1959
From Parsonage Colliery 6-1975

RESPITE 0-6-0STIC HE 3696 1950
From Ladysmith Colliery 11-1974. Ex shops by 8-6-1975. To Bickershaw Colliery

1977 HURRICANE 0-6-0STIC HE 3830 1955
From Bickershaw Colliery 8-1977. Laid aside and used for spares. Scrapped early 1981

1978 No 7 0-6-0DE YE 2749 1959
From Littleton Colliery 5-1978. To Bold Colliery 4-1979

1979 ALISON 0-6-0STIC HE 3163 1944
From Bold Colliery 10-1979. Renamed JOSEPH. To Bold 2-1980

D 5 0-4-0DH NBL 27876 1959
From William Pit. Noted in shops 4-79. To William Pit 8-1980

WOLSTANTON No3 0-6-0DM WB 3150 1959
Ex Wolstanton by 8-1979. To Wolstamton by 12-1980

1980 No 1D 0-6-0DH HE 6663 1969
Ex Granville by 3-1980. To Bersham by 12-1980

No 2 0-6-0DH EEV D1120 1966
Ex Lea Hall by 12-1980. To Lea Hall by 12-1981

1981 No 14D 0-6-0DH HE 7040 1971
Ex Hem Heath by 4-1981. To Point of Ayr by 12-1981

No 8D 0-6-0DH HE 7018 1971
Ex Hem Heath by 4-1981. To Bersham by 10-1982

1982 LO 52 0-6-0DH YE 2745 1960
Ex Agecroft by 12-1982. To Cronton by 5-1983

No 12D 0-6-0DH HE 7016 1971
Ex Hem Heath. To Bold by 6-10-1982

No 6D 0-6-0DH HE 7017 1971
Ex William Pit. To William Pit by 12-1982

1983 0-6-0DE YE 2713 1958
Ex Sutton Manor by 5-1983. To Booth, Rotherham, 3-1986

4wDH S 10097 1962
To Sutton Manor Colliery 10-1983

Astley Green Colliery Museum

Standard gauge

0-4-0STOC AE 1563 1908 12"x18"
Formerly Millom Hematite Ore and Iron Co Ltd, Hodbarrow Mine, Millom and left there 9-1968
Stored at various locations prior to coming to Astley Green

4wDM RH 244580 1941 48DS class
Formerly Park Webb Ltd, Ince Forge, Wigan, and left there about 1974
Stored at various locations prior to coming to Astley Green

2'0" gauge

120 4wDM RH 462365 1960
Ex North Western Water Authority, Bamber Bridge about 6-1982
To Penycuik Peat Co Ltd, Whim Moss, Lamancha Station, Cowdenburn

6 4wDM MR 8937 1944
Ex West Lancashire Light Railway, Hesketh Bank, about 7-1982
To Moseley Industrial Tramway Museum, Manor School, Cheadle 12-1986

24 4wDM MR 7498 1940
Ex Yorkshire Water Authority, Riccall Depot, about 10-1982
To Scottish Agricultural Industries Ltd, Bolton Fell Mill, near Hethersgill, Cumbria

4wDM RH 422573 1958
Ex North Western Water Authority, Lower Rivington Reservoir about 10-1982
To R & A Jenkins, Great Fransham, Norfolk, mid 1992

4wDM MR 22031 1959
Ex Lilley Waddington Ltd, Plant Dealers, Horwich by 3-1986
To Ashton Canal Carriers, Guide Bridge

7 4wDM MR 11218 1962
Ex Warrington Borough Council, Risley Moss 17-10-1989

MAVIS 4wDM RH 7002/0967/6 1962
Ex Knebworth Park and Wintergreen Railway, late 1992

4wDH HE 8834 1978
Ex British Coal, Bickershaw Colliery, 9-1992 (flameproofed underground locomotive)

2'6" gauge

3 4wBE EE
Ex British Coal, Agecroft Colliery 3-1991 (flameproofed underground locomotive)

References to Chapter 13

1 *"The Industrial Railways of the Wigan Coalfield - Part Two"* - Townley, Smith and Peden - Runpast Publishing, Cheltenham, 1992
2 FJ 17-2-1950
3 FJ 9-7-1954
4 FJ 13-12-1957
5 FJ 20-3-1953
6 *"Collieries in the Manchester Coalfields"* Geoff Hayes - De Archaeologische Pers, Eindhoven, nd
7 MG 7-9-68
8 BLN 119
9 *"From Walkden Records - Part One"* - Alex Appleton - in *"Industrial Locomotive"*, Vol 6, No 62, 1991
10 *"Industrial Locomotive Society Journal"*, Vol XVII, No 1, January 1963
11 *"Industrial Locomotive Society Journal"*, Vol XIX, No 1, February 1965
12 IRS Bulletin 2-8-1963
13 *"Walkden Yard Yarns - No 2"* - George L Booth - Streetgate Books, nd about 1993
14 IRS Bulletin 28-8-1965
15 British Railways Signal and Telegraph Notice dated 26-11-1966 to 2-12-1966
16 IRS Bulletin16-2-1963
17 IRS Bulletin 3-8-1964
18 FJ 7-12-1967
19 BLN 103
20 BLN 95
21 BLN 153
22 Information supplied by Philip Hindley
23 BLN 165
24 BLN 170
25 BLN 215
26 BLN 167
27 BEN 26-10-1983

APPENDIX 1

Locomotives Handled by Thomas Mitchell and Sons Ltd

About twenty years ago one of the authors, Frank Smith, was able to inspect the firm's archives, including an almost complete series of catalogues and ledgers.

Catalogue No 1 was issued in September 1891 and subsequent issues appeared at half yearly intervals to start with and later more frequently. Locomotives were featured regularly from No 4, mid 1893, until No 67, issued in 1924. The catalogues were supplemented by lists of plant which were issued from time to time. The office copies of both the catalogues and lists were often marked up in ink with additional information.

The ledgers which were examined started in January 1901, the first locomotive entry being item No 2366. They contained information about the plant which was bought, sold and hired out. The entries usually provide the dimensions of the locomotives and in most instances give the date of construction and the makers number. Sometimes the name of the engine is given as well.

Some information about locomotives handled by the firm prior to 1891 can be found in advertisements in the *"Colliery Guardian"* and other trade periodicals.

Unless otherwise stated, the information given below has been transcribed from advertisements and from the firm's records. Supplementary details, added by the authors, are enclosed in square brackets [ ].

Locomotives advertised in trade periodicals, 1871 to 1893

Second hand contractors locomotive, four wheels, 9" cyls, in good repair - Advertised for sale in CG 25-8-1871.

Standard gauge tank locomotive with 7¾" cyls, built by Adamson and Company, in good condition - Advertised for sale in CG 13-6-1873.

Standard gauge tank locomotive, four coupled with 10"x24" cyls - Advertised for sale in CG 18-7-1873. Also advertised for sale in CG 6-2-1874 where cylinder dimensions are given as 10¼"x24" and weight as 13¼ tons

Standard gauge tank locomotive, six coupled with 12"x18" cyls and 3'0" dia whls, built by Manning, Wardle and Co - Advertised for sale in CG 12-9-1873 and *"Engineer"* 26- 9-1873

Six coupled locomotive with 12" cyls, built by Manning Wardle and Co - Advertised for sale in CG 18-5-1877

Four coupled locomotive with 12" cyls - Advertised for sale in CG 18-5-1877

Six coupled locomotive with 12" cyls, built by Manning Wardle and Co - Advertised for sale in *"Engineer"* 27-5- 1881

Four coupled locomotive with 12" cyls, built by Manning Wardle and Co - Advertised for sale in *"Engineer"* 27-5-1881

Four coupled locomotive with 10¼" cyls - Advertised for sale in *"Engineer"* 27-5-1881.

There is also a record of a locomotive named ATALANTA which was either sold or hired to the Earl of Bradford's Great Lever Colliery in January 1890. (See Chapter 4)

Locomotives appearing in the firm's records 1891 to 1925

Standard gauge four coupled saddle tank with 9½" x 14" cyls, built by Manning, Wardle and Co and rebuilt by the makers in 1887

Shown in Catalogue No 3, probably July 1893. Price, as marked in office copy, £250
Included with contractors plant advertised for sale in CG 27-7-1894
Last appears in catalogue No 7, Jan 1895 (No 8 missing)

Four coupled saddle tank with 9"x14" cyls, 30" dia whls, 5ft wheelbase, boiler tested to 120 psi, weight empty 14 tons, built by Lewin and Co, Poole and rebuilt 2 years ago. Now in Manchester

Shown in catalogue No 10, July 1896. Price, as marked in office copy, £100
Advertised for sale in MM 1-3-1897
[Possibly the loco supplied by Lewin to the De Soto Alkali Co, Widnes - Liquidation sale of successor company, Lancashire Alkali and Sulphur Co Ltd, 28-7-1893]

Six wheeled, four coupled saddle tank with 11"x18" cyls, built by Sharp, Stewart and Co.

Shown in catalogue No 10, July 1896, or No 11,Jan 1897. Item No 818. Price, as marked in office copy, £150

Four coupled saddle tank with 10"x16" cyls and 2'9"dia whls, built by Manning, Wardle and Co No 1029 of 1887

Shown in catalogues Nos 10 July 1896 (or 11 Jan 1897 ?) to 13 Jan 1898 - Item No 833
Advertised for sale in MM 1-2-1897 and MM 1-8-1898
[New to T A Walker, Manchester Ship Canal contract as BARTON. Apparently sold by Mitchells to Jas Wrigley and Sons, Bridge Hall Mills, Bury. Repurchased by Mitchells, 12-17-1917, see item Mo 9153. Also see Chapter 5]

Four coupled saddle tank with 9" cyls and 2'10" dia whls, 3'6" gauge, built by Barclay No 272 of 1880

Shown in catalogues Nos 12 July 1897 to 26 July 1904 - Item No 1038
Advertised for sale in MM 1-2-1897

Four coupled saddle tank with 8" cyls, 2'6" gauge, built by Hughes of Loughborough

Shown in catalogues No 12, July 1897, to No 15, Jan 1899 - Item No 1175

Four coupled saddle tank with 9"x14" cyls and 2'9"dia whls, built by Manning, Wardle and Co in 1887 - JUBILEE

Shown in catalogue No 12, July 1897 - Item No 1213
[Possibly MW 990 of 1887 or MW 991 of 1887]

Saddle tank with 13"x18" cyls, 4 leading wheels 4'2" dia and 2 trailing wheels 2'6" dia, built by Black Hawthorn and Co - HEBE

Shown in catalogues Nos 13, Jan 1898 and 14, July 1898 - item No 1333. Price, as marked in office copies, £150
[BH 118-1869 Garstang and Knott End Railway 0-4-2ST]

Six coupled saddle tank with 13"x20" cyls, built Hudswell, Clarke and Co in 1883 - HOPE

Shown in catalogue No 13, Jan 1898 - Item No 1351. Price, as marked in office copy, £270
Note in catalogue says that it was working until recently as a passenger loco on a private company's line and that it would be available shortly
[HC 263-1883 Garstang and Knott End Rly]

Four coupled saddle tank with 9"x14" cyls, built by Sharp, Stewart and Co, just ceased work - LITTLE WONDER

Shown in catalogues Nos 14, July 1898, and 15, Jan 1899 - Item No 1440. Price, as marked in office copies, £200
Advertised for sale in MM 1-8-1898

Four coupled saddle tank with 10"x14" cyls, built by Manning, Wardle and Co in 1881 - OUTFALL
Shown in catalogues Nos 14, July 1898, and 15, Jan 1899 - Item No 1505. Price, as marked in office copies, £320
[MW 728 of 1881, new to T Monk, contractor, Boston, named OUTFALL]

Six coupled saddle tank with 10"x18" cyls and 2'9" dia whls, built by Barclay - BEDFORD
Shown in catalogues No 16, July 1899, to No 27, Jan 1905 - Item No 1833. Price, as marked in office copies, starts at £350 and falls to £180
Advertised for sale in CG 19-5-1899
Office copy of catalogue No 20, July 1901, had note in red ink "Bedford Leigh"
[See Chapter 9]

Four coupled locomotive with 12"x18" cyls and 3'4" dia whls, 5'6" wheelbase, 105 psi working pressure, built by Black, Hawthorn and Co - LILFORD
Shown in catalogue No 16, July 1899, - Item No 1882. Price, as marked in office copy , £360
Advertised for sale in CG 19-5-1899
Office copy of catalogue No 16 had note in red ink "Sold"
[This is obviously LILFORD, the well tank built by Hawthorns and Company of Leith in 1861 for John Fletcher and Others of Atherton - see Chapter 9. Mitchells were in error in saying that it was built by Black, Hawthorn and Co of Gateshead]

Four coupled saddle tank with 10"x16" cyls and 2'8" dia whls, built by Hunslet Engine Co, No 238 of 1880. Has been standing idle some years.
Shown in catalogue No 17, Jan 1900, to No 31, Feb 1907 - Item No 2143
Office copy of catalogue No 20, July 1901, had notes in red ink "Progress" and "Chesterfield"
Office copy of catalogue No 31, Feb 1907, had note in red ink "Sold"
Ledger entries show :
Sold 2-5-1903 to Thomas Robinson and Son, Rochdale, for £380, subject to working satisfactorily
[But the sale seems to have fallen through]
Hired 6-6-1904 to Jos Place and Sons, Darwen, for not less than 3 weeks at £7 per week, with option to purchase for £380
Hired 14-11-1904 to The Bolton Iron and Steel Co, for not less than 3 weeks at £6 per week, plus £4 for taking to and fro.
Sold 13-3-1907 to Harrison Blair and Co, Farnworth for £310, £25 allowed on old loco taken in part exchange (See item No 4188) [See Chapter 6]

Six coupled saddle tank with 11"x16" cyls, built by Hudswell, Clarke and Co
Shown in catalogues No 19, Jan 1901, to No 33, 1908 - Item No 2331. Price, as marked in office copies, starting at £400 and falling to £200
Advertised for sale in CG 14-9-1900
Office copy of catalogue No 20, July 1901, had note in red ink FARMERS FRIEND
List No 65, Dec 1901 says now on hire, seen working by appointment
Ledger entry shows :
Oct 11th 1901 - Agreed to lend to Thomas Fletcher and Sons - 1 locomotive "Farmers Friend" on hire for not less than three months at £6-10s per week, they paying carriage
[HC 173-1875, Garstang and KnottEnd Rly - Also see Chapters 5 and 6]

Four coupled saddle tank with 12" cyls, built by Manning Wardle and Co
Shown in catalogue No 19, Jan 1901 - Item no 2366
Ledger entry shows:
Sold 23-1-1901 to Ince Waggon and Ironworks Co, Wigan, as seen and inspected at Shakerley Colly, for £425
[MW 469 of 1873, new to William Ramsden, Shakerley Colliery, See Chapter 10]

Four coupled saddle tank with 12" cyls, built by Manning Wardle and Co, No 952 of 1886
Ledger entries, item No 2465, show :
Bought 15-2-1901 from J J Poole, Engineer, St Helens, for £335
Sold 3-4-1901 to Dunmores Ltd, Brick Works, Irthlingborough for £275, item No 2501 taken in part exchange
[New to T A Walker, St Fagans, named ST FAGANS, later Cannington, Shaw and Co Ltd, St Helens]

Tramway engine and boiler, 4'0" gauge, built by Kitson and Co, 1895
Ledger entry, item No 2495, shows:
Bought 6-4-1901 from Robert Finch, Hawthorn Villa, Clitheroe, for £90
Shown in catalogue No 20, July 1901, which says new in 1898, cost £840 and has just stopped work
List No 64, June 1901 says built 1898 and mentions pair of 8" engines
The following undated ledger entry of 1910, item 5055A, probably refers to the engine from the tram :
Sold to Clifton and Kersley Coal Co Ltd - "A" frame vertical tram engine about 6" cyls with flywheel, delivered to Outwood, for £11

Six coupled saddle tank with 12" cyls, built by Manning Wardle and Co, No 688 of 1878.
Ledger entry, item 2501, shows:
Bought 23-4-1901 in part exchange from Dunmores Ltd, Brick Works, Irthlingborough
Advertised for sale in CG 20-9-1901
Office copy of catalogue No 20, July 1901, had name DOVER inserted in red ink. Price marked in catalogue £400
Office copy of catalogue No 26, July 1904, had note in red ink "Sold". Price marked in catalogue £300
[New to T A Walker, Deal, named DOVER]

Six coupled saddle tank with 12" cyls, built by Hudswell, Clarke and Co, No 240 of 1880, requires overhauling
Ledger entry, item No 2672, shows:
Bought 24-1-1902 from Thomas Fletcher and Sons, Bolton for £120
Office copy of catalogue No 25, Jan 1904, had note in red ink "Sold". Price as marked in catalogues reducing from £180 to £150
[New to Thomas Fletcher, Bradley Fold. See Chapter 5]

Old standard gauge four coupled saddle tank, with outside cylinders 8½" x 15"
Ledger entry, item 2790, shows:
Bought 31-7-1902 from Bolton Iron and Steel Co Ltd for £45
Catalogue No 23, Jan 1903, gives maker as Hughes of Loughborough and notes that the loco requires repair
Advertised for sale in CJ 3-2-1904, which states built by Hughes
Office copy of catalogue No 26, July 1904, had note in red ink "Sold". Price as marked in catalogue £80.

Four coupled (altered from six coupled) saddle tank, with 15" cyls and 4'6" dia whls, makers LNWR - BEE
Ledger entry, item 3023, shows
Bought 14-8-1903 from The Hulton Colly Co, lying at Hulton Colly for £80
Advertised for sale CJ 3-2-1904 as four coupled loco with 15" cyls
Office copy of catalogue No 25, Jan 1904, had note in red ink "Sold". Price as marked in catalogue £350.
[SS 1137 of 1859. See Chapter 4]

Four coupled saddle tank, with 11"x22" cyls and 3'6" dia whls, make and date unknown - GLADYS
Ledger entry, item 3222, shows :
Bought 20-6-1904 from Gigg Paper Mills, Bury for £65
Catalogue No 27, Jan 1905, which is last catalogue entry, says ready for work, may be seen just as stopped work a few miles from here. Price as marked in catalogue £150.
[See Chapter 5]

Four coupled saddle tank with 13"x18" cyls and 36" dia whls, built by Hudswell, Clarke and Co, No 363 of 1892

Ledger entries, item 3518, show :

Bought 17-7-1905 from Mr Lawton, Pitshelf Collieries Nos 3 and 4 Pits, Notts for £170 free on rail at Tibshelf Town, Carriage £17-0-3d

Sold 15-11-1906 to R H Longbottom and Co Ltd, Wakefield for £390

[New to Babbington Coal Co, Tibshelf Colly. The reference Pitshelf in the ledger appears to be an error and should read Tibshelf]

Standard gauge shunting locomotive, vertical boiler and pair of vertical cyls, about 9 tons weight, as working at their works

Ledger entry, item No 4188, shows:

Bought 14-3-1907 from Harrison Blair and Co, Farnworth for £25

[In part exchange for item No 2143 - HE 238 of 1880. See Chapter 6]

Four coupled saddle tank, with outside cyls 12"x about 20" and 3'0" dia whls, built by Yorkshire Engine Co No 322 of 1880

Ledger entry, item 4245, shows

Bought May 1907 from Steel Peach and Tozer Ltd, Sheffield for £85

Office copy of catalogue No 32, July 1907, had note - in stock. Price as marked in catalogue £150. Last appears in catalogue No 33, early 1908.

Four coupled loco, with 14" cyls and 42"dia whls, built by Walkers, Wigan - GRAHAM

Ledger entries, item 4438, show :

Bought 15-10-1907 from Earl of Ellesmere, as lying at Little Hulton for £125

Sold 12-2-1908 to Geo Watkinson and Co Ltd, Buckley, Chester for £ 350, carriage paid to their siding

[See Chapter 11]

Four coupled saddle tank, with 12" cyls and 38" dia whls, built R W Hawthorn, rebuilt 1900

Ledger entries, item 4674, show :

Bought 22-4-1908 from Nuttall and Co, Contractors, Trafford Park for £120

Sold 4-5-1908 to Robert B Byass & Co, Port Talbot, as lying at Trafford Park, for £250 free on rail

Four coupled saddle tank, with 9"x14" and 2'6" dia whls, built by Manning Wardle and Co, No 880 of 1883, rebuilt about 1900 - WINNIE

Ledger entries, item No 4685, show :

Bought 29-4-1908 from Jos Pugsley, St George, Bristol for £155

Sold 1-6-1908 to Clifton and Kersley Coal Co Ltd, for £250, to be delivered to Astley, This entry crossed out and marked cancelled

Hired 12-8-1909 to Earl of Bradford Colliery, Bolton, at £4 per week and extra for delivery

Hired 14-5-1910 to Unsworth and Cowburn, for not less than 4 weeks at £4 per week, they pay carriage

Hired 29-6-1911 to Clifton and Kersley Coal Co Ltd at £5 per week, with option to purchase for £275. Blue pencil note says delivered to Astley.

Hired 11-3-1914 from Clifton and Kersley Coal Co Ltd, for one week at £5 per week, plus extra for loading and unloading

Hired to Gigg Paper Mills, Bury, for one week, at £10 pr week, plus extra for loading and unloading

Last shown in catalogue No 41, Jan 1912.

Ledger entry, item 8541, shows

Bought 20-5-1916 from Clifton and Kersley Coal Co Ltd, Astley, for £ 90, as sold to them, originally no 4685. Note says scrapped Feb 1917

Note in red ink in office copy of catalogue No 51, Jan 1917, also said scrapped Feb 1917

[New to J P Edwards, contractor, Aintree, named WINNIE - Also see Chapters 4, 5 and 10]

Saddle tank with 8"x16" cyls, built by Manning, Wardle and Co, No 577 of 1875, cracked cylinder, broken crankpin, boiler and firebox patched

Ledger entry, item No 5021 shows :

Bought 7-5-1910 from North Hendre Lime Co, near Mold, for £30, free on rail at Rhydymwyn

This locomotive is not shown in the Catalogues

[New to J Bayliss, contractor, Manchester, named BEATRICE]

Four coupled saddle tank, with 12" cyls, built by Yorkshire Engine Co No 260 of 1875, lying at Co-op Soap Works, Irlam

Ledger entry, item 5424, shows:

Bought 16-6-1910 from Peckett and Sons, Loco Works, Bristol, for £50

Appears in Catalogue Nos 38, July 1910, and 39, Feb 1911

Six coupled saddle tank, with inside cyls 14"x20" built by Manning, Wardle and Co in 1877, boiler new 11yrs ago, tyres new 12 months ago - WHARTON HALL

Ledger entry, item No 5698, shows

Bought 10-4-1911 for £130, Note says scrapped

Not shown in catalogues

[MW 838 of 1877, new to Wharton Hall Colliery Company. See Chapter 10]

Four coupled saddle tank with 15"cyls, built by Sharp, Stewart and Co - THE SQUIRE

Ledger entry, item No 5715, shows

Bought 29-4-1911 from The Hulton Colly Co Ltd for £75

Not shown in catalogues

[Presumed to be SS 2479 of 1875. See Chapter 4]

1'6" gauge locomotive, with 4"x7½" cyls, 1'6", built by Bagnall in July 1909, lying at Lostock

Ledger entry, item No 6044, shows

Bought 18-12-1911 from Darrell S Dobson, The Poultry Farm, Lostock Hall for £25

Hired 26-4-1915 to John Knowles and Co, Wooden Box, Nr Burton for 2 weeks at £4 per week [and later sold to them]

Advertised in CJ 10-7-1912

Last appears in catalogue No 48, mid 1915

[SCOUT WGB 1907 of 1909. See Chapter 3]

Four coupled saddle tank, with 10"x14" cyls, built by Hunslet Engine Co No 425 of 1887, rebuilt 1900, lying at Dolgarrog -INCE

Ledger entries. item No 6102, show

Bought 14-2-1912 from Geo N Dixon, Auctioneer, Liverpool for £126

Hired 1-11-1912 to Electrolytic Alkali Co, Middlewich for not less than eight weeks at £5-5-0 per week on rail Bolton

Sold 25-2-1918 to War Office for £600.

Four coupled saddle tank, with 10" outside cyls and 2'9" dia whls, built by Hudswell, Clarke and Co No 304 of 1888, has been lying idle 5 or 6 years - HULME

Ledger entry, item 6110, shows:

Bought 1-3-1912 from the Horrocksford Lime Co Ltd,Clitheroe for £65

Catalogue No 42, July 1912, says lying about 18 miles from here

Last shown in catalogue No 44, mid 1914. Price as marked in catalogues £300.

Four coupled saddle tank, with cyls 5½" (crossed out 5" inserted) x 7", 3'0" gauge, built by Bagnall - MILDRED

Ledger entries, item No 7857, show:

Bought 5-3-1915 from Greaves Bull and Larkin, Harbury, for £60

Sold 9-1-1917 to Armstrong Whitworth and Co Ltd, Newcastle on Tyne, for £160

Advertised in MM 16-4-1915, MM 17-9-1915, MM 17-11-1916 and MM 23-2-1917

[WGB 1844 of 1907]

Four coupled saddle tank, with cyls 5½" x 7", 3'0" gauge, built by Bagnall - MAUDIE
Ledger entries, item No 7858, show :
Bought 5-3-1915 from Greaves Bull and Larkin, Harbury, for £60
Sold 9-1-1917 to Armstrong Whitworth and Co Ltd, Newcastle on Tyne, but this crossed out and note inserted - order altered to one
Sold 14-3-1917 to A Merchant Jnr, late Taylor and Co, Bobbin Makers, Forres, NB, for £180
Advertised in MM 16-4-1915, MM 17-9-1915, MM 17-11-1916 and MM 23-2-1917
[WGB 1782 of 1905]

Four coupled saddle tank, with 14"x20" cyls and 3'6" dia whls, built by Hawthorn of Gateshead, overhauled about 3½ years ago.
Ledger entries, item No 8827, show :
Bought 13-12-1916 from Cochrane and Co, New Brancepeth Colly for £425
Sold 13-12-1916 to Brunner Mond and Co Ltd, Middlewich for £425
[RWH 1635 of 1873]

Four coupled saddle tank, with 10" outside cyls, built by Manning, Wardle and Co, No 1029 of 1887
Ledger entry, item No 9153, shows
Bought 12-7-1917 (as of 21st June) from J Wrigley and Sons, Paper Mills, Bury
Only appears in Catalogue No 53, Jan 1918
[See item No 833, above, and Chapter 5]

3'0" gauge locomotive, with 5¼" x 9" cyls and 18" dia whls, built by Bagnall, No 1632 of 1905
Ledger entry, item No 1628, shows
Bought 22-12-1920 from Greaves, Bull and Lakin, Birmingham, delivered for £96
Last appears in Catalogue No 66, June 1923. Price as marked in catalogues £400 reducing to £ 250
[WGB 1632 of 1900. The date of 1905 given in the ledger appears to be an error]

Four coupled saddle tank, with 14" cyls, built by Peckett in 1902, overhauled by Peckett in 1920 - BOBS
Ledger entries, item No 4701, show:
Bought 25-3-1925 from E Rushton Son and Kenyon, auctioneers, as lying in shed at Bridge Hall Mills, Bury, for £300
Sold 27-3-1925 to Withnell Brick Co Ltd, Withnell, for £425
[P 939 of 1902. See Chapter 5]

Locomotives from 1924 to 1939

Very few locomotives seem to have passed through the hands of the firm during this period and none appears in the catalogues after issue No 67 in 1924.

In the "*Contract Journal*" for 15th July 1931 the firm advertised that it wanted to purchase a 2'0" gauge engine, four coupled with cylinders about 6" diameter.

There is also an unconfirmed statement that the firm purchased the locomotive LAZARUS at a sale held by R Briggs and Sons Ltd at Chatburn in 1938. This was a four wheeled engine with vertical boiler and vertical cylinders, built by Atkinson Walker Waggons Ltd in 1928.

Locomotives after 1945

In the period after the second world war, a number of locomotives were broken up by Thomas Mitchell and Sons Ltd. Mostly were scrapped at the site where they were purchased, although it seems that one, CRITCHLEY, may have been brought back to Bolton from Lytham Gas Works.

Locomotives known to have been broken up by the firm include:

YORK	0-6-0STIC	MW	1295	1895	Preston Corporation, Preston Docks
EDINBURGH	0-6-0STOC	HL	2245	1893	Preston Corporation, Preston Docks
KING	0-6-0STOC	HL	2492	1901	Preston Corporation, Preston Docks
CRITCHLEY	0-4-0STOC	P	1621	1923	North Western Gas Board, Lytham Works

Thomas Mitchell and Sons Ltd also bought several standard and narrow gauge diesel locomotives, mainly as surplus from various war time establishments.

AMW 155 0-4-0DM RSH 6977 1940 150HP

This is thought to be the locomotive purchased, according to Mitchells records (item No 24794) in 1950.
Appears in catalogue No 92, Aug 1955
[AMW 155 was purchased according to IRS records from the Air Ministry Depot at Handforth, Cheshire.]

AMW 157 0-4-0DM RSH 6979 1940 150HP

This is believed to be the locomotive purchased, according to Mitchells records (item No 24929) in September 1950, from the Ministry of Supply at Hereford
Appears in catalogue No 91, June 1953
Sold to Geo Cohen and Co, London 1953
[According to IRS records it was sold by Mitchells to Round Oak Steelworks 13-7-1953]

4wDM Hunslet/Hudson 2280 1941 30HP 2'0"gauge

This is believed to be the locomotive purchased, according to Mitchells records (item No 24932) in September 1950, from the Ministry of Supply at Hereford
Appears in catalogue Nos 91, June 1953, and 92, Aug 1955
[Sold to National Coal Board, for use at Mosley Common Colliery, March 1960]

4wDm Simplex 35" gauge

Mitchells records, item 26523, show purchased from London Brick Co, Bedford and that loco had National diesel engine No 45165
Rebuilt by Mitchells to 31" gauge
Sold to W L Hobbs (Dyserth) Ltd, Hendre Limestone Quarries, near Mold
[Probably FH 1913 of 1935 or 1914 of 1935]

WTE No 3 0-4-0DM HE 2122 1940 150HP

Mitchells records, item No 27129, show purchased from Wales and Monmouthshire Industrial Estates Ltd, arrived Mitchells works from Wrexham Trading Estate 9-3-1956
[Hired Sept or Oct 1959 to Rea Ltd, Birkenhead]
[Hired Nov 1960 to Abelsons, Birmingham]
[Hired June 1964 to Grant Lyon Co Ltd, for use on railway contract at Carlisle]
[Hired April 1966 to W J Lee Ltd, Birkenhead and still there 23-2-1970]
[Noted 10-1-1971 at Walsh Transport Services Ltd, Darwen, stored on behalf of Thomas Mitchell and Sons Ltd]

The following are also believed to have passed through the hands of Thomas Mitchell and Sons Ltd, but do not appear in the records of the firm which were examined :

0-4-0DM HC D610 1939

Ex Burtonwood
1965 to Brown and Tawse Ltd, West Horndean Estate

MARGARET 0-4-0DM HC D1031 1956 128HP

Purchased in 1968 from Limestone Products Ltd, Abergele
Sent directly on hire to W J Lee, Seacombe
From W J Lee in 6-1971 to Walsh Transport Services Ltd, Darwen, for storage on behalf of Thomas Mitchell and Sons Ltd

APPENDIX 2

Locomotives Advertised for Sale

In addition to those described in the text and in Appendix 1, a number of other locomotives were offered for sale in the trade press. Those which have come to the attention of the authors are given below and are divided into two categories - contractors disposing of plant on completion of a job and dealers who traded in locomotives.

CONTRACTORS

George Gilbert, Little Hulton Branch

Sale of plant on 30-3-1871 on completion of Little Hulton Branch, including a six-wheeled loco with 13"x24" cyls, and tipping wagons. - BC 25-3-1871

Abraham Pilling, Back o' th' Bank, Bolton

Sale of plant at Back o' th' Bank on 8-8-1877 on completion of Astley Bridge Branch, including two tank locos, one built by Manning Wardle. - BC 21-7-1877

Scott and Edwards, Bury

Sale of plant at Bury on 13-2-78 on completion of L&YR contract, including one four coupled loco by Manning, Wardle, 9 ½" cyls and 2'9" dia whls, equal to new, and one large six coupled saddle tank, 18" cyls and 5'0" dia whls, by Sharp and Co of Manchester. *"Engineer"* 1-2-1878

Baker and Firbank, Cross Lane to Patricroft Widening

Sale of plant on 14-8-1883 on completion of LNWR contract, including a loco. - CJ 1-8-1883 and Engineer 3-8-1883

Monk and Newell, Walkden

Sale of plant on 17 to 19-7-1889 completion of Pendleton and Hindley Railway for L&YR, including sixteen four coupled and six coupled tank locos, with cyls 9" to 15", of recent date built by Hunslet Engine Co and Manning Wardle. - CG 5-7-1889 and *"Engineer"* 5-7-1889.

Sale at Walkden on 19-9-1917 of two six wheeled and two four wheeled standard gauge saddle tanks and one four wheeled 3'0" gauge saddle tank. - CJ 2-8-1917, *"Engineering"* 31-8-1917, MM 31-8-1917 and MG 1-9-1917

Sale at LMS Yard, Walkden, on 4-12-1929 of whole of plant and buildings, including two Simplex 2'0" gauge 20 HP petrol locos and a four coupled saddle tank, 2'6" gauge, by Bagnall. - MG 16-11-1929 and CJ 27-11-1929

Sale of plant at Walkden on 18-4-1934, Monk and Newell in liquidation, including two 20HP Simplex locos and one Bagnall steam loco, 3'0" gauge. - CJ 21-3-1934

John Strachan, Bullfield, Bolton

Sale of plant at Bullfield on 25-10-1905, on completion Bolton to Bullfield Widening for L&YR, including two 6 coupled saddle tanks, with 16" and 12" cyls, by Manning Wardle. - CG 13-10-1905, MG 14-10-1905 and CJ 18-10-1905 (which gives cyl sizes as 11" and 12")

George Ellis, Barton Rd and Worsley Rd, Worsley

Sale of standard gauge saddle tank and six petrol locos. - MG 5-10-1929

William Townson, Bolton

Sale of plant including 2'0" gauge Planet loco. - CJ 30-12-1942

M C Walker, Westhoughton

Sale of plant including one 2'0" gauge loco with Meadows petrol engine. - CJ 21-11-1951

County Borough of Bury

Sale of plant including one 2'0" gauge petrol tractor and bogie trucks. - CJ 3-2-1955

DEALERS

Thomas Dunn, Windsor Bridge Ironworks, Pendleton

For sale two powerful 6 wheels coupled goods locos, as new, and two old locos suitable for pumping purposes. - *"Herepath"* 22-6-1850

J & W Leigh, Patricroft

For sale narrow gauge tank loco, 10"x18" cyls and 3'2" dia whls, made about 3 years ago and just overhauled. Would suit contractor. - *"Engineer"* 16-6-1865

"JH" Post Office, Bolton

Wanted. Two tank locos, with cyls 11" to 13". - CG 1-1872

"HB" Post Office, Bolton

Wanted. Two tank locos with cyls 11" or 12". - CG 4-10-1872, CG 1-11-1872 and CG 8-1-1873

Wanted. Tank loco with 10" or 12" cyls. - CG 8-8-1873

Henry Parkinson, 44 Folds Road, Bolton also Foundry Street Boiler Works, Bolton

For sale tank loco, six wheels four coupled, 14 ½"x22" cyls, by Sharp, Stewart. Can be seen working. - CG 11-1869 and *"Engineer"* 25-2-1870

For sale bogie tank engine with 14 ½"x22" by Robert Stepehnson and Co. - CG 7-1870

For sale tank loco with 14 ½" cyls, by Sharp. Stewart, four coupled tank loco with 10" cyls, four coupled tank loco with 12" cyls and bogie tank loco with 14 ½"x22" cyls by Robert Stephenson. - CG 8-1870 and MJ 15-10-1870

For sale tank loco with 14 ½„ cyls by Sharp Stewart four coupled tank loco with 10" cyls, four coupled tank loco with 12" cyls, tank loco with 8 ½" cyls. - *"Engineer"* 7-7-1871 and Engineer 25-8-1871 (which says loco with 8 ½" cyls is 3'6" gauge)

For sale tank loco with 14 ½„ cyls by Sharp Stewart, four coupled tank loco with 10" cyls, four coupled tank loco with 12" cyls.- *"Engineer"* 23-2-1872

For sale four coupled tank loco with 10" cyls. - MJ 12-7-1873

For sale four coupled tank loco with 10" cyls, by Manning Wardle, nearly new. - *"Engineer"* 21-8-1874

For sale one four coupled tank loco with 13" cyls and one four coupled tank loco with 10" cyls. - CG 6-6-1879

Mr Wood, Engineer, Moses Gate

For sale tank locos, one four coupled with 15" cyls, one with 12" cyls, one with 10" cyls, one with 9 ½" cyls, one with 8 ½"cyls, two narrow gauge. - CG 13-10-1882

Stone and Hutchinson, Metal Merchants, Bolton

The Industrial Railway Society Lists state that this firm acquired two 2'0" gauge steam locomotives from the contractors John Dickinson and Co (Bolton) Ltd about 1937 and broke them up about 1940. Both were 0-4-0 well tanks, built by Hudswell, Clarke and Co in 1915, named BILLY and EDWARD, works numbers 1160 and 1170 respectively.

APPENDIX 3

Quotations for 10–ton Wagons July 1892

In 1892 the agent to the Earl of Bradford made enquires for 25 new 8-ton and 10-ton wagons for use at Great Lever Colliery. Eight firms replied [1,2] and the quotations are summarised below.

Wigan Wagon Co Ltd	
New	£50 each
Second Hand	£30 each
Lancashire and Yorkshire Wagon Co Ltd, Heywood	
New	£57-10s each
7 year purchase lease	£10-2s-6d per wagon per year
Cravens Ltd, Sheffield	
8 Ton wagons, new	£60 each
Midland Railway Carriage and Wagon Co Ltd, Midland Works, Birmingham	
8 Ton wagons	£58 each
10 Ton wagons	£58-15s each
North Central Wagon Co, Rotherham	
8 ton wagons	£36 each
7 year redemption hire	£6-5s-6d each per year
British Wagon Co, Rotherham	
No new wagons	
16 second hand 10 ton wagons	£8-5s each per annum for 5 years
10 second hand 8 ton wagons	£7-1s-6d each per annum for 5 years
McLauchlin and Co, Haughton Bridge Wagon Works, Darlington	
10 ton wagons	£62 each
Extra for bottom doors	£1-10s per wagon
Extra for one end door	£1-7s-6d per wagon
Second hand wagons	£30 each
Gloucester Railway Carriage and Wagon Co Ltd	
10 ton wagons	£60 each

References to Appendix 3

1 BMB ZBR 5/53/266

2 BMB ZBR 5/53/277

APPENDIX 4

Bradford, Ashton Moss and Moston Colliery Locomotives

BRADFORD COLLIERY

Locomotives used by Manchester Collieries Ltd 1936 to 1947

No 2 0-4-0STOC AE 1995 1928 14"x22" 3′6"
Taken over from Bradford Colliery Co Ltd 1936
To National Coal Board 1-1-1947

0-6-0STIC P 518 1890 13"x18"
Temporarily at Bradford Colliery in 1937 and returned to Wheatsheaf Screens 7-12-1937

Locomotives used by National Coal Board 1947 to 1956

No 2 0-4-0STOC AE 1995 1928 14"x22" 3′6"
Taken over from Manchester Collieries Ltd 1-1-1947
Transferred to Robin Hood Screens 7-2-1956; for later history see Chapter 6

ROBIN HOOD 0-4-0STOC CF 1200 1901 14"x19" 3′2"
Temporarily at Bradford Colliery late 1953 while No 2 under repairs at Bradford.
Returned to Robin Hood Screens early 1954

ASHTON MOSS COLLIERY

Locomotives used by National Coal Board 1947 to 1959

0-4-0STOC K 2251 1879 12"x10" 3′0 ½"
Rebuilt HC 1921
Taken over from Chamber Colliery Co Ltd 1-1-1947
Scrapped at Ashton Moss late 1950

KING 0-4-0STOC AB 1448 1919 14"x22" 3′5"
Taken over from Chamber Colliery Co Ltd 1-1-1947
To Walkden Yard for repairs 28-1-1947. Returned to Ashton Moss 9-1947. New Boiler from Hough
At Walkden Yard for repairs mid to late 1950 and returned to Ashton Moss
To Walkden Yard for repairs 2-6-1953. Returned to Ashton Moss 21-8-1953
To Walkden Yard for repairs 28-1-1955. Returned to Ashton Moss 9-6-1955
At Walkden Yard for repairs 10-1957 to early 1958 and returned to Ashton Moss
Transferred from Ashton Moss to Bank Hall Colliery, Burnley, 11-1959, after coal winding ceased at Ashton Moss
From Bank Hall to Walkden Yard for repairs late 1971 to early 1972 and then sent to Ladysmith Colliery, Whitehaven about 5-1972
Scrapped at Ladsysmith about 10-1976

ATHERTON 0-4-0WTOC H(L) 340 1867 12"x18" 3′6 ½"
Temporarily at Ashton Moss mid 1947, KING under repairs at Walkden.
From Howe Bridge Colliery and returned to Howe Bridge

ROBIN HOOD 0-4-0STOC CF 1200 1901 14"x19" 3′2"
Temporarily at Ashton Moss in 1951, KING under repairs.
From Walkden to Ashton Moss 4-6-1951. From Ashton Moss to Robin Hood Sidings 8-11-1951
Temporaily at Ashton Moss in 1952, KING under repairs.
From Robin Hood to Ashton Moss 5-3-1952. From Ashton Moss to Robin Hood 26-3-1952
Temporarily at Ashton Moss in 1953, KING under repairs at Walkden
Probably from Robin Hood Screens to Ashton Moss. Probably from Ashton Moss direct to Bradford Colliery

WESTWOOD 0-4-0STOC HC 1036 1913 16"x24" 3′8"
Temporarily at Ashton Moss in 1955, KING under repairs at Walkden.
From Walkden to Ashton Moss 6-1-1955. FromAshton Moss to Walkden 23-5-1955

KEARSLEY 0-4-0STOC KS 3123 1918 15"x20" 3′2"
Temporarily at Ashton Moss 6-1957 to early 1958, KING under repairs at Walkden
From Robin Hood Screens to Ashton Moss. From Ashton Moss to Walkden Yard

Production ceased about 1959 and coal subsequenlty wound at Bradford. Ashton Moss then used for winding men and materials

MOSTON COLLIERY

Locomotives used by National Coal Board 1947 to 1951

FAILSWORTH 0-6-0STOC HL 2727 1907 15"x22" 3′9"
Taken over from Platt Bros and Co (Holdings) Ltd 1-1-1947, under repair
To Wheatsheaf Screens, where arrived 1-2-1951
For subsquent history see Chapter 7

WESTWOOD 0-4-0STOC HC 1036 1913 16"x24" 3′8"
Taken over from Platt Bros and Co (Holdings) Ltd 1-1-1947
To Walkden Yard by 8-1948
For subsequent history see Chapters 7, 9, 10 and 11

ROBIN HOOD 0-4-0STOC CF 1200 1901 14"x19" 3′2"
From Outwood to Moston 12-1-1950. From Moston to Robin Hood by 5-1950

Colliery closed June 1950 and then used as a pumping station for Bradford Colliery

APPENDIX 5

The Small Landsale Collieries

A certain amount of information about the smaller landsale collieries came to light when we were preparing material for the present book. All were served exclusively by road transport and so do not feature in our main text.

What we have found is far from a complete record of all the small pits which at one time existed within the area of our study. Nevertheless, we think that it will prove of interest to industrial historians and we hope that it may provide a starting point for more detailed studies.

THE OUTSKIRTS OF BOLTON

Rumworth and Deane

The Church Pit, worked by Crompton and Vickers, was for sale in May 1858 [1] and what is described as their Rumworth Colliery seven years later, in June 1865 [2].

On Hunger Hill there was a colliery, together with a brick and tile works, owned by Moses Price and Company. Following Price's suicide in November 1862 [3], the plant was auctioned on 18th June in the following year [4], when the mine was said to be exhausted.

John Rosbottom with his son Thomas, opened his Victoria Colliery in 1867, on a site now occupied by the Barton Grange Garden Centre, adjacent to the Three Pigeons Public House. It became the property of Thomas Brocklehurst about 1872 and passed to Thomas Brocklehurst Ltd around 1906. It was taken over by the National Coal Board on 1st January 1947 and closed at the end of 1959, after nearly one hundred years of continuous operation [5].

Lever Edge and Fishpool

The first edition of the 6" map, surveyed in 1844 to 1846, marks Lever Edge Colliery, adjacent to Lever Edge Lane. It seems to have closed for a period and does not appear in the Mines Lists until 1874, when Joseph Rothwell is shown here. The occupiers are given as the Lever Edge Colliery Company from 1875 to 1879, Barlow, Atherton and Rothwell in 1880 and 1881 and the Lever Edge Coal Company from 1883 to 1886. It seems to have been known later as Morris Green Colliery, which is shown as worked by the Morris Green Coal Company Ltd in the Mines Lists in the mid 1890s.

There was a small colliery at Fishpool, on a site later occupied by the workhouse and the hospital. It was taken over in the 1820s or 1830s by James Roscoe from the Grundy family, for whom he had previously been the manager [6]. The mining rights were evidently subleased by Roscoe from the Bridgewater Trustees [7]. The pits are marked on the first edition of the 6" map, but it is not shown in the Mines Lists for 1853/4.

There was a short lived venture in the same locality in the 1890s. The Winsey Colliery at Plodder Lane only appears in the Mines List for 1893, in the occupancy of John and James Smith. What is described as John Smith's Farnworth Colliery, near Plodder Lane Station, was put up for sale on 14th March 1894 [8].

Farnworth

Robert Urmston worked a small colliery at Dixon Green, which is marked on the first edition of the 6" map to the east of the Bridgewater Trustees' Lord's Moss and Balance Pits. By 1852, the colliery was worked out and the plant was auctioned byhis executors [9,10].

Crompton and Haslam's High Stile, Riley Row and Darley Street Collieries were advertised for sale in 1858 [11]. Some of the pits were taken over by William Haslam; they later passed to Ellis Crompton, who worked them until about 1865. This was possibly the same Farnworth Colliery which Edward Wilson advertised for sale on 25th November 1868 [12].

There are also fragmentary references to a colliery at Halshaw Moor worked by Ellis Fletcher in 1829 [13] and to Robert Armstrong's colliery at Farnworth in 1848 [14].

Burnden and Rose Hill

Coal at Burnden was leased from the Earl of Bradford by the brothers Thomas, Samuel and John Scowcroft, who seem to have worked two collieries. The first edition of the 6" maps, surveyed in 1844 to 1847, shows one Burnden Colliery to the west of the Manchester road. The other is to the east of the road on both sides of the Bolton to Bury railway.

By 1853 [15] all the original partners had died and the colliery was offered for sale on 25th July [16]. It was acquired by Samuel Scowcroft Junior and continued in his occupation until 1860, when the lease reverted to the second Earl of Bradford.

Rose Hill Colliery, a little further to the north, is first shown in the occupation of Samuel Scowcroft in 1860. His new sinkings here replaced an earlier colliery, which the first edition of the 6" map marks alongside the River Croal, at the bottom end of Orlando Street. Rose Hill Colliery is last shown in the Mines Lists for 1925.

Raikes Colliery and the Great Lever Five Quarters Pit

The original Raikes Colliery was situated to the north of Hacken, with pits on both sides of the Manchester Bolton and Bury Canal. An estate plan of 1820 [17] shows that the coal was then leased by the Earl of Bradford to the executors of John Horridge and that there were four shafts in operation - the Ladder Pit, the Great Coal Pit, the Cannel Pit and the Deep Engine Pit. Although John Horridge, presumably the son of the former occupier, is shown at Raikes in a directory of 1824 [13,18] the colliery appears to have closed soon afterwards. The coal here was subsequently worked by the Earl of Bradford himself.

John Smith's Great Lever Colliery, not to be confused with the Earl's later colliery of the same name, was worked by the proprietor of the adjacent bleachworks. It was listed in a directory for 1824 [18]. It is also shown on a Deposited Plan dated 1830 for a proposed railway from Manchester to Preston, which would have had a branch to the bleachworks [19,20]. The colliery was later known as the Great Lever Works Pit or the Five Quarter Pit. It was taken over by the third Earl of Bradford in 1869 and is last shown in the Mines Lists for 1872, when presumably it was closed.

Little Bolton, Halliwell and Doffcocker

The first edition of the 6" map marks what is described as Little Bolton Colliery on the banks of the River Tonge, alongside the present Slater Lane. Presumably this was the Little Bolton Colliery shown in the Mines List for 1853/4 to 1863 as being occupied by Andrew Knowles and Sons.

The map also shows a Long Lane Colliery on the west side of the Blackburn Road, to the north of the junction with Halliwell Road, and another pit and engine house is marked on the north side of Halliwell Road in the vicinity of the present Weymouth Street. This may have been the Astley Bridge Colliery, leased from a Mr Tipping and worked by George and Thomas Grundy, which is shown on two plans of 1848 [21,22].

Two Brownlow Fold Collieries are marked, one near the junction of the present Darley Street and Escrick Street, the other near the junction of Elgin Street and Vallets Lane. A plan of 1844 [23] suggests that part of the property was leased from John Escrick. The collieries were possibly worked by Longworth and Scowcroft who are shown at Halliwell in in 1848 [14] and 1851 [24]. Brownlow Fold Colliery was up for sale on 22nd July 1853 [25].

Gabriel Garbutt is shown in the Mines Lists at the Eight Houses Colliery, Halliwell, in 1856 and at Holden's Colliery, Halliwell, from 1857 to 1858.

Pits at Doffcocker are shown as being worked by Longworth and Scowcroft in 1853/4, by Thomas Cross from 1855 to 1870 and by James Rothwell from 1871 to 1874. Thomas Cross is also shown at Vallets Colliery in 1869. The pits at Doffcocker may have been what the first edition of the 6" map marks as Midge Hall Colliery, on Chorley Old Road, near Montserrat, where there were also extensive sandstone delfs.

The pits at Montserrat seem to have been reopened in the 1890s and are shown as Doffcocker Colliery on the second edition of the 6" map, published in 1894. The Mines Lists show Samuel Rothwell as here in 1896. J H & S Rothwell Ltd had taken over by 1908 and the property had passed to C J Schofield Ltd by 1920.

Eagley Bank and Sharples

Coal mining here seems to have been started by Robert Knowles (died 1780) in the first half of the eighteenth century. The pits were inherited in turn by his son Andrew (1735- 1810), his grandson Robert (1756- 1819) and his great grandson Andrew (1783-1847) [26,27]. The family was still recorded as working a colliery at Eagley Brook in 1824 and1829 [13,18].

Apart from the Little Bolton Colliery, mentioned earlier, there is only one instance of mining by Andrew Knowles and Sons in districts north of Bolton in later years. The firm is shown in the Mines Lists at a colliery at Sharples from 1864 to 1870.

North of Sharples, Edmund Ashworth and Sons, proprietors of Egerton Mills worked a colliery at Chatham Close from 1874 to 1885.

There was also a short lived venture at Brian Hey, at the top end of Smithills Dean Road, actually in the old Little Bolton Township. Here, in an area where there had been a number of small pits in the eighteenth and early nineteenth century, the Mines Lists for 1858 to 1860 record a colliery worked by James Sewart.

Bradshaw and Harwood

A study of coal mining in Bradshaw and Harwood, which goes back to at least the seventeenth century, has recently been published by the Turton Local History Society [28].

Baines' directory of 1824 [18] records that there were mines at Bradshaw worked by two separate proprietors, Thomas Lomax and Thomas Scowcroft. There was also a Bradshaw Colliery Company, consisting of Thompson, Swift and Cole of the Hope Foundry, Bolton, together with with Robert Barlow and James Cross. We know that William Swift retired from the partnership on 18th December 1832 [29].

James Hardcastle, who had inherited Firwood and Harwood Bleach Works from his father in 1839 [30], later took over the collieries. The Mines Lists show him as working pits Harwood from 1853/4 to 1855 and again from 1858 to 1860. Between 1861 and 1872 he is shown with pits at both Harwood and Bradshaw.

RADCLIFFE AND BURY

Ainsworth

Thomas Fletcher's Ainsworth Red House Colliery was situated on the north side of the Bury New Road, to the east of the junction with Ainsworth Hall Road. It is not shown on the first edition of the 6" map, surveyed in 1844 to 1847, but appears in the Mines Lists for 1853/4. The colliery was flooded when water ran into the workings from a new reservoir built by John Rylands, who owned the nearby Ainsworth Mill. Rylands and Son took over the colliery and are first shown as occupiers in the Mines Lists for 1862.

Moorside Colliery, which the 1929 geological map marks near the intersection of Church Street and the lane leading to Old Barn, first appears in the Mines Lists for 1874 in the occupation of Ellwood, Jones and Spedding. It passed to W and J Spedding 1875 and to the Moorside Firebrick, Tile and Coal Co 1876. George Hargreaves and Company, who worked the Round Hill Colliery at Outwood during the period from 1874 to 1876, had taken over at Moorside by 1881. The colliery is not shown in the Mines Lists after 1881.

Radcliffe in 20th century

A new pit was sunk in 1900 at Coney Green, which was owned and managed by Mr Arthur Fletcher, late of Outwood [31]. The colliery is shown as discontinued in the Mines List for 1902, although Fletcher was still recorded as being the occupier in 1904. It was taken over by the Radcliffe Colliery Co Ltd in 1905 or 1906. It subsequently became the property of the Brynn Hall Colliery Co Ltd, a firm based near Wigan, and is shown under these owners for the first time in the Mines Lists for 1908. Later lists show that it was abandoned in October 1919.

In 1909 the Brynn Hall Colliery Company sank new pits at Wilton, on Turks Road. According the Mines Lists the colliery was closed in 1926 and abandoned in 1929. The Brynn Hall company sank new pits at Countess Lane and Turks Road which were opened in 1926. The former closed down the same year.

The Mines Lists show that the property was taken over by the Turks Road Colliery Co Ltd in December 1929. A new pit was sunk at Bradley Lane, which opened in 1930 or 1931, only to be closed in 1932. Turks Road Colliery was abandoned in May 1932.

There was also a short lived mine, worked by the Bury Road Colliery Co Ltd, which appears in the Mines Lists for 1933 and 1935.

Affetside and Elton

The Turton Local History Society's study of the Bradshaw and Harwood Collieries [28] also provides some information about mining in Affetside. The Mines Lists record that Jethro Scowcroft had a pit here in 1853/4, but it is not shown later.

At Elton the first edition of the 6" map marks Venture Colliery, located to the east of Starling Road, midway between the Ainsworth and Bolton Roads. The 6" Geological Map of

1929 shows an Elton Colliery on the south side of the Bolton Road, with the No 2 Engine Pit, perhaps incorrectly, on the Ainsworth Road, adjacent to its junction with the present Haig Road. The Venture and Elton Collieries had closed before the survey for the second edition of the 6" map in 1889 and 1890.

The Mines Lists show that William Thornton Parks was mining at Elton from the early 1860s to 1872. By 1874 he had moved to the Alderbarrow Colliery, which the geological map identifies on the Walshaw to Bury road, near its junction with the present Brookthorpe Road. Alderbarrow Colliery is not shown in the Mines Lists after 1876.

KEARSLEY

Scowcrofts' Pits

John Scowcroft was a partner in the firm of Peter Rothwell and Company, which had been mining coal in Kearsley from at least 1834 [32]. Peter Rothwell retired from the partnership in 1846 [33], leaving Thomas Scowcroft, Samuel Scowcroft and the executors of John Scowcroft to carry on. The first edition of the 6" map, surveyed in 1844 to 1846, shows Rothwell's Pits to the north of Moss Lane. They appear only in the Mines Lists for 1853/4 and are not shown on the Kearsley Tithe Map, dated 1855 [34].

The Scowcrofts seem to have acquired an interest in pits worked by the Grundy family. George Grundy and Brothers are shown at Kearsley in 1834 [32] and George and Thomas Grundy appear in directories of 1848 [14] and 1851 [24]. The Kearsley Tithe Map marks three pits, recorded as being occupied by Thomas Grundy, on land owned by the Trustees of the Duke of Bridgewater. Two were towards the upper end of Singing Clough and the third near the vitriol works.

Stoneclough

A Stoneclough Colliery was offered for sale, along with its steam engines and other plant, on 22nd November 1811 [35]. The colliery was stated to be near the turnpike road and short distance from the Manchester, Bolton and Bury canal.

The first edition of the 6" map, surveyed in 1844 to 1846, marks a quite extensive colliery and coke oven complex on the east side of the Manchester to Bolton railway, between the River Croal and the road to Whitefield. The 6" Geological Map shows the Paper Mill, Cotton Tree and Railway Pits here. The colliery seems to have been closed before the first List of Mines appeared in 1853/4.

Clamerclough Pottery

The Clamerclough Pottery, owned by the Dorning family, was located to the east of the town, near the Manchester to Bolton railway. There was a coal pit here as well and Jonathan Dorning was shown as a coal merchant in an 1834 directory [32]. The Mines Lists show that Peter Dorning had taken over by 1855 and that the pit was worked by his representatives from 1856 to 1859.

The pit is not shown in the Mines List again until 1869, in the occupation of John Gerrard, who had taken over the pottery. It is last recorded in the Mines Lists for 1884. The pottery was closed down at about this date and is shown disused on the second edition of the 6" map, surveyed in 1889 to 1891.

WORSLEY

Mesne Lea Colliery

Mesne Lea Colliery was located to the east of the main road from Walkden to Worsley, in the centre of an area worked by the Bridgewater Trustees.

The colliery is said to have started in 1824 [36]. In directories for 1848 [14] and 1851 [24] Catherine Nightingale is shown as the proprietor. The Mines Lists for 1853/4 and 1855 record the occupiers as the representatives of the late P Nightingale. Between 1856 and 1883 the colliery was worked by the firm of Peter Nightingale and Company. Nathaniel Grundy is recorded here in 1885. Part of the plant was auctioned on 24th February 1888 [37] and there was a further sale on 19th February 1888 [38].

References to Appendix 5

1 BC 22-5-1858
2 BC 10-6-1865
3 BC 8-11-1862
4 BC 13-6-1863
5 BEN 16-11-1959
6 BC 2-8-1890
7 LRO NCBw 19/1
8 BC 4-3-1894
9 BC 1-5-1852
10 BC8-5-1852
11 BC 23-1-1858
12 BC7-11-1868
13 BC 25-1-1879
14 *"Royal National Commercial Directory and Topography of the County of Lancaster"* - Isaac Slater, Manchester, 1848
15 LG 25-10-1853
16 BC 23-7-1853
17 BMB ZJA 338/1 Plan of Raikes Hall Estate, dated 22nd April 1820
18 *"History, Directory and Gazeteer of the County Palatine of Lancashire"* - Edward Baines, Liverpool, 1824-5
19 LRO PDR 195
20 LRO PDR 196
21 BMB ZJA 335/1
22 BMB ZJA 335/2
23 BMB ZJA 476/1
24 *"Royal National Commercial Directory and Topography of the County of Lancaster"* Isaac Slater, Manchester, 1851
25 BC 16-7-1853
26 Biographical Notes BMB B1, p159
27 Biographical Notes BMB B1, p231
28 *"Bradshaw and Harwood Collieries"* - James J Francis - Turton Local History Society Publication No 5, 1982
29 LG 1-1-1833
30 *"Bradshaw Works"* - James J Francis - Turton Local History Society Publication No 4, 1979
31 FJ 16-2-1901
32 *"National Commercial Directory for the Counties of Chester, Cumberland, Durham and Lancaster "*- James Pigot and Co, Manchester, 1834
33 LG 4-9-1846
34 LRO DRM 1/61
35 LRO DDHu 53/83/204
36 BC 1-6-1867
37 BC 19-2-1887
38 BC 14-2-1888

APPENDIX 6
Bridgewater Collieries Wagon Stock

The Bridgewater Archives held at Lancashire Record Office (LRO NCBw 11) contain two valuations of the Bridgewater colliery plant. The following extracts provide details of the railway wagons in use on 13th July 1914 and on 31st December 1920. The authors have made no attempt to correct the titles of the various wagon building firms given in the inventories, nor to reconcile discrepancies between the two lists.

On 13th July 1914 the stock included :

2 6-ton ballast wagons, wood frames and dumb buffers. Built before 1870, reputedly by Metro Wagon Co. (Internal user)

9 7-ton ballast wagons, wood frames and dumb buffers. Built before 1870, reputedly by Olive and Co. (Internal user)

121 8-ton wagons, wood frames and dumb buffers. Built before 1874, reputedly by Olive and Co and Ashburys. (Internal user)

4 4/5-ton flat wagons, wood frames and dumb buffers. Built before 1870 by Worsley Yard.

4 8-ton flat wagons, wood frames and dumb buffers. Built before 1874, reputedly by Olive and Co. (Internal user)

2 10-ton flat timber wagons, wood frames and dumb buffers. Built before 1874 by Worsley Yard.

90 8-ton wagons, wood frames. Purchased 1893. Built by Birmingham Wagon Co. (49 have spring buffers, the remainder for internal use only have dumb buffers)

3 8-ton wagons, wood frames. Purschased 1880 from John Gigson [Gibson ?]. Rebuilt Walkden Yard.

100 10-ton wagons, wood frames. Purchased 1904. Built by S J Claye.

100 10-ton wagons, wood frames. Purchased 1905. Built by S J Claye.

100 10-ton wagons, wood frames. Purchased 1906. Built by S J Claye.

238 8-ton wagons, wood frames. Purchased 1879 to 1886. Gigson [Gibson ?] Colliery, Ashburys and Claye. Reconstructed and converted to spring buffers 1907.

100 10-ton wagons, wood frames. Second hand. Built 1908, reputedly by Davies and Co.

30 10-ton wagons, wood frames. Purchased 1908. Built 1902/3, reputedly by Davies and Co.

150 10-ton wagons, wood frames. Purchased 1911. Built by S J Claye.

50 10-ton wagons, wood frames. Purchased 1912. Built by S J Claye.

100 10-ton wagons, wood frames. Purchased second hand 1913. Reputedly built by Davies and Co

100 10-ton wagons, wood frames. Purchased 1913. Built by S J Claye.

10 10-ton wagons, wood frames. Built Walkden Yard 1913.

50 10-ton wagons, wood frames. Built Walkden Yard 1914.

6 8 and 10-ton wagons, wood frames. Purchased second hand 1913. (3 since broken up)

5 8 and 10-ton wagons, wood frames. Purchased second hand 1913. (2 since broken up)

10 8-ton wagons, steel frames. Purchased 1893. Built by Birmingham Wagon Co.

100 10-ton wagons, steel frames. Purchased 1899. Built by S J Claye

200 10-ton wagons, steel frames. Purchased 1902. Built by Ashbury Carriage Co.

200 10-ton coke wagons, steel frames. Purchased 1902. Built by Midland Carriage Co.

On 31st December 1920 there were 2907 wagons, comprising :

3	8-ton dumb buffer wagons, obsolete (internal user).
478	8-ton dumb buffer wagons, wood frames, reconstructed with laminated spring buffers 1906 to 1914. Originally purchased 1879 to 1886. Various makes. Numbers between 926 and 1699.
669	8-ton dumb buffer wagons, wood frames, reconstructed with self contained spring buffers 1906 to 1914. Originally purchased 1879 to 1886. Various makes. Numbers between 102 and 1699.
100	8-ton wagons, wood frames. Rebuilt by Walkden Yard. Originally constructed by Birmingham Wagon Co in 1893 and purchased in that year. Numbered 1700 to 1799.
100	10-ton wagons, wood frames. Purchased 1904. Built by S & J Claye. Numbered 1800 to 1899.
5	10-ton wagons, steel frames. Purchased 1899. Built by S & J Claye.
95	10-ton wagons, wood frames, rebuilt Walkden Yard 1916-1920. Purchased 1899. Built by S & J Claye. Numbered 1900 to 1999.
194	10-ton coke wagons, steel frames. Purchased 1899-1910. Built by Midland Carriage Co.
6	10-ton coke wagons, wood frames. Rebuilt 1913-1919. Purchased 1899-1900. Built by Midland Carriage Co. (The above 200 coke wagons Nos 2000 to 2199 are included the wharves valuation)
200	10-ton wagons, wood frames. Rebuilt by Walkden Yard 1911-1920. Purchased 1902. Built by Ashburys. Carriage Co. Numbered 2200 to 2399.
200	10-ton wagons, wood frames. Purchased 1905 and 1906. Built by S & Claye. Numbered 2400 to 2599.
130	10-ton wagons, wood frames. Purchased second hand from W R Davies and Co. Built 1902-1903 by Cardiff Rolling Stock Co. Numbered 2600 to 2729.
150	10-ton wagons, wood frames. Purchased 1911. Builders S & J Claye. Numbered 2730 to 2879.
50	10-ton wagons, wood frames. Puchased in 1912. Builders S & J Claye. Numbered 2880-2929.
100	10-ton wagons, wood frames. Puchased in 1913. Builders S & J Claye. Numbered 2930-3029.
10	10-ton wagons, wood frames. Built by Walkden Yard 1913. Numbered 3030 to 3039.
100	10-ton wagons, wood frames. Purchased 1913 from Messrs Griffiths. Built 1900-1902 by Chorley Wagon Co and Ince Wagon Co. Numbered 3040 to 3139.
90	10-ton wagons, wood frames. Built by Walkden Yard 1914. Numbered 3140 to 3229.
80	10-ton wagons, wood frames. Built by Walkden Yard 1915. Numbered 3230 to 3309.
23	10-ton wagons, wood frames. Built by Walkden Yard 1916. Numbered 3310 to 3332.
12	8-ton flat wagons. Built 1870 to 1874, reputedly by Worsley Yard and Olive and Co. Numbers 63, 72, 88, 171, 180, 199, 232, 233, 241, 323, 581, 629.
1	10-ton goods van, wood frames. A spring buffer wagon built by the Lancashire and Yorkshire Wagon Co, Heywood in 1903 and converted to a covered van at Walkden Yard in 1915. Number 06.
111	8-ton and 10-ton wagons, purchased from Messrs S Wheeler and Sons, 1920. Made up of self contained and laminated spring buffer wagons.

The following details of wagons purchased by Manchester Collieries Ltd in the 1930s have been supplied to the authors by Peter Fidczuk, based on records held at the National Railway Museum:

Nos	8690	to	8789	12-ton wood framed wagons supplied by Charles Roberts and Co in 1934
Nos	10332	to	10431	12-ton wood framed wagons supplied by Lancashire and Yorkshire Wagon Co in 1936
Nos	10432	to	10706	12-ton wood framed wagons supplied by Central Wagon Co in 1936
Nos	10707	to	10781	12-ton wood framed wagons supplied by Lancashire and Yorkshire Wagon Co in 1936
Nos	10782	to	10931	12-ton wood framed wagons supplied by Charles Roberts and Co in 1936
Nos	10932	to	11131	12-ton wood framed wagons supplied by Charles Roberts and Co in 1939
Nos	11132	to	11281	12-ton wood framed wagons supplied by Central Wagon Co in 1939
Nos	11282	to	11431	12-ton wood framed wagons supplied by Lancashire and Yorkshire Wagon Co in 1939
Nos	12001	to	12004	12-ton wagons of various types to compare steel and wooden designs, supplied by Charles Roberts and Co in 1934
No	12005			12-ton wood framed wagon suppplied by Lancashire and Yorkshire Wagon Co in 1935
Nos	12006	to	12010	12-ton all steel wagons supplied by Butterley Co in 1937

Corrections and Additional Information Relating to Part 1

The Salford Mining Museum is now known as the Lancashire Mining Museum. The abbreviation SMM has been retained in the References.

Page 18 7th paragraph and page 24 7th paragraph for "Manchester, Bury and Rawtenstall Railway" read "Manchester, Bury and Rossendale Railway"

Page 52 under heading "Castlefield to Ordsall Lane" for "Ashton under Lyme" read "Ashton under Lyne"

Page 80 under heading "Bolton Iron and Steel Works" for "Rushton and Sharp" read "Sharp and Eckersley"

Page 81 under heading "Back o' th' Bank Power Station" alter designation of third locomotive from 4w-4wWE to 4w-4wOHWE

Page 111 5th paragraph for "T H and T Scowcroft Ltd" read "T and H T Scowcroft Ltd"

Page 113 The inference, under the heading New House Colliery, that John Fletcher was probably the son of Matthew the Elder is incorrect. It seems likely that John was the son of Ralph Fletcher of the Haulgh (1787-1832) and was the same person who was a trustee at the Clifton and Kersley Collieries, during the minority of Charlotte Fletcher, and also had interests at Atherton and Ladyshore.

Page 149 6th paragraph for "Bury Making Co Ltd" read "Bury Papermaking Co Ltd"

Page 154 1st paragraph for "Ince Waggon and Iron Ltd" read "Ince Waggon and Ironworks Co Ltd"

Page 155 under heading "Dobson and Barlow Ltd" alter designation of first two locomotives from 4wWE to 4wOHWE

Page 158 under heading "Heap Bridge Paper Mills" for "Yates Duxbury and Son Ltd" read "Yates Duxbury and Sons Ltd"

Page 166 2nd paragraph and page 168 1st paragraph for "Outwood Colliery Co Ltd" read "Outwood Collieries Ltd"

Page 175 1st paragraph for "(1707-1832)" read "(1757-1832)"

Page 188 2nd paragraph Delete "until closure" after "Bradford Colliery". Bradford Colliery did not close until 6th September 1968.

Page 191 6th paragraph for "T and S Scowcroft" read "T S Scowcroft"

Page 199 under heading "Outwood Colliery" delete "Thomas Fletcher until about 1875". For "Thomas Fletcher and Sons Ltd from 11th May 1868" read "Thomas Fletcher and Sons Ltd from 11th May 1898".

Page 200 In table under "ROBIN HOOD" add "From Outwood to Walkden Yard for repairs 10-3-1951 and thence to Ashton Moss Colliery on 4-5-1951"

Page 200 In table under "OUTWOOD" add "From Outwood mid 1950 to Walkden Yard for repairs, which took until 1954. New boiler received 3-12-1953, repairs complete 28-2-1954 and sent to Wheatsheaf Screens 2-3-1954"

Page 202 In table under "KEARSLEY" add "Under repairs at Walkden Yard in late 1946 and early 1947. Returned to Robin Hood 2-1947"

Page 202 In table under "ROBIN HOOD" alter second line to read "To Walkden Yard for repairs 13-3-1947 and then sent to Outwood on 1-9-1947". Also add "From Robin Hood 18-8-1955 to Walkden Yard for repairs. From Walkden Yard to Robin Hood 26-11-1956"

INDEX TO INDUSTRIAL FIRMS AND PROPRIETORS

INDEX TO INDUSTRIAL LOCATIONS

INDEX TO RAILWAYS AND CANALS

INDEX TO LOCOMOTIVE BUILDERS

The following are listed in the Locomotive Summaries and in the Appendices

Additional information can be found in the text about the following builders

Published as separate volumes in the same series

Industrial Railways of the Wigan Coalfield

Part One - South and West of Wigan

Orell and Norley Hall; Pemberton; Ince; Amberswood and Strangeways Hall; Platt Bridge, Bamfurlong and Mains; Low Hall, Maypole and Wigan Junction; Edge Green, Brynn and Garswood; Skelmersdale and Bickerstaffe; Rainford and Upholland.

Part Two - North and East of Wigan

Haigh and Aspull; Kirkless; Wigan Coal and Iron Company; Wigan Coal Corporation; Shevington, Appley Bridge and Gathurst; Douglas Bank and central and northern Wigan; Standish; Coppull; Chorley and Adlington; Blackrod and Westhoughton; Westleigh and Swan Lane; Bickershaw and Hindley Green.

Industrial Railways of Bolton, Bury and the Manchester Coalfield

Part One - Bolton and Bury

Central Bolton; Hulton, Dean Moor and Farnworth; Great Lever; Smithills; Tonge and Breightmet; Darcy Lever and Little Lever; Ladyshore and Stopes; Bradley Fold; Radcliffe; Bury; Heap Bridge; Tottington, Woolofold and Summerseat.